Little Ohio

100 Towns POPULATION **BELOW 500**

A NOSTALGIC LOOK AT THE BUCKEYE STATE'S SMALLEST TOWNS

Written and Photographed by Karen Robertson

Adventure Publications
Cambridge, Minnesota

Dedication

For Jake, without you this would not have been possible.

Acknowledgments

I would first like to acknowledge the countless dedicated individuals who work tirelessly to preserve their local history through written volumes, websites, historic buildings, historic markers, and more. A book like this one would not be possible without the tireless work of local historians. For each village in this book there is at least one (often more than one) person who has spent their free time documenting what matters to their hometown. These people are too countless to list here. The work of preserving history is often thankless, but to each and every one of you I offer a sincere thank you.

I would also like to thank Brett Ortler and the entire AdventureKEEN team. Brett's hard work and keen eye for detail pushed *Little Ohio* from an unassuming manuscript to a well-polished book that I can be proud to have in print. Thank you for the easiest and most enjoyable editing process I have ever experienced.

Last, but certainly not least, I would also like to thank my father, John Robertson, and my husband, Jake London, for accompanying me on my many trips through Ohio. I truly enjoyed getting to know the state with both of you.

Photo Credits

All photos by Karen Robertson unless noted.

Back cover green buckeye, Ivaschenko Roman/shutterstock.com; vintage baseball glove, eurobanks/shutterstock.com

Page 19 disc golf basket, Joe Ferrer/shutterstock.com; **Page 20** American flag flying, Lucy Clark/shutterstock.com

Cover and book design by Jonathan Norberg

Edited by Brett Ortler

10 9 8 7 6 5 4 3 2 1

Little Ohio: A Nostalgic Look at the Buckeye State's Smallest Towns
Copyright © 2019 by Karen Robertson
Published by Adventure Publications
An imprint of AdventureKEEN
330 Garfield Street South
Cambridge, Minnesota 55008
(800) 678-7006
www.adventurepublications.net
All rights reserved
Printed in China
ISBN 978-1-59193-849-1 (pbk.); ISBN 978-1-59393-850-7 (ebook)

Table of Contents

Introduction

Over the past year, I have had the privilege of both researching and visiting 100 Ohio towns and villages. I traveled around the entire state, at one moment standing on the northern border in Beulah Beach overlooking Lake Erie, and the next driving along the Ohio River, Ohio's southernmost boundary, to the village of Moscow. I solemnly looked upon sites of tragedy in Ohio's history, such as the Sunday Creek Coal Mine in Millfield or the site of the Great Kipton Train Wreck. But I also saw joy and triumph in every single stop on my journey in brand new small businesses, beautiful parks, and a plethora of historic markers gushing with local pride. I even had some once-in-a-lifetime experiences such as attending a Welsh Gymana Ganu in Venedocia and standing directly on the state line in College Corner.

Writing this book has taught me a lot. I've lived in Ohio my entire life, but I've never seen *this much* of the Buckeye State. As a historian, when I embarked upon my research, I was incredibly intrigued by the similarities between the villages in this book and what that meant for understanding the history of Ohio and small towns as a whole. However, I was also excited by the sheer amount of diversity present in the stories of these towns. Every single village in this book offers a unique perspective.

Hopefully as you read through *Little Ohio*, you will see, as I did, that there is no one way to define "small town." Just as Cleveland is not Toledo or Cincinnati is not Dayton, Lockbourne is not Lockington and Mount Eaton is not Mount Pleasant. When I first stepped foot in Fresno, a rural town in the eastern part of Ohio, I was immediately hit with a sense of appreciation for the silence around me. When I walked along Fresno's streets, admiring the unique homes on either side of me, I could hear nature in a way I was not accustomed to, but certainly could get used to. In comparison, the streets of Put-in-Bay were a cacophony of conversation and color. A tourist destination for many Ohioans, Put-in-Bay is perhaps only silent in the off-season. Yet Put-in-Bay and Fresno have almost the exact same population! (138 and 136 respectively.)

The 100 villages in this book are each unique, but ultimately the story of Ohio's small towns is the story of the unique people that live there. I hope that, whoever you are, even if you aren't from Ohio (yet), you will be able to see yourself somewhere in these pages. The story of Ohio's small towns is the story of Cathecassa traveling from his home in St. John's to Washington, D.C., to advocate for the rights of American Indians in the Ohio territory. It is also the story of Dutch migrants coming to Celeryville, using their well-honed skills to make the soil profitable, and the migrant workers, who now, over a hundred years later, continue to plant on that land. The story of Ohio's small towns is the story of freedom and self-reliance in abolitionist strongholds like Mount Pleasant and the settlement of freemen at Gist. It is the story of stepping up and getting things done, like the many small-town women who ignored societal norms and ran for mayor anyway (and won).

Despite the differences that make each village unique, they also have their similarities. Many are connected intimately with nature, from the natural marvels of Rockbridge and the Zaleski National Forest to the treehouses of Glenmont. Many of these villages also share similar origin stories. In eastern portions of Ohio, many villages were founded by migrating Quakers, while in the north, Lake Erie and the Canadian border lent itself to a history of bootlegging. By and large, it was transportation that brought new villages to Ohio, be it Zane's Trace, the National Road, canals, railroads, or highways. Unfortunately, it has also been transportation that has stunted the growth of many villages. As each village is bypassed by new forms of transportation, fewer travelers spend money in town, and its population naturally shrinks.

However, the biggest similarity amongst these villages is a strong sense of pride that keeps the locals in town and allows life to carry on. It is this pride that has made it so easy for me to chronicle the history of these villages. Residents are doing this work on the ground every day, from the Adams family preserving the stories of Morgan County's African-American families at the Multicultural Genealogical Center in Chesterhill, to John Jurko II building a wealth of primary sources to document his family's founding of Yankee Lake. It is perhaps this pride that made me certain I had never left Ohio no matter how far I traveled. I've always felt surrounded by that pride wherever I am in the Buckeye State. However, part of the joy of being an Ohioan is our diversity and the opportunity to experience so much without leaving our borders. I hope as you read you will see, as I did, that when we embrace both our diversity and our local pride, Ohio is truly at its best.

Locator Map

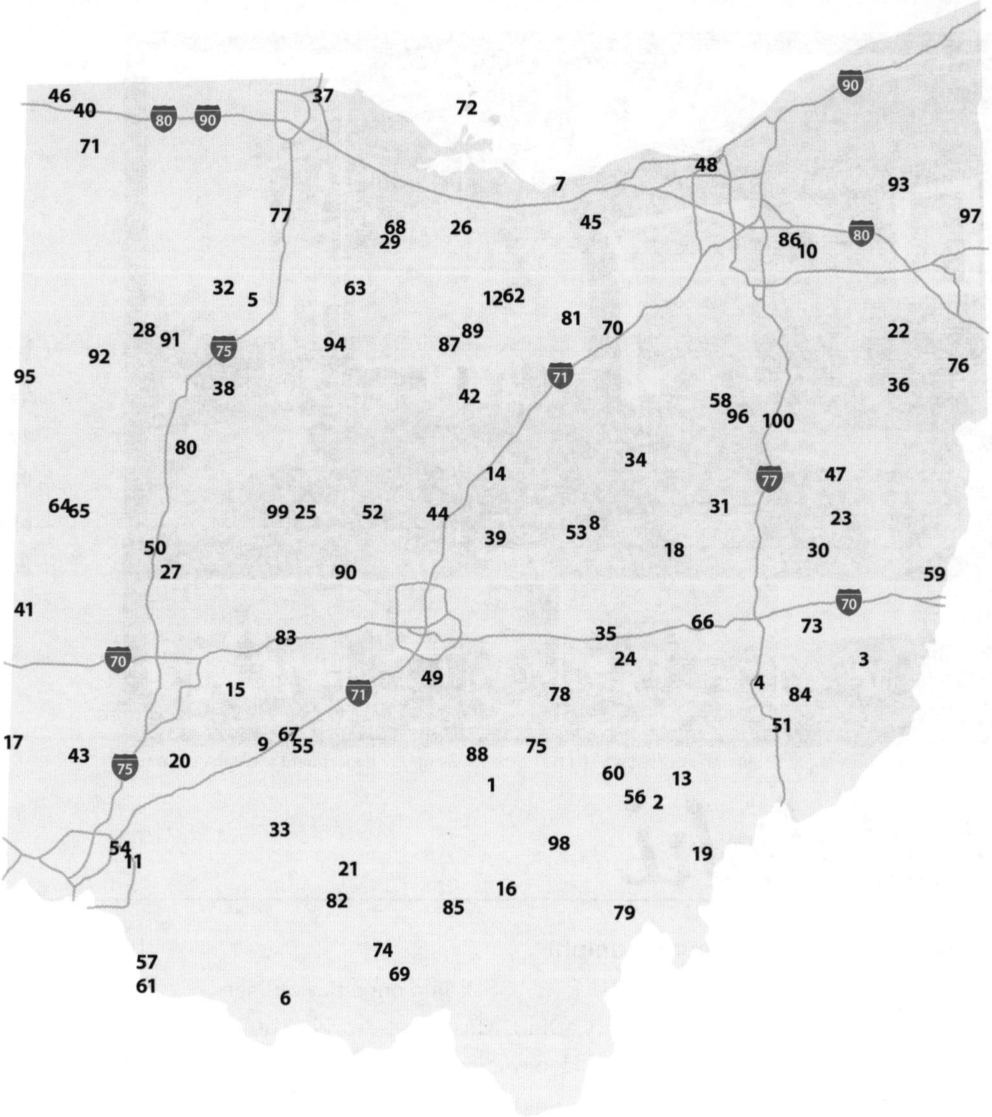

1 Adelphi
2 Amesville
3 Beallsville
4 Belle Valley
5 Benton Ridge
6 Bentonville
7 Beulah Beach
8 Bladensburg
9 Bowersville
10 Brady Lake
11 Camp Dennison
12 Celeryville
13 Chesterhill
14 Chesterville
15 Clifton
16 Coalton
17 College Corner
18 Conesville
19 Coolville
20 Corwin
21 Cynthiana
22 Damascus
23 Deersville
24 East Fultonham
25 East Liberty
26 Flat Rock
27 Fletcher
28 Fort Jennings
29 Fort Seneca
30 Freeport
31 Fresno
32 Gilboa
33 Gist Settlement
34 Glenmont
35 Gratiot
36 Hanoverton
37 Harbor View
38 Harrod

39 Hartford
40 Holiday City
41 Hollansburg
42 Iberia
43 Jacksonburg
44 Kilbourne
45 Kipton
46 Lake Seneca
47 Leesville
48 Linndale
49 Lockbourne
50 Lockington
51 Lower Salem
52 Magnetic Springs
53 Martinsburg
54 Miamiville
55 Milledgeville
56 Millfield
57 Moscow
58 Mount Eaton
59 Mount Pleasant
60 Murray City
61 Neville
62 New Haven
63 New Riegel
64 New Weston
65 North Star
66 Norwich
67 Octa
68 Old Fort
69 Otway
70 Polk
71 Pulaski
72 Put-in-Bay
73 Quaker City
74 Rarden
75 Rockbridge
76 Rogers
77 Rudolph

78 Rushville
79 Rutland
80 Saint Johns
81 Savannah
82 Sinking Spring
83 South Vienna
84 Stafford
85 Stockdale

86 Sugar Bush Knolls
87 Sulphur Springs
88 Tarlton
89 Tiro
90 Unionville Center
91 Vaughnsville
92 Venedocia
93 West Farmington

94 Wharton
95 Willshire
96 Wilmot
97 Yankee Lake
98 Zaleski
99 Zanesfield
100 Zoar

Population: 374   **Incorporated:** 1838

INSETS L to R: Adelphi United Methodist Church •
Kingston National Bank • A community park
in Adelphi • Adelphi Opera House

Nathaniel Massie, the man who laid out the village, designed it so that all of its streets ran directly east and west or north and south. Adelphi is the only village in Ross County to be laid in such a grid. Even today, this makes navigating the streets of Adelphi very simple.[14]

TOP: The Adelphi Community Center, which also hosts the village fire department and village council.

Adelphi

The Adams Brothers Found Adelphi

IN 1804, GENERAL NATHANIEL MASSIE laid out a new village in Colerain Township, Ross County, Ohio. Massie was working on behalf of two brothers, Reuben and Henry Adams. The Adams brothers named their new village Adelphi, a name it still holds today.[1] Some sources believe that it was named in homage to the ancient Greek sanctuary of Delphi.[2] Others believe the name was chosen because it's derived from a Greek word meaning "brothers."[3] Either way, it stuck.

In 1838, the village of Adelphi was officially incorporated. A group of citizens apparently attempted to form a new Ohio county and elect Adelphi as the county seat, but the attempt was unsuccessful. Nonetheless, the village began to grow. In 1879, Daniel F. Shriner moved from

the city of Chillicothe to Adelphi to begin the Adelphi Border News, which remained in print until about 1944. Beginning in 1882, the Cincinnati, Hocking Valley & Huntington Railroad began building a railway arm into the village. When construction finished in 1885, the area economy blossomed.

Adelphi's Signature Experiences

The village of Adelphi is well known for two things: bologna sausage and its community band. The history of Adelphi's famous bologna is very hazy, likely by the design of its original creator. As the story goes, during the 1800s a man named Gus Santo lived in Adelphi and made a style of trail bologna sausage so popular that it took on the village's name. He took the recipe to his grave, but bologna was still made in Adelphi until the 1940s. For a time the nearby Laurelville Meat Packing plant took over, keeping their version of the recipe a secret as well. During the 1970s and 1980s, the village of Adelphi celebrated the famous bologna with a summer festival.[4] Sadly, the recipe has been lost to history.

The Adelphi Community Band was first founded in the village in 1880. The band soon became well known around the area, playing at local events and county fairs. Now well over 100 years old, the Adelphi Community Band continues to entertain the community.[6]

Tella Denehue Kitchen

In 1920, one of Adelphi's most famous residents first came to town. Tella Denehue was born in Londonderry, a Ross County village near Adelphi, on February 14, 1902. In 1920, Tella Denehue married Noland Kitchen, and the couple moved to Adelphi. The couple had four children, a farm, a used-car business, a gas station, and a greenhouse. On top of all of these commitments, Noland Kitchen was also the mayor of Adelphi.

In 1963, Noland Kitchen passed away, and Tella Denehue Kitchen took over as mayor. She was the first female mayor of the village (and the first female mayor in Ross County).[7] Around this time, Tella's son, Denny, gave his mother a painting set, probably hoping to lift her spirits after she became a widow. She put the set away for a few years but eventually put it to use. Kitchen worked with oil paints, creating a style of folk art known as memory painting. She painted from her memories of rural life in the Midwest, sometimes specifically painting Adelphi.[8]

News of Kitchen's work spread as she aged. In 1980, she was inducted into the Ohio Women's Hall of Fame.[9] Her son, Denny, contacted a museum professional, Robert Bishop, to speak about his mother's art. Bishop was very interested, and he made sure that examples of Kitchen's work were preserved at the American Folk Art Museum.[10] Today her paintings have sold frequently at auction, with buyers being moved by her representations of her own way of life.[11]

The Namesake of Purdue University: A Household Name

In October 1802, John Purdue was born in Pennsylvania. The Purdue family moved to Adelphi in the early 1820s, but unfortunately, John's father and one of his sisters died shortly thereafter. Purdue became responsible for supporting his family, so he began teaching in Pickaway County schools and apprenticing with a local merchant. After Purdue began helping his neighbors sell crops and livestock on commission, he became interested in the business world. Purdue and James Fowler, the brother of one of Purdue's students, opened a general store in Adelphi in 1833. By 1834, Purdue had left the village, moving to Lafayette, Indiana, with dreams of opening more stores under his name.[12]

By the mid-1800s, John Purdue was a well-known, successful businessman in the state of Indiana. In 1869, the federal government gave the state of Indiana funds (via the Morrill Act) to establish a land-grant college. Upon hearing this news, Purdue offered up his own money as well as a large plot of land. All he asked was that his name be attached to the college and that he keep a lifelong appointment on the board of directors. Purdue held its first classes in 1874 and is highly regarded today around the country.[13]

Tella Kitchen wasn't the first member of the Kitchen family to serve as mayor. Tella took over the post after her husband, Noland, died, but previous to Noland's service, his father, E. E. Kitchen, a schoolmaster, also served a few terms.[15] E. E. Kitchen's name appears in one of Tella Kitchen's artworks, where he's noted as the owner of the village's first school bus.

Population: 157   Approx. Founding: 1837

INSETS L to R: A mural on the side of the post office honoring Amesville's history • The Ames Academy Bell (1852-1955) in Gifford Park • The Coonskin Library Museum seen from the playground of Amesville Elementary School • Amesville Elementary School

One of Amesville's most well-known former residents is Thomas Ewing. Ewing was born in 1789 in what is now the state of West Virginia. His family moved to Ames Township in 1798, becoming some of the first settlers to call the area home. As an adult, Ewing set up a successful law practice in Lancaster, Ohio, represented Ohio in the United States Senate, and served as the Secretary of the Treasury, the first Secretary of the Interior, and as a foster-father to future Civil War general William Tecumseh Sherman.[12]

TOP: The front of Amesville's post office

Amesville

The Founding of Ames Township

IN 1786, THE OHIO COMPANY OF ASSOCIATES formed in the state of Massachusetts. Like other land companies popping up at this time period, the company's goal was to purchase and resell land in the then-Northwest Territory for profit. Led by a man named Reverend Manasseh Cutler, the Ohio Company of Associates purchased approximately 1,600,000 acres of land in the southeast corner of the future state of Ohio from the United States.[1]

In 1797, about a decade after the formation of the company, Reverend Cutler's son, Ephraim Cutler, age 29, made a home in the lands his father had acquired. Settling in the future Athens County, Cutler helped form the township of Ames, which was the future home of the village of Amesville. Others soon followed, including George Ewing and his son Thomas, and Sylvanus Ames. Ames, the village's future namesake, arrived in 1800. He became the second sheriff of Athens County, a trustee at Ohio University (formed in 1804), and a representative to the 16th and 17th Ohio General Assembly.[2]

After the founding of Ames Township, Ephraim Cutler frequently had to leave town on official business. In 1801, he was elected to the legislature for the Northwest Territory, and in 1802, he was made a delegate to Ohio's Constitutional Convention. While serving at this convention, Cutler helped ensure that the new state's constitution forbade slavery on Ohio soil.[3]

The Origins of the Coonskin Library

Even when he was home in Ames Township, there was no time for Cutler to rest. The early settlers of the township met in 1803, with the intent of discussing improved roads; however, conversation quickly turned to the desire for readily available books. There was also a lack of funds to build a village library. Early residents of Ames Township hungered for an understanding of the world beyond their borders, whether it was obtained by an improved road enabling them to travel to a nearby settlement or by settling in to read a good book.[4]

As was common elsewhere in the U.S., physical currency was very rare among early Ames Township settlers. There was no market in town, and the nearest town was 20 miles away. Most cash was spent on taxes or debts still owed to the Ohio Company of Associates for the settlers' land. The settlers lived off the land and bartered for whatever else they needed. One man who grew up in Ames Township later stated, "So scarce was money that I can hardly remember ever seeing a piece of coin till I was a well-grown boy. It was with difficulty we obtained enough to pay our taxes and buy tea for Mother."[5]

Still, the town was committed to obtain a library, and a man named Josiah True proposed a way to raise the funds. He suggested that the settlers catch raccoons and sell the skins for the cash required to purchase the desired tomes. This was something the residents of Ames Township were good at—they regularly hunted in the forests, as did members of various American Indian nations, most likely the Shawnee and the Lenape. There was no shortage of raccoons ready to be caught for this purpose.[6]

As it happened, one man, Samuel Brown, had been planning the 700-mile trip to Boston, Massachusetts, in his wagon. By the time he was ready to leave, the township's residents had supplied Brown with a bounty of skins to be sold. Thomas Ewing, a boy of 15 at the time, remembers contributing 10 skins himself.[7] Brown was able to trade the skins for about 74 dollars, which in turn enabled him to buy 51 books. Brown purchased books based on a list that focused mostly on reference texts, historical and religious writings, and the works of Enlightenment-era philosophers.[8]

While Brown was on his journey, the interested residents of Ames Township began purchasing shares in an organization they decided to call the Western Library Association. Members paid 25 cents a year to fund regular library needs. This subscription-based funding system was common for early libraries, but it also meant that those without the means to afford a membership couldn't use the library's resources. Late fees were assessed at 50 cents, although with "a just appreciation of the difficulties of backwoods traveling and the knowledge that with his best efforts the shareholder from seven or eight miles away might be delayed by swollen creeks, fallen trees or bottomless mud holes." Ephraim Cutler was declared the first official librarian in 1804.[9]

While they stuck with their official name, the Western Library Association became well known in Ohio's history books as the Coonskin Library, thanks to its unique funding mechanism. Today the books that Samuel Brown originally brought home to Ames Township can be found at the Ohio History Connection and Ohio University's Alden Library. What's more, the Coonskin Library Museum opened in 1994 in the old cafeteria of Amesville Grade School.[10]

A Village of Entrepreneurs

Modern-day citizens of Amesville are just as industrious as the early settlers who built the village's first library. Amesville is filled with businesses, including the Green Edge Gardens, Kasler's County Kitchen, Homecoming Farms, and Village Productions (a dance studio). The village also has multiple wineries and a brewery in development. For those interested in spending some time absorbing all that Amesville has to offer, Lance Rentals provides multiple bed-and-breakfasts right in town.[11]

One of Amesville's modern-day businesses, Homecoming Farms, is run by Amesville native John Wood and his family. In addition to providing the citizens of Amesville with fresh produce straight from the farm, Wood creates and sells bowls and furniture produced in his wood shop.[13]

INSETS L to R: Beallsville High School • The Historic Beallsville Diner • Veterans Memorial Community Park, nearby a historic marker lists the names of the Monroe County residents who gave their lives in Vietnam • Beallsville's main road stays active even in the depths of winter

Everyone in Beallsville knows Jeff Rich. The minister at the Beallsville Church of Christ, he is selflessly involved in every aspect of town life. He brings church services to anyone who wants them, by traveling to those who cannot get to a service or picking up those without access to transportation. To augment his ministerial salary, Rich maintains a job as a substitute teacher at Beallsville schools. He also works with the Beallsville High School football team. Rich was featured in *The Christian Chronicle*, a publication of the Church of Christ, in 2013.[19]

TOP: A monument bearing the names of the Beallsville residents who died in Vietnam

Beallsville

The Beginnings of Beallsville

THE VILLAGE OF BEALLSVILLE WAS PLATTED IN 1824, but an 1867 courthouse fire meant the village had to be platted again as the platting documents were lost. The village grew at a respectable pace. By 1825, it had its own post office. By 1841, the village was incorporated, but the official paperwork listed the village as "Elva." After incorporation, residents petitioned for their former name, succeeding in 1851.[1] In 1874, the Monroe County Commissioners appointed John B. Noll to replat the village.[2] Noll reported that the village had first been platted in 1824 by Citizen Beall. The village took on Beall's name thereafter.[3]

In 1879, the village became the site of a train depot, leading to swift growth. It was home to many dairy farmers, cigar factories, and the Beallsville Shirt Factory, which burned down in the early 1900s and was never rebuilt.

Hudson's General Store and Beall's Descendants

One of the most well-known establishments in the village of Beallsville was Hudson's General Store, which was built in 1880 by Addison Hudson (Citizen Beall's grandson). After his store grew, he relocated. Hudson's descendants operated the store until 1985, when it was sold. The original building can still be seen in Beallsville today.[4]

Vietnam Comes to Beallsville

Unfortunately, Beallsville's largest claim to fame was born out of immense tragedy. During the Vietnam War, reporters continually descended upon the village of Beallsville, asking residents to speak about the recent loss of their brothers, friends, and sons.[5] By 1969, the small village of Beallsville, home to only about 450 people at the time, had lost more residents per capita in the Vietnam War than anywhere else in the U.S.

The first resident of Beallsville to fall in the Vietnam War was Jack Pittman. Pittman graduated from Beallsville High School in 1964 and was drafted at the age of 19.[6] He died in July of 1966 and was buried in the Beallsville Cemetery, in a plot reserved for his parents.[7] Pittman was injured in the line of duty and flown to a military hospital, but he did not survive. His family, frustrated at the loss of their only son, refused a military funeral.[8]

The next three men taken from Beallsville were all graduates of the 1965 class of Beallsville High School. In August 1966, Duane Greenlee, the only casualty from Beallsville who enlisted rather than being drafted, died in the course of duty. Greenlee was a Marine. In December 1967, Charles Schnegg became another casualty from the 1965 class. Only a few months later, on Memorial Day of 1968, the Beallsville class of 1965 lost a third member, Richard Rucker.[9]

Bad news continued to roll into town. In March of 1969, William "Bobby" Lucas was killed by a sniper while trying to save a fellow soldier.[10] Finally, the village of Beallsville had had enough. With Lucas's death, the village had officially lost the most men per capita of any tow in America, and the national media descended on Beallsville.[11]

After the death of Lucas in 1969, Keith Harper, a funeral director in Beallsville, and Raymond Starkey, the Monroe County Treasurer, joined together to attempt to put a stop to the loss of life in Beallsville. The men approached their congressional representatives to ask for help. These congressmen, Clarence Miller and Wayne Hays, attempted to speak with the Defense Department, the Selective Service, and even President Nixon himself.[12]

Miller and Hays unsuccessfully requested that soldiers from the village be brought home and that Beallsville's young men could stop registering for the draft. In March 1971, Phillip Brandon became the sixth soldier from Beallsville to die in the Vietnam War.[13]

Reactions to the Tragedy

Beallsville's relationship to the Vietnam War was (and still is) complicated. As reporters returned during the 1970s, residents expressed a mix of frustration with both the war and the reaction of their fellow Americans. There were never any protests in Beallsville—the residents overwhelmingly felt that protesting would be disrespectful to the men who had given their lives. Yet some residents were clearly frustrated that their brothers and sons had given their lives for what they felt to be a useless endeavor. As Jack Pittman's mother stated, "...our boy's life wasn't worth all of Vietnam."[14]

The residents of Beallsville, particularly the Pittman family, also felt a class-based source of frustration. They felt that rural Beallsville had suffered more than its fair share because their residents often could not afford a college education. Because university students could receive draft deferments, high school graduates were more likely to be drafted into service. Earl Pittman, Jack Pittman's father, grew frustrated watching college students protest a war that they never had to serve in while his son was brought home in a casket. As he told NBC news in 1967, "The bigger towns, they don't get no place in it."[15]

Beallsville has always managed to balance its frustration with pride. On Memorial Day 1968, the village came together to dedicate a memorial at the Beallsville Cemetery in honor of the men they had lost.[16] Today the monument still stands in pristine condition. Nearby is the Beallsville Veteran's Memorial Park, dedicated to the memory of all of the Monroe County men who died in Vietnam. An official state historical marker is in the parking lot, bearing the names of these men.

Beallsville isn't pronounced the way it looks. It's actually "BELLS-vale" or sometimes "BELLZ-vihl," depending on whom you ask.[17] During the 1950s, the Scripps School of Journalism at Ohio University put together a running list of Ohio town name pronunciations.[18] This list was likely useful to the news reporters descending on Beallsville during the 1970s.

TOP: While it is no longer in use, this Russian Orthodox Church is still very present in Belle Valley.

Population: 217   **Incorporated:** 1905

INSETS L to R: From the parking lot of the Faith Baptist Church, at a high point in Belle Valley, you can see for miles • Belle Valley American Legion Post 641 • A convenience store in the valley • Faith Baptist Church

During the early 1900s, the Belle Valley Slavish Band played for village residents, and even at auspicious events, such as the inauguration of Governor James Cox in 1917. 1917 was a dramatic year for the band. About a week before they led the Noble County delegation to the gubernatorial inauguration, the band performed in Belle Valley. Their recently fired leader, angry at this state of affairs, arrived at the performance and fired a shotgun at the group, hurting a few band members and damaging the bass drum.[16]

Belle Valley

The Founding of Belle Valley and the Coal Beneath

DURING THE EARLY 1870s, the Cleveland and Marietta Railroad made its way through Noble County, Ohio, passing near the farmland of a man named Benton Thorla. In 1872, Thorla opened a store on his property, and in 1875 he hired William Lowe to survey his farm. Thorla began to sell lots, forming a new village, known as Belle Valley. It grew quickly, as other railways built stations in Belle Valley, making it an important transfer point for shipping, as well as a telegraph station for railway communication.[1]

In addition, coal was found beneath the ground of Thorla's former farm, generating mining jobs and bringing new families to the area.[2] The Imperial Mining Company of Belle Valley first found coal in North Belle Valley on January 13, 1904, ushering in a new era for the local economy. Soon Noble County was dotted with coal mines and new homes for the men who risked their lives to retrieve the area's black gold.[3]

In 1905, the villages of Belle Valley and North Belle Valley decided to consolidate and incorporate under the name Belle Valley. The new village continued to grow, hitting a peak population of 1,050 in 1920.[4]

Immigrants Come to Belle Valley

Many of the men who came to work in Noble County's mines were of Eastern European descent. These newcomers were largely welcomed in the local economy.[5] In many cases, immigrant mine workers were sending their wages overseas to a family waiting to follow their path to the United States. Unfortunately, mining was a very dangerous business, and sometimes the superintendent of a mine had to send the miner's last paycheck himself. For example, in 1913, in the Imperial Mining Company's Belle Valley mine, Nicholas Bilkovish of Russia was killed by falling slate. Compounding the tragedy, Bilkovish had a wife and child back in Russia.[6]

Noble County's Deadliest Mine Explosion

On May 17, 1913, the deadliest mine explosion in Noble County history took the lives of 15 men in Belle Valley.[7] It was a Saturday evening, and 20 men were in the Imperial Mining Company mine. Around 7 p.m. a small tremor was felt at a nearby residence, but it wasn't large enough to cause any concern until the mine engineer received a signal from below to help bring the men to the surface.[8]

Five men arrived at the surface when the mine engineer hoisted the cage. They informed the engineer that two explosions had occurred, the second of which was especially deadly. These five men, and another, J. R. Yeager, had been working closest to the mine shaft, a fact that had saved their lives. When they reached the surface, the five men likely knew that their coworkers wouldn't make it out alive. However, they quickly sent for a rescue crew to retrieve Yeager who was still breathing.[9]

Yeager was closer to the explosion than the other four men, recalling that "When the blast came—there wasn't an instant's warning—I was hurled over and over against rocks and slate and coal for a distance of 300 feet. Big things came crashing at me and I thought I was a goner for sure." When a mine explosion occurs, the toxic gases it produces, known as afterdamp, can prove just as deadly as the initial blast. Yeager, suffering a broken hip, was able to drag himself closer to the other men, staying low where the air quality was best. Yeager survived the afterdamp until a rescue crew arrived, but unfortunately one of his rescuers, Henry Fairhurst, was killed by this toxic air.[10]

After Yeager's rescue, almost all of Belle Valley's 1,000 residents arrived outside the mine, waiting and mourning until the afterdamp cleared.[11] They all knew that there would be no more rescues. Around 3:30 in the morning, hoping the afterdamp had dispersed, crews literally took a canary into the coal mine and began to clean up the mess. Finally at 5 o'clock in the morning, 10 hours after the explosion, rescue crews retrieved the bodies of the victims, as their distraught families looked on.[12] As one newspaper observed, in the week that followed, "business is entirely abandoned and this place is indeed a village of sorrow."[13]

Investigating the Explosion

The State Mine Inspector arrived in Belle Valley shortly after the explosion, attempting to find a cause for the tragedy. At first, all fingers pointed to Sam Saltis, the fire boss and one of the five survivors of the accident. Each day, the fire boss was supposed to arrive early to check the mine for dangerous gases. He carried a lamp, and if its flame burned blue, he was meant to mark a room as possibly dangerous. Saltis hadn't done his job that day, claiming that the assistant superintendent, now dead, had pushed him to get to work instead. Fortunately for Saltis, the inspector declared the explosion was caused by the movement of a brattice, a partition used for ventilation, that blocked a new track the miners were laying. Brattices are used to direct airflow and prevent the buildup of dangerous gases in underground mines. Changing this airflow created a pocket of gas, which exploded when a miner walked into the area with an open lamp.[14]

The mine reopened a month later, while the Imperial Mining Company continued to settle claims with victim's families, an especially challenging task for miners with family overseas. Despite the danger, Noble County residents continued to return to the mines. In Belle Valley alone, tens of thousands of tons of coal were produced each year. Stores, hotels, and businesses cropped up around the mines as workers continued to flood into the village of Belle Valley.[15]

In May 1930, former Noble County resident Christopher Lippett returned home to dig for gold. Lippett had had a dream that inspired him to rush back to the area to look for gold on an area farm. Unfortunately for Lippett, very little gold has been found in Ohio.[17]

TOP: The Benton Ridge Community Park, featuring the Veterans Walkway

Population: 292   Incorporated: 1875

INSETS L to R: Post office boxes outside town hall where residents of Benton Ridge retrieve their mail. Also at this spot is a drop off for village sewer payments. • A bell cast in 1889 that now sits outside the Calvary Church of Benton Ridge • The Good Shepherd United Methodist Church • An entrance to the expansive Village of Benton Ridge Community Park

During the mid-1950s, Jerry Solt, of Findlay, Ohio, finally gave up on his engineering degree. Instead, he turned to his true passion: kart racing. Solt and his father became very well known for building, racing, and selling karts. Their karts were unique, using Jerry's creative ideas and engineering knowledge to push the envelope. In the early 1990s, Jerry and his wife, Marylyn, purchased a large plot of land just north of Benton Ridge, where, among other things, they built a racing track, which later closed. With encouragement from former racer Matt Cramer, the Solts reopened their track to the public in 2017 under the name Solt Speedway.[12]

Benton Ridge

Benton Ridge and Thomas Hart Benton

IN NOVEMBER 1835, William Mires laid out the village of Benton Ridge on top of a ridge that runs east and west through Ohio's Hancock County. A post office was established in 1840, and in March 1875, the village was incorporated. By 1880, only 189 people called it home.[1] Because Benton Ridge was never home to a railway or a highway, it has always been very small.

Benton Ridge was partially named for a United States Senator from Missouri, Thomas Hart Benton.[2] During the 1830s, when Benton Ridge was founded, Thomas Hart Benton was known nationally for his support of westward expansion and the gold standard. He was a Democrat, like President Andrew Jackson, and often pushed the president's positions on the Senate floor.[3] Any Ohioan keeping up on the news would have known Benton's name.

But why would Ohioans name their town for another state's senator? It's likely that the citizens of Benton Ridge were interested in Benton's support of westward expansion. During Ohio's earliest years, most Americans considered Ohio to be part of the "West." Most early Ohioans were born on the East Coast and struck out to settle in Ohio. Benton also supported the distribution of publicly owned land to new white settlers. Many early Ohioans purchased public land or received Ohio lands through a military pension. The citizens of Benton Ridge were likely using their name to pay tribute to a man that supported the policies that had made their village possible.

Thomas Hart Benton held his seat in the United States Senate until 1851, when he lost the support of Missourians due his changing beliefs on slavery. As a Democrat, and a slave owner, he had spent most of his career as a pro-slavery advocate. As white Americans began loudly and publicly arguing over the future of slavery, Benton began speaking out frequently against its expansion into new territories. Benton did not object to slavery on moral grounds, but rather he wished to stop the arguing that was tearing the United States apart. After losing his Senate seat, Benton served a brief time in the House of Representatives. He passed away in 1858. Despite voting him out of the Senate, Missourians still appreciated Benton's legacy, sending a statue of him to the National Statuary Hall in 1864.[4]

The Benton Ridge Telephone Company

In 1902, a telephone company came to Benton Ridge, thanks to founders Peter A. Kemerer and George W. Brown. The Benton Ridge Farmer's Mutual Telephone Company (in 1957, the "Farmer's Mutual" was dropped when the business became for-profit) remained small, moving from building to building in Benton Ridge with a small staff. Brown and Kemerer served as president and secretary, respectively, while Pete Baldwin served as a lineman and Carrie and Molly Hughes as operators.[5]

When Benton Ridge residents wanted to make a phone call, they would pick up the phone, and the first voice they heard would be Carrie's or Molly's. The caller would provide the necessary phone number for their connection, and then Carrie or Molly, operating a switchboard, would connect the callers. During the late 1800s, as telephones increasingly came into style in the United States, many telephone companies hired teenage boys as operators. Some of these boys were often rude to their customers, so companies turned instead to young women, who were considered naturally polite and thus fit for the position. By the time the Benton Ridge Telephone Company opened in 1902, it was standard to hire female switchboard operators.[6] While Carrie and Molly likely moved on to new careers or maybe even out of the village, the company would have hired operators until 1959, when Benton Ridge made the switch to dial telephones.[7]

In December 1965, Benton Ridge Telephone Company made news across the state when they began publicly feuding with the American Telephone and Telegraph Company (AT&T) over a possible defense contract. Both parties were interested in providing the infrastructure for a local portion of the nationwide Cold War network known as the Automatic Voice Network (AUTOVON). This network allowed for calls to travel across the country in the case of a nuclear attack.[8]

AT&T had approached the Department of Defense without the Benton Ridge Telephone Company's knowledge to propose an AUTOVON link in the village. AT&T assumed the federal contract would go to them and began building AUTOVON infrastructure right away. The Benton Ridge Telephone Company and their lawyers became concerned that this new infrastructure could be easily transferable to civilian service and that AT&T could eventually take away their nearly 300 subscribers in the region. The president of the Benton Ridge Telephone Company told reporters that he felt his company had the "duty, responsibility, and prerogative" to build the AUTOVON link in Benton Ridge.[9] In 1967, the Benton Ridge Telephone Company was successful in winning the Department of Defense contract and becoming the responsible party for the AUTOVON link in the village.[10]

The Benton Ridge Telephone Company continued to expand during the second half of the twentieth century. Today, based in the nearby city of Lima, the company provides telephone, internet, and television services to the village of Benton Ridge and the surrounding area.[11]

Parishioners of the Benton Ridge Calvary United Methodist Church were well acquainted with the puppet Buddy Woodenhead during the latter half of the twentieth century. Reverend Marion L. Hanover, a Bucyrus native and ventriloquist, used his handmade puppet in his performances. This brought a "light, entertaining" touch to sermons and community events.[13]

TOP: There are multiple monuments to the Bentonville Anti-Horse Thief Society in town

Population: 287   Approx. Founding: 1839

INSETS L to R: Bentonville Community Church • A main road in Bentonville • A painted barn on the edge of the village • Benton Village Apartments

The Naylor family has been instrumental in Bentonville's history, and it has also helped record it. Linda Sue Naylor, daughter to Verna and Harry Naylor and sister to James Naylor, has written a book titled *A Brief History of Bentonville, Ohio.* As Linda Sue Naylor once told a reporter, "Our little town has a lot more history than a lot of people might think."[15]

Bentonville

A Family Affair

THE FIRST WHITE SETTLERS IN THE AREA that became Bentonville were the Eddington and Leedom families, who were related by marriage. Around 1796, George Eddington, Isaac Eddington, and William Leedom, George's son-in-law, all brought their families to Adams County. Isaac in particular decided to settle on a creek that runs from modern Bentonville into the Ohio River. The water is still known as the Isaac Creek in his memory. George Eddington settled on Zane's Trace, where he would entertain travelers at his residence.[1]

In 1839, Joseph Leedom, likely a descendant of William, laid out the new village of Bentonville, naming it for Senator Thomas Benton of Missouri.[2] Right around the same time, many miles north of Bentonville, other settlers were giving a similar name to the village of Benton Ridge (page 14).[3] While Thomas Hart Benton was from Missouri, not Ohio, his support of western expansion earned him many fans among the early Ohio settlers.

The Murder of Sanford Phillips

Bentonville made news in Adams County in 1867, thanks to a very public murder case. One morning that December, not too far from the schoolhouse in the north part of town, while school was in session and residents moved about on the street, a man named Sanford Phillips was murdered. Despite the fact that Phillips was murdered in broad daylight, no one came forward with any evidence to help local law enforcement. Phillips, about 45 years old at the time, was known as a generally unsavory character, and no one in Bentonville was very fond of him.[4]

Phillips had recently become fond of a local girl named Lydia Purdin. Lydia was 17 years old, and Purdin had taken to visiting her when her widowed mother and brother were not at home, almost as if he was courting her. Purdin did not seem to take to Phillips and his advances, as it was known that she was interested in a young gentleman by the last name of Burbage. When Phillips learned of this, he beat poor Burbage and threatened his entire family.[5]

On the December morning in question, Phillips came into Bentonville early in the day, going to visit Lydia Purdin, whose family was away. Around noon, Lydia went to a neighbor's house for a visit, staying about an hour. When Lydia arrived home around 1 p.m., her family was still away. She came screaming from the house, yelling that a murder had occurred inside.[6]

When law enforcement entered the Purdin home, they found Sanford Phillips sitting in a chair, with his head partially detached from his body. He had been hit twice with an axe and had clearly been dead for a few hours. It seemed almost obvious that Lydia had murdered Phillips before visiting with her neighbor, and she was quickly arrested. However, likely due to the overwhelming negative sentiment towards Sanford Phillips, Lydia Purdin was released.[7]

The Bentonville Anti-Horse Thief Society

Bentonville is home to an organization with a name that seems odd today: the Bentonville Anti-Horse Thief Society. Formed in 1853, its members sought to protect a valuable asset for local farmers: their horses. During this time period, horses were a main source of transportation and part of the workforce on a farm. In 1860, the average American made less than $500 a year, but replacing a horse would cost about $150–200, a huge portion of the annual income. Losing a horse could be a huge blow to a family's economic status.[8]

When the organization formed, the trustees elected a captain and a crew of riders to be responsible for catching horse thieves. For each thief they caught, they were awarded $10. In that era, most captured horse thieves were executed by the riders without a fair trial.[9] In the twentieth century, automobiles took hold in America, and the family horse became less important to farmers. With this technological shift, the Bentonville Anti-Horse Thief Society's mission shifted. With no horse thieves to chase, the members began helping out their community, mostly through donations, such as the first set of electric lights installed in Bentonville.[10] The Bentonville Anti-Horse Thief Society still exists today. It is now the oldest organization of its type, and members get together one day a year, at the end of April, for an annual banquet. They have a meal together and hire a speaker to address the crowd. Membership in the organization is not limited to residents of Bentonville. Anyone can join, simply by sending in the membership dues of one dollar.[11]

The Naylors of Bentonville

One of the longtime members of the Bentonville Anti-Horse Thief Society was Verna Naylor.[12] A community standout, Naylor served as the postmaster of Bentonville from 1968 until her death in 2010. She ran the post office out of her home. At the time of her death, Naylor was the oldest postmaster and the oldest postal worker in the United States.[13] The Bentonville Post Office was a family affair for the Naylors. Verna Naylor originally took over the role of postmaster when her husband, Harry, passed away in 1968. He had served as the postmaster since 1949. After Verna Naylor passed away in 2010, her son James took over the post. According to relative Linda Sue Naylor, in Bentonville, the post office is "a place for congregating with friends and neighbors to discuss the happenings in our community."[14]

Despite its reputation, to this day it remains unclear how many thieves were actually caught by the Bentonville Anti-Horse Thief Society. As one longtime member said in 1976, "To be honest, I think we only had three horses stolen in the history of the society." It seems no official record of the organization's activities was ever kept or preserved.[16]

Population: 53   **Approx. Founding:** 1920

INSETS L to R: A playground overlooking Lake Erie • A view of the lake that is ubiquitous at Beulah Beach • Space for a cookout for Beulah Beach summer camps • Summer cottages line the streets of Beulah Beach

While Beulah Beach offers a retreat from day to day life, the Christian Missionary Alliance has still embraced the conveniences of technology. Visitors to one of Beulah Beach's many year-round camps can download the Beulah Beach app on their cell phones for updates about events, maps of the campus, and even menus for the food available that week. Devoted guests can register for their next retreat right from the app before they head home.[9]

TOP: The main office at Beulah Beach

Beulah Beach

The Beulah Beach Institute

IN 1928, IN THE SMALL COMMUNITY OF BEULAH BEACH, the first graduating class of the Beulah Beach Institute collected their diplomas, packed up their dorm rooms, and inscribed precious memories and bittersweet goodbyes in their classmates' yearbooks. At first glance, that yearbook, the *Beulah Beach Beacon*, looks like any other yearbook from the early twentieth century. It includes many common features of the time that have faded in recent years, such as a class will, a class history, and a class prophecy.

The *Beulah Beach Beacon* even included a class poem, written by Miss Miriam Hazlett after seeking inspiration on the sandy shores of Lake Erie. As the *Beacon* recorded at the time, Miriam Hazlett "is a poet but doesn't know it. Her perspiration exceeds her inspiration but she gets there just the same."[1]

Every member of this tight-knit class of 10 received a small biography in the yearbook, written by a fellow classmate, just like the summary of Miriam Hazlett's poetic prowess. Even without skipping ahead to the class history, these biographies make it clear that these 10 men and women had spent three years in close quarters and had the inside jokes to show for it. Apparently Raymond Moore had a bright future ahead of him, especially "in the matrimonial field." Naomi Jordan, or Nemo as her friends called her, was "the girl from the big city" and the "self-styled belle of Beulah Beach."

However, Beulah Beach Institute wasn't quite like other boarding schools. Further on in the *Beulah Beach Beacon*, each new graduate weighed in on what Beulah Beach meant to them. The first comment came from Carrollton Clause, originally of Aurora, Indiana (although apparently he was quite sweet on a girl he had met in Cleveland, and the class prophecy suspected he would settle down there). Clause wrote that during his time at Beulah Beach, "Jesus has revealed Himself to me as the all-satisfying and all-sufficient one for all needs of spirit, soul, and body."

The Christian Missionary Alliance

The small community of Beulah Beach in which the Institute was based was founded by the Christian Missionary Alliance in 1920.[2] The Beulah Beach Institute was a short-lived institution, but the Christian Missionary Alliance has always been a fixture in Beulah Beach.

In 1887, Reverend A. B. Simpson, a Presbyterian pastor in Canada, began forming a nondenominational network of religious missionaries. By 1919, adopting the "tabernacle strategy," the growing Christian Missionary Alliance began building centers for training their missionaries—including at Beulah Beach.[3] One of the men involved in this growing strategy also had Ohio roots.

A. W. Tozer moved to Akron, Ohio, with his family as a young man. As a teenager, he found a job at one of Akron's biggest businesses: Goodyear. One day as Tozer walked home after his shift, he heard a preacher speaking nearby. Tozer caught a few words that he always remembered: "If you don't know how to be saved, just call on God." These few words were enough to change Tozer's life. He spent his life working as a pastor and writing constantly about his relationship with God. Tozer traveled as a representative of the Christian Missionary Alliance, and audiences at Beulah Beach may have been lucky enough to catch a sermon of his in the early twentieth century. Today he is buried in Akron near Ellet Church.[4]

Despite the annual advertisements for missionary conferences in local newspapers, other Beulah Beach residents were never quite sure what went on in the Christian Missionary Alliance buildings. In fact, one man who attended religious summer camps at Beulah Beach as a child now recalls that his friends assumed the "private" sign out front meant it was a nudist beach![5]

Eleanor Smith and Chuck Russell

By the 1950s, the community of Beulah Beach was barely large enough to maintain a post office. However, two of the community's most interesting residents made sure the mail continued to run on time. Mrs. Eleanor H. Smith managed post office boxes in a partitioned room in the front of her home. At the height of summer season, Smith still only saw 75–200 customers. However, she was still incredibly busy, as the mailings of the Christian Missionary Alliance created at least five mail deliveries each day![6]

When she wasn't managing the post office, Mrs. Smith was often spending time with her foster son, Chuck Russell. Despite being nearly blind, Chuck created and sold jewelry, often made from the interesting stones he could find on Beulah Beach. Handicapped by a surgery he had at the age of two, Chuck had to refrain from too much exertion, as he told the *Sandusky Register*, "I expended myself a bit more than usual one day a couple of weeks ago in cleaning up the shop and I was sick for a week!"[7]

Beulah Beach Today

Today the post office of Beulah Beach is gone, as the community is a Census-designated place. It has all but been consumed by the city of Vermilion. However, the Christian Missionary Alliance continues to maintain its residency at Beulah Beach, offering a large campus for visiting groups, conferences, field trips, and summer camps.[8] While Beulah Beach is no longer populated with poetic boarding school students or determined postmistresses, the Christian Missionary Alliance continues as a fixture on the sandy shores of Lake Erie.

The Christian Missionary Alliance has always made good use of their spot on Lake Erie. Over the years, the lake has been used for baptisms. An early postcard, which can be seen online at Massachusetts's *Digital Commonwealth*, shows hundreds of people gathered around the lake for baptisms at a convention.[10] Baptisms are still performed in Lake Erie today.[11]

Population: 191   Approx. Founding: 1833

INSETS L to R: The Dilley-Lasater Funeral Home, first opened in
1925 • Businesses dot a main road in Bladensburg • Bladensburg
Church of Christ • The main road in Bladensburg

One of Bladensburg's oldest businesses is the Dilley-Lasater Funeral Home. First opened in 1925 by Alva Harris as the Harris Funeral Home, the business was purchased in 1975 by John T. "Pete" and Mary Dilley. In 1979, the Dilley's expanded their business through the purchase of a funeral home in the nearby city of Mount Vernon. In 2008, Brent and Gloria Lasater, long-time employees of the funeral home, purchased the business from the Dilleys. Today they manage both the Mount Vernon location and the Dilley-Lasater Funeral Home on South Church Street in Bladensburg.[15]

TOP: The Bladensburg Post Office

Bladensburg

Maryland Veterans Come to Knox County

DURING THE 1830s, many Maryland-born veterans of the War of 1812 were moving west, largely into Ohio and Indiana. One of these men was Samuel Davidson, a veteran who came to the future village of Bladensburg in 1831 (by way of Coshocton).[1] The village of Bladensburg was laid out in 1833 by John Wheeler, Samuel Wheeler, and Washington Houck, but most histories agree it was Samuel Davidson who gave the village its name.[2]

In the summer of 1814, Davidson found himself with about 6,500 other enlisted men in his home state of Maryland, under the orders of General William Winder. The Napoleonic Wars were coming to an end in Europe, and many battle-hardened British soldiers were arriving to fight in the United States, where the War of 1812 was well underway. These experienced troops represented a threat to American troops. Winder prepared to defend two key cities in the northeast: Baltimore, Maryland, and Washington, D.C., the capital of the fledgling nation.[3]

To best defend both of these cities, Winder brought his men to the strategically located Maryland town of Bladensburg. Around midday on August 24, 1814, British forces under General Robert Ross met Winder's men, including Samuel Davidson, at Bladensburg. The American forces soon began to crumble, and in a panic, many men ran from the battlefield, leaving the British forces an open path to Washington, D.C.[4]

British troops passed through Winder's men into the capital city on the evening of August 24, bringing destruction with them. Flames filled the night sky as Washington burned. The presidential mansion (known today as the White House), the Capitol Building, the Treasury Building, and the War Office were all victims to the blaze. President James Madison and his cabinet quickly left town, but his wife, Dolly, and Paul Jennings, a man held in slavery at the presidential mansion, famously stayed behind to rescue some of America's earliest relics.[5]

What's in a Name?

Why exactly would Samuel Davidson name his new hometown after one of America's biggest military embarrassments? Almost 200 years after Washington burned, Samuel Davidson's great-great-great-great-granddaughter, Christina Davidson, would be asking herself just that question. Generations after Samuel moved west to Ohio, Christina turned back toward the East Coast, where, in 2014, working as a writer, photographer, and editor, she wrote about her early ancestor for the *Baltimore Sun*.[6]

Christina, who recalled hearing Samuel's story repeated many times "during picnics of [her] childhood," admitted that until she moved east in her twenties, she assumed the name of Bladensburg, Ohio, "commemorated a glorious triumph." As the 200th anniversary of the battle approached in 2014, Christina took to the archives to attempt to uncover why Samuel Davidson may have suggested naming a new village for such a large loss.[7]

Unfortunately, Christina wasn't able to find a definitive answer, but she was able to weave a fascinating reflection on his life for the *Baltimore Sun*. As it turns out, Samuel's unit had stayed in Bladensburg until the bitter end, refusing to run. As Christina wrote, "the most important thing Samuel did on Aug. 24, 1814, was survive."[8]

Christina does have one idea about Bladensburg's name. Samuel was one of many War of 1812 veterans moving into Knox County in the 1830s. Christina surmised that a "new town named after that scar could feel like forgiveness and an invitation to communion, fellowship and healing for troubled souls."[9]

Oil in Bladensburg

During the mid-twentieth century, oil wells in Bladensburg began drawing visitors from all over. Businesspeople even came from Texas, where oil was plentiful and profitable. What was so attractive about the Bladensburg oil fields? The oil was just 2,000 feet below the ground.[10]

As Harry Dugan of the Associated Oil Investments and Chief Drilling Co. told the *Newark Advocate* in 1965, 2,000 feet was actually a comparably shallow distance to drill compared to other oil fields. Combined with twentieth-century developments in hydraulic fracturing (fracking), this shallow distance made finding oil in Bladensburg almost a sure thing. Each project would yield less oil than prospectors may have found in Texas, but there was never any risk of coming up empty.[11]

The oil supply in Bladensburg came from a geological formation known as Clinton Sandstone, which actually spans most of eastern Ohio and continues north along the Appalachian Valley. This sandstone was deposited more than 400 million years ago, on top of a layer of Utica shale. This shale contained oil and gas, which flowed upward and was captured in the very porous sandstone. Bladensburg is situated on one of the shallowest parts of the Clinton Sandstone formation: it varies from about 2,000 to 6,500 feet deep. As of 2013, 80,000 wells had been drilled throughout the Clinton Sandstone formation.[12]

Oil was discovered in Bladensburg at the end of the 1800s, but it did not become a popular business opportunity until 1948, when several wells were built in the village.[13] The first Americans to pump oil from the formation were actually based quite a ways south of Bladensburg, in the city of Lancaster. Interested citizens began drilling in 1886, and in February 1887, the first oil spilled forth onto the surface from a Clinton Sandstone well.[14]

Bladensburg is home to the Bladensburg Fire District, an almost exclusively volunteer group serving Bladensburg and nearby Martinsburg (page 110). Via their Facebook page, residents of the village can learn about training exercises, get to know emergency responders, and keep tabs on everything from dangerous weather situations to community gatherings.

TOP: Bowersville Methodist Church

Population: 337   Approx. Founding: 1848

INSETS L to R: Bowersville Church of Christ • Bowersville Police Station • The home base of Premier Grain in the middle of Bowersville • Bowersville Post Office

On May 31, 1898, Norman Vincent Peale was born in Bowersville, Ohio. While Bowersville was his birthplace, Peale moved quite a lot as a child, due to his father's job as a Methodist preacher. Peale attended classes at Ohio Wesleyan and followed in his father's footsteps, becoming ordained in the Methodist Episcopal Church in 1922. Peale is best known for his work with religion and psychiatry, the publication of *Guideposts* (a religious magazine), and his book *The Power of Positive Thinking*.[16]

Bowersville

Bowersville and the Bowermaster Family

IN 1848, there were only three or four houses to be found in the area that would become the village of Bowersville. One of these homes was owned by Christopher Hussey, probably the first white settler in the area.[1] He officially platted the new village in 1848, using a survey from Samuel T. Owens, the Greene County Surveyor. The village grew slowly, as many of the first land sales were to speculators, rather than individuals interested in moving to the new village.[2]

Although the village was small, it already had at least one store, opened by a man named Peter Bowermaster, before the village was even platted. Most local histories agree that the village of Bowersville was named for Peter, who was also the village's first postmaster and probably had some say in the name for the purpose of mail delivery.[3] At least one history of Greene County states that the name was actually suggested by a man named D. L. Reaves, as a reference to the great shade trees in the village.[4] While these shade trees did exist, it seems more likely that the name Bowersville was a nod to Peter.

Peter Bowermaster was born in Pennsylvania in 1787. He moved to Greene County, Ohio, in 1810 and soon after joined up with a Greene County unit serving in the War of 1812. After the war he returned to Bowersville, where he served as postmaster from 1848 until his death in 1859.[5]

It is believed that about a year before he died, Peter Bowermaster had the privilege of naming the township he resided in. In 1858, the residents of Bowersville felt that their village had grown large enough to necessitate the formation of a new township in Greene County. Perhaps selfishly, the residents knew that this would make their village the largest and most powerful community in this new township. They went to the county government to ask for this new separation and were happily greeted with an affirmative answer. Peter Bowermaster, a big fan of Thomas Jefferson, suggested they name the new township Jefferson. This name stuck and is still in place today.[6]

Peter's son Reason A. Bowermaster briefly took over the postmaster position after his father's death, but his real talents were as a woodworker. He sold his works, including furniture and barrels, in the village of Bowersville. The Bowermaster family grew with Bowersville—as of a history written in 1918, members of the family were still living in the village.[7]

The Fickle Railroad

During the latter half of the 1800s the fickle nature of local railroads put Bowersville's economy on a metaphorical roller coaster. During the early 1870s, thanks to a rumor that a railroad would soon pass through the village, Bowersville's economy boomed. Unfortunately, these rumors proved to be false, and the promised railroad never came into existence.[8] In the late 1870s, the village finally did get a smaller railway, known as the Detroit, Toledo & Ironton Railroad.[9] This was great news for the many farmers in the community attempting to move their grain out of the village. However, the railroad track was not up to expected standards and was pulled up in the early 1880s, again stymieing the trade opportunities of Bowersville residents.[10]

In 1894, the railroad was finally permanently replaced, and Bowersville was allowed to flourish. Two grain elevators were built in town. They were so successful that even though one elevator burned to the ground on several different occasions, the owners continued to rebuild. In 1916, Jefferson Township spent $50,000 building a school in Bowersville that would serve the entire township. Children of all ages came to the village each day for their lessons.[11]

An Explosive Bank Robbery

In 1895, as Bowersville began to boom yet again, the village built a bank.[12] Known as the Bowersville Bank, this institution was the site of a dramatic robbery in 1933. A gang of bandits was first noticed by Mrs. Merle Arnett, a telephone operator for the village who worked on the second floor of the bank. She heard an unusual sawing noise, so she went downstairs to see what was the matter. She could see that the bandits were sawing through the telephone wires, keeping the villagers from calling for outside help while the thieves worked. They threatened Arnett, and she was forced to wait out the entire ordeal in her second-floor office.[13]

According to one account, the gang of bandits was made up of about eight men, with four assigned to the bank and four assigned to patrolling the town in their car. The patrollers threatened the villagers to keep them from seeking help. They sent up a few flares to let their partners at the bank know that everything was safe and sound. The men at the bank used a huge amount of explosives to blow open the bank vault. When the explosion erupted, the vault door flew about 15 feet, and the interior of the bank was destroyed. The bandits grabbed a few thousand dollars of cash and escaped, never to be seen again.[14]

The bandits' methods were fairly similar to those of John Dillinger, who terrorized Ohio and other midwestern states during the 1930s. However, records can confirm that Dillinger was in prison in Indiana at the time of the Bowersville robbery. He would not rob his first bank until a few months after the Bowersville incident. In 1984, the village of Bowersville purchased the former bank building and turned it into a senior center.[15]

In the 1970s, Bowersville made national news. In 1972, inspired by citizens of nearby Jamestown, Bowersville residents formed a club devoted to investing in the stock market. In 1977, 27 percent of residents had some stock investment. Residents were most interested in Bob Evans Farms Inc., and Kroger Co., both Ohio food companies, something familiar for Bowersville farmers.[17]

Population: 464
Incorporated: 1927 (unincorp. 2017)

INSETS L to R: Brady Lake Village Hall • A playground for the
children of Brady Lake • The local fire department • A unique
building for the local post office

The dissolution of Brady Lake was bureaucratically complicated for politicians and citizens alike. Because of the way the village and township were formed, the neighboring Franklin Township had to annex the village and the lake separately. Residents then had to wait for their vote to be recognized by Portage County before much changed in the village. Confused motorists were still issued speeding tickets by the Brady Lake Police Department a few weeks after they had voted to dissolve their village. However the transfer of responsibilities to Franklin Township was a slow and gradual process.[19]

TOP: The lake at the center of Brady Lake

Brady Lake

The Tale of Captain Samuel Brady

UNTIL 2017, PORTAGE COUNTY, OHIO, WAS HOME to a village known as Brady Lake. After a vote for dissolution, Brady Lake has become a census-designated place. The village, first incorporated in 1927, didn't quite last 100 years.[1]

Brady Lake is named for the tale of Captain Samuel Brady, passed down for generations near Kent, Ohio, less than two miles from Brady Lake. As the legend goes, Captain Samuel Brady, of western Pennsylvania, a known Revolutionary War soldier and an "Indian fighter," brought a crew of men to Northeast Ohio in 1780 on a mission to antagonize American Indian communities in the area.[2] Because many American Indians had sided with the British during the ongoing

American Revolution, it is possible that Captain Brady was sent to assess any possible threats from the West.

Brady and his men treated the American Indians that they encountered very poorly. Brady's legend was once retold as a heroes-versus-villains story, where the heroic civilized white gentleman, Brady, is victorious over the Indian "savage." These unfounded characterizations are damaging to American Indians even today. Such tellings seem to omit the fact that Brady and his men, not the "savages," were actually the initial aggressors in their story.

According to most tellings, Brady and his men arrived in Northeast Ohio and soon mounted an attack on a group of American Indians near present-day Kent (the name of the Indian nation has been lost to time).

Brady and his men believed themselves to have the upper hand, but reinforcements soon arrived, and Brady was captured.[3]

Brady escaped his captors, running miles through the woods. At one point, with many men on his heels, Brady famously leapt over a gorge on the Cuyahoga River that was about 20 feet wide.[4] Today, "Brady's Leap" is a popular spot to visit.

The leap bought Brady some time, as his pursuers had to cross the river that he had seemingly soared over. By this time, Brady was exhausted. Unsure how much farther he could go, Brady submerged himself in a nearby lake, using a hollow reed as a snorkel to breathe. The men pursuing Brady assumed that he had either escaped or drowned. Once they left the scene, Brady fled. Thanks to that fateful day, the lake just outside Kent, Ohio, has long been known as Brady Lake.[5]

A Summer Getaway

Brady Lake was just another body of water until 1891, when an amusement park brought many Northeast Ohioans to the lake's shores.[6] The park was a popular spot for summer cottages or an after-work getaway.[7] A large dance hall featured exciting musical performances and a lively social scene, while the lake provided a tranquil moment of peace.[8]

As the park prepared to open for each summer season, local newspapers would print the names of individuals who would be renting out the cottages for the summer, letting visitors know whom they could spend their summers playing and partying with.[9] In particular, students from the nearby Kent State Normal School began regularly renting out cottages on the lake.[10]

During the 1890s, Brady Lake also became associated with a nineteenth-century American movement known as spiritualism. Spiritualists believed that it is possible to contact the supernatural, particularly the spirits of recently departed friends and loved ones.[11] At Brady Lake, an organization known as the Lake Brady Spiritualist Camp Association began holding annual gatherings as soon as the Brady Lake Park opened in 1891. The schedules for these gatherings looked like any other large conference; however, conference attendees were also given the opportunity to meet with mediums on site so as to host seances.[12]

With thousands of visitors coming to Brady Lake each summer, residents decided to form a village. In 1927, the village of Brady Lake was officially incorporated.[13] In 1993, the village would be joined by a Brady Lake Township, when it was discovered that the village had never properly annexed its own lands from the bordering Franklin Township.[14]

By the time that Brady Lake Township was formed in 1993, the amusement park on the lake was long gone. During the 1950s, the park became known as a particularly seedy place, thanks to illegal gambling and influence from the Cleveland mob.[15] In 1946, Ohio Governor Frank Lausche began the process of removing Brady Lake Mayor Joseph D. Cox from office for his part in the illegal gambling schemes. Lausche then locked down all the slot machines at Brady Lake while he investigated.[16] It wasn't long before Brady Lake Park was shuttered for good.

Dissolving a Village

In the spring of 2017, the 458 residents of Brady Lake (or at least the adults among them) were asked to make their way to the ballot box and decide the village's fate. A vote about dissolution had already occurred in 2013, but the citizens of the village had decided to remain incorporated. However, in the years following the vote, taxes continued to rise, and issues like poor road conditions worsened. In 2017, by a vote of 106–88, the village and township of Brady Lake were both dissolved.[17]

Despite the dissolution, members of the community still feel a strong attachment to each other. The lake in Brady Lake is now owned by Franklin Township, but it will hopefully one day be managed by a local association of folks from the former village.[18] Brady Lake may no longer be incorporated, but it is still a community.

On November 19, 1914, Eddie Morgan was born in what would become Brady Lake. A right fielder and a first baseman, Morgan was signed by the Saint Louis Cardinals at the age of 18.[20] On April 14, 1936, in his first major league at bat, Morgan hit a home run.[21] Playing in 39 games in all, he was later traded to the Brooklyn Dodgers and the Philadelphia Phillies.[22]

Population: 375   Approx. Founding: 1796

INSETS L to R: A sign marking Camp Dennison's Civil War museum, one of multiple stops in the village for anyone interested in the story of the original camp • Sitting down for a meal inside the Schoolhouse Restaurant • The Waldschmidt Homestead • An all purpose trail runs directly behind the Schoolhouse Restaurant

Any visitor to Camp Dennison has to visit the Schoolhouse Restaurant and General Store. Originally built in 1864, this building was one of the first two-story schoolhouses built in the Midwest. It housed local students from 1870 to 1952 and then briefly served as office space for the Dravo Gravel Company. In 1961, Donald and Phyllis Miller purchased the building and turned it into a restaurant. Visitors can enjoy a meal of comfort food followed by a stroll out back to visit with the goats and geese.[13]

TOP: A realtor and a barbecue restaurant share space in Camp Dennison

Camp Dennison

The Waldsmith Settlement

THE HISTORY OF THE VILLAGE OF CAMP DENNISON, OHIO, begins before Ohio gained statehood. Sadly, like that of many modern Ohio villages with deep roots, the origin story of the village begins with American Indian removal. During the late 1700s, early white settlers in the Northwest Territory began to push American Indians from the land they had long called home.

In 1794, a group of men traveled from their home in Pennsylvania to inspect area land that was available for sale. The group included Christian Waldsmith, George Harner, and Levi Buckingham, among others.[1] Within the next year, many of the men made land purchases in the same region of the Northwest Territory known as the Symmes Purchase. John

Cleves Symmes was a New Jersey congressman who created a company to buy land from the federal government with the intent of reselling to interested businessmen and settlers. The land Symmes acquired in southwestern Ohio became known as the Symmes Purchase or the Miami Purchase. The purchase included the future city of Cincinnati.[2]

Of the Pennsylvanians who traveled to Ohio together in 1794, Christian Waldsmith was the biggest land purchaser. He made his purchase in 1795, and he brought his family, which included six children, to the area in 1796. The Waldsmith family soon became the largest economic engine in the area. The small community they formed was known as the Waldsmith settlement. Christian Waldsmith opened mills, a general store, and a whiskey distillery. In 1810, the region's paper mill burned down, and desperate residents convinced Waldsmith to get into the paper business as well.[3]

When Waldsmith died in 1814, most of his business interests were taken on by his eldest son-in-law, Matthias Kugler. In 1837, Matthias's son, John Kugler, invested in the Little Miami Railroad, purchasing $10,000 in stock to ensure that track was laid through the Waldsmith settlement area. By this time, the Waldsmith settlement had taken on the name of Germany, due to the common ancestry of its early settlers. When the Little Miami Railroad arrived in Germany, it damaged the Waldsmith's empire, forcing its businesses to compete with those in the larger city of Cincinnati.[4]

The Original Camp Dennison

As the American Civil War began in 1861, President Abraham Lincoln called for troops from each state. Thousands of Ohio men flooded recruiting centers. By the end of the war, Ohio contributed more individual soldiers than any other state in the Union. The new recruits soon overwhelmed the military infrastructure. Troops began flooding into Columbus and even resorting to building small local camps to get started. Ohio's governor at the time, William Dennison, had little military experience, so he approached General George B. McClellan. McClellan took control of the state's troops and began to organize.[5]

McClellan began by establishing reliable training camps for recruits. He focused on the southwestern portion of Ohio. Dennison and McClellan anticipated that Kentucky might join the Confederacy, and they needed a line of defense on the Kentucky-Ohio border. McClellan sent one of his officers, William S. Rosecrans, to investigate.[6]

Rosecrans suggested locating a new camp in the village of Germany, thanks to its nearby rail depot and many promising physical attributes. McClellan agreed and named his new camp for Ohio's governor. On April 30, 1861, Brigadier General Jacob Cox arrived at the new Camp Dennison, coming from Columbus with 1,500 men. Rosecrans brought a large supply of lumber and the tools he needed to lay out the camp. Between Rosecrans's know-how and the strength of 1,500 men, the team had the camp established quickly. Unfortunately, as one historian later wrote, the "first night spent in Camp Dennison will never be forgotten by any who had the misfortune to be there..." Soldiers were met with a torrential downpour, soaking their tents and making for a miserable evening.[7]

Soon many more soldiers came to Camp Dennison. At one point, the camp was the sixth largest "city" in the state. The early group of trainees was a ragtag assembly, showing up in many different outfits and colors while they waited for uniforms to arrive. Disease became a problem, and nurses often traveled from Cincinnati to aid the men. After the summer of 1861, the original trainees at Camp Dennison began to filter out to battle, and new regiments arrived.[8]

After the spring of 1862, Camp Dennison became a military hospital. Unfortunately, this meant that when Confederate General John Hunt Morgan and his raiders came through Camp Dennison in July 1863, the troops at the camp were not well prepared to mount an offensive. Morgan came to Ohio with the intent of distracting Union troops and damaging Union infrastructure. Despite their illnesses and injuries, the residents of Camp Dennison defended the area. Morgan's men did destroy a supply train that was mostly carrying military musicians and their instruments (the musicians survived), but they were unable to take the camp or destroy the important railway system.[9, 10]

Camp Dennison was officially closed in September 1865, although the village of Germany permanently adopted the camp's name.[11]

During the 1870s, the residents of Camp Dennison attempted to change the town's name to Grand Valley, to attract tourists and new residents. However, the local railroad station insisted on keeping the name Camp Dennison. This is why the village is still known as Camp Dennison today.[12]

Visitors can still see Christian Waldsmith's home in Camp Dennison. Before he moved to Ohio, Waldsmith participated in the American Revolution. The Ohio Society of the Daughters of the American Revolution operates the historic site, located on Ohio Route 126. It is open to visitors on Sundays between May and October from 1 to 5 p.m.[14]

Population: 210   **Approx. Founding:** 1896

INSETS L to R: Wier's Farms, family owned since 1891 • Celeryville Christian School • A community health center for migrant workers on the property of Buurma Farms • A quiet street in Celeryville during the winter season

TOP: Christian Reformed Church in Celeryville

A few of the migrant workers who come to Celeryville each spring have found a permanent home in the village. One such worker is Romeo Perez. Perez, originally from Mexico, first arrived in Celeryville in 2004. By the time *The New York Times* arrived to profile Celeryville in 2017, Perez was living in the village year-round and running his own business: Romeo's Bakery. The bakery's most popular product? Pan dulce, a traditional Mexican sweet bread.

Celeryville

Henry Johnson Brings a New Community to Huron County

THE WILLARD AREA OF HURON COUNTY, OHIO, has always been known for its swamp-like conditions. It is marked by a dark, wet soil known as black peat, or more simply, "muck." In the mid-1890s, a local man named Henry Johnson realized that this soil, a plentiful resource in what was then known as Willard Marsh, was perfect for growing celery and similar vegetables. Johnson didn't have the expertise to maintain Willard Marsh, but he was pretty certain he knew who might.[1]

Celery requires consistently damp conditions as it grows or it yields the wrong taste and consistency when harvested. The muck of the Willard Marsh could provide suitable conditions, as long as it could be drained during the autumn wet season.[2]

As 1895 came to an end, Henry Johnson headed north to Kalamazoo, Michigan, where a Dutch community had formed. The Dutch were well known for expertise in drainage and flood control systems. Many farmers in the Netherlands used these drainage systems to maintain successful peat farms, similar to the ones Johnson hoped would grow in the Willard Marsh. Johnson offered a group of Dutch immigrants in Kalamazoo a plot of land in Willard Marsh if they could bring their knowledge to the region.[3]

As winter drew to a close in early 1896, about 36 Dutch families left Kalamazoo and traveled to their new home in Huron County. They arrived on March 4, 1896, and got to work improving the land.[4] Once the drainage systems were in place, the families split up the land so each had their own farm. With so many celery farms popping up, the area became known as the village of Celeryville.[5]

Celeryville's farms continued to see success for the second generation of Dutch farmers. In 1934, the village contained 37 families and 27 farms.[6] As the twentieth century progressed, farms consolidated, and today three remain: Buurma Farms, Wiers Farms, and Holthouse Farms.[7]

Celeryville's Farming Families

These farms are owned and operated by the descendants of original Dutch migrants to the area. Each farm has expanded in recent years by purchasing area farms as well as new land outside Celeryville, and outside Ohio.[8, 9, 10] It is very likely that most Ohioans have purchased produce grown on one of these farms at some point in their lives.

Buurma Farms originated with Frans Buurma, a Dutch immigrant who was working as a laborer on a celery farm in Kalamazoo, Michigan, when Henry Johnson arrived in 1896. Buurma decided to follow Johnson to Huron County so that he could try his hand at running a farm. In 1896, Buurma Farms was founded on a small 4-acre plot of land in the future village of Celeryville.[11]

In 1891, Henry and Kathryn Wiers left their home in Groningen, Netherlands, and resettled in Kalamazoo. The descendants of Henry and Kathryn Wiers have continued to grow their farm, much like the Buurma family.[12] Each new Wiers generation has a choice to pursue a career away from the family business, but as Ben Wiers told a reporter in 1988, "...there's something about the land. If I went somewhere else, I'd feel like I was missing something."[13]

Holthouse Farms had a bit of a slower start, but it is just as successful in Celeryville today. In 1870, Jan Holthuis was born in the Netherlands, and in 1889, he arrived in Kalamazoo. Together with his sons, Rudy and Jacob, Jan set up a celery farm in Celeryville in 1903. It was Jacob and Rudy who really grew Holthouse Farms, as Jan moved to Tiffin not long after its founding.[14]

Migrant Workers in Celeryville

As the farms in Celeryville grew during the twentieth century, they began to require a larger labor force. The farms subsequently began to hire migrant farm workers. The migrant workers have become a regular part of the fabric of the Celeryville community. During the winter months, their homes sit empty, but each spring, a largely Hispanic migrant workforce arrives to sow the fields of Celeryville, not leaving until each vegetable has been harvested in the fall. As Ben Wiers told *The New York Times*, "Without the Hispanic labor force, we wouldn't be able to grow crops."[15]

However, Celeryville, and the nearby Willard, have not been immune to growing national tensions concerning immigration. About 7 in 10 field workers in the United States are undocumented. Previously, the wages that farm work provided made working in the muck an attractive prospect. However, as the national discourse around immigration has grown increasingly vitriolic, many migrant workers fear coming to the United States. Celeryville's farms have suffered as a result. Locals are not interested in doing this laborious work, so fields have been left unharvested, and profits are at risk. In 2016, Celeryville's farmers left millions of dollars of produce sitting in their fields. As Ken Holthouse told the *Times*, "We pray and hope the workers come."[16]

Celeryville made national news in 2017, when the Willard Area Chamber of Commerce attempted to throw a welcome-back party for migrant workers. As soon as a local paper published an article about the event, as Ricky Branaham, the chamber's executive director said, "It took on a life of its own. It got political." So many residents disapproved of the welcome-back party that it was canceled, largely out a fear of protestors.[17]

In 1906, Henry Wiers helped finance and build the village's first church, where services were only offered in the Dutch language. The Celeryville Christian School has also been open since 1931. The school grew quickly, opening up a new facility in the 1950s, with additions during the 1980s. Today, the school serves students from preschool through 12th grade.[19]

Population: 210   Incorporated: 1899

INSETS L to R: Branch of the Morgan County Library • The Stone
Matheney Funeral Home • Chesterhill Cemetery • The Triple
Nickel Diner is nestled into the back streets of Chesterhill

Why do local families find themselves purchasing
fresh produce at wholesale prices at the Chesterhill
Produce Auction? Chesterhill is located in a food
desert, many miles from any grocery stores.
Auctions like Chesterhill's help local families get
access to fresh food. Many families will buy in
bulk at the auction and then preserve their purchases for use year-round, by canning, freezing,
or other methods.[14]

TOP: A mechanic and a convenience store along a main road in Chesterhill

Chesterhill

The Boswells of Belmont Build a Village

IN 1829, ELIJAH AND ANN HIATT left their home in Belmont
County, Ohio, and set out to build a home in Dublin, Indiana. Not long
after, Ann's father, Dempsey Boswell, wrote asking that they return. Boswell and his nephew, Exum Bundy, were interested in starting their own
new village, and they wanted Elijah's assistance. Elijah and Ann decided
to make the trek back to Ohio. The three men traveled to Marietta,
where they met with Rufus Putnam of the Ohio Company and purchased
100 acres of land in Morgan County for about one dollar per acre.[1]

In 1834, the extended Boswell family finally arrived to live on the
land they had purchased and began the process of building a village. J.
B. Pruden was hired to lay out lots, and Boswell opened the first village
store, using financial contributions from all of the new settlers.[2]

When it was time to pick out a name for the village, many new residents suggested the names of the three founders, however all three men
objected. Dempsey Boswell then suggested the name of Chester, because
he and the other early residents of this new village were all members of
the Society of Friends. Many Quakers in the United States could trace
their ancestry to the village of Chester, England.[3] The name Chester
was chosen, but it was quickly changed when the founders realized a
nearby town had that name. They settled on Chesterfield, which also
was changed for the same reason. Finally, the village chose its permanent name: Chesterhill.[4]

The village of Chesterhill never experienced a large boom, but it
did serve as a residence for many oil workers during the 1890s, when oil
fields in the area were offering plenty of work. Histories of the village

make it clear that the oil workers weren't viewed as permanent residents. As one history recorded, "The town was full of strangers, oil workers of all classes, and no one knew to what class his neighbor belonged."[5]

Building the Chesterhill Produce Auction

Today the village of Chesterhill is known for the Chesterhill Produce Auction. Open twice a week, from May until October, it involves local farmers, many of them Amish or Mennonite, who meet at the beginning of each season to plan out the produce they will sell, to avoid any unnecessary competition. Then each week they pack up their vehicle, be it a truck or a buggy, and transport large amounts of fresh produce to the auction. Here, more than 1,300 registered bidders get a chance to purchase some of the best products Ohio has to offer.[6]

The Chesterhill Produce Auction is one of nine produce auctions in Ohio. These auctions, including Chesterhill's, have been largely successful thanks to lots of hard work and passion in the local community.[7] The Chesterhill Auction began in 2003, when retired couple Jean and Marvin Konkle, originally of Bainbridge, retired to the village. The couple had seen an auction in Bainbridge that was very successful, and they wanted to transfer the idea to their new hometown.[8]

Most of Ohio's produce auctions are designed to serve rural areas like Chesterhill and Morgan County. Many rural Ohioans are stuck in food deserts with no grocery store nearby, and certainly no farmers' markets. This makes selling produce very difficult, especially for Amish farmers whose beliefs may preclude access to modern transportation.[9]

In 2003, the Konkles began talking to the residents of Chesterhill about an auction, slowly gaining local support. By the summer of 2004, they began broaching the topic specifically with their Amish neighbors. The key to success in most produce auctions in Ohio is the involvement of the Amish and/or Mennonite communities. The format of most auctions allows for the preservation of the tight-knit, local, and labor-intensive farms that are prized by Amish culture, and in turn, the generational dedication that the Amish community is able to provide ensures continued product for the auction to sell.[10]

Finally in 2005, the Chesterhill Produce Auction's inaugural sales took place under a tent in the village, with a building still on the way. The cost of establishing the auction reached about $150,000, most of which came from a mortgage on the Konkles' house. Despite the fact that they funded the auction, the Konkles never made decisions alone. They worked with a steering committee made up of members of The Ohio State University Extension Educators, the nonprofit Rural Action, and local farmers. This enabled certain issues to be ironed out before the auction even opened. For instance, it is typical during an auction to assign each seller a number. The steering committee noted that most Amish families have a religious objection to the use of numbers for personal identification. The auction opted to use letters instead.[11]

The Multicultural Genealogical Center

Around 2010, Ada Woodson Adams, Al Adams, and their nephew, David Butcher, opened the Multicultural Genealogical Center in the village of Chesterhill. The center works hard to tell the stories of African-Americans in Morgan County. This history was often passed down through an oral tradition that can be complicated to preserve.[12]

The Adams family of the Multicultural Genealogical Center has contributed much research to the history of Chesterhill's Underground Railroad. They have even compiled a tour of the local sites. The tour includes Henman's Cave in Chesterhill and a privately owned residence in Millfield (see page 116).[13]

The first non-Quaker resident, George C. King, of Chesterhill arrived in the village in 1836. Due to their pacifist beliefs, none of the Quakers felt comfortable serving as the justice of the peace, so King was elected into the position almost as soon as he set foot in town. He went on to serve for over 30 years, taking on the nickname "Squire King."[15]

TOP: The Chesterville General Store sits on a busy intersection in town

Population: 232   **Incorporated:** 1859

INSETS L to R: The Chesterville Post Office • Chesterville United Methodist Church • Chesterville Town Hall • The Enos Miles House maintains many of the features crafted by its original owner in the 1830s

Interested in learning more about the historic buildings of Chesterville? Head to the internet. The Selover Public Library of Chesterville, in addition to providing access to their collection and planning community events, has published a history of many of the village's buildings on their website. This list includes many of the buildings listed on the National Register of Historic Places and beyond! Studying the architecture of Chesterville truly is one of the best ways to understand the stories of its earliest residents.[12]

Chesterville

The Oldest Community in Morrow Count

THE VILLAGE OF CHESTERVILLE, in Morrow County, Ohio, is the oldest community in the county. White settlers came to the future Chesterville, mostly from Pennsylvania, during the earliest days of Ohio's statehood. Many of these settlers were given land in the area through the military pensions they earned after service in the Revolutionary War. In 1807, Chester Township was first surveyed by one of these early settlers, Joseph Vance. In 1812, Chester Township was officially established, taking its name from Chester, Pennsylvania, the original home of many of the new Morrow county inhabitants.[1]

During the 1810s, Enos Miles, a teacher and surveyor (among many other prestigious talents), arrived at his new home in Chester Township. Here he began to lay out a village that the locals called "Miles Crossroads." In 1829, J. C. Hickman officially laid out the village, which was named Chesterville, after the township.[2] In 1832, with Enos Miles as postmaster, village residents were officially told to have their mail addressed to Chesterville.[3]

Naming a New County

In 1845, the state of Ohio formed a new county that included Chester Township. Chesterville residents petitioned the state legislature to make their village the county seat. Even though it was the oldest settlement in the county, the village faced competition from nearby Marengo and Mount Gilead. The county had yet to be named, and each village had their own ideas about the possible moniker. Chesterville preferred Chester

County, Mount Gilead promoted Gilead County, and Marengo suggested Bennington County.[4]

After three years of debate, Marengo gave up, throwing its support behind Mount Gilead. Chesterville and Mount Gilead remained devoted, and the Ohio legislature could not come to a decision. Finally, residents of Mount Gilead struck a deal, agreeing to name the county Morrow, after former Governor Jeremiah Morrow. This won the vote of one extra legislator, allowing Mount Gilead to win the race for Morrow County seat by one vote on February 24, 1848.[5] Due to this loss, Chesterville was largely ignored by incoming railways and highways in the future. Without the important trade and travelers that these modern modes of transportation provided, Chesterville was stuck with permanent small-town status.[6]

A Village Made for the National Register of Historic Places

Because Chesterville's growth was frozen in the 1850s, today it is something of an architectural destination. Multiple buildings in the village have been added to the National Register of Historic Places (NRHP). It is rare to see so many antebellum buildings still in use in one village, but Chesterville's lost bid for county seat was actually a blessing. As the village's growth slowed during the 1850s, fewer new structures went up, so historic structures were passed on through generations. During the late 1970s, residents of Chesterville organized to preserve and recognize the historic architecture in their hometown. They formed a group called Chesterville Community Concerns that requested a survey of the village by the NRHP and began restoring Chesterville's Town Hall.[7] The Town Hall is actually one of the youngest buildings in town on the Register. It was originally constructed in 1867 by village officials and the Independent Order of Odd Fellows. The building was a center of village entertainment, hosting traveling shows, school plays, and family parties. The building has been completely owned by the village since 1968. It continues to host community events, such as summer reading programs sponsored by the village's library.[8]

Also listed on the NRHP is the home that Enos Miles, Chesterville's best-known founder, built during the 1830s. Upon his arrival in the area, Miles built a log cabin, but by the 1830s he built a more permanent home at the corner of South Portland and Mill Streets. Miles and his large family (including an Enos Jr.) lived there until Miles's death in 1840. The home has traded hands often since 1840 but remains almost unchanged.[9]

The Life of a Village Founder

Enos Miles was trained as a teacher and devoted much of his life to education. He taught the children of Chesterville before a public school was founded, giving lessons in churches or cabins. Around 1820, Miles sold a portion of his land to the village for only a pint of oats, so it could erect an official schoolhouse. This log structure wasn't very efficient—in the winter, students near the fireplace sweated while those in the back could see their breath. However, interest in the school increased, and soon the village built a new two-story building for the students.[10]

In 1830, Enos Miles expanded his business operations when he opened a hotel and tavern known as the Leonard House. Not long after, embracing his roots as a teacher, Miles built an adjoining brick building that he deemed the "Academy." This academy was meant as a finishing school for young women in the community. Unfortunately, Miles died not long after the academy was established, and there was a lack of interest from local students. The academy was combined with the Leonard House and served as a part of the hotel. According to town history, President Grover Cleveland spent a night at the hotel in 1885. Unfortunately, two years later in 1887, the hotel burned down. In 1924, Daniel Selover, a member of a long-time Chesterville family, gave a large endowment for construction of a library on the former hotel site. The Selover Public Library is still an active institution in town, providing the educational resources that Enos Miles so prized.[11]

In 1885, Hugh Dillman McGaughey was born in Chesterville. He became an actor on Broadway and even appeared in a few silent films, including *An Amateur Widow*. He enlisted in the U.S. Navy during World War I. Afterward, Dillman married Anna Dodge, the widow of a former auto magnate. They divorced in 1947.[13]

TOP: The historic Clifton Mill

Population: 151   **Incorporated:** 1835

INSETS L to R: A view along the hiking trail at Clifton Gorge • The Clifton Garden Cabin • Clifton Opera House • The Clifton Mill sells flour made on site

In 1849, the village of Clifton suffered greatly from a cholera outbreak. Residents were first warned of the impending emergency when a traveler staying at a local tavern became ill overnight and died first thing the next morning. On the southern end of the village, residents had placed privies near the Clifton Gorge, assuming the water would drain into the canyon. However, it actually began to drain into their wells. As a result, between 15 and 40 people in the village died.[16]

Clifton

The Early Years of Clifton—A Mill and a Missed Opportunity

IN EITHER 1802 OR 1803, a man named Owen Davis built a mill within walking distance of a large and rocky gorge in southwestern Ohio, which was perfectly suited for harnessing the power of the Little Miami River. This location began to attract other mill proprietors, including Colonel Robert Patterson, ancestor to John Patterson, the future founder of the Dayton National Cash Register Company (page 37).[1]

These mills began to attract new settlers, including Timothy G. Bates and Bennett Lewis, who bought much of the land that made up the town and built a general store in 1826. In 1833, Bates and Lewis had a surveyor by the name of Robert Watson lay out the town of Clifton, said to be named for the gorgeous cliffs on the gorge.[2, 3] Many agree that the town was incorporated in 1835, though some sources note an informal town charter from 1816; the village's official website notes an 1838 charter.[4, 5]

The new village of Clifton began to grow, because it was located on the Cincinnati, Lebanon, and Columbus Stagecoach Route, also known as the Accommodation Line. As visitors passed through the village, residents were ready to accommodate their needs. Furthermore, manufacturers in Clifton could use this route to trade their goods.[6] This route was quickly overshadowed in the 1840s, as talk of the Xenia-Springfield Railroad came to southwestern Ohio. Unfortunately for Clifton, the nearby village of Yellow Springs was chosen as the local stop on the rail line. The railroad bypass forever stunted Clifton's growth.[7]

The History of the Clifton Mill

Despite the disappointment concerning the railroad, residents of Clifton continued to persevere. The mill first opened by Owen Davis in the early 1800s was eventually sold to the Patterson family. During the Civil War, the mill provided Union troops with cornmeal and flour. Around 1869, the Armstrong family took over the mill, and in 1908 they began using the water-powered turbine to provide electricity to local towns and villages. From 1908 until 1937, the turbine ran constantly. For only $1 per month, a family could purchase electricity. According to various sources, the mill burned down at least twice in its long history, and it changed hands across many Clifton families. Finally, in 1988, Tony Satariano, originally a Pittsburgh resident but a huge supporter of history in the village of Clifton, became the owner of the mill.[8]

The Satariano family still uses the Clifton Mill to mill flour; however, they have also preserved a historic site for residents and visitors alike. Today visitors to the Historic Clifton Mill can step inside to view how exactly the mill works, stop by the restaurant for a home-cooked meal, or visit the country store inside the restored building. Every year as fall comes to Ohio, workers at the Historic Clifton Mill spend three months putting up approximately 4 million Christmas lights on the site. From the day after Thanksgiving until New Year's Eve, visitors can enjoy the Legendary Lights, recognized in 2018 by *USA Today*.[9]

The Clifton Gorge

The magnificent Clifton Gorge is just a quarter of a mile west of the village boundaries and on the edge of John Bryan State Park. The site includes gorgeous hiking trails that wind through the canyon carved out by glaciers. Hikers can view waterfalls on the Little Miami River and some of the best springtime flowers in the state. Clifton Gorge is owned by the Ohio Department of Natural Resources and has been registered as a National Natural Landmark.[10]

The Clifton Opera House

Since 1893, the village of Clifton has been home to its own opera house. The building was designed by Charles Cregar, an architect from Springfield, Ohio, who also designed the municipal building in his hometown. The Clifton Opera House was likely one his smaller commissions. The building was built to hold 500 audience members, a number that has always been larger than the population of the village.[11] Unfortunately, in 1925 a part of Cregar's original design, a tower on the top of the opera house, had to be removed. Apparently bats had taken up residence in the tower and residents had no other option to remove them. In 1963, the opera house became a town hall and police station. Unfortunately, by 1987 the village was ready to have it torn down. However, the Clifton Historical Society, led by Howard Printz, began leasing the building and making repairs.[12] Today the Clifton Opera House is completely functional. Its calendar of events and shows can be found on its website, and it can also be rented for private functions.[13]

Famous Faces in Clifton

The village of Clifton is the birthplace of a few very famous Ohioans. In 1839, just a few years after Clifton was incorporated, Isaac K. Funk was born in the village. Funk grew up to found and operate the Funk & Wagnalls Company with partner Adam Willis Wagnalls. The company became famous for their encyclopedias.[14] Also born in Clifton, many decades later, in 1913, was Woody Hayes. Hayes is most well known for his time as the head coach of the Ohio State University football team, from 1951–1978.[15]

Many small towns no longer have hotels or inns available in town, but this is not the case in Clifton. The Clifton Garden Cabin, located in the heart of downtown, sleeps up to six guests. Visitors to the Historic Clifton Mill or hikers of the Clifton Gorge will find that the cabin is conveniently within walking distance of both attractions.[17]

TOP: First Baptist Church in Coalton

Population: 470   **Incorporated:** 1880

INSETS L to R: The James Rhodes Community Center • A railway that runs through the center of Coalton • The Coalton Volunteer Fire Department • Governor James Rhodes's birthplace

Located in both Coal and Liberty Townships, the Coalton Wildlife Area was first established as a camp for Boy Scouts, then sold to the Mead Corporation in 1959. Mead, a large manufacturer of paper and office supplies, used the land for logging. The trees from this area were used to produce Mead products at a Chillicothe paper mill. In 2007, the Ohio Department of Natural Resources (DNR) acquired the wildlife area, which is now available for recreational hunting. The site is home to a number of interesting trails and a thriving forest that the Ohio DNR works hard to preserve.[18]

Coalton

A Village Built on Coal

WHITE SETTLERS FIRST MOVED into the northern end of Jackson County, Ohio, from Virginia and Pennsylvania during the 1810s, but without fertile soil for agriculture, population growth remained stagnant. However, once coal was discovered in the late 1800s, investors and miners alike moved into the area. In fact, by 1882 the population had grown so much that a new township was established. Fittingly, the new Coal Township took its name from the rock that enabled the area to boom.[1]

By 1877, construction of the Ohio Southern Railroad was nearly complete in what would become Coal Township. Interested in capitalizing on this new development, John F. Shook and Adam Scott laid out a village nearby named Eurekaville.[2]

In 1879, J. H. Wilson and Joseph Gooding laid out a town on the border named Coalton. Eventually the two towns merged, and the name Coalton stuck. The village of Coalton grew in its early years, reaching a population of about 2,000 people by the 1890s. In 1880, the village was incorporated.[3]

Governor James Rhodes, Son of Coalton

Quite a few famous people have come from the village of Coalton over the years. Among the most well known was James A. Rhodes. Rhodes was born in Coalton on September 13, 1909, to a local coal-mining family.[4] Unfortunately, in 1916 when Rhodes was only a boy, a mining accident took his father's life. A young Rhodes was forced to seek out work. Eventually the family moved to Springfield, Ohio, where Rhodes finished up high school.[5]

After high school, Rhodes and his family moved to Columbus so he could attend The Ohio State University. Unfortunately, college life interfered with his ability to support his family. He dropped out before he was able to graduate.[6]

Despite dropping out of school, Rhodes eventually set his sights on politics. In 1937, he was elected to the Columbus School Board, as a Republican. He soon served as the city auditor, eventually becoming mayor of Columbus, a position he held from 1944 to 1952.[7]

From 1952 to 1962, Rhodes served as the Ohio State Auditor, with a short break for a failed bid at the governor's office in 1954. Undeterred, Rhodes ran again and won, serving as governor from 1963 to 1971 and again from 1975 to 1983. Rhodes died in 2001 and is buried in Columbus.[8]

During his time as governor, Rhodes was known for lowering taxes while increasing education funding. In 1970, Rhodes attempted to run for the United States Senate; however, his primary election occurred only two days after the Kent State Massacre. As governor, Rhodes had ordered the Ohio National Guard to Kent State University, where they shot and killed four student protestors. Rhodes lost the primary and didn't try again.[9]

"Ritty's Incorruptible Cashier"

The village of Coalton played a role in the development of a familiar piece of technology: the cash register. In 1878, James Ritty, a cafe owner in Dayton, inspired by the mechanisms that drive a ship's propeller, invented a device to help him balance his books, calling it "Ritty's Incorruptible Cashier."[10] Meanwhile in Coalton, a brash businessman named John H. Patterson was dismayed to see that every year his books reported a loss. Wanting to fix the problem, Patterson purchased a few of Ritty's machines. By the end of the year he was reporting huge profits.[11]

Convinced that Ritty's invention represented the future of business, Patterson quickly purchased all of the stock available for the National Manufacturing Company, the owners of the patent. In 1884, he obtained

total control of the company, even though the cash register was a device for which there was then no discernible demand. No one wanted a machine that would count their cash: they could do that for free. When Patterson finally managed to inspect the National Manufacturing Company's poorly maintained factories, he had buyer's remorse and attempted to give his purchase back, but he was stuck with it.[12]

Patterson decided it was time to convince potential customers that they needed his product. In doing so, he not only led the business, now named the National Cash Register company to success, but helped popularize the modern model of a sales team, with an emphasis on sales territories, "canned" talks, and frequent, targeted mail advertising. In fact, one company received so many mailed flyers that they wrote Patterson back insisting, "For Heaven's sake let up. What have we done to you?"[13]

Patterson also revolutionized employee relations. He built a new factory with a multitude of windows to allow for natural light, landscaped lawns for lunchtime walks, a lending library, and a cafeteria. Employees received free health care. When asked about these perks, Patterson insisted "…it pays." With happy employees, his production numbers went up and so did his profits.[14]

Nonetheless, Patterson was obsessive about controlling his business, and he employed "knock out men" to keep businesses from buying cash registers from his competitors. Thanks to these tactics, Patterson and 29 other executives were brought to court on antitrust charges in 1913. Luckily for Patterson, just before his trial, the city of Dayton experienced a life-altering flood. Patterson was one of the first residents to begin organizing rescue crews. This act of goodwill made indicting Patterson politically difficult, and he was let off on all charges. Perhaps trying to save face, he fired the other 29 employees who had also been charged. One of these men, Thomas Watson, would go on to help found IBM.[15]

Isham Jones was born in 1894 in Coalton. He became a successful saxophone player, orchestra conductor, and composer. One of his best-known songs is "It Had to Be You."[16] Pat Duncan, a player with the Cincinnati Reds from 1919 to 1924 was born in 1893; he won a World Series in 1919, the year baseball was tainted by the Black Sox Scandal.[17]

JOHN H. PATTERSON,
FOUNDER OF
THE NATIONAL CASH REGISTER COMPANY,
FIRST USED A CASH REGISTER
OF THIS EARLY TYPE
IN HIS STORE
HERE IN COALTON, IN 1881
★ ★ ★
IMPRESSED WITH THE MACHINE,
HE BOUGHT THE COMPANY
THAT BUILT IT
AND DEVELOPED A
WORLD-WIDE BUSINESS SAVING

TOP: Union School

Population: 418 **Approx. Founding:** 1837

INSETS L to R: The College Corner Post Office (located on the state line and serving both sides, the post office uses two zip codes) • Hueston Woods Park • Downtown College Corner near the state line • College Corner United Methodist Church

In 1935, the Cincinnati office of the Federal Bureau of Investigation (FBI) was investigating George Barrett for stealing and reselling vehicles. Special Agents Nelson Klein and Donald McGovern tracked Barrett to College Corner. A shootout occurred. Klein hit Barrett's legs and incapacitated him, but Barrett fatally wounded Klein. The shootout occurred very close to the Ohio and Indiana border, but ultimately Barrett was tried in Indiana courts. Although hanging had been outlawed in Indiana, killing an FBI officer had recently been declared a federal crime, and hanging was still allowed at the federal level.[19]

College Corner

Two Small Towns in One Place

THE VILLAGE OF COLLEGE CORNER is unique. That's because the village of College Corner is actually in two states. Straddling the western boundary of Ohio and the eastern boundary of Indiana, the village of College Corner encompasses four townships, three counties, two zip codes, and one post office.[1] When combined with the population of West College Corner, Indiana, the village of College Corner, Ohio, reaches a population well over 1,000. However, on its own, the Ohio village is technically only home to 407 people.

The village of College Corner was originally located exclusively in Butler County, Ohio. It was laid out in May 1837 by a local man named Gideon T. Howe. Howe became well known in College Corner as a tavern keeper (in 1976, Howe's tavern was added to the National Register of Historic Places).[2, 3] Later extensions to the village pushed its boundaries into Preble County, Ohio, and Union County, Indiana.[4]

Throughout the village's entire history, the lines between the Ohio side and the Indiana side of College Corner have been blurry. While operating together and working as neighbors, each side is bound by their own state laws, and each village was incorporated separately.[5] Next-door neighbors even have two different state power companies.[6]

College Corner is found in College Township, Butler County, Ohio, an area specifically set aside by the state for an institution of higher learning.[7] When it was laid out, College Corner was found quite literally in the corner of College Township.[8]

Union School: One of a Kind

Students on both sides of College Corner have been attending classes together since 1893, the year Union School was first built. This school has become somewhat of a marvel, with frequent local and even national media coverage. Remodeled in 1926 on its campus on State Line Street, half of the Union School sits in the state of Ohio and half in Indiana. The official border? The half-court line on the school's basketball court.[9]

Today Union School exclusively serves elementary school students, but during its days as a high school, it hosted many basketball games. As two players waited eagerly for a jump ball at the beginning of a game, they were standing in completely different states. This split has caused some unique problems over the years. For example, during the infamous Blizzard of 1978, there were many snow days. The state of Ohio allowed for fewer snow days for its students than Indiana, so the students at Union who lived on the Ohio side of College Corner had to attend a handful of field trips to a local park to accumulate the required in-school hours.[10]

More recently, when the school sponsored a visit by a group of Indiana dentists to provide checkups for students, the staff mistakenly reserved a classroom on the Ohio side of the school. When the dentists arrived they moved to the Indiana side of the building, as they were only licensed to practice in Indiana.[11] Similarly, early teachers at Union were required to be licensed in both states (specific education requirements have been worked out in recent years).

One of the biggest problems for the entire village of College Corner was dealing with conflicting time zones. The Ohio side of the village has always been in the Eastern Time Zone and observed Daylight Saving Time.[12] And from 1918 until 1961, the Indiana side was in the Central Time Zone.[13] The Indiana side finally moved to the Eastern Time Zone but did not observe Daylight Saving Time, meaning that for a portion of the year, the time was different depending on where you were in the village. The school and most organizations adhered to Indiana time (Eastern Standard Time), but there were still many missed appointments and constant queries of: Is that Ohio or Indiana time?[14]

In 2006, the state of Indiana finally began using Daylight Saving Time, meaning that for the first time in the village's long history, watches all across College Corner are always set to the same time.[15] Most village residents were strong proponents of the switch to Daylight Saving Time, anxious to finally live in a standard time zone. The only downfall was for bar owners on the Indiana side whose bars had been able to stay open an hour later than bars on the Ohio side for a portion of the year. However most bartenders agreed, the lost hour was worth it to finally stop being asked for the time.[16]

Students in College Corner continue to go to school together, making the Union County-College Corner Joint School District truly one of a kind. The joint school district was formed in 1921, in an attempt to add some order to the chaos that occurred when one school spanned two states. Today, preschool through fifth grade is held in the old Union School (updated in 2004), while other students are spread among various buildings in both Ohio and Indiana. During the 1980s, the state of Indiana required the students that were residents of Indiana go to high school in a school completely in their own state. Ohio students acquiesced and began traveling farther for classes. However, the state of Ohio threatened to pull their half of the school district's funding, since their students were not being educated in Ohio. Finally, in 1995, the school district was reorganized, still allowing for joint education across state borders, but largely adhering to Indiana's laws.[17]

Residents of the village almost always speak positively about the Union School. It ties the town together. All of the other issues that come with maintaining a village in two states are handled so that the students can continue to go to the school their community values. The Union School keeps this community united.[18]

In 1835, Ambrose E. Burnside, a future Civil War general, may have worked as a tailor in the village. It's also possible that Benjamin Harrison once passed through town. His father-in-law, Dr. John W. Scott, helped build the Presbyterian Church in 1845.

TOP: A view of Conesville

Population: 344   Approx. Founding: 1847

INSETS L to R: Conesville United Methodist Church • The
Conesville Post Office • A railroad town • Conesville School

The two groups lobbying against the Conesville
Power Plant in 2009 were the Environmental Integ-
rity Project and Earthjustice.[12] The Environmental
Integrity Project was originally founded in 2002 by
Eric Schaeffer, former director of the Evironmental
Protection Agency. The nonprofit has headquarters
in Washington, D.C., and Austin, Texas.

Conesville

The Founding, Fall, and Founding (Again) of Conesville

THE EARLY HISTORY OF CONESVILLE, OHIO, is a story of
ups and downs, booms and busts. The village can be found in Franklin
Township of Coshocton County. During most of the Ohio's first century
of statehood, Franklin Township was tiny. The township was home to
three small villages, each supporting about twenty homes. Sometime
during the early- to mid-1800s (the exact date seems to be lost to history), a man by the last name of Cones set up a distillery in Franklin
Township. The families of his employees began to move in near the
distillery, and thus the village of Conesville was born.[1]

During the height of the distillery's business, it looked as if the village of Conesville would grow. Interested in the new community, a man
named James Johnson built a cooper (barrel-making) shop in the village.
Johnson, originally born in Massachusetts in 1815, did not learn the
trade until 25. He moved around a lot as a child, living in New Jersey
and New York, and found early work on the Erie Canal. After working
on the Canal, Johnson trained to become a cooper and began working
in his new field in 1848. In 1852, he came to Conesville, producing barrels for Cone's distillery, as well as for other buyers.[2]

Johnson's cooper shop brought additional business and employees
to Conesville, leading to a short boom for the village. Unfortunately,
the distillery went out of business, Johnson closed his shop in 1868, and
many families left the village. By 1881, as one history stated, Conesville
had become, "merely a railroad station, with a country store attached."

Although the village had shrunk, Conesville maintained a post office and a station on the Pittsburgh, Cincinnati, and St. Louis Railway during the 1880s.[3]

Conesville's fortunes turned in 1894, when the Oden Valley Coal Company opened a mine just northwest of the village. Soon after, Arnold Coal Company and Burt Coal Company opened mines south of the village.[4] These new mines brought workers back to Conesville and made certain that the village would never again be simply "a railroad station, with a country store attached."

Caught Red-Handed

In 1935, the village of Conesville was the site of some interesting detective work. That fall, Ransom Smith and James Cox of Conesville decided to steal a car belonging to Albert Cox while it was parked outside the building that housed the *Coshocton Tribune*. Ransom Smith had already done some time at the Mansfield reformatory, so his actions were no surprise.[5]

The local police spotted the missing Chevrolet the day after it was stolen, but they decided not to take it into custody right away. Instead, they were able to confirm that someone took the car out each night and always returned it to the same spot in Conesville for the day. The police began to plan a stakeout, arriving in Conesville after dark and waiting for a few hours for the car to return to its parking spot.[6]

A car finally arrived, with Ransom Smith and James Cox inside. However, the car no longer matched the description of the missing vehicle. It's license plates held a new number, and the body of the car was now painted red. However, upon inspecting the car, the police found cans of red paint under the seats. Smith and Cox weren't exactly "caught red handed" but they were pretty close. The men were arrested and sent to jail to await a trial. Smith was still on probation for a former theft charge.[7]

The Conesville Power Plant

With so many coal mines nearby, it made sense that in 1957 Columbus Southern Power Company, now a part of American Electric Power (AEP), opened a power plant in the village of Conesville. At its height, the company employed about 600 people.

In 1985, AEP opened a coal preparation plant in Conesville to support the work at the main power plant. The plant washed and readied coal for firing at the power plant, moving through about 3 million tons of coal each year. The plant had a remarkably safe history, until closing in 2012 with 22 employees, a sign of what was to come for AEP in Conesville.[8]

Since the early years of the 2000s, environmental groups have openly discussed their concerns about the Conesville Power Plant. Their concerns were complicated. The plant was central to Conesville's economy, but it was also putting the community at a significant health risk. In 2009, the power plant was listed as one of twelve in Ohio that the Environmental Protection Agency (EPA) had deemed an unacceptable cancer risk. In addition, the Conesville Power Plant didn't monitor groundwater pollution, potentially leaving residents at risk of arsenic poisoning.[9]

As researchers have continued to learn more about the dangers of coal ash and as the priorities of AEP Ohio have changed, the Conesville Power Plant's days became numbered. The plant's costs have begun to outweigh their profits, and they found few buyers for the plant. One of the plant's main suppliers, Westmoreland Coal, has recently filed for bankruptcy.[10] In October 2017, the state of Ohio officially devalued the Conesville Power Plant. Unfortunately, this has taken a huge cut out of the funding received by Franklin Township and the local schools. The plant has been slated to close for a while now, but recently the date was moved up. The plant will close on May 31, 2020. Many of the 165 employees have found jobs elsewhere in the AEP organization.[11]

Despite the issues stemming from the Conesville Power Plant, American Electric Power (AEP) has played a positive role in the Conesville community. One of AEP's contributions has been the Conesville Coal Lands, a 10,635-acre public hunting and fishing area with more than 100 lakes and ponds, as well as horse trails, camping, and mountain biking options.[13]

TOP: Coolville Town Hall

Population: 498   **Incorporated:** 1835

INSETS L to R: The Healing Chapel, the smallest church in Ohio •
Coolville Elementary • "Coolville: Building Community One Block
At A Time" • Grace Brethren Church on the site of the former
Coolville Male and Female Seminary

Does Coolville, Ohio, sound familiar? It might be
because of the cartoons you watched as a kid. In
the animated series, *Scooby-Doo*, Scooby and the
gang hail from a town named Coolsville, Ohio (note
the addition of an "s.") While the real Coolville
can be found in Athens County in southeastern
Ohio, Scooby's dog house lives in Erie County in the
Northwestern part of the state. There is no known
connection between Coolville, Ohio, and the drafting
of Scooby's backstory.[11]

Coolville

A Journey From New England

IN 1798, A GROUP OF ABOUT 40 TRAVELERS from New England
embarked on a journey west, toward what would soon be the state of Ohio.
The travelers stopped for a time in the city of Belpre, likely to avoid winter
travel. After starting out again in 1799, the group reached the future Athens County.[1]

One of these travelers was a man named Asahel Cooley. Many years
after his initial move to Ohio, the Revolutionary War veteran had a village
laid out in Troy Township in 1818. The village eventually took his name,
becoming known as Coolville, Ohio; it was officially incorporated in 1835.[2]

In 1815, before the village of Coolville was even surveyed, two of
Asahel's sons, Simeon and Herman, built a dam across the Hocking River.

This dam helped provide power for various economic pursuits that would
allow the town to thrive. Thanks to the dam, the village of Coolville was
able to support a flour mill, a grist mill, a sawmill, and a distillery.[3] Unfortunately, the dam that the Cooleys built is now underwater. Despite this, a
mill remained in business in Coolville into the 1980s, beginning to rely on
electric power after 1945. In 2004, the mill was torn down.[4]

Coolville Male and Female Seminary

During the 1840s, the citizens of Coolville decided to provide the best
education possible for their young residents, who at the time could only
acquire an eighth-grade education in the village. The Methodist Episcopal
Church sponsored the opening of a seminary that was financed by the
village residents. Like most seminaries, the Coolville Male and Female

Seminary prepared students for a life of ministry. However, secular course schedules were available for students preparing for a college education. It's not clear how long the school was open, but most sources suggest it was from the 1840s to the 1860s. When it closed, the building was rented out for meetings, briefly used as a private residence, and then sold to the Troy Township Grange. In 1969, the Grace Brethren Church acquired it, razed the building, and built a new church on site.[5]

A Record-breaking Church

Coolville is home to more than one church, including the smallest one in the state of Ohio. The Healing Chapel, owned and operated by Janice Middleton, only seats about 8 worshippers at a time. Middleton and her late husband, Lloyd, acquired the church around 2002 and relocated it to Route 63, just south of Route 50. The Middletons placed the church there to provide a respite for weary travelers. Despite the fact that her husband has since passed away, Janice Middleton continues to work diligently on the upkeep of the church. Unfortunately, visitors sometimes steal portions of the church (Middleton says she doesn't mount anything to the wall, so thieves don't cause more damage). However more often than not, visitors come for a chance to see the unique building or for a moment of peace.[6]

Changing Transportation Affects Business in Coolville

From the mid-1800s until the late 1960s, Coolville was an important trade stop in southeastern Ohio. Many of the goods that Coolville citizens produced were sent out on flatboats along the Hocking River. The B & O Railroad also ran through Coolville from 1874 to 1967. Known by some locals as the "Doodle Bug," this railroad connected residents of Coolville to the larger cities of Athens and Belpre. Coolville residents were able to jump on the train to travel to jobs outside of the village limits. This especially came in handy in the early 1900s, when the village's agricultural lifestyle began to give way to industrialization. In 1963, a highway passed through Coolville, but there was no exit into town. With this new mode of travel, Coolville began receiving fewer and fewer visitors.[7]

With fewer visitors, Coolville has seen a decrease in village businesses. Many businesses formerly relied on piquing the interest of passing travelers or meeting their needs during a long journey. One business that remains is White-Schwarzel Funeral Home on Fifth Street. This funeral home has long-standing roots in Coolville, beginning in 1858 with J. Leander White, a photographer and furniture dealer. Likely due to carpentry knowledge acquired from his furniture business, White was asked by residents to make caskets. White would arrive at the home of the deceased, measure the body in height and width, then fashion the casket to precisely fit.[8]

White's son, Charles Everett White, inherited the family business at the age of 19. Following with the trends of his own time, Charles began embalming bodies and eventually made the switch to offering ceremonies in the funeral home rather than at the home of the deceased. Charles passed the family business to his sons, who in turn passed it along to one of their step-sons, a man named Lee Ethridge. The White funeral business remained in the family until Ethridge passed away in 1985. In 1996, Mike Putnam, a lifelong Coolville resident who had been working at the White Funeral Home since 1983, purchased the business. Putnam and his business partner, Kevin Schwarzel, still operate the funeral home today.[9]

A Unique Headstone

In 1797, the Barrows family arrived in Troy Township, settling in the future Coolville area. Today the family is best known for their headstone near Coolville, which includes a large carving of a turkey, along with arguments in favor of the bird's superior nature. Mr. and Mrs. Clayton E. Barrows long argued to have the turkey made the United States national bird, rather than the eagle. They noted that the turkey only fights when attacked, whereas the eagle is much more aggressive than the United States should be. Mr. and Mrs. Barrows believed this so strongly that they quite literally took it to their graves.[10]

If you're interested in a day out on the water, Coolville is a great place to visit. Located almost on top of the Hocking and Ohio Rivers, the village offers a great excuse to escape into nature. Just outside of Coolville, visitors can find the Blue Heron Campground, located directly on the Hocking River, with docks available for those who bring their own boat.[12]

TOP: Clint Fultz Memorial Park.

Population: 467   **Approx. Founding:** 1844

INSETS L to R: Corwin Town Hall, atop the hill that runs through Corwin • The Little Miami Scenic Trail • Waynesville Lumber Supply Company • The entryway to Miami Cemetery

What did Thomas Corwin say when he spoke out against the Mexican-American War? In one of the most powerful portions of his speech, Corwin compared the lands that America attempted to take from Mexico to the many places that Americans associate with the Revolutionary War, saying "...had one come and demanded Bunker Hill of the people of Massachusetts...Is there a river on this continent that would not have run red with blood?...But this same American goes into a sister republic, and says to poor, weak Mexico, 'Give up your territory, you are unworthy to possess it...'"[11]

Corwin

A Railroad Brings A Village

DURING THE 1840s, exciting news reached Warren County, Ohio: a railroad was coming to Wayne Township! In anticipation of the economic boom that this railroad would bring, in 1844 John and Joel W. Johnson laid out a new village on the site of the future depot. They settled on the name Corwin, honoring another Warren County man, Thomas Corwin, who had recently served as Ohio's 15th governor.[1]

In 1845, the Little Miami Railroad came through the newly appointed village, on its way from Cincinnati to Xenia. The depot in Corwin took the name Waynesville, after another more established village nearby. Corwin and Waynesville were only barely separated by the new railway track, and they existed in parallel. The citizens of Corwin were happy to be involved with Waynesville, but they also took pride in their own accomplishments.[2]

The citizens of Corwin had many accomplishments to be proud of as their village boomed. The Little Miami River brought both passengers and freight into the village. The Panhandle Hotel opened up next door to the depot, providing passengers on a rail journey with a comfortable evening in Corwin. A coal yard to supply incoming trains was built near the depot by Seth Cook. The villagers also built a lumberyard, a canning business, two grain elevators, and a sawmill. As the village grew it also acquired a blacksmith shop and two water towers, among many other localized services.[3]

Modern Landmarks in Corwin

The Waynesville Depot is long gone, but its former location is easy to spot, as it was next door to the Miami Cemetery. The cemetery saw its first burial in 1833, when a man named Gaines Goode carried his daughter Narcissa up the east ridge of the Little Miami Valley and to her final resting place in a meadow on his farm. Goode gave a tract of land near this grave to the Waynesville Methodist Church, allowing it to become a cemetery. In 1866, the Miami Cemetery Association was formed. It has grown greatly over the years. The cemetery is now marked by a large arch at the entrance, erected by the Wayne Township Veterans Association in 1876. In 1893, a gothic chapel was built in the cemetery. It has since been restored.[4]

Where the Little Miami Railroad once cut through the village of Corwin, there is now a bike trail. Known as the Little Miami Scenic Trail, the bike path passes through former railroad villages and is more than 70 miles long, offering both short- and long-distance bikers an exciting experience. Corwin is a great place for bikers to stop, because it has public restrooms, water, and available parking.

The Life of Thomas Corwin

Corwin's namesake was born in Bourbon County, Kentucky, in 1794. Thomas Corwin actually spent most of his life in Warren County, Ohio. Corwin's father, Mathias, served 11 consecutive terms as a state representative, leading Thomas to develop an interest in a career of public service.[5]

Corwin passed the Ohio Bar Exam in 1817 and began practicing law in Lebanon. In 1818, he became the prosecuting attorney of Warren County, a position he held until 1828. In 1822, he married Sarah Ross. The two started a family in Lebanon, raising five children. Corwin served in the Ohio House of Representatives while his children were small, in two separate terms from 1821 to 1823 and again from 1829 to 1830.[6]

In 1830, still with young children at home, Corwin was elected to the U.S. House of Representatives and began splitting his time between Lebanon and Washington, D.C. Serving for five consecutive terms, he became known as the "terror of the House," thanks to his talent for debate.[7]

In 1840, Corwin retired from the House of Representatives and ran for Governor of Ohio. He beat out incumbent Wilson Shannon and served a two-year term as the 15th governor of Ohio. Corwin, a Whig, faced stiff opposition from his Democratic counterparts in the Ohio Congress, and he wasn't able to accomplish much. Wilson Shannon ran against Corwin again in 1842, and Shannon won.[8] However, when the Johnsons named the village of Corwin in 1844, the glory Corwin had brought to Warren County was still fresh in their minds.

In 1844, Thomas Corwin was elected as a United States Senator from Ohio, serving until 1850. As a senator, Corwin made perhaps the most important speech of his life. On February 11, 1847, Corwin stood up on the Senate floor to express his displeasure with the Mexican-American War. In this speech, Corwin also referenced the coming American Civil War and the tensions that he predicted would lead to an internal conflict.[9] Corwin is known today for this speech.

In 1850, Corwin was made Secretary of the Treasury, a position he held until 1853, when he attempted to retire to his law practice in Lebanon. However, Corwin returned to the U.S. House of Representatives as a Republican in 1859 and helped campaign for Abraham Lincoln, who, once elected, made Corwin the United States Minister to Mexico. Corwin thrived in this position, having curried much favor in Mexico when he spoke out against the Mexican-American War. Corwin retired in Washington, D.C., in 1864, practicing law until his death on December 18, 1865, not long after the end of the Civil War.[10]

Corwin is home to Hisey Park, a former farm owned by the Hisey family, which was first dedicated in 2005. It covers 158 acres with restored wetlands and space for kayaking, biking, bird-watching, fishing, and hiking. Nearby Bowman Park covers about 50 acres of land and is the result of a donation from Woody Bowman.[12]

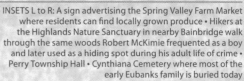

Population: 68   **Approx. Founding:** 1840

INSETS L to R: A sign advertising the Spring Valley Farm Market where residents can find locally grown produce • Hikers at the Highlands Nature Sanctuary in nearby Bainbridge walk through the same woods Robert McKimie frequented as a boy and later used as a hiding spot during his adult life of crime • Perry Township Hall • Cynthiana Cemetery where most of the early Eubanks family is buried today

After his guilty verdict, John Jones made one last attempt to escape the authorities. Thanks to the large number of McKimie's accomplices in the Waverly prison, Jones was relegated to an extra room upstairs. Jones began to attempt an escape when he was left unguarded at suppertime. When his guard returned from his evening meal, he found Jones attempting to saw his way out using a stove leg and a case knife.[23]

TOP: Mendlebrights, a fabric and craft store in Cynthiana

Cynthiana

An Auspicious Family

ON OCTOBER 26, 1780, IN QUEEN ANN COUNTY, Maryland, George Eubanks and Rebecca Harrington were married. Their union produced most of the well-known citizens of the early years of Cynthiana, Ohio. The couple moved to Kentucky in 1797 with four of their children in tow and eventually settled in Perry Township, Pike County, in 1804.[1] David, the Eubanks's second-eldest child, laid out the village of Cynthiana between 1835 and 1840. Needing a name for the new village, David chose to combine the names of his wife, Anna, and his daughter, Cynthia. David eventually left Cynthiana, dying in Missouri in 1857.[2] David's sisters Rebecca and Rhoda, were the youngest of the family's 11 children. Being significantly younger, they outlived the rest of the Eubanks family, living together in the family home in Cynthiana during their senior years.[3]

Robert "Little Reddy" McKimie

In 1878, as October ended and Halloween night fell on the village of Cynthiana, Rebecca and Rhoda came face-to-face with one of Southern Ohio's most famous outlaws: Robert "Little Reddy" McKimie.[4] McKimie was an accomplished burglar and conman who made his start out West, but during the fall of 1878 he was terrorizing southwestern Ohio, where he had been born and raised.[5]

Growing up, Robert lived with his aunt in Rainsboro, Ohio, a town in Highland County neighboring Cynthiana. By 1869, Robert was 14 years old; he enlisted in the Army and was sent to Texas to be a cavalryman.[6]

McKimie soon showed his true colors when he shot down a man on his horse, stole the steed, and rode away, deserting his military post. Caught and sent to prison in Utah, he escaped within a year. Robert rode through the Black Hills, violently robbing stagecoach travelers and earning himself the name "Little Reddy" due to his red hair.[7]

Despite his violent career out West, the residents of Rainsboro were none the wiser. In 1871, McKimie sent his aunt $50 from his spoils, indicating to her that he had left the military and joined a cattle business somewhere in Kansas. McKimie's family assumed he was making an honest living on the new frontier.[8] In 1877, having sufficiently built a fortune in his "cattle business," Robert McKimie returned to Rainsboro to show off his success. He soon bought a house, started a legitimate business, and married a well-known local woman named Clara Ferguson. Somehow, McKimie shared his stories of his time out West without revealing his villainy. Unfortunately for McKimie, his stories reached the ears of one Seth Bullock, sheriff of Deadwood, South Dakota.[9]

Bullock recognized McKimie for the criminal he truly was. In danger after this dramatic revelation, Robert and Clara McKimie ran to Bermuda. Unfortunately for the happy couple, McKimie was arrested for not paying his hotel bill. The McKimies were asked to leave, so Robert went ahead to find money he could send for Clara's return ticket.[10]

McKimie returned to Ohio where he quickly put together his own little gang, including friends John Jones, "New York Charley," and Frank Messmer.[11] In order to find the cash to send Clara home from Bermuda, McKimie's gang began terrorizing much of southwestern Ohio, including the Eubanks sisters in Cynthiana.[12]

McKimie's Gang in Cynthiana

In the dark of night on October 31, 1878, McKimie's new gang slid on their masks and slipped into the Eubanks home, the same house built by George and Rebecca Eubanks in 1804.[13] The men roughly threw the elderly Eubanks sisters about; as one sister later testified, "that fellow made up the bed and put us both in it."[14] The gang made off with $900.[15]

One month later, in November 1878, Detective John T. Norris of Springfield, Ohio, captured McKimie, John Jones, "New York Charley," and Frank Messmer.[16] The group had many crimes to answer to, but for their crimes against the Eubanks sisters, McKimie's gang faced trial in the nearby town of Waverly.[17] In a time before television, movies, or rock concerts, the trial of Robert McKimie was the event of the year for Cynthiana's residents.[18]

It was almost impossible to find a jury unbiased against Robert "Little Reddy" McKimie. Likely knowing his fate, McKimie seemed to enjoy his trial, laughing along with the audience as his exploits were uncovered. Newspapers reported that McKimie was particularly gleeful when his lawyers forced Detective Norris to recount his own ill-gotten gains and the year he had spent in the Ohio Penitentiary.[19]

McKimie was found guilty within the first five minutes of the jury's deliberations. After his sentencing to five years for his crimes against the Eubanks sisters, McKimie spoke plainly and openly about his crimes, providing aid for his friend Henry O. Clegget. Clegget had provided a hiding spot and some hair dye for McKimie, but ultimately he was declared not guilty as he had no direct hand in the crimes. Unfortunately for John Jones, Frank Messmer decided to turn on his fellow member of McKimie's gang. His testimony helped the jury put Jones behind bars.[20]

Despite his many escapes, somehow the Ohio Penitentiary held McKimie safely within its walls for his combined 14-year sentence. In true Robert McKimie fashion, he disappeared after his release, and no one knows what became of him.[21] As for the Eubanks sisters, the women adopted two large guard dogs at the end of the trial.[22]

Robert McKimie's childhood reads almost as if it was written by Mark Twain himself. Not unlike Tom Sawyer, McKimie loved exploring caves as a boy. After the Eubanks robbery, McKimie managed to evade capture by hiding out in the Seven Caves that he had enjoyed exploring as a child.[24]

Population: 443   **Approx. Founding:** 1808

INSETS L to R: The former Damascus Grade School, now a museum. Nearby is a historic marker for Ervin G. Bailey • The Damascus Fire Department • Heath's Barber Shop and the Dragonfly Spa and Salon • Goshen Township Park

On Christmas Day of 1800, Ervin G. Bailey was born in the village of Damascus. As a child, he began experimenting and inventing on his father's farm. Bailey became well regarded in his field for inventions, such as his Bailey Boiler Meter, that helped improve the efficiency of steam technology.[13] In 1948, he was given the highest award of recognition bestowed by the American Society of Mechanical Engineers.[14]

TOP: The Damascus Friends Church as seen from the former Lot 17 Burial Ground, now a parking lot

Damascus

Promoting a New Village

IN 1806, Horton Howard, Samuel Woolman, and Anthony Morris arrived in what was then Columbiana County, Ohio. The three men and their families, all Quakers, likely came from Virginia and New Jersey. They were soon followed by a Mr. Hoopes of Pennsylvania, who made significant land purchases in the area.[1]

Hoopes hired Howard, Woolman, and Morris to lay out a village on his land. In 1808, they platted it, naming it Damascusville (and reserving three large lots for themselves). Howard, Woolman, and Morris were tasked with enticing new residents to move to Damascusville. To do so, they ran an advertisement in a Philadelphia newspaper, offering lots in Damascusville for $5 to $6. Payments could be made in cash or with dressed hogs.[2]

The promoters, devout Quakers, took the name of their town from the Bible. The village is bordered by two tributaries of the Mahoning River. In the Old Testament, particularly in the story of Namaan, Damascus is described as a fertile plain between two rivers. On December 31, 1881, the post office in town, first established in 1828, simplified the village's name, changing it to Damascus. The new village grew steadily. By the 1810s, residents began to make their own bricks, and brick homes soon appeared around the village.[3] By 1827, the villagers transitioned from a log meeting house to a sturdier brick building.[4] In 1829, Pleasant Cobbs purchased a plot of land that soon became a village inn, meant to accommodate stagecoach travelers coming through Damascus.[5]

An Event at the Inn

In June of 1856, in the nearby village of Salem, the owners of the Farquar House were charged with violation of local liquor laws. They couldn't find a lawyer to represent them, so they promised the Salem Temperance Committee that they wouldn't sell liquor again. As a sign of good faith, all of their liquor stores were transferred to the Temperance Committee. A man named Bloom then approached the Salem Temperance Committee demanding two barrels of the Farquar House's whiskey that had already been sold and needed to be shipped to Boardman. As Bloom prepared to ship the whiskey barrels, he left them on the front porch of the Damascus Inn, much to the dismay of Mr. Delzell, the inn's owner. Believing that Bloom intended to take the whiskey back into Salem to sell by the glass, residents of Damascus stole the barrels and rolled them to the west end of town, where they set the barrels on fire and rolled them down a hill.[6]

Changing Travel

During its early years, the village saw many stagecoach travelers. Travelers continued to pass through Damascus when, in 1852, the Ohio and Pennsylvania Railroad built a depot in the village. However, the conventional railroad was abandoned in the early 1900s when the Stark Electric Railroad arrived. Unfortunately the electric railway was short lived. The rails were officially abandoned in 1939, leaving Damascus with only a slow bus service and fewer visitors.[7]

The Lot 17 Burial Ground

The Quakers in town eventually split into two separate sects, but they have a common history. This history was brought to light in 2001, when the Damascus Friends Church wanted to expand their parking lot. The space chosen had been used as a burial ground in the early 1800s, so before digging or building, they called in a professional archaeologist from Youngstown State University. Professor John R. White and his many students and colleagues began to investigate the site, known as the Lot 17 burial ground, in March 2001.[8]

Members of the Damascus Friends Church knew the site was a burial ground, but there were no remaining markers or headstones. The archaeologists began by digging only three feet into the earth. Burying bodies six feet underground is not a new tradition, so they knew that staying at three feet would help ensure that they did not accidentally disturb any burials below. The next step was to spray the entire area with water. As the uncovered earth was sprayed, the shapes of six-sided coffins began to appear. The water revealed to archaeologists the differences between untouched soil and the holes that had been dug for these coffins hundreds of years ago.[9]

When archaeologists began to dig deeper, they found stray pieces of bone, some metal hinges, and pieces of wood. Using church records, forensic science, and the few human remains they could find, the archaeologists were often able to determine who had been buried in a specific place. In one case, the archaeologists discovered a set of bones "all catawampus in the grave." They were able to determine that this was the burial of a man who had been killed by a tree during a storm. He was buried as he was found, with no straightening of his limbs for a funeral.[10]

By the end of the Lot 17 project, all of the former burials were moved to the Damascus Cemetery.[11] Local residents were able to have a historical marker placed both on the original Lot 17 and in the new Damascus Cemetery to honor all 118 individuals who were exhumed overall. Among these individuals was Samuel Coppock Jr., father to Edwin Coppock, who was hanged for taking part in John Brown's raid on Harper's Ferry in 1859.[12]

Many of Damascus's early residents belonged either to the Stanley or Cobb families, which frequently intermarried, and early residents constantly had to fend off squirrels that destroyed their corn crops. Thanks to these two facts of life, the following became a common saying in town: "The squirrels took the corn and the Stanleys took the Cobbs."[15]

TOP: Deersville United Methodist Church

Population: 75   **Approx. Founding:** 1815

INSETS L to R: Bell's Vacation Rentals • Mary Jobe Akeley's headstone • A main thoroughfare in Deersville as seen from Hazel's House, a local bed and breakfast • A historic marker noting the Moravian Trail

Some of the earliest white families in Deersville almost ended up in Illinois. In 1819, a group of Virginia families, intent on settling in Illinois, happened upon a Mr. Norris as they traveled. Mr. Norris assured the families that Illinois was full of low land where malaria was quite common. Norris also happened to own a large amount of land in Brownsville, the town neighboring Deersville. He made sure that these families safely made their way to Brownsville where he could sell them land. A few of these families stopped off early and settled in Deersville.

Deersville

Moravian Missionaries Travel Through the Future Deersville

IN 1802, A YEAR BEFORE OHIO'S STATEHOOD was officially declared, surveyors began to record the details of Franklin Township, a part of Harrison County. Soon the township began to break into smaller villages. By Thanksgiving of 1815, Deersville had been platted by John Cramblett.

In 1952, Homer C. Poulson, a lifelong resident of Deersville, accustomed to frequent questions about his memories of the community, decided to record the history of Deersville. He begins his narrative long before the 1815 platting of his hometown, "Far enough back that there were no white inhabitants, even in Harrison County…" As Poulson goes on to note, many of the first residents of his hometown were American Indians, members of the Lenape (Delaware) and Wyandotte Nations.[1]

Deersville is part of an Eastern Ohio area that was visited by white Moravian missionaries from Germany in the early 1770s as they attempted to convert American Indians. To that end, a few more permanent settlements were founded, including Schoenbrunn and Gnadenhutten.[2]

The Struggles of the Lenape

Within a few years, residents of these settlements were being attacked on all sides. During the American Revolution, British soldiers aligned with members of the Lenape Nation who had not converted to Christianity. Meanwhile, members of the Lenape who had converted couldn't participate in the war because of their religious beliefs, but the British worried they were aligned with the rebellious Americans.[3] This fear forced the American Indian people living in the Moravian settlements to move to northern Ohio.[4]

However, a group was sent back to Gnadenhutten in 1781 in an attempt to stave off food shortages by harvesting previously planted crops.[5] Unfortunately upon their return, they were captured by Pennsylvania soldiers and 96 of the 98 members of the Lenape Nation were brutally murdered.[6] As Poulson described, "About 100 men under Col. Williamson made peaceful overtures, deprived them of their arms, bound them, then butchered all save two boys who made their escape."[7] Colonel Williamson's men falsely accused the Delaware people at Gnadenhutten of leading raids into Pennsylvania.[8]

While Poulson only offered a few paragraphs summarizing the history of American Indians in Deersville, he was shockingly prescient for his time, comparing the treatment of American Indians by white Ohio settlers to modern totalitarian regimes, writing, "Hitler did likewise. Stalin now does. They usurp the homes of other people and they call it 'civilization.'"[9] Perhaps Poulson's awareness was due to the continued upkeep of the Moravian Trail, passing through Harrison County, and specifically through Deersville. This path marked the steps Moravian missionaries took on their way through Eastern Ohio.[10]

The Tappan-Moravian Trail Today

Today parts of the Moravian Trail are still marked in the Deersville area. Visitors can learn more about Deersville and Harrison County history by following the signs erected by the Ohio Scenic Byways Program on the Tappan-Moravian Trail.[11] One of the stops on this trail is the Union Bell Hotel. Built in 1835 as the Union Hotel, this building provided an important stop on the stagecoach trail between Wheeling, WV, and Wooster before the Civil War. Over time, Deersville lost its importance as a travel hub, and the town's population shrank. The Union Hotel remained open through the 1880s, but by the time the local Bell family acquired the property in 1984, it was empty and falling apart. After years of hard work, the Union Bell Hotel reopened for business in 2013.[12]

Today the Moravian Trail has also taken on the name Tappan, due to the Tappan Lake, a body of water that did not exist when Moravian missionaries first walked the land. Tappan Lake is technically located in Deersville today, but that is only because two other small towns are submerged underneath it.[13] In 1933, Ohio decided to take on statewide flood control. From this effort was born the Muskingum Watershed Conservancy District (MWCD). The official plan of the MWCD, approved in 1934, called for 14 dams and reservoirs to be built.[14] One of these, the Tappan Reservoir on Little Stillwater Creek, required the villages of Tappan and Laceyville to be completely covered by the reservoir. Residents were given time to move, but the project began so quickly that some remnants of the two towns can still be found submerged in the water.[15] Along the Tappan-Moravian Trail, visitors can get a small glimpse into the history of Tappan by visiting the Pleasant Valley Church. This building (and its accompanying cemetery) were moved uphill when the project began.[16]

Mary Jobe Akeley

One of Tappan's most famous residents is buried in Deersville. Beginning in the early 1900s, Mary Jobe Akeley mounted many expeditions to the remote Canadian Northwest. She became known internationally for her work, and the Geographical Board of Canada named a mountain peak in the Canadian Rockies (Mount Jobe) in her honor. While not mapping and exploring new territories, Mary Jobe was busy opening a camp for girls, Camp Mystic, in Connecticut. In 1924, Mary Jobe married Carl Akeley, a fellow explorer who is now known as the "father of taxidermy." Together they explored the Belgian Congo where Mary bravely continued to lead an expedition after her husband died in the middle of their journey.[17] When she wasn't exploring, Mary made a home in Mystic, where she died in 1966.[18]

A Deersville native, Harry Hazlett went on to coach the Canton Bulldogs, a pro football team, from 1913 to 1915. Hazlett also was only the second Harrison County resident to be promoted to Major General—George Custer was the first. Hazlett took part in both World Wars. He is buried in Arlington National Cemetery.

WELCOME TO TAPPAN LAKE PARK

TOP: East Fultonham United Methodist Church

Population: 335   **Approx. Founding:** 1815

INSETS L to R: A view of Lake Isabella • The driveway to Lake Isabella: summer fun lies directly ahead • The East Fultonham Post Office • Another view of Lake Isabella

In 1903, the Zanesville and Western Railway constructed a boarding house to host their workmen. After the building fell out of use around the 1920s, it was purchased by O. E. Shrider, who opened a hotel. Unfortunately, in February 1929, the hotel caught fire and couldn't be saved, resulting in an $18,000 loss. Once realizing the hotel was a total loss, firemen from Zanesville focused on saving nearby buildings. The fire was caused by a defective flue on the second floor. Shrider himself noticed the fire while showing a group of guests to a nearby room.[17]

East Fultonham

A Village Built on a Railroad

THE EARLY HISTORY OF EAST FULTONHAM is tied to its namesake, the neighboring village of Fultonham. In 1815, in Muskingum County, Ohio, the village of Uniontown was laid out. By 1828, the village was interested in opening a post office. There was more than one Uniontown in Ohio at this time, so the village needed a new name. The first postmaster of the village was Lyle Fulton. His name was adopted for the entire village, which took on the name Fultonham.[1]

Sometime around 1883, the Zanesville and Western Railway came to Muskingum County, passing near Fultonham.[2] A new village sprung up to take advantage of this, taking on the name East Fultonham. The village of East Fultonham eventually grew to the point that its population outnumbered the nearby Fultonham.[3]

Columbia Cement Builds a Business and a Lake

For most of Muskingum County's history, Newton Township, where East Fultonham is located, was well known for its mineral deposits. In the early 1800s, quite a bit of pottery came out of the area. Locals also began to mine limestone for use in construction. In 1918, the Swingle-Robertson Company opened up a strip mine in East Fultonham to retrieve and sell this limestone.[4] By 1919, the quarry had been purchased by the Pittsburgh Plate Glass Company. The Pittsburgh Plate Glass Company quickly realized that there were other materials in the area. To capitalize on this opportunity, the company opened a cement plant, known as Columbia Cement, in 1924.[5]

The Columbia Cement Plant became a large employer for residents of East Fultonham. By 1950, it employed about 350 people. In

1924, when the plant had just opened, it turned out about 2,500 barrels of cement each day, more than doubling this number by 1945. During World War II, some of this cement helped create runways for military airplanes.[6] For much of the twentieth century, the cement plant was a basic part of life in East Fultonham.

Eventually, the company's original quarry, no longer useful for business, was turned into a recreation destination. In the early 1940s, the quarry was filled with water and turned into a lake. The lake was named Lake Isabella, after the deceased wife of Columbia Cement Plant superintendent, Robert W. McAllister. An organization was formed to maintain the grounds, but residents were more than willing to assist. When planting needed to be done, a sign went up that said "Come and bring your own spade."[7]

Lake Isabella is still a popular destination in East Fultonham today. To visit, you need to be a member. For $90 a year, interested individuals can purchase a single membership. Family memberships are $130. The lake covers about 28 acres and is stocked with catfish, bass, walleye, bluegill, and perch. Members can come to the lake for swimming, fishing, kayaking, or camping, among other activities. There are also fireworks on the Fourth of July. Members can rent the lake for picnics with outside groups or on special occasions.[8]

The Columbia Cement Plant is now gone, but the land where the plant was once located is now owned by the Quasar Energy Group, a Cleveland-based business. As well as generating renewable electricity, Quasar specializes in recycling organic waste, such as sewage sludge and leftover food scraps, and creating fertilizer. Of course, the East Fultonham community has not always been pleased with the resulting smell.[9]

A New Type of Business Comes to Town

In 2017, the Quasar Energy Group began working with a new company, Grow Ohio Pharmaceuticals, LLC, that will cover 10 acres.[10]

What exactly does Grow Ohio need such a large space for? Growing medical marijuana.

In November of 2017, the state of Ohio granted a handful of businesses the right to operate medical marijuana grow sites. Grow Ohio was one of these lucky businesses.[11] Construction began on the company's 55,000-square-foot building in Spring of 2018. Grow Ohio hopes to produce about 18,000 pounds of dried marijuana each year. They will rely heavily on Quasar Energy's support. The energy group will be supplying a large amount of the electricity that the site needs around the clock. The site will be surrounded by an eight-foot-high fence and monitored constantly by security. They hope to create around 40 new local jobs.[12]

Grow Ohio is only licensed for production, so it will need to send its product away to licensed retailers for actual sale.[13] This doesn't mean there haven't been concerns from the community about what will happen once Grow Ohio begins operations. Muskingum County's Commissioners are concerned about the strain the new business will have on local law enforcement, especially in a state already fighting an opioid crisis. However, others are in favor. When asked about the issue, many of the Newton Township trustees and the Muskingum County Sheriff felt the business was secure and likely to bring money to the area.[14] As the *Zanesville Times Recorder* uncovered, "According to a 2016 study by the National Institute on Drug Abuse, the presence of medical marijuana dispensaries correlates with a higher level of recreational marijuana use but a reduced rate of opioid addiction and overdoses." The owners of Grow Ohio are hopeful that their presence might help fight Ohio's opioid addiction.[15]

Thomas A. Hendricks, Vice President under Grover Cleveland, was born in between the villages of Fultonham and East Fultonham in 1819. His family moved to Indiana just after he was born. Hendricks and Cleveland were elected in 1884; however, Hendricks died in 1885, after less than a year in office.[16]

TOP: East Liberty United Methodist Church

Population: 366 **Approx. Founding:** 1834

INSETS L to R: Moore's East Liberty Grocery • The East Liberty
Auto Plant • Pop's Pizza Parlor • The East Liberty Fire Department

In 1988, Jay Ackley of East Liberty, a fourth-generation dairy farmer, began working with his father to manage about 50 cows and a little over 800 acres. Today, with his wife Kristy and their two sons, Jay manages the Ack-Lee Holstein farm, caring for 110 cows and 2,800 acres. The farm produces large amounts of dairy products as well as wheat, corn, and soybeans. They maintain one full-time herdsman and some part-time help, but the majority of the work on the farm is managed by the Ackley family themselves.[15]

East Liberty

A Village Built Around a Mill

SOMETIME IN THE 1830s, a man named John Bower laid out a village in Logan County, Ohio, that would go on to take the name East Liberty. Sources don't agree on the exact date that Bower laid out the village. Some claim 1834, while others use 1838. Either way, Bower was likely reacting to population growth in the area due in large part to a nearby mill owned by a man named John Garwood.

After Garwood built his mill in the future East Liberty area, other businesses and families followed.[1] The first post office established in the village was fittingly named Garwood's Mill. Once Bower laid out the town and the post office moved, the village officially took on the name East Liberty.[2] At least one source claims that the village was also once known as Otter Slide, but there's no explanation for this interesting name.[3]

Alonzo Skidmore and the Central Ohio College

The village of East Liberty grew quickly during the nineteenth century. In fact, by 1875 the village even hosted an art gallery. In 1882, capitalizing on this growth, a man named Alonzo Skidmore decided to open an institution of higher learning in the village, known as Central Ohio College. The residents of the village were very supportive of his project, raising $1,500 to help bring it about. Skidmore successfully matched these funds and got to work on his new school.[4]

Tuition at Central Ohio College during its opening year was 10 dollars for 12 weeks of instruction.[5] By 1887, students could take courses in six main areas: science, literature, business and commercial, music, art, and normal (teacher training). Skidmore himself served as not only president of the college but also as a professor. All students could also take penmanship courses, regardless of specialization.[6]

The college always remained a rather local institution. Most students either came from East Liberty itself or other nearby Ohio towns and villages. The name Skidmore was common among the class lists and teaching staff. In 1887, a woman named Lillian Skidmore, likely Alonzo's cousin by marriage, was listed as teaching the music courses, while three other Skidmores were actively attending classes. Central Ohio College remained coeducational, with a high number of women on the student list.[7] Unfortunately, by the 1890s enrollment at the Central Ohio College had declined, and it shut down in 1894. The village of East Liberty purchased the building and used it to open a three-year high school.[8]

The East Liberty Honda Plant

Today East Liberty is known in the central Ohio area for its large Honda manufacturing plant. The East Liberty Auto Plant was built in 1989, following Honda's success in the nearby city of Marysville. Thanks to plants in East Liberty, Marysville, and the village of Anna, the central Ohio area has become an international leader in Honda production. In 1982, the first American-made Honda Accord came off the line in Marysville. Today almost all new Acura models (Honda's luxury brand) are produced in the state of Ohio.[9]

When Honda decided to expand to East Liberty in 1989, they asked workers how to make the workday more enjoyable and productive. A total of 822 suggestions were received. Honda has since made its East Liberty Plant an incredibly flexible manufacturing center. The plant was also built with the environment in mind. It uses a special waterborne painting system to reduce emissions and has focused on returnable parts containers, to cut down on waste.[10]

Although the East Liberty Plant was built with flexibility in mind, Honda recently invested $54 million to enable the plant to produce the Acura RDX. This new car requires a new style of paint, a new foam-injection system, a unique moonroof, and brand new structural adhesives. The plant's employees needed to work over the course of four years to carefully calculate a plan for adding these new tasks while maintaining high production numbers for their other vehicles.[11] The work was worth it. The Acura RDX is the very first Honda vehicle that was not only produced in the United States but also designed and developed stateside. The East Liberty Plant is the only plant in the country making this new, sought-after vehicle.[12]

In 2018, the state of Ohio followed Honda's example and moved a new transportation research project to the village of East Liberty. On July 9, 2018, then-governor John Kasich led a groundbreaking for a new Smart Mobility Facility in East Liberty. This site, boasting 540 acres, will include a live model of normal road conditions to help researchers produce self-driving vehicles. The facility in East Liberty should hopefully generate jobs, and if successful, stimulate Ohio's economy.[13]

Local History Written by a Local

Interested in learning more about the history of East Liberty? In 2017, village resident Janet Akey Blank published a new account of East Liberty's past, titled *Why Small Townships Produce Big Character: The History of East Liberty, Ohio ... One Small Town With Big Character*. Blank grew up in East Liberty before pursuing a career as a pharmacist. Now retired, she lives on the same property where she grew up. When writing her new book, Blank relied not only on her own memories but interviews and conversations with other former residents of East Liberty. The book can now be purchased via the publisher's website.[14]

John Garwood's mill has not been forgotten. The Logan County Historical Society has erected a historical marker where it's believed the mill once was. According to the marker, John Garwood and his 13 children moved to the future East Liberty in 1805.[16]

TOP: A portion of the original Ebenezer Orphan Institute that survived the Blizzard of '78

Population: 233   **Approx. Founding:** 1841

INSETS L to R: The Flat Rock Post Office • Flat Rock Ebenezer United Methodist Church • The entryway to the Seneca Caverns • The Bishop Seybert Cemetery, Bishop John Seybert's final resting place

Just outside of Flat Rock lies an underground geological marvel known as the Seneca Caverns. Underground caverns are well noted in the history of the Flat Rock area. Some histories even posit that very early white settlers entered the caverns to hunt rattlesnakes.[11] Since 1933, Seneca Caverns has been open to the public for tours. Interested visitors will travel 110 feet below the Earth's surface, where they can see the Ole Mist'ry River, an underground stream that is actually part of the Flat Rock water table.[12]

Flat Rock

Albright People Settle Flat Rock

THE STORY OF THE VILLAGE OF FLAT ROCK in Seneca County, Ohio, begins in eastern Pennsylvania with a man named Jacob Albright. In 1790, Albright converted to Methodism and began organizing other German Methodists in the area. This new group, known as the Evangelical Association after Albright's death, called themselves the Albright People during the early 1800s. The group was organized into classes, including the Thomas class in McClure, Pennsylvania. In 1841, a large group from this class moved to Ohio, where they had a new village laid out by a local surveyor.[1]

The new settlers quickly built a church and began to engage with other evangelicals around the region. The village also served as a stopping point for circuit riders who traveled around the United States, spreading the message of the Evangelical Association. One of the best known circuit riders, Bishop John Seybert, stayed in Flat Rock often during his journeys. In fact, Seybert was in Flat Rock in 1860 when he passed away. The village hosted his funeral, and he is buried nearby in the aptly named Bishop Seybert Cemetery.[2] The Evangelical Association eventually merged with the United Brethren of Christ to form the Evangelical United Brethren Church, which has since been absorbed into the larger United Methodist Church.[3]

Flat Rock's Name

The village of Flat Rock was originally known as Lewisville; however, when a post office was opened, it was given the name Flat

Rock. The name stuck, and now it is the official name for the village.[4] One volume, penned in 1911, suggests that the town's odd name came from an actual smooth stone found on the farm of Samuel Horner a mile east of the village. As the story goes, Horner had a spring on his property, but due to overuse, it fell into ill repair. Horner began to dig a well, but at about six feet deep he hit a flat rock. Frustrated, Horner hit the rock, and as it broke, a huge stream of water burst forth, filling the well and creating a clean, running stream to replace the dirtied spring. According to this telling, the village was named for this miraculous flat rock.[5]

Ebenezer Orphan Institute

In 1864, as the Civil War wound to an end, members of the Evangelical Association in Ohio sought to help the orphans the war had left behind. Originally an orphans' home was opened in the city of Tiffin, but it was quickly outgrown. In 1867, 170 acres of land were purchased in Flat Rock with the intent of building a new, larger orphans' home. The new building, erected at a cost of $12,000, was opened in May 1868, taking the name Ebenezer Orphan Institute of the Evangelical Association.[6]

The new institute, a source of pride for Evangelicals around the country, was well-supported, well-funded, and greatly needed. This need lead to many expansions during the late 1800s and early 1900s. By 1912, the institute had seen multiple land purchases and various renovations on the main building, but the children were still overcrowded. The girls slept in four rooms at the front of the building and the boys in four rooms at the back. At one point the home was occupied by 65 girls, meaning rows and rows of beds, often with multiple children sharing a bed each night. In May 1912, the construction of a new Girls' Cottage helped ease some of this congestion.[7]

The institute reached its largest size–500 acres–in 1921. This year two new Boys' Cottages were constructed, along with a new school building. When they were not in class, the children of the Ebenezer Orphan Institute helped manage the farm that they lived on. The institute was able to sell some of the products made on the farm to raise even more funds to support the children. In 2006, the memories of two former residents of the Ebenezer Institute were recorded in a book titled *The Orphan Home, Flat Rock, Ohio, 1910–1916: The Memories of Laurence K. and John H. Buchholz.*

Unfortunately the Blizzard of '78 was not kind to the Ebenezer Institute. In January 1978, an unforgettable winter storm struck Ohio, leaving residents snowed in for days. The force of this blizzard destroyed the institute's main building, almost forcing the institution to close. However rather than shuttering its doors, the institute's leadership decided to promote a change in mission instead.[8]

The Flat Rock Care Center

Since 1978, the Flat Rock Care Center has served children with intellectual and developmental disabilities. Thirty-four children were able to be accommodated at once in the original institute structures. As this first group of children began to reach adulthood and leave the Flat Rock Care Center, the Flat Rock Community Services Program was born. Starting in 1992, this new program provides services to adults with intellectual and developmental disabilities who desire a community-living lifestyle.[9]

In 2004, an entirely new, modern facility was officially opened at the Flat Rock Care Center. (Many of the historic buildings from the original Ebenezer Orphan Institute were also left standing.) In October 2003, as construction was completed on the new facility, a group of former residents gathered to reminisce about their childhoods and look with excitement toward the future for Flat Rock.[10]

The modern discovery of Senaca Caverns is credited to two young Flat Rock boys, Peter Rutan and Henry Komer. While the boys were hunting rabbits in 1872, their dog ran off and disappeared into the brush. The boys ran after him, and fell into a sinkhole that led to the cave. They ran home with the exciting news. Thanks to their discovery, we can visit the caverns today![13]

TOP: The Fletcher Covered Bridge

Population: 482   **Incorporated:** 1848

INSETS L to R: Jack's Garage on the street in Fletcher • The Suber Shively Funeral Home • Fletcher United Methodist Church • A street in Fletcher

Today Fletcher is largely a farming community. One of the farms in town is known as the End of the Road Farm, owned and operated by the Ruff family. The Ruffs cultivate 20 of their 21 acres carefully using draft horses (including 30-year-old Jane) and shun synthetic pesticides. The farm specializes in sorghum syrup and unique items like Grandpa's Ugly Tomatoes. End of the Road Farm has Certified Naturally Grown certification. You can find their products at the Piqua Community Farmers Market.[15]

Fletcher

John Malloy Founds Fletcher

IN 1821, IN MIAMI COUNTY, OHIO, a man by the name of John Malloy purchased a plot of land of about 80 acres. After nine years on his farm, Malloy began to lay out a new village in 1830.[1] The village went unnamed for about five years, until it was decided in 1835 that it should bear the moniker of the second merchant in town, one Samuel Fletcher. In 1848, interested residents of Fletcher met in the home of Isaac Kiser where they officially incorporated their village and elected its first leaders.[2]

The village of Fletcher sits near the Great Miami River (it flows through the nearby city of Piqua), which eventually flows into the Ohio River and finally to the Mississippi. During the early years of the village, it is said that John Malloy and John Davis used this waterway for their successful lumber business. They made multiple trips all the way to New Orleans, Louisiana, to sell their wares. These trips were always at the mercy of the weather and the water—sometimes all of the fine lumber was tossed into the river before it could be sold. However, Malloy was successful enough that he became, as one county history noted, "a bonanza king" and moved to California where he died with a large fortune.[3]

The village of Fletcher became a station on the Pittsburgh, Cincinnati, and St. Louis Railway and grew accordingly.[4] While it has never been very large, the village boasted a population of 567 in the early 1950s, being the only incorporated village in all of Brown Township.[5] In recent years, as rail travel has been significantly reduced, the population of Fletcher has fallen and it is again a small rural village.

Mischief Makers in the Village of Fletcher

Fletcher has had some mischief makers in its past, including a village burglar who was never found. In December 1908, Fletcher residents awoke to find that all but one establishment in the village had been robbed. The perpetrator got away with a decent amount of cash from each register in town and a large amount of stamps from the safe at the post office, where they had blown the safe open. While the criminal was never uncovered, newspapers of the time suspected a local job.[6]

Perhaps this local flair for mischief is why, beginning in the 1960s, Fletcher mayors began implementing a Halloween curfew for residents under 18 years of age. At multiple points in the late twentieth century, the local newspaper reported that from October 1 to October 31, kids were required to be inside by 8 p.m. Fletcher was all about the treats, no trick involved.[7, 8]

The Fletcher Fire Department

In 1930, Fletcher experienced the worst fire the village has ever seen. It completely consumed a local grocery store and one floor of a nearby home. Luckily for the mostly volunteer fire department, there were no high winds to carry the flames around the village. Firemen emptied an entire cistern attempting to fight the fire and then were forced to waste valuable time obtaining the muddy water of the river. As the men fought the fire, phone operators answered calls from concerned friends and family members in nearby Piqua. Preferring to watch in person rather than make a call, many people from all over the county began to crowd into the small village of Fletcher. Rumors began to fly. Some believed that the fire had consumed the entire southern half of the village! Certainly the rumors got worse when an oil tank inside the grocery store caused a huge explosion. Luckily no one was hurt, the fire was extinguished, and the grocery store was well insured.[9]

Today the village of Fletcher still operates a fire department made mostly of volunteers. As a very small village, Fletcher has often struggled to maintain city services. For a while, a resident named Howard Suber, the owner of Suber Funeral Homes, was able to respond in emergencies, and an ambulance was not needed. However in 1976, a new law made it so that Suber could no longer serve as the village's emergency contact.[10] At this point village trustees began raising funds for a combined Fletcher-Brown Township Ambulance Service. They went door-to-door to ask for funds and hosted a pig roast to fund it.[11]

The Fletcher Presbyterian Church Cemetery

Also in 1976, township trustees faced another crisis: taking responsibility for the dead. The Fletcher Presbyterian Church had disbanded in 1974 and sold its land to a man named Kenneth Kennedy.[12] After a few years, Kennedy offered to hand over the deed to either the village or the township, but legal complications kept them from accepting his offer.[13] With no clear owner, the cemetery fell into disrepair until 1995, when the Fletcher Cemetery Association, the managers of another cemetery in the village, finally took over the deed.[14]

In 1861, Thomas Charles Munger was born in Fletcher, Ohio. In 1907, President Theodore Roosevelt nominated him as a United States District Court Justice, a position he held until his death in 1941. Munger's grandson is Charlie Munger, business partner to Warren Buffet and vice chairman of Berkshire Hathaway.[16]

TOP: The bridge from Fort Jennings Park into downtown Fort Jennings

Population: 486   **Incorporated:** 1881

INSETS L to R: Fort Jennings State Bank • A monument marks what is believed to be the original site of Fort Jennings • The Fort restaurant, "the only stop in town" • St. Joseph Catholic Church

Some of the earliest white settlers in Fort Jennings traveled across an ocean to reach their new homes. In 1833, in his mid-twenties, Henry Joseph Boehmer left his home in Oldenburg, Germany, for the United States. He and his traveling companions settled in Fort Jennings, making a home there in July 1834. Boehmer often wrote to his relatives in Germany, and the letters have been preserved and translated for modern readers. Boehmer lived in Fort Jennings until his death in 1868. During his time in the village he served as the first teacher at Fort Jennings School and dammed the Auglaize River to build a water-powered grist and flour mill.[14]

Fort Jennings

The Original Fort Jennings

ON SEPTEMBER 1, 1812, in Frankfort, Kentucky, the 2nd Regiment of the Kentucky Volunteer Militia was raised. Lt. Colonel William Jennings immediately led his regiment to St. Marys, Ohio, to join General William Henry Harrison (future president and a future Ohioan). Harrison ordered Jennings to proceed north, and he did, following the Auglaize River. However, not too far along their journey, the 2nd Kentucky learned from loyal spies that if they continued north along the river they would run into British forces at Fort Defiance. Jennings made the decision to stop and make camp, ordering his men to begin construction on a blockhouse.[1]

Fort Defiance was built in 1794 on the Auglaize and Maumee Rivers by Anthony Wayne. It was used as a base of operations by various American generals, including Wayne and Harrison, during warfare with American Indians who lived in the western portions of Ohio. Sadly, the destruction of nearby American Indian villages was often planned within the fort's walls. Today the city of Defiance, Ohio, sits where Fort Defiance once stood.[2]

The fort that Jennings and his men began to construct was known as Fort Jennings in his honor. After 1812, Jennings was very rarely at the fort, but it became an important stop for American troops as they moved between Fort St. Marys and Fort Defiance.[3] It was used to store supplies, and soldiers stationed there even started building boats for the troops. While they had an important role to play, soldiers hated being stationed there and often were incredibly bored.[4]

After the war, around 1820, white settlers began to move into the area.[5] The fort's original location has since been lost to time. The village of Fort Jennings was platted in 1847 and began to grow as the Cloverleaf Railroad was built through the area in 1876. After the growth caused by the railroad, the village was officially incorporated in 1881. By 1910, the village had a population of 336.[6]

Honoring the War of 1812, Then and Now

During the centennial of the War of 1812, construction began on a Memorial Hall to mark the occasion. Residents of the village attempted to locate the hall as close as possible to the fort's original site. Finished in 1916, the hall became a central feature in the community. It eventually fell into disrepair, but in 2012, Dr. Wesley Klir led a successful effort to reopen the hall for the bicentennial of the War of 1812.[7]

Since this rededication in 2012, each summer, residents of Fort Jennings and the area gather at Fort Jennings Park to remember the military history of the village and celebrate modern veterans. This weekend-long event, called Fort Fest, features an encampment of War of 1812 reenactors. The weekend includes opportunities to learn about the history of the war, including a day camp for elementary school students. The celebration also boasts live music and beer and wine tastings. Fort Fest even includes an annual duck race sponsored by the local Lions Club.[8]

Education in Fort Jennings

The village of Fort Jennings has always been very serious about education. In 1840, the first classes were held in a log cabin. By 1856, a school system was established for Jennings Township, and by 1910, a local high school had been chartered. In 1912, the first three graduates graduated from the new Fort Jennings High School. In 1921, Fort Jennings purchased buses to be sure that every student could get to school. By 1938, the village had already outgrown the high school. Even though it was the depths of the Great Depression, a new school was built, costing $100,000 (about $1.8 million in 2019).

In 2004, a new school again made its way into Fort Jennings. For the first time since the original log cabin schoolhouse was built in 1840, all of the students in Fort Jennings would be housed in one building, which was built to accommodate preschool through twelfth grade.[9] The village's dedication to education has paid off. Today the 165 high school students in Fort Jennings boast a 98 percent graduation rate and test scores above the state average.[10]

An Image of Colonel Jennings Surfaces

Oddly enough, residents of Fort Jennings had no idea what Colonel William Jennings looked like until 2001. Historians could not find any depictions of Jennings in local archives or libraries. Luckily in February 2001, town officials answered the phone and a Mr. William Williamson of Madison, Wisconsin, was on the other end, offering to donate an image of his great-great-great-grandfather, Colonel William Jennings.[11]

Williamson, 81 years old, only had a hand-drawn portrait, which was passed down to him. The image had been in Williamson's home since the 1960s, but he did some searching online and learned that a small Ohio village bore his ancestor's name. A former professor well-trained in library science, Williamson immediately understood how important this image might be to the village.[12]

The original drawing of Colonel Jennings remained with the Williamson family, but in April 2001, Williamson and his wife traveled to Fort Jennings to pass on a reproduction of the image. The village was ready to celebrate and greeted Williamson with a musical performance by the Fort Jennings High School Band. Williamson and his wife were then taken on a tour of the town, met with several local representatives, and received lunch and a plaque. Today the image of Colonel Jennings is displayed proudly at the Fort Jennings State Bank.[13]

In 1918, Leo J. Wildenhaus, a former teacher at Fort Jennings High School, opened The Fort Jennings State Bank. The bank has remained a local establishment (with the addition of a few local branches) and is owned completely by stockholders. The Fort Jennings State Bank still operates today in the village.[15]

BICENTENNIAL PROJECT OF FORT JENNINGS AREA SEPTEMBER 1976

TOP: Fort Seneca Community Church

Population: 254   **Approx. Founding:** 1836

INSETS L to R: A main road in Fort Seneca • Fort Seneca's large community park • A sign marking Pete Mellott Memorial Field with Mellott's picture • The Pete Mellott Memorial Field

In 1877, citizens of Fort Seneca had become tired of crossing the Sandusky River by wading through shallow portions, so they approached Seneca County for the funds necessary to build a bridge. The new bridge stood over the Sandusky River until it was destroyed in the infamous 1913 flood that damaged much of Ohio. This flood also destroyed a nearby dam that had supported the mills in the village. Before the flood, it was common for residents to hold skating parties near the bridge, where water often pooled and froze due to the slack from the dam. In 1914, a new bridge was built, standing higher above the water to avoid future flood damage. The bridge still stands today.[10]

Fort Seneca

A Saloon Story

AFTER THE AMERICAN REVOLUTION, members of the American Indian nation known as the Seneca came to what would soon be called Northwest Ohio and began to build communities along the Sandusky River.[1] Decades later in 1819, white settlers first came to this area, naming their new community McNutts, after an early white settler named A. McNutt.[2]

For about a decade, the new white settlers and the members of the American Indian community shared this space in Pleasant Township. In fact, it was a common occurrence to see members of the Seneca community patronizing the saloons run by newly arrived white settlers. As one village history recalls, "Saloons were common in [what would become] Ft.

Seneca, each having a barrel of whiskey with a good supply of tin cups. In a remarkably short time, the whiskey level would become low and the crowd high. Songs were sung, and for some obscure reason, rarely a night went by without a wild melee breaking out…"[3]

Generally these wild melees were resolved outside the courtroom, with both parties admitting their faults and mending their friendships. However, likely thanks to growing anti-American Indian sentiment in the United States, one of these fights ended with an American Indian man of the Seneca Nation being locked in the Ohio Penitentiary. This incident, while not documented in any primary sources, has been recalled time and time again by many local histories. The story says that on October 4, 1829, a group of Seneca men were drinking at the tavern of Benazah

Parker. At this point, the government had outlawed the sale of whiskey to American Indians, but Parker was known to break this law: he was probably making more money for the sales than he was being fined when he got caught.[4]

That evening, Parker denied a cup of whiskey to a man named Peter Pork for some reason. Pork became angry, and Parker asked him to leave. When Pork would not leave the saloon, Parker grabbed a hot stick from the fireplace and brandished it at Pork, who in turn stabbed Parker, then dropped his knife and fled the scene. According to local stories, many citizens and even justices gathered together to capture Pork, who was tried and sent to the Ohio Penitentiary. Pork was viewed as a "mean, ill-tempered savage" who needed to be restrained. While it is very possible that Pork was mean and ill-tempered, it is more likely that this characterization and Pork's quick arrest were due to the racism against American Indians, so prevalent in Ohio at the time. Pork stayed at the Penitentiary until 1831, when the entire Seneca Nation was forcibly removed from their Ohio homes by the United States government. At this time, Pork was released and allowed to move to a Western reservation. Parker lived for about 15 more months, but it is said he eventually perished from the ill effects of the wound he sustained that evening at the saloon. Eventually, due to the work of the Women's Christian Temperance Union (a now international organization founded in Ohio during the 1880s that served as a precursor to many women's suffrage organizations), the village of Fort Seneca was declared dry and the sale of alcohol banned.[5]

A Confusing Name

Sometime in the 1830s, the village of McNutts was renamed Swope's Corner, probably for a local white settler named Samuel R. Swope. In January of 1836, Erastus Bone and Vincent Bell officially had the village surveyed, as the population had grown large enough to support multiple businesses and a post office.[6] The post office was established in the village in the early 1830s, moving from its original location about three miles north of the village. Before and after this move, the name of the post office that served the region was "Fort Seneca." This name came from a War of 1812-era fort located near the original post office site (for more on the fort, see page 140).[7] In retrospect, it's quite odd that the village of Fort Seneca is named for a fort that never actually existed within the village's boundaries, but this postal move may explain the situation. The village was likely renamed for the post office that moved into its jurisdiction.

The 1875 Tornado

In 1875 the village of Fort Seneca was hit by a tornado so bad that it is still frequently recalled today. Many homes and businesses were destroyed, with some lifted from their foundations and thrown across the village. As one history recalls, "the Methodist Church was moved bodily from its foundation 20 feet, tipped over and smashed to stones…" Dr. Nighswander, a local physician, saw his office picked up by the wind, leaving his medications strewn about, bottles broken, and liquid cures mixed together into an unsalvageable mess. A man named Eph Ambrose owned a smokehouse in Fort Seneca. The day after the tornado his smokehouse was gone and his yard almost comically strewn with hams. Even the shoe store was destroyed.[8]

Somehow, all of the residents of Fort Seneca escaped the tornado of 1875 unscathed. Even many of the village's animals survived. Apparently a man named Davidson had a few horses hitched in his barn during the tornado, and perhaps fearing the worst, went to look for them after the storm. According to one history, "he found them about 40 feet away, quietly standing hitched to a remnant of the manger." As the horses could not tell him what had occurred, Davidson was left to assume that they had been lifted up by the high winds, and then simply placed back on the ground, after flying quite a distance.[9]

In 1826, a general store was built in Fort Seneca. It operated well into the 1970s. In 1916, after a train wreck in the nearby village of Maple Grove, men arrived to purchase food for the clean-up crew, nearly emptying out the entire store after a few days.[11]

TOP: The Raider, a favorite restaurant in Freeport

Population: 353   Approx. Founding: 1810

INSETS L to R: Freeport Presbyterian Church • A sign marking the Clark Memorial Branch Library in downtown Freeport • A mural on the side of the Freeport Volunteer Fire Department • The Freeport Press

Many features in Tuscarawas County are known by the name "Post Boy" (e.g. Post Boy Road) because of an infamous area murder. On September 9, 1825, William Cartmell began his day at the Freeport Post Office before delivering the mail to Coshocton. He was shot and killed by John Funston, who framed the only witness, a man named Johnston. The Freeport postmaster stepped in with a clue. He had given Cartmell a $10 bill and kept a record of the serial number. This bill was found in a local gun shop where Funston had recently had his weapon serviced. Funston was taken into custody, Johnston identified him, and Funston was hanged.[16]

Freeport

A Navigable Stream

THE VILLAGE OF FREEPORT, in Harrison County, Ohio, was first platted in 1810 by William Melton and Dan Easly on the Big Stillwater Creek. It is believed that the name of Freeport was a reference to a recent decision by the Ohio General Assembly to designate the creek as a navigable stream. This designation would have made the village a prime location for a growing trade center.[1] Freeport never did develop into a booming trade metropolis, but it did see success as a timbering and quarrying area. The Cleveland, Lorain and Wheeling Railway also constructed track through the village.[2]

John J. Ashenhurst and the Freeport Press

In 1880, a man named John J. Ashenhurst founded the *Freeport Press*. Ashenhurst was born in 1848 in Wheeling, West Virginia, but moved to Hayesville, Ohio, in 1856. Ashenhurst's father was a minister with the United Presbyterian Church and had been assigned to a job in Ohio. The ministry was a noble calling, but unfortunately did not come with a large paycheck. Ashenhurst spent much of his childhood in Hayesville, working to help his family pay the bills.[3]

At the age of 15, Ashenhurst acquired a printing press. An industrious teenager, he started his own newspaper, the *Hayesville Chronicle*. Soon he took a permanent position at the *Ashland Times*.[4] After leaving his parents' house in Hayesville, Ashenhurst was a very busy man. In 1869, he joined Ohio's Prohibition Party, and in 1872, he started a Prohibition-themed newspaper, *The Ohio Valley News*. After a few years Ashenhurst traveled to Virginia, where likely inspired by his upbringing in a religious and abolitionist household, he began the Thyne Institute, a school for freedmen run by the United Presbyterian Church. By 1880, Ashenhurst was back in Ohio, starting the *Freeport Press*.[5] Within two years, Ashenhurst was on his way again, taking on leadership of a leading prohibition paper, the *Wayne County Herald*. From there he traveled to Nebraska and then back to Canton, Ohio, taking on two other publications. In 1891, Ashenhurst paused publishing to run for Ohio governor on the Prohibition ticket; he came in fourth.[6]

The Williams Family Takes on the Press

After Ashenhurst left town, the *Freeport Press* was purchased by L. B. Williams. The Williams family ended up owning the *Freeport Press* for four generations.[7] In 1957, Anne Williams Buck and her husband Maynard, fourth-generation Williams family members, took over. During their tenure, the *Freeport Press* greatly expanded, developing the printing business that it is well known for today. The Press also began to acquire other local publications.[8] In 1961, the *Freeport Press* purchased the *Scio Weekly Herald* to form the *Press Herald*. When the *Press Herald* first began its new run, it was edited by a Freeport native named Ann Miller. Miller was not only a resident of Freeport but also a graduate of Kent State University's school of journalism.[9]

In 1968, the new *Press Herald* acquired the *Cadiz Republican*, merging further into the *Harrison News Herald*.[10] However, the *Freeport Press* began to focus more on the printing business, eventually separating itself from the *Harrison News Herald*. Today the *Herald* is published separately from *Freeport Press*, which has transitioned fully into a production business, rather than a news publication.

Unfortunately, after their big expansion, Anne and Maynard Buck began to struggle financially. With concerns growing over a possible bankruptcy, the couple began to reach out to possible buyers in the late 1980s. They were concerned that the dissolution of such a large company in the village of Freeport could have lasting impacts on the many

residents who would lose their jobs and the tax dollars that the village relied on.[11] In 1987, they were able to sell to Suburban Graphics. The business changed hands quite a few times, but by 2003, the current owner of *Freeport Press*, David Pilcher, was the sole owner.[12]

David Pilcher and the Freeport Press Today

Pilcher actually arrived at *Freeport Press* with Suburban Graphics in 1987. Much like the original founder of the *Freeport Press*, John Ashenhurst, Pilcher stumbled into the publishing business after high school and found that he had a knack for it. Starting in 1987, Pilcher quickly grew the business, which is now one of the nation's top printers, printing and shipping for magazines and catalogs.[13]

Pilcher began by purchasing equipment, using liquidation sales, plant closings, and auctions to acquire modern equipment at decent prices. He was able to maintain the staff at the plant, many of whom had been working there for 40 years or more. In 1987, when Pilcher first arrived, the plant was making about 7 to 8 million dollars in annual sales. Within 15 years, he had surpassed 33 million dollars annually.[14]

In 2015, *Freeport Press* acquired a new building in the nearby city of New Philadelphia. The company invested between 15 and 20 million dollars on new infrastructure, including the new building and state-of-the-art equipment. Today, *Freeport Press* operates in both Freeport and New Philadelphia, with sales continuing to roll in under Pilcher's watch.[15]

The Skull Fork Covered Bridge and the 16-sided barn are both found near Freeport and the nearby Buckeye Trail, a hiking trail, which spans all of Ohio.[17] The 16-sided barn was built in 1924, renovated in 2008, and is believed to be one of only three 16-sided barns in the United States.[18]

Population: 140 **Approx. Founding:** early 1800s

INSETS L to R: Fresno United Methodist Church • A pavilion at Fresno Park • A memorial to the Fresno School, 1896-2007 • White Eyes Fuel provides gasoline for travelers stopping through Fresno

The residents of Fresno are great at seeing the opportunities in their historic buildings. In 1932, the village built White Eyes Rural School #2 on County Road 171. However, the school closed its doors in 1950.[15] Still intact, the building today hosts one of Fresno's most popular businesses: White Eyes Pizza and Carry Out. Customers can drive up to a window at the old school building and pick up their pizzas.

TOP: The former White Eyes Rural School, now White Eyes Carryout

Fresno

Koquethagechton Leads the Lenape in Ohio

TODAY, THE VILLAGE OF FRESNO, OHIO, now a census-designated place, is located in White Eyes Township. This township, and the creek that runs through it, are named for one of the area's early residents, an American Indian man named Koquethagechton.[1] Koquethagechton was known as "White Eyes" to many white English settlers in the Ohio country, purportedly due to the light color of his complexion.[2]

Koquethagechton was born around the year 1730 and grew up in what is now the state of Pennsylvania. Here he became an influential leader for the Lenape, or Delaware, Nation. In the early 1770s, he moved to what is today Coshocton County, Ohio. He formed his own town near the present-day city of Coshocton, where he hoped the Lenape people could live without encroachment from white settlers. Lenape settlers in Koquethagechton's new town did come into contact with some settlers, in the form of Moravian missionaries. However, partially due to Koquethagechton's successful leadership, the two groups were able to live in harmony. Some members of the Lenape Nation converted to Christianity with the aid of the missionaries, but not all of the residents of Koquethagechton's town abandoned their former religious traditions.[3]

Negotiating with the Colonists

In 1776, the Delaware people chose Koquethagechton as their official representative to the Continental Congress. Here he promised aid to the American Colonies in the coming revolution. He also pushed his biggest goal: securing a place for the Lenape Nation as the 14th state in the new United States of America.[4]

In September 1778, Koquethagechton was one of a handful of representatives from the Lenape Nation who attended peace talks with the United States Continental Congress. These talks ended in the Treaty of Fort Pitt. In this document, the Lenape representatives and the colonists' representatives agreed that the Lenape in the area would aid the colonists in the war, while the colonists would recognize Lenape sovereignty.[5] Not long after this treaty was signed, Koquethagechton was named a lieutenant colonel in the Continental Army.[6]

In 1778, Koquethagechton served as a guide for the Continental Army as they traveled through the Ohio Country. During this trip, Koquethagechton mysteriously died. His traveling companions claimed he suffered from smallpox, but according to many tellings he was assassinated by American colonists unhappy about the promise of Lenape sovereignty in the recent treaty. After Koquethagechton's death, the relationship between the Lenape and the American colonists disintegrated, and many Lenape supported the British during the rest of the war.[7]

A Village of Many Names

In the early 1800s, at the junction of the White Eyes Creek and Middle Fork, a town began to form, taking the name Jacktown for Bill Jack, a local blacksmith. In 1831, William M. Boyd built a mill here and the town became known as Boyd's Mill. The town grew slowly and was home to only two families in 1863. In 1875, the town's name changed to Avondale. By 1883, the population of Avondale had reached 96.[8]

In 1905, the town of Avondale experienced its final name change. A well-known neighborhood in the Cincinnati area was known as Avondale, and it was causing confusion at the post office. According to local histories, a former resident of the Coshocton County Avondale, Dr. Harry Wallace, had recently moved from Fresno, California, and loved his new home. In a letter, he suggested the name Fresno. Residents took his advice, and the village was renamed.[9]

Business in Fresno Today

Pearl Valley Cheese is located just three miles north of Fresno on Ohio Route 93. In 1928, Ernest Stalder, a young Swiss immigrant in his late twenties, purchased the cheese business for $700 (a little over $10,000 today). A year later, Stalder married Gertrude Bandi, a fellow Swiss immigrant, and the two pursued the businesses together.[10] In the early years, all milk was delivered to Pearl Valley Cheese by horse and wagon. However in 1932, the milk finally started arriving by truck. The businesses grew quickly from this point, with a new electric-powered factory going up in 1938. By 1947, Pearl Valley Cheese was the largest cheese plant in the state of Ohio.[11]

While it's no longer Ohio's largest cheese manufacturer, Pearl Valley Cheese is still very active today. Visitors can watch the cheese-making process and then step into the store to buy the delicious products of this process. Can't make it to Fresno? You can shop online via their website.[12]

Fresno also has a stake in the craft beer movement. In 2014, Kevin Ely, a brewmaster formerly with Uinta Brewing Company of Salt Lake City, Utah, along with his wife, Jael Malenke, and her brother and his wife, purchased a farm in Fresno to start a brewery. Jael grew up just down the road and knew it was a great spot to set up shop. Today the family operates a brewery in a converted barn, using water from a nearby natural spring in their many brews.[13] The brewery is known as the Wooly Pig Farm Brewery, for the curly-haired mangalitsa pigs that Kevin encountered in Bavaria while learning his trade. The farm now is home to a number of these wooly pigs, which sometimes end up on the tasting room's menu. In the meantime, the pigs enjoy foraging on the grain waste left over from the brewing process.[14]

There's lots to do in the Fresno area. About two miles southwest of the main part of the village is the Forest Hill Lake & Campground, which boasts a lake fed by a natural freshwater spring.[16] Fresno is only 20 minutes away from Coshocton and its Roscoe Village, a canal town restored to what it looked like in the 1830s.[17]

TOP: The Gilboa Quarry

Population: 178   Incorporated: 1848

INSETS L to R: A plane to be sunk at the quarry for divers • The famous Gilboa bull • Little Red's brand new storefront • A village park

One of the most-recognizable landmarks in Gilboa is a 16-foot-tall fiberglass bull which has stood at the corner of Route 224 and Pearl Street in Gilboa since the 1970s. Gilboa resident Pete Diller can recall when his father first spotted the bull outside a bar in Toledo and offered to buy it. The village of Gilboa was attempting to draw in visitors, and the elder Diller figured this was just the way to get noticed. Pete Diller and his brother took a semi, with a forklift onboard, to Toledo to pick up their father's new purchase. He remembers that "Its head was so high that we had to jockey around every stoplight...The first stoplight...we hit right on its forehead."[19]

Gilboa

The Early Years of Gilboa

IN 1833, THE VILLAGE OF GILBOA in Putnam County, Ohio, was first surveyed by a man named Elisha Stout. Soon many tradesmen began moving to the new town and setting up shop, leading to a population boom. By 1848, the village of Gilboa, named for the story of Mount Gilboa in the Old Testament, was officially incorporated.[1]

One of the best-known businesses in Gilboa was the Chambers Hotel, built in 1840 by Matthew Chambers, an early white settler. A social hotspot, many men in the village also treated the hotel more like a tavern, gathering around for conversation about the news of the day. Matthew Chambers himself enjoyed regaling visitors with tales of his service in the War of 1812, whether they wanted to listen or not.[2]

The Challenges of 1852

The year of 1852 was particularly challenging for Gilboa. The town was thriving, and a railroad was rumored to be coming to town. Unfortunately this new project, known as the Dayton and Michigan Railroad, passed by Gilboa, hurting the town's business interests.[3]

In the summer of 1852, the village of Gilboa was struck with a deadly outbreak of cholera. About 19 villagers became ill, with 14 succumbing to the disease. No one knows for sure how the disease made its way into Gilboa, but many posit it had something to do with Chambers Hotel. Some say that when Chambers had sent an employee by the name of Sanchel to Sandusky that summer to retrieve groceries, Sanchel had become ill and brought the disease back to town with him. Others believe a visitor at the hotel brought the disease in with them while passing through the village.[4]

Many residents of Gilboa began to flee during the cholera outbreak, but it is believed that three medical professionals stayed behind to treat the ill. Unfortunately, one of these doctors fell ill himself. This man, Dr. Gustav Thatye, was a Hungarian immigrant. It is believed he came to the United States as a political refugee after supporting Louis Kossuth's failed revolution. Thatye lived with John Kisseberth and his family. When he passed away, Mrs. Kisseberth saw to it that a headstone was placed in the local cemetery.[5] The stone is still there today.

Despite the unfortunate events of 1852, the village of Gilboa persevered. In 1888, things began looking up for the residents. Finally a new railroad came to town, the Findlay, Ft. Wayne, and Western Railroad, bringing economic growth.[6]

Little Red Bakery

In May 2010, a tasty new business arrived in Gilboa.[7] Kelly Wolfe, a Gilboa native, and her business partner, Brandi Smith, opened a new bakery called Little Red, inspired by the recipes Wolfe had learned from her grandmother.[8]

While she is inspired by her family's recipes, Wolfe is a well-trained chef in her own right. After graduating from high school in Gilboa in the late 1990s, Wolfe immediately went to culinary school in Pittsburgh, Pennsylvania. After some time as a savory chef, she applied to Le Cordon Bleu in London, England, where she earned a pastry degree.[9]

For the first eight years of their new business, Wolfe baked at home, and Smith, managing the financials, sought out venues to sell Little Red's baked goods. Soon their products were for sale in nearby towns, and not long after people started calling with requests.[10] In July 2018, Little Red had grown so large that Wolfe and Smith were able to open a storefront bakery on Main Street in Gilboa.[11] But why "Little Red?" As Kelly Wolfe

told reporters, "My last name is Wolfe...I have three little kids, red hair, and my recipes are from my grandmother. It just kind of stuck."[12]

A Destination for Divers

The village of Gilboa has always been a popular destination for divers. Just west of town is a large limestone quarry, which reaches 130 feet in depth.[13] It's popular with divers who plan to take on the cold Great Lakes, since the quarry's waters are generally between 40 and 70 degrees Fahrenheit.[14] The Gilboa Quarry also provides suspended platforms on which teachers and students can rest for a moment of instruction.[15]

The quarry features many interesting sunken treasures to explore. The managers of the quarry have purposefully sunken such items as a plane, a helicopter, and a school bus, so divers may swim in and out of each machine. For those more interested in natural beauties, divers can pick up a bag of fish food before embarking on their journey. With this bag in hand it is possible to attract a few bass or rainbow trout.[16]

For those interested in visiting Gilboa Quarry, there is a campsite located on site. The managers of the quarry also keep a cottage open with a handful of beds for visitors. Luckily, when it gets busy, there are still a few hotels nearby.[17] In 2009, Gilboa Quarry was its busiest when a group of divers assembled to attempt to break the world record of most divers submerged at once. In all, 794 divers participated, but unfortunately, a good number of no-shows left the group a few hundred people short of the record.[18]

Many victims of Gilboa's 1852 cholera outbreak were buried in a separate cholera cemetery. Some fans of the paranormal believe the cemetery is haunted. Visitors have reported hearing the voices of children when there were no kids present. And according to rumor, some of the graves were exhumed but there were no longer any remains inside.[20]

TOP: The Carthagenia Baptist Church

Population: unknown, not counted
Approx. Founding: 1832

INSETS L to R: A special marker for Lester J. Robinson, veteran of the U.S. Army • A state historic marker notes the importance of the Gist Settlement • A dog keeps watch as the grounds of the Gist Settlement Cemetery are cared for • The cemetery at the Gist Settlement is dotted with historic family names and the headstones of many veterans who served in a segregated military, including during the Civil War

Who was Samuel Gist? Why did he adjust his will? There is no certain answer. Between 1808 and his death in 1815, Gist revised his last will four times.[16] In the final version of the document, this man, who had made a career selling insurance to slave traders, somehow decided to change his ways. Born an orphan, Gist first came to the United States as an indentured servant, and he only moved up the social ladder through marriage.[17] Perhaps an aging Gist reflected on his early days or the many slaves upon whose back his fortune was built and had a change of heart.

Gist Settlement

Waiting for Freedom

IN 1804, A BOY NAMED HANNIBAL TURNER was born on a plantation in the state of Virginia. Turner and his family were enslaved by a man by the name of Samuel Gist. Hannibal Turner himself would never even meet the man that held him in bondage. Gist, an Englishman, had once lived in Virginia but was upset by colonial unrest during the American Revolution and moved back to England in 1776. Despite the distance, Gist continued to maintain ownership of his land and the men and women who worked in his fields.[1]

In 1815, Gist died. Quickly, rumors began to spread amongst the slaves on his three Virginia plantations. It was said that in recent edits to his will, Gist had decided to free all of his slaves upon his death.

Hannibal Turner, 11 years old by this time, began to hear whispers that he might be freed.[2]

Gist's will did free all of his slaves, but it would be 1832 before Hannibal Turner and his family saw freedom. Turner would be nearly 30 years old by the time he was free.[3]

Managing Freedom and Moving to Ohio

Gist appointed a few friends to manage the manumission of about 300 slaves and the trust that he had left behind to finance their needs. The first step was determining a new place that the freed slaves might live. Staying in Virginia was not an option, as Gist's former slaves would almost certainly be kidnapped by slave catchers.[4]

Gist's friends were able to find land for sale in Brown and Highland Counties in the state of Ohio, where slavery was forbidden. They were also able to find local Ohio Quakers who were willing to act as executors of the large trust that Gist had left behind. Unfortunately, Gist's friends did not believe that the former slaves could manage the money and land on their own. They expressed a concern that if the newly freed men owned their own lands, they would sell and simply move away.[5]

Gist's former slaves were slowly moved in groups, and all attempts were made to reunite any families that had been split up amongst Gist's three plantations. Hannibal Turner and his family were among the final group to leave. Finally, when their time came in 1832, they walked from Virginia to Highland County, Ohio, where they were able to build a new home.[6]

This new community in Highland County, known as the Gist Settlement, prospered. When the new residents arrived, the Quakers had established some infrastructure: crops were already growing in the fields, and a few buildings had been constructed. One of the first things the new settlers did was build a church, known as Carthagenia Baptist Church. With a school, church, and land, the community grew and new generations were welcomed into the Gist Settlement.[7]

For many years the settlement was self-sufficient; however, there was reason to leave the community once in a while. For example, many men from the Gist Settlement served with the Union Army during the Civil War.[8] Eventually, during the early 1900s, the children of the Gist Settlement began going to school in the nearby town of New Vienna.[9]

One of these children was Paul Turner, born in 1931. He is the descendant of Hannibal Turner, one of Gist's original slaves. After leaving the settlement for a career in the Navy, Turner returned to his family's land, where he still lives today.[10]

The Gist Settlement Today

From 1840 to 1930, the settlement's population remained around a steady 75.[11] However, in recent years the population has dwindled. While Paul Turner still pays the electric bill at the Carthagenia Baptist Church, there hasn't been a service in the building since 1999.[12]

One of the reasons for this decline is disappointment in the local legal system. Paul Turner spent many years entwined in legal complications as he attempted to gain full ownership of the land his ancestors should have been the owners of in 1832. Because Gist's friends didn't trust his freed slaves to manage their own land and finances, the deeds were never passed on to their rightful owners.[13]

During the mid-1800s, it was found that the Quakers who had been put in charge of the Gist trust were mismanaging the funds. The white men who had been left in charge took advantage of the fact that freed black people were not considered full citizens in the eyes of the Ohio law. There was no easy way for residents of the Gist Settlement to wrest control of the money and land that was rightfully theirs.

In 1851, Highland County officials stepped in, and the county took control of Gist's trust. This wasn't much of an improvement. In 1948, led by the Turner family, Gist residents hired an attorney and attempted to retrieve the deed to their lands. The case dragged out for decades, never reaching a conclusion. When Paul Turner returned to the settlement in 1976, he immediately began paying property taxes, despite the fact that he did not have a deed. He was desperate to ensure that his home was not taken away.[14]

Today, Paul Turner owns most of the Gist Settlement. In a case that finally settled the century-long confusion, Turner was given 19 of the settlement's 31 lots, while 2.5 were given to Dale Robinson, another Gist descendant.[15]

The Gist Settlement was never officially incorporated. In fact, residents of the settlement lived "an entirely separate…life from their white neighbors…"[18] Most maps completely missed the Gist Settlement."[19]

TOP: Glenmont Tavern

Population: 296   **Incorporated:** 1896

INSETS L to R: A street view of Glenmont with St. John's United Church of Christ in the foreground and St. Peter's and St. Paul's Catholic Church in the background • One of the many treehouses hidden away in Glenmont • A veterans memorial in downtown Glenmont • St. Peter's and St. Paul's Church, made with stone from the Glenmont Quarry

Ever dreamed of spending the night in a treehouse? The Glenmont-based company, The Mohicans, may be able to make that dream come true. The company has now built six treehouses in the nearby Mohican Forest with all the comfort of home, including beds, televisions, kitchens, and plumbing.[17] If you aren't interested in spending the night, you can check out The Treehouse Brewing Company, a bar built in a treehouse in Glenmont. The treehouse itself, like some of the Mohican treehouses, was built and designed by Pete Nelson, host of the show *Treehouse Masters* on Animal Planet.[18]

Glenmont

The First Village in Richland Township

IN MAY 1841, after a survey by Samuel Robinson, a new village was laid out in Richland Township, Holmes County, Ohio. The village had many names, among them Napoleon, Black Creek, Manning, and Pictoria.[1] It was finally incorporated in 1896 as Glenmont. Not long after it was platted, the village of Glenmont grew into a trade center for the mostly rural area.[2]

Of all the settled areas in Richland Township, Glenmont grew the fastest thanks to the Cleveland, Columbus, and Cincinnati Railroad that passed very near the village and crossed Holmes County.[3] Holmes County residents encouraged county officials to use public funds to pay for the railway, but Ohio law didn't allow that. To get around this law,

county residents called an election in which they approved a purchase of $75,000 of railway stock using public money. The railroad was finished in May 1854, passing just south of Glenmont, making the village a trade hub. The railroad was in service until 1979, although freight trucks eventually diminished its influence.[4]

Blum's Briar Hill Stone Company

In 1917, Robert Blum came to Glenmont to visit a local quarry run by the Purdy Brothers. The Glenmont quarry was the source of the stone for St. Peter's and St. Paul's Catholic Church (still standing in Glenmont). Blum was a stonecutter based in Amherst, Ohio, and he was in search of a particular material.[5]

Blum found more than just that: he developed an interest in the quarry itself. Upon returning to Amherst, Blum consulted his business partner. They soon purchased the quarry and opened Briar Hill Stone Company. The company was supposedly named by a visiting salesman who commented on the briars on the hill that surrounded the quarry.[6] Blum's new business provided some jobs for Glenmont residents, but he also brought much of his staff with him from Amherst. Both Blum's sons and a grandson ended up joining the firm. Many of these tradesmen were immigrants who had settled in Amherst and now moved to Glenmont. This was the village's first experience with a large group of immigrants and a chance to embrace new traditions.[7]

Briar Hill Stone Company is still in business today. The company is based in Glenmont, but it maintains eight quarries across north-central Ohio. Briar Hill works exclusively with sandstone, providing five different color ranges for various projects.[8]

The Battle of Fort Fizzle

In 1863, as the Union Army faced a recruiting shortfall, the United States passed the Conscription Act, requiring states to furnish a certain number of soldiers based on their population. Able-bodied men were allowed to find someone to serve in their place or pay a fine to avoid service, but those who couldn't had no choice but to serve. Draft officials often traveled throughout the state to enforce the new law. This often lead to rioting, most famously in New York City in the summer of 1863.[9]

Many residents of Holmes County objected to being drafted into military service for the Union Army, either because they were Peace Democrats who favored negotiation with the Confederacy or because they were Copperheads who favored a Confederate victory. When a draft agent named Elias Robinson came into the county on June 5, 1863, he was not greeted kindly. What happened next isn't at all clear, but it remains an important legend in Holmes County.[10]

Robinson was soon attacked. As one source records, a man named Peter Stuber started the commotion by throwing a rock at Robinson. Soon after, another man named William Greiner drew his pistol and fired into the air. In reaction to this event, Captain James Drake of the Provost Marshal's office was sent with a group of men to Holmes County to arrest the attackers. Four men were arrested, but a small mob followed Drake out of town and recovered their four friends.[11]

It would take more force to counter the Holmes County draft resistors. Officials in the capital city of Columbus ordered Colonel William Wallace and about 420 men of the 15th Ohio Volunteer Infantry to march on Holmes County. When they arrived on June 17, they were met by about 900 local men who had fortified themselves in what they called Fort Vallandigham, for Clement Vallandigham, a famous Ohio Copperhead.[12, 13] The fort was located in Richland Township, on the farm of a man named Lorenzo Blanchard.[14]

The soldiers immediately advanced, and the rioters sent one volley towards the 15th Volunteers before running in fear. The soldiers pursued them, wounding two, but soon the fighting ended. On June 18, a group of Peace Democrats, led by Daniel P. Leadbetter, arrived in Holmes County to negotiate a peace. The 15th Volunteers refused to leave if the four men who assaulted Robinson did not surrender. Fortunately, the four turned themselves in, and Colonel Wallace's men returned to Columbus. Eventually 40 rioters were indicted, but only Lorenzo Blanchard was found guilty.[15]

Today this incident is known as the Battle of Fort Fizzle. The draft resistors were largely mocked after the event. As one journalist wrote, the rioters ran from the battle like a "flock of quail taking flight." The term "fizzle" was meant as an insult, but it stuck.[16]

What ever happened to Peter Stuber, the man who started the Battle of Fort Fizzle? In an ironic twist, Stuber was drafted into the Union army in 1864[19] and discharged one year later in 1865 after serving in Company A of the 126th Ohio Volunteer Infantry. He died in Glenmont in 1893.[20]

Population: 224   **Approx. Founding:** 1830

INSETS L to R: Gratiot Town Hall • The Gratiot United Methodist Church • The sun sets over the park in Gratiot • The Gratiot United Methodist Church office

Jesse Yarnell, born in Gratiot in June 1837, moved to California in 1862. Upon arriving in California he opened the *Daily News* in Placerville. In 1866, Yarnell moved to Los Angeles, where he began the *Weekly Republican*, which eventually became the *Evening Express*. He then became a leader at the *Weekly Mirror*, which merged with the *Times* to form the Times-Mirror Company. After the merger, Yarnell assisted the new company in continuing to publish the still-influential *Los Angeles Times*. Yarnell died in Los Angeles in January 1906.[15]

TOP: A park maintained by the Gratiot United Methodist Church

Gratiot

A Village on the National Road

AROUND THE YEAR 1830, Adam Smith laid out a new Ohio village, directly on the border between Licking and Muskingum Counties. Why such an awkward location? The settlement of this new village, soon to be known as Gratiot, was largely driven by the construction of the National Road, the first highway in the U.S. Smith began laying out the village only when he had official word that this new thoroughfare would cut a path through his farmland.[1] Many new towns across Ohio and the United States quickly appeared on the National Road, with hopes of economic success from trade and travel.

The village of Gratiot was named for a man named Colonel Charles Gratiot, originally of St. Louis, Missouri.[2] First appointed as a cadet by Thomas Jefferson in 1804, Gratiot became a member of the Army Corps of Engineers after graduating from the Military Academy in 1806. Gratiot made a name for himself during the War of 1812, when he served as William Henry Harrison's Chief Engineer. In 1828, Gratiot was appointed the Chief Engineer of the entire Army Corps of Engineers.[3]

This promotion put Gratiot in charge of planning and constructing roads, harbors, and fortifications across the United States. The National Road, a federally funded project, would have received support from Gratiot's engineers. It was fitting that a village built around the National Road would take the name of the nation's chief engineer. In fact, it is said that Gratiot spent many an evening in inns and taverns along the National Road, speaking with the residents his new project affected. It is believed

Adam Smith was one of these residents that Gratiot spent many hours with when he visited Zanesville, inspiring Smith to name his new town after the man he had gotten to know so well.[4]

Unfortunately, Gratiot did not see the end of the construction of the National Road. In 1838, President Martin Van Buren dismissed Gratiot after lengthy arguments with the War Department over proper benefits.[5]

The Sad Fate of Cornelius Hamilton

In January 1821, before Adam Smith had officially laid out the village of Gratiot, a boy named Cornelius Hamilton was born in its future borders. Hamilton was raised in the area, attending Denison University in Granville (now only a 30-minute drive from Gratiot) as an adult. Hamilton passed the Ohio Bar Exam in 1845 and moved to the city of Marysville, where he began his own practice.[6]

In 1850, Hamilton had the privilege of serving as a delegate to Ohio's second constitutional convention. Hamilton and the other delegates met to work through the problems that had arisen from the state's original constitution and draft a new basis for law in the state. While heavily amended since, this 1850 constitution still governs Ohio.

1850 was a big year for the state of Ohio and for Cornelius Hamilton. Hamilton purchased the fledgling *Marysville Tribune* that year, which he owned until 1853.[7]

After his many accomplishments, it was no surprise that Hamilton was elected to serve as a representative from the 8th district of Ohio in the United States House of Representatives. Hamilton was elected as a member of the Republican Party in 1866. He arrived on the job in Washington, D.C., in March 1867, but tragically, his service was cut short in December of that same year.[8]

When Hamilton traveled to Washington to attend congressional sessions, he left his wife and children behind in Marysville. During the winter of 1865–1867, Hamilton was in the nation's capital, when his eldest son, Thomas, began to express that he felt uneasy and wished his father would come home. Thomas was about 18 years old at the time. Hamilton's wife wrote to his offices in Washington, D.C., and the two decided it was best for Cornelius to make a visit to the family. By early December, Hamilton was back at home in Marysville.[9]

Within two weeks of his visit, after observing Thomas's behavior, Hamilton had begun filing papers to have his son admitted to the nearest insane asylum. However, the events of December 22, 1867, prevented that from happening. That morning, Cornelius and his eldest sons, Thomas and John, went out to feed the animals in the barn. John turned back early, sent to the house to prepare for Sunday school at the behest of his father. John recalled turning back as he neared the house and noticing that his brother was carefully watching him.[10]

Not long after John arrived back at the house, Thomas returned as well, alone. His mother asked where Cornelius had gone. As an answer, Thomas raised an axe he was carrying, as if to attack her. John ran between the two, and Thomas began to chase his younger brother with the axe. John slipped as the two raced through the house, and Thomas managed to hit his shoulder with the axe. John crawled out of the house, escaping with his life, and Thomas turned again to his mother.[11]

Mrs. Hamilton had run across the street to a neighbor's household. When he left the Hamilton house, Thomas was accosted by multiple neighbors, attempting to get him to drop his weapon. As this chaos ensued in the street, John returned to the house and, even with his likely dislocated shoulder, began to carry his two younger sisters from their home. Thomas noticed his siblings and walked back in their direction. Witnesses recalled John screaming, "Save my two little sisters!"[12]

Finally, Thomas was captured by a neighbor, and a search was made for Congressman Cornelius Hamilton. He lay near the barn, covered in feed, where Thomas had left him after hitting him with a large wooden board that caused his death.[13]

Ohio is well known for "mispronouncing" the names of its cities, villages, and towns. If you're from Ohio, Lima doesn't sound like the city in Peru, Russia is not pronounced like the country, and Bellefontaine doesn't address that "e" on the end. So how do Ohioans pronounce Gratiot? As if they are saying "gray-shot."[14]

TOP: A view of the gorgeous brick lined sidewalks and historic buildings of Hanoverton

Population: 391   **Incorporated:** 1836

INSETS L to R: The Hanover House, available for rent via the Spread Eagle Tavern • The rear entrance to the Spread Eagle Tavern • Hanoverton Presbyterian Church • The first public well dug in town in 1845

As one of the oldest buildings in Hanoverton, the Spread Eagle Tavern most certainly comes with ghost stories. One of the most popular stories concerns a daughter of the original owner, a woman named Olevia. According to the local legend, she left Hanoverton with dreams of a life on stage. She found herself in New York City, happily engaged. However, her fiancé left her, and she returned to Hanoverton, heartbroken. Olevia could not overcome her sadness and eventually took her own life. Stories abound of Olevia appearing in her former bedroom on the third floor and pulling the sheets from guests' beds while they sleep.[18]

Hanoverton

Hanover Becomes Hanoverton

THE VILLAGE OF HANOVERTON was first platted in 1813 by James Craig. Craig was part of a group of Quakers who settled in the area. In 1813, Craig purchased 24 acres and platted a new village. Craig and his friends immediately opened a store and a few mills on site.[1]

The village was originally called Hanover. However, the name quickly changed in 1827, when the village residents attempted to open a post office and learned that a village in Licking County, Ohio, had already claimed the name. Many early Ohio towns experienced this problem, and it generally required a complete name change. In Hanover, however, the residents simply tweaked their name, changing it to Hanoverton.[2]

The Sandy and Beaver Canal

The village of Hanoverton began to grow quickly during the 1830s, peaking at a population of about 2,000 residents.[3] This growth was almost exclusively due to the construction of the Sandy and Beaver Canal in the village. Construction began on this 73.5-mile-long canal in 1828. When construction finished 20 years later, the canal connected the Ohio River and the Ohio and Erie Canal.[4, 5] The village of Hanoverton itself only saw construction crews for about 5 years, from 1832 to 1837.[6] However the promise of the canal was enough to bring many new residents to town.

The first canal boat to come through Hanoverton arrived in January 1848. Residents rushed to meet the boat, excited about the village's new era. Hanoverton was an interesting stop on the canal journey thanks to a location known as "the Big Tunnel." During canal construction, workers blasted through sandstone to form a hole 18 feet in diameter. Local history tells that when the workers first managed to open the tunnel from end to end, a young boy named Jimmy McIntyre sprinted through the tunnel, so he could be remembered as the first person to completely cross through it. Once construction was completed, a chain laid through the tunnel helped pull boats through its entire length.[7]

When the first boat came through the tunnel in 1848, a large stone fell into the water, blocking passage. The boat had to wait while the stone was removed. However, one man onboard couldn't delay. As the story goes, Ed Sinclair was set to be married that day at 3 pm. He jumped from the boat and swam to shore so he could be on time.[8]

In 1852, the Sandy and Beaver Canal officially closed, thanks to a break in a dam at the Cold Run Reservation in Columbiana County. The fallout from this break destroyed a large amount of personal property and the infrastructure of the canal itself. By 1854, the company managing the canal declared bankruptcy.[9]

"Just Near Enough for You to Hear the Whistle..."

Right around the time that the canal was closing, the Cleveland and Pittsburgh Railroad came to Columbiana County. In 1852, a representative of the railway came to town to speak to Hanoverton residents. The railway wanted $10,000 from the village to ensure that the railroad was built within Hanoverton boundaries.[10] The Hanoverton representatives declined the offer. They felt that building the railroad through their village was inescapable. Angry at this attitude, the railway representative left with one last promise, stating "We'll show you. We'll build it just near enough for you to hear the whistle." He kept his promise. The railway bypassed Hanoverton, and the village began to shrink.[11]

Without the railroad, the town's tunnel had no real purpose. Instead, young couples in the nearby village of Dungannon (at one end of the tunnel), kept a rowboat near the tunnel, turning Tunnel Hill into a tunnel of love. Eventually the boat was left untied one night and floated into the tunnel, never to be used again.[12]

Historic Plymouth Street and the Spread Eagle Tavern

Today, visitors to Hanoverton can enjoy many historic buildings on Plymouth Street. Once the village's main roadway, Plymouth Street was left behind when the canal was built and business moved to Canal Street. This move helped preserve these buildings, as they weren't used as much.[13]

One of the most-visited buildings on Plymouth Street is the Spread Eagle Tavern. The tavern was first built in 1837, under the supervision of a man named Will Rhodes. Many of the men who built the tavern were likely canal builders put out of work during the Panic of 1837. This economic downturn is largely what caused the construction of the Sandy and Beaver Canal to drag on for 20 years. The tavern is an excellent example of Federalist architecture.[14] Because many of the buildings on Plymouth Street are architecturally significant, the entire district was placed on the National Register of Historic Places in 1977.[15]

Today, the Spread Eagle Tavern still operates as a tavern. A huge restoration project was undertaken after Peter Johnson bought the tavern at auction in 1988, lengthening the lifespan of the building while retaining its historic character.[16] Visitors to the Spread Eagle can eat in seven themed dining rooms. Some rooms, such as the William McKinley room, are more formal, while others, such as the log barn room, are more rugged. For after-dinner drinks or an enjoyable cocktail hour, visitors can travel to the Patrick Henry Tavern Room or Gaver's Rathskeller (a German word for a bar in the basement of city hall). Five overnight guest rooms are also available.[17]

In the village of Hanoverton, March 21, 1954, was officially declared Ella Tate and Pearl Carle Day. Ella and Pearl had served a combined 95 years as telephone operators in Hanoverton, and with the arrival of dial telephones in 1954, they were able to retire. Ella had been working as an operator since the age of 11.[19]

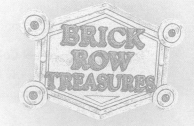

TOP: The Harbor View Historical Society

Population: 107   **Incorporated:** 1921

INSETS L to R: A mural marks Harbor View Park • Boats line the harbor off of Maumee Bay and Lake Erie • Post Office boxes for the residents of Harbor View and their unique zip code • The Harbor View Yacht Club

According to census records, when Mayor Levi Shovar was arrested for defying the Volstead Act, he had two young sons at home, James and Ernest. Both boys ended up serving their country in the military. James served as a Master Sergeant in the Marine Corps during both World War II and the Korean War. Ernest, an infant at the time of his father's arrest, served as a Corporal in the Marine Corps during World War II.

Harbor View

Completely Surrounded

JUST OUTSIDE TOLEDO, on the coast of the Maumee Bay, lies Harbor View. Oregon Township was once home to about half a dozen different villages and towns; however, by 1950, most villages were annexed by the larger village of Oregon. Only Harbor View stayed independent, leaving the village almost completely surrounded by Oregon.[1]

The early history of Harbor View is not well documented.[2] It is likely that Lucas County residents began to build cottages in the area in the early 1900s, with a hope of living a comfortable life on the water.[3, 4]

"The Coolest Summer Colony"

It's possible that early settlement of Harbor View was driven by real estate companies capitalizing on the waterfront. The 1930 census records show that early village residents came from all over: Ohio, as well as Kentucky, Tennessee, Pennsylvania, Michigan, Maryland, Poland, Canada, and Germany. In 1913, the E.H. Close Realty Company ran an advertisement in the *Lima News* offering a plot of land on Harbor View Beach ("the coolest and most popular Summer Colony on Maumee Bay") in exchange for a lot purchased in Lima's new Gardendale neighborhood.[5]

A diverse village began to form. Some were in Harbor View to vacation, while some residents of lesser means called Harbor View home year-round. As the *Toledo News-Bee* described in 1923, Harbor View was "a one street village, formed in the shape of a horseshoe, with small and large, cheap and elaborate, well-furnished and shabbily outfitted cottages vying with each other...."[6]

March 1924 Rocks Harbor View

In March of 1924, crime in Harbor View was a hot topic in town. March began with an article in the *Toledo News-Bee* bemoaning local teenagers' after-midnight parties in the cottages of Harbor View. A resident named J. A. McKelvey had complained for several years to Harbor View police about break-ins at his cottage: furniture was broken and trash was left behind. Local police hadn't been helpful, so residents turned to the Lucas County Probate Court.[7]

After interviewing many Toledo teenagers, a judge found that after downtown dance halls closed at midnight, the teens would find somewhere to purchase liquor, make their way out to Harbor View, and break into a cottage to continue the party. This discovery was no mystery to Harbor View's residents. On their way out on Sunday mornings, the revelers would yell goodbyes from the windows of their cars.[8]

On March 27, 1924, the *Coshocton Tribune* reported of the arrest of Harbor View Mayor Levi H. Shovar for the breaking of the Volstead Act, the law that enforced Prohibition. The night before this article ran, the Mayor had asked his deputy marshalls, Herbert Crane and Karl Neipp, to take five confiscated cases of beer and resell them to a local soda shop, telling them only to "be careful." The three conspirators were caught in the act by federal authorities and quickly arrested.[9]

Only two days later, the *Marysville Journal-Tribune* reported the arrest of the marshal of Harbor View, J. W. Hoffman. Hoffman had arrested a man for transporting liquor, taken his truck, and then offered to sell the truck back to the man for $300. The angry man found his way to a local judge, reported the incident, and Hoffman followed his deputies into the local jail.[10]

Ohio Attorney General C. C. Crabbe promoted Mayor Shovar's arrest. At the time of the incident, Crabbe was in Harbor View investigating the "kangaroo courts" that allowed the free flow of liquor near Maumee Bay and Lake Erie. Crabbe, and the Ohio based Anti-Saloon League, wanted to rid the area of such leaders. Many residents of Harbor View felt differently. They didn't believe Mayor Shovar had done anything wrong and attempted to crowdfund his bail money.[11]

Deputy Marshal Ralph J. Zahnle

Illegal liquor running was a problem for Harbor View until the end of Prohibition. Unfortunately, in November 1929, one Harbor View police officer lost his life in the line of duty.[12] Deputy Marshal Ralph J. Zahnle, a World War I veteran, had been on the force for only three months when he and his partner stopped two suspicious cars passing through town. One of the cars rammed their police vehicle. The suspects then fired more than 20 rounds from their rifles straight into the police car. Zahnle's partner avoided injury, but Zahnle was not so lucky. At only 33 years old, Zahnle died from the gunfire, leaving behind a wife and three small children.[13]

The suspects ran away from the scene of the crime on foot, but they were eventually apprehended.[14] Two of the men, Joe "Red" Sullivan and Lewis Taylor, confirmed in court that they were rum smugglers who'd been caught.[15] Unfortunately, only one man saw time for manslaughter; he was sentenced to just 19 years and 11 months.[16]

Harbor View Today

Harbor View remains an interesting town today. In 2012, construction began on the Harbor View Historical Museum, in the former Harbor View Missionary Baptist Church. Here visitors learn about the history of each town that once made up Oregon Township, including the still-independent Harbor View.[17]

Despite its small size, the village of Harbor View still maintains its own post office and its own zip code: 43434. A palindrome, the number reads the same backwards and forwards. The post office occasionally gets requests from out-of-towners who want a letter postmarked with these numbers.[18]

TOP: The Snack Shack near Railroad Heritage Park

Population: 399   Approx. Founding: 1883

INSETS L to R: A sign in Harrod advertising the annual Pork Rind Heritage Festival • Inside the "little red building" at the Railroad Heritage Park • Climb onto the red caboose to see a typical passenger car • Harrod State Bank, home of the Auglaize Township Historical Society

How does the Auglaize Township Historical Society fund its activities? A portion of the organization's funding comes from the annual Harrod Pork Rind Heritage Festival.[15] Co-sponsored by the village of Harrod and Rudolph Foods Company, the event takes place each year on the second weekend of June. The festival includes a parade, live entertainment, a hog roast, crafts, and, of course, pork rinds.[16] Money raised at the festival is donated to local schools, the fire department, and the historical society, among other causes.[17]

Harrod

A Delayed Founding for the Village of Harrod

THE HARROD FAMILY, led by patriarch William Harrod, first arrived in Allen County, Ohio, in 1841. The family, originally of Pennsylvania, stuck around for generations.[1] In 1883, James B. Townsend officially laid out a village near William Harrod's original home in Allen County. Townsend, a lawyer by trade, served as a director of the Lima and Columbus Railroad. Townsend knew that the railway planned to lay track near the old Harrod family homestead. Hoping to capitalize on the railroad's presence, Townsend laid out a town, choosing to name the village for the area's earliest white settlers.[2]

Preserving the History of Harrod

Thanks to the Auglaize Township Historical Society, the history of Harrod is ever-present in the village in the combined Harrod Veteran's Memorial Park and Harrod Railroad Parks. The Veteran's Memorial Park is impossible to miss thanks to its battle tank and helicopter. The helicopter is particularly eye catching, as it has been mounted atop a large metal pole, making it appear as if it is flying through the air. Both vehicles were in service during the Vietnam era.[3] However, the park is dedicated to all veterans and contains reminders of other important American military moments, such as the attack on Pearl Harbor.

The particular "Huey" helicopter on display is Huey tail number 587, which was flown by the 176th Assault Helicopter Company from

1966 to 1967, during their service in Chu Lai. The Huey was used for medical evacuation, cargo movement, and active fire.[4] The Huey in Harrod is maintained by the Auglaize Township Historical Society.[5]

Nearby, in the Railroad Park, visitors can find a 1905 Shay locomotive, manufactured nearby in Lima, Ohio. The railroad continued to boost the local economy until it was abandoned in the 1970s.[6,7] Visitors to the park can climb onto the locomotive and look inside the attached red caboose. Nearby stands a renovated railway workman's shanty and the "little red building," which originally belonged to Samuel T. Winegardner. In the late 1800s, Winegardner owned a sawmill and lumber yard where the building once stood. Winegardner provided lumber for many new homes in the village. Winegardner's office was moved to the park in 1994 and has since been restored.[8]

Harrod also has a museum, run by the Auglaize Township Historical Society. The historical society was first founded in 1988, by childhood friends and longtime Harrod residents Lucy Winegardner Lovett and Suzanne McPheron Archer. In 1988, Lovett suggested the installation of a mural representing the village's past. While doing research for the mural, the friends discovered that in 1989, Harrod would officially be 100 years old. This spurred the creation of an official historical society, which is still active today.

Two Famous Women from Harrod

On July 17, 1920, Reverend Willis E. Smith and Mrs. Sybil Irwin Smith, new residents of the village of Harrod, welcomed a daughter, Dorothy June, into the world. Dorothy June, or "D.J." to her friends, didn't get to spend much time getting to know Harrod: her family moved around quite a bit during her childhood. D.J. finished high school at the age of 16 in Keene, New Hampshire. During her high school years, she had begun performing on stage almost constantly. After graduation, D.J. returned to Ohio for a year at Oberlin College. She soon left school and moved to New York.[9]

Once in New York, Dorothy June Smith adopted a new stage name, June Vincent, and began working as a model to pay the bills. In 1943, while she was working as an understudy for the show "The Family" on Broadway, an actress fell ill. Vincent took over for her, attracting the notice of a talent scout from Universal Pictures. Vincent started her career with Universal in the movie *Honeymoon Lodge*.[10]

Vincent performed in dozens of movies and made more than 115 television appearances. She appeared in *In A Lonely Place*, which featured Humphrey Bogart, in 1950, and starred in *Black Angel* in 1946. By the end of the 1950s, Vincent mostly appeared as a guest star on television programs. She did not care for fame and would give up roles for the sake of her husband and children. Vincent married William M. Sterling, a World War II pilot, in 1944, and the two had three children together.[11]

During her time in Hollywood, Vincent was noted for her unusually candid nature. She told a reporter that she was in fact a natural brunette, not a blonde. She also resisted studio executives who wanted her to appear younger. At the beginning of her career, when she found out her age was being given as 18, she eagerly told *The Boston Post* that she was, 23.[12]

Vincent last appeared on television in 1976, before retiring to Colorado with her husband. She passed away in Colorado in 2008, at the age of 88.[13]

Louise Clapp was also born in the village of Harrod, sometime in the early 1900s. Unfortunately, her life has not been as well documented. Clapp played in the All-American Girls Professional Baseball League from 1953 to 1954, the league's last years of operation.[14] The All-American Girls Professional Baseball League was formed during World War II, and its story was adapted in the film *A League of Their Own*.

Kendra Kesner runs the Belevedere Emporium, a large white home originally built between 1883 and 1892. Once abandoned and slated for demolition, Kesner took possession of the home and spent three years restoring it. Today she sells gifts and home decor in her very unique boutique.[18]

TOP: A view from the center of town

Population: 409   Incorporated: 1866

INSETS L to R: Croton Church of Christ • Hartford Town Hall • The post office in Hartford which still goes by the name "Croton" • Croton United Methodist Church

Interested in getting married near Hartford? The village is home to a large venue that maintains high accolades from many wedding websites. The Irongate Equestrian Center, originally a private training facility for a professional horse rider, opened to the public in 2014. The staff at Irongate spend much of their time caring for and breeding horses, but they are also dedicated to renting out the 105-acre facility for private and corporate events and celebrations.[13]

Hartford

A Town With Many Names

IN SEPTEMBER 1824, the village of Hartford was officially platted by Ezekiel Wells and Elijah Durfey, two early white residents of the area.[1] The new village was located in Hartford Township, which had first become home to white settlers in 1812.[2] These settlers gave the township the name Hartford to honor the city in Connecticut from which they originated.[3]

In 1833, a post office was established in the new village of Hartford, under the name of Granby. The village residents wished to change their name to Hartford, but another village in Ohio had already claimed the name. During the 1840s, the village began using the name Hartford colloquially but named the post office Croton. Today they continue to use both names; Croton for the post office and Hartford for the village.[4]

A town hall was built in Hartford in 1857, at the cost of $600. The village continued to grow, seeking incorporation in 1866. As railways came through the state, Hartford's economy prospered. However, once the freeway made railroads obsolete, Hartford's population shrank.[5]

The Hartford Independent Fair

Despite its size, Hartford is still the location of the county fair at the end of each summer. The fair, known officially as the Hartford Independent Fair, first began in the fall of 1858. The event was planned by the Hartford Fair Society and held on land leased to the village by a man named Taber Sharp. The fair grew quickly, soon demanding an official fairgrounds and infrastructure. In 1868, the first official building was added to the fairgrounds. By popular demand this building provided meals for fair visitors for only 25 cents. In 1883, the fairgrounds gained an amphitheater, and in 1901, a sheep barn. In 1895, the fair board of directors planted a large number of shade trees, which still benefit visitors fighting the summer heat. Today over 40 buildings stand on the 183 acres of fairgrounds, much larger than Taber Sharp's original 25 acres.[6]

The fair has always focused on agriculture and youth involvement. Displays of farm equipment are popular, as are 4-H competitions featuring local youth. In 1948, the Hartford Fair had the very first 4-H band. Eventually dorms were built on the fairgrounds so that young competitors could keep on an eye on their livestock during the entire run of the fair.[7]

Early in fair history, visitors were drawn to Hartford to view a few different types of races. In 1858, horse racing began, including the Free-For-All Trot. During this race, some horses are ridden, and others run all on their own. Foot racing among people was also a popular pastime. The very first foot race at the Hartford Fair was held between William Lane and Maggie McComb. It was expected that Lane would be the victor, but in the end McComb left him behind and claimed the first-place spot. Apparently this victory was "to the disgruntlement of the men."[8]

While the village and township of Hartford are still the main sponsors of the annual fair, other townships within Licking County have been given an opportunity to participate in the planning. Around the 1870s, a board of directors formed and each township was able to send a representative. By 1908, 14 townships were represented on this board, each with one elected director, except for Hartford Township, which was allowed two representatives. In 1970, the board added five at-large directors to represent other Licking County townships that were not yet involved. The list of directors has only continued to grow. As of 2012, the board of directors included 27 people. Even so, Licking County locals still feel as if each visit to the fair is one big family reunion—a bookend on another summer.[9]

Run Out By A Mob

While many of the white settlers in Hartford Township came from the New England area, this was not true of all of the early residents. Many also came from the slave-holding states of Virginia and Maryland. Multiple times during the 1830s, when abolitionist speakers came into the village of Hartford, they were run out by a mob. A man named Reverend R. Robinson was quite literally dragged from the pulpit and through the streets of the village. Another abolitionist speaker, Hon. Samuel White, was threatened with a tarring and feathering. Apparently a strong-looking man, he threatened the mob, and was allowed to leave town. The abolitionists of Hartford reportedly remained fearfully indoors during these incidents.[10]

Narrowly Avoiding Dissolution

In 2014, the village of Hartford was nearly dissolved by its residents. A small group of individuals began circulating a ballot measure for dissolution, and ultimately 91 residents of the village signed it. The voters of Hartford overwhelmingly decided to vote against the measure, which failed at a vote of 19 for and 133 against.[11]

Despite the huge support for the village of Hartford, the village struggled to find funding. During the time period that the dissolution issue remained on the ballot, village officials were barred from applying for any sort of grant funding. A number of tax levies have failed— though one recently passed in 2019—and the budget was affected by funding cuts from the state. Frustrated with the lack of necessary monies, village officials decided to sell the village recreation center. In reaction to the dissolution measure, the mayor of Hartford was hopeful that residents might ride the momentum into a larger engagement with the village and its government. He asked residents to understand funding concerns and to come to more council meetings. In one particular interview, the mayor commented that the individuals who attempted to dissolve the village actually attend village council meetings frequently.[12]

Doyt L. Perry was born in Hartford. As a young man, Perry attended Bowling Green State University in northwestern Ohio, playing football, basketball, and baseball. He's best known for later coaching the Bowling Green Falcons football team to victory after victory. The university's stadium was renamed in his honor.[14]

TOP: Holiday City Village Hall

Population: 47 **Incorporated:** 1997

INSETS L to R: As a prominent stop off the Ohio Turnpike, Holiday City has multiple gas stations • The Four Seasons restaurant is a must for visitors to Holiday City • Econo Lodge, one of Holiday City's many hotels • Hotels line the very busy Route 20 that is central to life in Holiday City

Unfortunately, in 2010, the village of Holiday City became involved in an unsolved missing persons case. In November of that year, John Skelton, of Morenci, Michigan, brought his three young sons through Holiday City. After that November day, the boys were never seen again. Their father is in prison but unwilling to divulge any helpful information. Early in 2019, Lynn Thompson, a reporter for the *Bryan Times* who covered the case from day one, published a book with all of the information he can recall, in the hopes that one day the boys will be found. Thompson believes that "if justice is all we have left, we need to finish it."[18]

Holiday City

A New Community

HOLIDAY CITY, OF WILLIAMS COUNTY, OHIO, is the youngest of the 100 towns, villages, and communities featured in this book. Incorporated in June 1997, the village was founded in order to provide public electricity to nearby businesses in a more cost-efficient way.[1,2]

It can be easy to miss Holiday City. The small village only measures about three square miles and is located directly on the Ohio Turnpike and the Norfolk Southern Railroad.[3,4] Traffic moves quickly, and the area does not immediately appear to be residential.

Holiday City may be an unusual village, but it has become very important to Williams County residents in the past few decades. While Holiday City only boasted 34 residents during its 20th anniversary in 2017, the village supported at least 1,500 jobs in the same year.[5]

Jefferson Township-Holiday City Visitors Bureau

There are four hotels located within the village limits of Holiday City. Located on the turnpike, the village has always sought to grow their tourism base. Since 1997, the same year Holiday City was founded, the village has helped operate the Jefferson Township-Holiday City Visitors Bureau.[6] The bureau is funded through a six percent lodging tax paid by any guests in the village's four hotels. Half of this tax is allocated directly to the village of Holiday City, with one fourth to Jefferson Township and another fourth to the bureau. As of 2015, the tax was bringing in about $42,000–$50,000 of each year for the visitors bureau.[7]

The current executive director of the bureau, Kellie Gray, is only the second person to ever serve in her position. She has focused on encouraging bus tours to stop and see the sites in Williams County, with a night spent in a Holiday City hotel. As the bureau's slogan boasts, Holiday City is "Halfway to Everywhere." And as Gray explains, "We're a great stopping point for bus tours and travelers heading from New York and Chicago and anywhere in between."[8]

Gray has also seen success in partnering with local events to encourage participants to stay in Holiday City. She has even planned her own events in Holiday City, such as the wildly successful Holiday City Wine and Arts Festival.[9]

Holiday City Employers

Two of Holiday City's biggest employers today are 20/20 Custom Molded Plastics and Menards. Employees come from around Williams County to work in Holiday City. 20/20 Custom Molded Plastics is based in Holiday City, with a recent 2017 expansion in Bluffton, Indiana. The Holiday City plant supports about 220 employees, with about 150 more at the new factory in Indiana.[10] 20/20 works with a variety of industries, providing a unique injection molding process to make a diverse set of plastic-based products. They have built pallets, pool ladders, doghouses, store displays, tool boxes, and even caskets.[11]

Menards first opened a distribution center in Holiday City in 2007, just in time for the village's 10th anniversary. In 2017, Menards began construction of a plant that produces doors. This new investment, adjacent to the distribution center, is anticipated to add about 90 new jobs for the village of Holiday City, with a total of about 1,000 employed at Menards in the near future. With both its original construction and its recent expansion, Menards has received funding and resources from Williams County and the State of Ohio. There is a large interest in keeping this employer in the area.[12]

Twenty Years of Milestones

Holiday City and its village council have hit many major milestones over the last 20 years. When the village was first founded, its village council met in a resident's barn. In fact, the council continued to meet in the barn for eight years until an official building was designated in 2005. Much of the village council is still made up of original founders of the village, but they have slowly begun stepping down from their positions, encouraging a new generation to take the reins.[13]

In 2010, when the state of Ohio reviewed the newest census numbers, Holiday City was officially declared large enough to be called a village.[14] In 2017, when the village celebrated its 20th year, a representative from the governor's office delivered a state proclamation recognizing the important event.[15] Holiday City continues to grow and prosper.

The Spangler Candy Company

Perhaps one of the most exciting stops for a visitor to Holiday City and Williams County is the nearby Spangler Candy Company. Located in Bryan, Ohio, the candy factory is a quick ride from Holiday City. Spangler Candy Company began as Spangler Manufacturing Company in 1906, headed by Arthur G. Spangler in the city of Bryan. In 1908, Arthur's brother Ernest suggested that he add candy to his company's offerings. By 1914, the company was in its current location, and by 1920 candy had become the company's sole focus.[16]

Today the Spangler Candy Company manufactures some of the nation's best-known confections, including Dum Dums and circus peanuts. Each day, the company's nearly 800 employees make at least 12 million Dum Dums and 2.7 million candy canes. On most weekdays, visitors to Williams County can take a trolley tour of the factory and visit the on site museum.[17]

There is no shortage of food to enjoy in Holiday City. For those preferring a fancy evening out, JJ Winns serves up high-quality food in a trendy environment. And for comfort food, there's the Four Seasons Family Restaurant. The restaurant's huge menu and convenient location make it a perfect spot for breakfast, lunch, or dinner.

TOP: Hollansburg Christian Church

Population: 218   **Approx. Founding:** 1838

INSETS L to R: Hollansburg Fire Department • A soldiers' monument in Hollansburg • The Hollansburg Post Office • This sign welcomes visitors to Hollansburg and celebrates the village's record as the first rural location with a motorized fire engine

The Mote family of Hollansburg made the local news quite a few times in the mid-twentieth century. Laura Louise Mote, daughter of Wendell and Virginia Mote, was an incredibly talented sharpshooter, competing during the 1960s and 1970s. At the age of 15, while still a sophomore in high school, Laura became the youngest competitor to ever win the Women's North American Clay Target Championship. She continued to win title after title during her illustrious career.[13]

Hollansburg

Higher Than Beef Steak When the Cow Jumped Over the Moon

AFTER THE WAR OF 1812, an influx of white settlers began moving into Darke County, Ohio. In March 1838, in Harrison Township, James Stewart began to lay out a town he called Union.[1] As the new village took shape, Stewart began to offer land for sale within the village's boundaries.

One of Stewart's customers was a man by the name of William Holloman, who lived about a mile north of Union, on his own farm. Holloman, an impulsive and opinionated yet soft-spoken man, was known to his neighbors as "Uncle Billy" Holloman. When negotiating a price with James Stewart, the two couldn't agree on a price for the lots Holloman wished to purchase, so Holloman decided that he would create a rival village on his farmland. Speaking of Stewart's village of

Union, Uncle Billy is said to have said, "I will knock that town higher than beef steak was when the cow jumped over the moon."[2]

Unfortunately for James Stewart, William Holloman did just that. His new village continued to grow, as Union eventually disappeared from the map. Fortunately for Holloman, after he began to lay out a village, a man named Valentine Harlan made a few additions. Early residents of the village combined the names of Holloman and Harlan to create the name Hollandsburgh. Over the years, letters have dropped from the name, leaving the modern village of Hollansburg.[3]

Uncle Billy Holloman lived in Hollansburg until his death in 1877. He was known by many generations of Hollansburg residents for his love of animals (he always had one or two dogs on his farm) and his cherry trees. He even kept a pet crow in his later years. His neighbors noted that he was distraught upon its passing.[4] Holloman never quite left Hollansburg; he was buried in Hollansburg Cemetery.

Hollansburg continued to grow after Holloman's death, thanks to the arrival of the Indiana, Bloomington, and Western Railway just north of the village. As with many small towns, the railway provided a constant stream of travelers and traders. With the rise of the automobile, rail travel declined. This meant fewer passersby, and the population of Hollansburg began to shrink.[5]

The First Rural Motorized Fire Engine in the Nation

One particular motorized vehicle actually provided the village its biggest claim to fame. In 1916, members of Hollansburg's Volunteer Fire Department were fed up with their hand-drawn equipment. The firefighters had to physically pull all of their equipment to each emergency call, even in winter, when the streets could be covered in half a foot of snow. The volunteers could not move fast enough and often arrived too late to help. Out of this frustration was born the first rural motorized fire engine in the United States.[6]

In late 1916, the men of the Hollansburg Volunteer Fire Department began to work on a creative solution to their biggest problem. They began by purchasing the frame of a 1916 Model T and mounting one of their hand-drawn tanks on the back. Work began on an engine, which took about five months to construct. After months of labor and supply purchases, the entire project reached a cost of $1,025 (about $24,930 in 2018). Donations helped pay for the project.[7]

Finally, on July 18, 1917, at a "Jubilee Celebration," the Hollansburg Volunteer Fire Department rolled out their new fire engine, the first of its kind, to a street filled with excited village residents. The streets were so filled with revelers that "it was impossible for the men to determine how fast the pumper could actually travel." After this exciting first, the village continued to invest in its Volunteer Fire Department.[8]

The Downing Fruit Farm

One of Harrison Township's oldest businesses is located just outside of Hollansburg. The Downing Fruit Farm, now run by Scott Downing, a seventh-generation member of the Downing family, originally opened for business in 1838. That year an orchardist named John Downing left his home state of South Carolina and built a new home in Darke County. Today the Downing family still works that land, producing about 10,000 bushels of apples each year in about 70 different varieties. The farm grows other produce as well, but they are best known for their apples and their ciders.[9]

The orchard has produced a large number of apple varieties in its 180 years of business. In 2015, Scott Downing told reporters about this development process, saying, "It's a lot of cross pollination; Downingland—our most popular variety—is a cross between a Golden Delicious and a Rome Beauty. My great uncle developed that. He went through over 1,000 of the exact same cross pollination until he came up with one he liked."[10] Scott himself has continued to operate with creativity. He recalls that one year a hailstorm destroyed his crop, making the apples suitable for cider, but not much else. To recuperate on the lost profits, Scott brought a slushie machine to the county fair and introduced Darke County to the apple cider slushie.[11]

The apple business has changed over time, but the Downing family has adapted with it. Today, Scott Downing works with his daughters, the eighth generation of the Downing family in Darke County, to pass on the tools of the trade. It doesn't look like Downing Fruit Farm is going anywhere anytime soon.[12]

Doug Mote, son of Tom and Rachel Mote and a former pilot at Skyways, Inc., of Dayton, appears in about six minutes of the 1964 James Bond movie *Goldfinger*. Mote and four other pilots flew in costume for about eight hours of filming, portraying a group of stunt girls hired to spray nerve gas over Fort Knox, Kentucky.

TOP: Iberia Presbyterian Church, the last remaining building from Ohio Central College

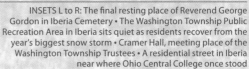

Population: 452   **Approx. Founding:** 1832

INSETS L to R: The final resting place of Reverend George Gordon in Iberia Cemetery • The Washington Township Public Recreation Area in Iberia sits quiet as residents recover from the year's biggest snow storm • Cramer Hall, meeting place of the Washington Township Trustees • A residential street in Iberia near where Ohio Central College once stood

In 1956, Tom Smith's father opened Smittie's Tires in the village of Iberia. More than a half-century later, Smittie's name is well known and trusted around Morrow County. In fact, Tom often saw third-generation customers come through his doors. However, in 2018, Tom decided to retire. It is not common for a chain to successfully take over a local shop without some controversy, but Van's Auto Service & Tire Pros seems to have done just that. The local chain purchased the business from Tom Smith and picked up right where he left off, providing excellent service right in Iberia, Ohio.[14]

Iberia

The Fosters and the Myers Found Iberia

ON MARCH 9, 1832, Samuel and Margaret Foster along with Frederick and Rachel Myers officially platted the village of Iberia. The Foster and Myers families were the first white landowners in the area, so they used their land to start a village. In much of the nineteenth century, women couldn't own property; still, Margaret and Rachel's signatures appeared on the official documents filed to lay out Iberia.[1]

The new village of Iberia began to grow as businesspeople moved in to support nearby farmers.[2] In 1851, the Cleveland, Columbus and Cincinnati Railroad passed through Morrow County. Track was laid about a mile and a half outside of Iberia, but the local station still bore the village's name.[3] The railroad helped the village, but it was a bit too far away to generate exponential growth.

The Beginnings of Iberia College

Iberia is perhaps best known for the college that once operated in the village. The college, known by many names during its short history, has its origin with Reverend John B. Blayney. In 1842, Blayney, a Presbyterian minister, worked with Hugh Elliot to conduct high school classes in the village. In 1849, thanks to Elliot's financing, the two were able to open a female seminary, run by Mary J. Haft.[4] Elliot's Female Seminary, as it was known, soon allowed men as well. From this point on, the school, even as it changed names and owners, would always maintain about half female and half male enrollment.[5]

In 1854, the seminary was chartered under the laws of Ohio as Iberia College, with Reverend George Gordon appointed as the first college president. Gordon was a known abolitionist and supporter of the Underground Railroad, as were two of his college trustees, Allen McNeal and Archibald Brownlee. When enslaved Africans seeking freedom came through Iberia, they were offered shelter until they could be transported to a safe house in Oberlin, Ohio, another college town.[6]

Declining a Presidential Pardon

In 1850, the United States passed the Fugitive Slave Law, which obligated northerners to aid in the capture of any slaves traveling north to seek freedom. After 1850, southern slave-catchers became a much more common sight in the North.

Not surprisingly, slave-catchers eventually made their way to the village of Iberia. In the summer of 1860, Deputy U.S. Marshal Joseph L. Barber and a few of his aides arrived to look for a few enslaved individuals who had been reported as runaways. When Barber arrived, abolitionists in town knew that three travelers on the Underground Railroad were being hidden at a nearby farm. At the first news of Barber's arrival, Iberia residents raced to the farm, sounding the alarm.[7]

Unfortunately, the abolitionists were too late. Barber arrived right on their heels and was able to grab one of the former slaves. The abolitionists began to angrily beat Barber's aides and held Barber down while they cut off his hair. Reverend Gordon arrived at the farm while the violence was occurring.[8]

Gordon did not take part in the violence, but he did not stop it either. He was tried as a complicit party, and as a well-known abolitionist was essentially made an example of. Gordon was fined and set to be sent to federal prison in the city of Cleveland, when President Abraham Lincoln attempted to issue him a pardon. Gordon refused Lincoln's pardon, "on the grounds that it did not exonerate him." He was sent to prison where he soon came down with sciatic rheumatism, forcing him to accept the pardon. Gordon died in 1868, never quite recovered from his time in prison. The residents of Washington Township buried Gordon in the township cemetery with veterans who had served during the Civil War.[9]

Educating a President

Sometime after Reverend Gordon departed Iberia College, the institution changed its name to Ohio Central College and educated a man who would one day sit in the Oval Office. Future-president Warren G. Harding graduated from Ohio Central College in Iberia on July 21, 1882. While at the college, he was active in literary programs and the Philomathic Society (dedicated to the sciences), and he co-edited the college paper, *The Spectator*, with his roommate F. H. Miller.[10] Not long after he left Ohio Central College, Harding acquired another newspaper, the *Marion Star*.

The End of Ohio Central College

Classes ended for good at Ohio Central College in the mid 1880s. At this time, the remaining buildings were sold to the Working Home for the Blind, which opened in 1887. This home was meant as a way to aid the blind in finding work. The residents were all graduates of the State Institution for the Blind in Columbus. Some were married couples. They were taught to make brooms, which were sold for a profit.[11] Unfortunately, a fire struck the Working Home in 1894. While no one lost their lives, the home was shut down. Despite the fact that they originally moved from Columbus, some of the residents of the home had become at home in Iberia and continued to live in the community.

After sitting dormant for a while, the remains of one building from Central College were successfully renovated into apartments. These apartments were occupied until 1915, when the local school district put the building to use. The building became a local high school until 1932, when it was finally razed.[12] The only trace of Ohio Central College left in Iberia is the Presbyterian Church, which once served as the college chapel.[13]

Iberia's name is attributed to a Robert Rowland, a visitor around the time of the village's founding. Rowland claimed he'd visited a town named Iberia in South America and liked the name. The trouble is, there's no Iberia in South America; the Iberian Peninsula is in Europe. The name stuck and is still in use today.[15]

TOP: Jacksonburg United Methodist Church, where Governor Cox spent many Sundays

Population: 63   Approx. Founding: 1816

INSETS L to R: A Wayne Township municipal building • Marcum's Carry Out • Jacksonburg United Methodist Church • A main road passing through the center of Jacksonburg

As a child, Governor James Middleton Cox's parents taught him and his siblings that the saloon in the village was a negative influence. The Cox children weren't even allowed to have playing cards in their house when growing up. As Cox said, "the diversion was usually history and geography tests." Cox took this lesson to heart, and as Governor, he had the saloon in Jacksonburg "condemned as a fire menace and torn down by the state marshal."[15]

Jacksonburg

A Rural Lifestyle

JACKSONBURG, OHIO, HAS BEEN one of the smallest incorporated villages in the state for quite some time. Jacksonburg residents are interviewed often by local and national media because of their place on Ohio's smallest village list. At its height, the village held 302 people, but by 1900 the population was 77. In 2000, it was around 67.[1,2] While Jacksonburg is mostly populated by descendants of earlier citizens, the village also draws the occasional new resident looking for a rural way of life. Even as some residents leave, the population is maintained by this interest in the quiet, intimate lifestyle Jacksonburg provides.

Very few people run for office in Jacksonburg, and council seats are normally filled by write-ins. However, Jacksonburg is not ready to give up its politically independent status. As Mayor Michael Sword once told the *Cincinnati Enquirer*, "We want to keep the town's identity." Sword has been mayor since 1980.[3]

Luckily for Jacksonburg's residents, almost the entire village remains zoned A-1 by Wayne Township. Because of this, homes can only be built on two-acre plots, limiting the amount of development that can encroach upon this rural way of life.[4]

From Jacksonburg to Columbus: A Governor is Born

The best-known citizen of Jacksonburg was James Middleton Cox, Ohio's 46th and 48th governor. Cox was a lifelong Democrat, writing in his memoir that "there must have been some Democrats in the vicinity" when Jacksonburg was named, due to its taking of the name of President

Andrew Jackson.[5] Cox also served in the House of Representatives, and in 1920, he ran against Warren G. Harding for President of the United States (Harding was educated in another small town, Iberia, featured on page 88).[6] The two men had quite a bit in common. Both were from Ohio, and both were known for successful careers in the newspaper business. Unfortunately for Cox, it was Harding that won the election.

James Middleton Cox was born in Jacksonburg in 1870. Both of his parents had also grown up in the small village. Cox maintained his grandfather's family home well into his adulthood. Cox worked hard as a young boy on his parents' farm, also taking on salaried positions as a janitor at his school and a sexton at his church by the age of 10. Despite the hard work, Cox maintained many positive memories of his childhood, including running barefoot in the summer with "stone bruises," maple sugar season, trips to Elk Creek for baptisms, McGuffey Readers from the nearby city of Oxford, and cold Sundays at church services hoping the wood fire would burn warmer.[7]

As Cox describes it, he just happened to take the Butler County teacher's examination on a whim. Surprised, he earned a two-year certificate, and Cox began teaching while delivering newspapers for his brother-in-law on Saturdays. Cox quickly switched gears and began working at the newspaper full-time, because, as he wrote, "printer's ink had moved in my blood." Beginning with the purchase of the *Dayton Evening News* in 1898, Cox built a media company that still provides daily news for much of Ohio's Miami Valley.[8]

Cox left a mark on the entire state of Ohio during his time as governor, but he also left a very personal mark on his hometown of Jacksonburg. A religious man since his childhood, Cox helped the Jacksonburg United Methodist Church build a new sanctuary in 1924, replacing the building where Cox had spent many a cold Sunday as a child. Based upon a gothic-style building Cox had seen in England, the building is still in use today.[9]

Fifty Stagecoaches Each Night

Jacksonburg was first laid out in February 1816. The village quickly boomed, becoming an important stagecoach station on the path between Darke and Preble Counties and the city of Cincinnati. Upwards of 50 stagecoaches could be found at any given night outside Jacksonburg's two hotels in the early nineteenth century.[10] The town grew to accommodate its boom, at one point even providing a home to four tailors.[11]

Technology quickly changed, and canals and railroads ruled the transportation industry. By the late 1800s, Jacksonburg's economic boom had come to an end. The village transitioned into the quiet, rural hometown that it is today.[12]

An Impromptu School Reunion

In 2013, upon the demolition of the Wayne School in Jacksonburg, a handful of former students showed up outside the construction gates to share memories. A construction worker unexpectedly found a time capsule buried by students almost 100 years earlier, in 1914. When the time capsule was opened and photographs found inside, one man on site exclaimed, "Hey, that's my grandfather!"[13]

Unfortunately, former students also shared a few sad memories of their time at Wayne School. In 1977, just over the Ohio River past Cincinnati, a deadly fire occurred at the Beverly Hills Supper Club on Memorial Day Weekend. Thirteen of Jacksonburg's residents perished in this fire, including an entire third of the Wayne School staff. Former students reminiscing around the construction site in 2013 recalled the impact these men and women had made on their lives.[14]

When James Cox ran for the presidency against Warren Harding, Franklin Roosevelt served as Cox's running mate. It was quite a star-studded campaign. Of the four men on the ticket (Cox with running mate Roosevelt and Harding with running mate Calvin Coolidge), only Cox would never make it to the Oval Office.[16]

TOP: C Dee's Lil' Store

Population: 139   Approx. Founding: 1817

INSETS L to R: James Kilbourne's final resting place, about 20 miles South of Kilbourne in Worthington, Ohio • The new Brown Township Hall • A sign on the busy main road that runs through Kilbourne to direct families to the baseball fields • The Kilbourne Ball Field

While it may only be a Census-designated place, Kilbourne provides many services for its residents. Just behind the new Brown Township Hall can be found the Kilbourne Ball Field. Here each summer, children from the ages of 5 to 15 come to play baseball. Kilbourne faces off against teams from the communities of Ashley, Bellepoint, Ostrander, and Radnor in a league known as Buckeye Valley Summer Baseball.[13]

Kilbourne

James Kilbourne's Eden

THE VILLAGE OF KILBOURNE, OHIO, now a census-designated place in Delaware County, owes its name to James Kilbourne.[1] Kilbourne was born in 1770 in New Britain, Connecticut. In the early 1800s, Kilbourne and other residents of the Farmington Valley area in Connecticut formed a group called the Scioto Company, with the intent of purchasing land in the West. In 1803, Kilbourne purchased and laid out the town of Worthington, Ohio. By 1805, Kilbourne was working as an official surveyor of public lands.[2]

Kilbourne became well known as a surveyor, playing a role in the founding of many early Ohio towns and villages. His positive reviews of Ohio life helped attract other migrants to the area.[3] In one instance, on a trip from Ohio to New York, Kilbourne came across a native New Yorker named Captain William Drake. Drake was traveling from New York to Ohio in hopes of settling in a new village called Norton, in Delaware County. Kilbourne himself had laid out this town, and he said to Drake, "I congratulate you sir, you are going to a perfect Eden." Unfortunately, Kilbourne may have become too accustomed to the rough Western lifestyle, for when Drake arrived in the village of Norton, all he saw was "a little log cabin, on the side of which were stretched some half a dozen partially dried raccoon skins." Drake apparently commented, "Well, I must say that if this satisfies Kilbourn's ideas of Eden, I never want to hear his conception of hell."[4]

In 1817, when the first settlers came to what is now the village of Kilbourne, they gave their new home the name of "Eden." Laid out by Isaac Eaton for Daniel G. Thurston and Isaac Leonard, this village was deemed to be a good investment, as it contained a major thoroughfare traveling in each cardinal direction. The village grew slowly. Its first merchant was Joseph Leonard, who cornered the market until other businesses came through in 1838. This was the same year the village established a post office, with C. M. Thrall as postmaster. The post office was called Kilbourn (a common second spelling of James Kilbourne's name).[5] It is likely the village eventually took on its postal name and dropped the original name of Eden.

Closing the Kilbourne Post Office

Unfortunately, in August of 2017, Kilbourne's post office was closed due to structural problems. The little building's owner passed away, and the structure needed repairs. When it closed, it didn't have running water or a restroom: employees had to go across the street to a neighboring store.[6] Despite these issues, residents loved their post office, as did other members of the Delaware County community. The Kilbourne Post Office allowed locals to skip waiting in long lines in nearby Delaware when they wanted to ship packages. As one employee noted, the holidays were a busy time, as people came from around the county to avoid long lines.[7]

Until the post office closed, many Kilbourne residents were retrieving their mail from post office boxes. When the change happened, postal customers had to learn how to place mailboxes at their own homes and how to rewrite their addresses. Kilbourne's former zip code, 43032, is gone, replaced with the 43015 of Delaware. And if a package is undeliverable? Now Kilbourne's residents have to wait in line at the Delaware Post Office with everyone else.[8]

Breaking Ground on the Brown Township Hall

Just as Kilbourne's post office was closing, the village was breaking ground on a new hall. The new Brown Township Hall was largely funded by Charles and Betty Sheets. Charles Sheets, now in his early 90s, comes from a long line of Kilbourne residents. His family first settled in town in 1835. Sheets himself attended the Brown School in Kilbourne, from 1932 to 1944. The Sheets family's donation came with a few requests, one being that the new township hall be built on the site of the old Brown School, first built in 1917 and torn down in 2010.[9]

The Brown Township Hall was officially dedicated in November 2017. Charles Sheets attended the opening events, stating, "I'm just real happy with the building. I've always felt close to Kilbourne because of growing up here for 25 years. I just feel a part of the Kilbourne community." For those interested in learning more about his family's long Kilbourne history, a display case in the new hall depicts their story.[10]

"I am content. I feel free."

A man named Bruno Abersfeld once worked just down the street from the new Brown Township Hall, operating Kilbourne Pizza. Abersfeld passed away in May 2017, but not before leaving behind a captivating life story. Born in Poland, Abersfeld lived under Communist rule with his father until 1969. Finally able to emigrate, the two moved on to Vienna and then quickly to Rome. They settled in Rome for about a year, before making it to their final goal, the United States, in 1970. Here the Abersfelds settled in Columbus, Ohio, where Bruno attended Eastmoor High school. He continued to live in the central Ohio area, finally settling in Kilbourne in 2004.[11]

Due to his time in Rome, Abersfeld enjoyed surrounding himself with art. He purchased many pieces at auction, becoming a collector. Despite spending a portion of his youth with easy access to some of Europe's greatest artworks, Abersfeld truly enjoyed his life in Kilbourne. As he said in 2010, "It is safe and peaceful here, and I am content. I feel free."[12]

The first death of a white settler in Brown Township of Delaware County occurred in Kilbourne. In 1828, James Longwell's infant child died. The village's cemetery had just been laid out earlier that year, giving the child a fitting place to be interred. The cemetery can still be found on the edge of town.[14]

TOP: A street view in Kipton lined with historic buildings

Population: 236   Approx. Founding: 1853

INSETS L to R: Kipton Community Park • The playground at Kipton Community Park sits next to the North Coast Inland Trail • Kipton Community Church • The North Coast Inland Trail marks where the Lake Shore and Michigan Southern Railroad once passed through Kipton

One of the postal workers who died in the train accident in Kipton was F. F. Clement of Ravenna, Ohio. Clement was in his late 20s when he died, leaving behind his mother, father, sisters, and a fiancée in Ravenna. Clement had gotten into the postal business in 1882 as an assistant postmaster in Ravenna. The postal clerk there had taken an interest in Clement, getting him swiftly promoted within the Cleveland postal system. Clement had been offered a position with the ocean postal service but turned it down to remain near to his family. Clement was well-liked in Ravenna, and the local newspaper published an extensive obituary upon his death.[19]

Kipton

A Village Built on a Railroad

AROUND 1852, the Toledo Norwalk and Cleveland Railroad established a train depot in Lorain County, Ohio, west of the college town of Oberlin. In 1853, William W. Whitney laid out the village of Binghampton near the depot, which was assigned the name Kipton, as was the local post office. Quickly the name of Whitney's village was changed from Binghampton to Kipton to follow suit.[1]

Today where the railroad once stood in Kipton, one can find "the Skinniest Park in Lorain County." About 13 miles of railway have been removed and the paths paved over by the Metro Parks system. Known as the North Coast Inland Trail, Kipton is at the westernmost part of the trail, with Elyria on the easternmost portion.[2]

The Infamous Kipton Train Wreck

Unfortunately, the village of Kipton is best known for one of the most disastrous train wrecks in Ohio history. Trains regularly passed through Kipton, traveling both east and west. When two trains traveling opposite directions were planned to travel on the same day, the Lake Southern Railway (the successor of the Toledo Norwalk and Cleveland), like all railways at the time, would communicate the plans to the conductors of both trains to be sure they did not crash. All parties would agree upon a location that the trains would meet and decide upon which train had the right of way and which train would pull aside at the Depot to allow the other train to pass.[3]

On April 18, 1891, the *Fast Mail No. 14*, traveling east, and the *Toledo Express No. 21*, traveling west, would meet at Kipton. This was a routine meeting place for Lake Shore trains—a regular day of business for the conductors and engineers. However, the *Toledo Express* arrived a few minutes late, and had yet to pull off the track when the *Fast Mail* train came hurtling toward the depot at full speed. The Kipton Depot building obscured the engineer's view of the situation, and he didn't see the other train. The *Toledo Express* had slowed down to pull off the track, but the *Fast Mail* train could not brake fast enough to avoid a collision.[4] The two trains met head on, destroying the depot building and killing at least seven men instantly.[5]

The scene of the collision in Kipton was chaotic and horrifying. Both trains had been carrying parlor cars with passengers. In these parlor cars almost all of the seats had been torn from the floor, throwing the passengers against the walls. Luckily, none were severely injured. Many passengers rushed from the trains to see if they could assist those who had been hurt.[6] When they left their train cars, they saw the front cars and engines of the two trains completely destroyed and piled on top of each other, with shredded mail and parcels strewn about the depot.[7] Kipton physicians also rushed to the scene, but unfortunately there was not much they could do.[8] All six of the postal workers on the *Fast Mail* train were dead, as were both engineers. The fireman on the *Toledo Express* left the accident alive for a time, but he was fatally injured (the fireman on the *Fast Mail* train had jumped to avoid certain death). The bodies were almost unrecognizable as they were pulled from the wreckage.[9]

As the regular passengers of the *Toledo Express* and the *Fast Mail* train caught other rides out of Kipton that day, the story of the accident began to spread. Some news accounts were based upon word of mouth from the arriving travelers.[10] The use of railcars to deliver mail was still fairly new the United States, and the disaster at Kipton marked the first real tragedy for the postal service.[11]

Staying "On the Ball"

The Lake Shore Railway quickly mounted an investigation. Early news accounts suspected that a late telegram instructing the two trains to meet at Kipton rather than Oberlin had caused the wreck.[12] However, it was soon found that it was the *Toledo Express* that had caused the problem. The engineer's watch had stopped for four minutes that day and then restarted, without the engineer realizing it. The conductor, confident and likely lackadaisical, did not check or compare his watch to the engineer's once that day, so the error went unnoticed. The *Toledo Express* showed up four minutes late to Kipton, meaning they did not have the necessary time to pull off the railroad track before the *Fast Mail* train arrived.[13]

The General Superintendent of the Lake Shore Railway turned to the nearby city of Cleveland to find a solution. Here he found a jeweler named Webb C. Ball, operating at the corner of Superior Avenue and West 3rd Street.[14, 15] He tasked Ball with investigating the problem of keeping watches standard and accurate on the often bumpy and unpredictable course of a train's journey. Ball adapted strict standards for conductors and engineers and built a watch that would be practical for railway use. The Ball Watch became a standard on railways across the United States.[16] In 1891, Ball incorporated his business, and in 1911 he was able to move to a larger building on Cleveland's Euclid Avenue. Here Ball managed his jewelry and watch businesses while also maintaining the national Railroad Time and Watch Inspection Service.[17] Because Webb C. Ball's innovations revolutionized the railroad industry, Americans began to use the phrase "on the ball" to indicate an eye for detail.[18]

Interested in owning a Ball Watch? The company is still around, though it is now based in Switzerland. The company boasts a robust collection on their website and an online order may be worth the hassle, considering they retain Ball's original technology. As the company's logo states, "accuracy under adverse conditions."[20]

TOP: A memorial called "Memory Point" sits near the front drive into the Lake Seneca community

Population: 465   **Approx. Founding:** 1965

INSETS L to R: Lake Seneca itself • Lakeside Cafe • A sign
near the entrance to Lake Seneca lets residents know about
upcoming events • The Lake Seneca Lodge

Lake Seneca has a long history of land speculation and investment, starting at a least a century
before American Realty Service Corporation even
existed. Long before Bridgewater Township was
ever settled, land speculators purchased lots in the
area from the government and held onto them,
hoping the price of land in the area would swiftly
rise. It wasn't until the mid-1830s that white settlers even moved into Bridgewater Township. The
first permanent settlers, led by Asa Smith, came
from Michigan in 1836.[16]

Lake Seneca

Building the Lake at Lake Seneca

COUNTING THE POPULATION OF LAKE SENECA can be a
little complicated. The census-designated place is a permanent residence
for some, but it was actually designed for Ohioans looking to purchase a
vacation home. Regardless of how often they stop by, property owners in
Lake Seneca are required to maintain membership in the Lake Seneca
Property Owners Association (LSPOA). The association, with an elected
board of directors, uses regular payments from the residents to maintain
the lake and roads and fund the town's community events.[1]

The community of Lake Seneca was first founded in 1965 by the
American Realty Service Corporation, a property-development business
based in Memphis, Tennessee.[2, 3] Lake Seneca, in extreme northwest
Ohio, near the Michigan border, is located in an area popular with

those seeking a second home. The many lakes and gorgeous natural sur-
roundings make it a great place to relax and disconnect.[4]

There is one major difference between Lake Seneca and other
nearby vacation communities: in Lake Seneca, the lake is man-made.[5]
The lake, covering 266 acres, was formed by building a dam across the
St. Joseph River. (This river water also makes Lake Seneca murkier
than your average lake.)[6] In 1966, when the Lake Seneca project was
finished, the American Realty Service Corporation had spent about
three million dollars.[7] With their lake built, it was time to ask new
residents to begin investing.

During the late 1960s, residents of nearby Ohio cities, particularly
Toledo, became accustomed to the print and radio advertisements that
developers began running. Radio jingles enticed new buyers to Lake

Seneca, ensuring that "Your dreams can come true at beautiful Lake Seneca." There was competition for sales from other nearby lake resorts, but new residents began moving in.[8]

Rescuing the Lake at Lake Seneca

Things went well at Lake Seneca for almost an entire decade. But then in 1975, American Realty Service Corporation went bankrupt, leaving Lake Seneca, and 54 other properties around the U.S., behind.[9]

Despite the bankruptcy, Lake Seneca was still a beautiful place to spend the summer. New residents were still charmed by walks along Seneca Drive, a six-mile road throughout the community that winds around the lake. Things changed in the late 1990s, when suddenly, the lake that gave Lake Seneca its name disappeared.

While doing some routine maintenance in 1996, Donald Bowen discovered that the dam keeping Lake Seneca together was falling apart. The clay that filled the seams of the dam had either washed away or never existed in the first place. Large holes in the dam were shoved full of old tires and other materials, rather than clay. The dam was at risk of collapsing and flooding other villages in Bridgewater Township.[10]

Lake Seneca's dam had failed before, but during its first failure, the development firm that built the dam had still existed. Now with American Realty Service Corporation in bankruptcy, the residents of Lake Seneca didn't have anyone to call. Members of the LSPOA had to keep watch on the dam day and night, relying on each other. Williams County emergency management stepped in and began slowly opening the dam to avoid a flood. Suddenly, the lake was completely dry.[11]

Residents of Lake Seneca became understandably bitter. As prices for vacation homes rose across the country in the late 1990s, they "couldn't give lots away" without the lake. Finally, at the turn of the new millennium, residents were able to get a loan from the Ohio Water Development Authority to construct a new dam. This $1.6-million dollar loan will be paid off by residents for years to come, but the residents of Lake Seneca were forced to take on this loan to regain their property values. Until the 2030s, residents of Lake Seneca will each pay $350 annually to defer the cost of the loan.[12]

In 2001, Lake Seneca got its lake back. Excited about the new prospects for the community, the property owners association invited local real estate investors to come celebrate. The flyers they sent around read, fittingly, "Hot Dam, Let's Party."[13]

Lake Seneca Today

Today, the residents of Lake Seneca are slowly reclaiming the years that they missed when the lake ran dry. Property prices remain low, but for some new buyers, that's just what they are looking for. In 2003, JoAnn Wietecha and her husband were looking for a year-round lake home, but were striking out with high prices in Michigan. Then they found Lake Seneca. Despite the fact that JoAnn's husband began driving 55 miles each day to commute to Toledo, the couple was thrilled with their purchase. As Wietecha told the *Toledo Blade* in 2004, "He tells people, 'It's not a long drive when this is what you're coming back to.' We love it here."[14]

Almost all of the lots in Lake Seneca are approved for single family homes. However, just off the lake, there is one lot dedicated to business use. Here residents can visit the Lakeside Cafe for breakfast, lunch, or dinner. The cafe is located conveniently off the lake, so that residents can stop in for a bite to eat while they enjoy the day on the water. The cafe closes over the winter but reopens each spring.[15]

The closest village to Lake Seneca is Bridgewater Center, the first village established in Bridgewater Township. Now unincorporated, the village was laid out in 1871 and named for its location at the center of the township. In the mid-1800s, both Bridgewater Center and Lake Seneca became important spots for trade.[17]

TOP: Leesville United Methodist Church

Population: 147   **Approx. Founding:** 1812

INSETS L to R: Leesville Volunteer Fire Department • A view of the roundabout in the center of town • Leesville Cemetery • A view of Leesville Lake frozen over in the winter

The village of Leesville was known as a safe place for abolitionists and runaway slaves during the pre-Civil War era. Many well-known abolitionists, including Frederick Douglass, came to speak in the village.[16] It has also been recorded that Leesville served as an important link along the Underground Railroad in Carroll County. Many histories mention the home of John Millisack as a stopping point for escaped slaves seeking freedom farther north.[17]

Leesville

Leesville's Early Years

IN AUGUST OF 1812, the town of Leesburg (later Leesville) in Carroll County, Ohio, was platted by Thomas Price and Peter Saunders.[1] Little is known about Saunders, but the Price family originated in Harrison County, Kentucky. In 1804, Price's father moved to Ohio, settling in Licking County. Around the same time, Thomas Price's father-in-law, William Rippeth, also resettled in the new state of Ohio. Thus, Thomas and his wife decided around 1812 to travel north to Ohio, to visit both sets of parents. While there, he purchased a piece of land in the land office at Steubenville. It would become the village of Leesburg.[2]

Leesville was quite the place for Carroll County's social butterflies during the 1890s. According to local newspapers, by 1896 the Wheeling and Lake Erie Railway stopped in town four times every Sunday. At the end of the nineteenth century, the village of Leesville even had its own newspaper, *The Leesville Review*. It was unique for its time, because its publisher, Judson O. Rivers, was African-American.[3]

Beginning in 1894, Leesville attracted thousands of visitors each fall for its annual October street fair. The fair would always begin with a parade through the streets of Leesville, featuring live music and many exuberant locals. The 1896 fair also featured an evening ball at the opera house.[4]

Lake Leesville

During the Great Depression, Leesville was impacted by New Deal programs. Formed in 1935, the National Youth Administration (NYA)

attempted to provide training and work for the youngest members of America's struggling workforce.[5] Coincidentally, just a few years earlier in 1933, the Muskingum County Conservancy District had formed to establish "flood control, conservation, and recreation."[6] In 1936, Bryce Browning was the chief executive of the Muskingum Watershed Conservancy District. He met with S. Burns Weston, Ohio's director of the National Youth Administration, and asked that a NYA camp be considered in the conservancy district. By 1937, the project was approved, and by 1938 the conservancy district was building a dam in Leesville, forming the Leesville Lake. In December of 1938, the NYA officially decided to locate a worker's village on this new lake.

Young men moved into the new village in 1940. Living at the NYA camp in Leesville wasn't work all the time. The men hosted young women for dances on site, and they even road-tripped together to Cleveland to see the Browns football team play. However, in 1942, to accommodate the growing war effort, the NYA camp was transitioned into a training camp for Navy construction workers, known as Seabees. By 1943, the camp was vacant.[7] From 1944 to 1965, the Tuscarawas Philharmonic rented the Lake Leesville camp for their performances. Since 1942, the Ohio Future Farmers of America have run the camp, now known as Camp Muskingum.[8]

The Muskingum Coal Company

On Halloween of 1947, the Muskingum Coal Company and Earl Jones of Zanesville opened a new mine and coal-washing plant in Leesville. The village, and Jones's famous dog "Chubby," greeted the new mine happily. In fact, the *Daily Times* of nearby New Philadelphia claimed that December that "'Black Diamonds' Will Bring a Merry Christmas."[9] Up to that point, the Ohio Department of Education had considered closing the village school. However, thanks to the anticipated growth from the mine, the closing orders were rescinded.[10] The famous

dog could not be found by news reporters for a comment on opening day. Mine workers reported that he was likely off chasing rabbits.[11]

A Piece of History is Lost

In 2016, the village of Leesville became the center of Carroll County news, when construction of a natural gas pipeline led to the demolition of one of the village's historic structures. After Rover Pipeline began plans for construction in Leesville in 2014, the company purchased the historic Stoneman House to be used as an office building. The structure was up for nomination for the National Register of Historic Places, and the State Historic Preservation Office warned Rover that they couldn't adversely affect the site.[12]

Unbeknownst to the preservation office or the citizens of Leesville, Rover Pipeline began to tear down the Stoneman House in May 2016. In June 2016, the company then contacted the preservation office, notifying them of the intent to tear down the building (without noting that the building was already gone). Upon learning that it was too late to save the Stoneman House, the Ohio State Historic Preservation office asked that Rover Pipeline pay for its mistakes. The company put $2.3 million dollars into a fund for preservation activities around the state, primarily in the counties affected by the new pipeline.[13]

Why was the Stoneman House historic? It was designed in 1843 for the Stoneman family by architect J. L. Kilgore. Kilgore was known locally for his stone work. The Stoneman House had 14-inch-thick walls and unique carvings in each step of the winding main staircase. Kilgore was also known for his work on headstones in local cemeteries. Besides Kilgore's work, the Stoneman family was also significant to Carroll County. John Stoneman was one of the first white settlers to come to the area, and it was his son, Rezin, who had the house built on the family's land.[14]

When did Leesburg become Leesville? In 1887, residents learned that there were too many villages in Ohio claiming the name Leesburg. In an effort to ensure that they received the correct letters and packages, the residents of Leesburg very casually changed over to Leesville.[15]

Population: 172   Approx. Founding: 1872

INSETS L to R: New Hope Baptist Church • A street in Linndale • A traffic camera in Linndale • A sign welcoming visitors to Linndale, without which travelers may not have realized they left the bustling streets of the city of Cleveland next door

When Mayor Ann Lakawitz was elected in Linndale, she started a trend. After her term in office began, women in Linndale started running for office—and winning. Mayor Lakawitz's cabinet was almost completely made up of women from Linndale. When asked about being a woman in politics, Lakawitz said, "I have to make my way the same as a man, so why not in politics?" She also reported that residents of Linndale had always taken her seriously and never questioned the large amount of women leading their city.[19]

TOP: Linndale's Peace Memorial

Linndale

Robert Linn Creates a Cleveland Suburb

LINNDALE, CUYAHOGA COUNTY'S SMALLEST VILLAGE, has always been known for its enterprising citizens, beginning with the village's founder, Robert Linn. In 1872, Linn and a few associates from Cleveland purchased about 300 acres of land bordering the city in Brooklyn Township.[1] From his home office at 236 Superior Avenue, Linn sold these lots at prices ranging from $3 to $30. Linn advertised his new community in local papers, bragging about its proximity to Cleveland.[2]

Soon Linn's lots sold and the town began to boom, hitting 800 residents at its height. Unfortunately, the nationwide financial crisis of 1873 caused problems for Robert Linn. Linn had formed a land company to absorb the interest he owed when starting the town. He began to default on his loans, and the residents became frightened of losing their homes. Many left, and the town's population plummeted.[3]

A Village with Criminal Tendencies

During the early 1900s, Linndale was known for its gambling houses and saloons. Because most Linndale police officers looked the other way, the small town of Linndale became affiliated with vice.[4] In 1930, the son of the Linndale Justice of the Peace was tried for murder when he shot and killed a man who had threatened his brother with a butcher knife.[5] During Prohibition in 1926, both Mayor Harry Dorsey and his deputy marshal were indicted by a federal jury for involvement in bootlegging. Dorsey pled guilty to charges of liquor conspiracy and smuggling.[6] Dorsey was ousted from his office by the Linndale City Council after he declined to resign the office.[7] He was sentenced to 18 months in a workhouse.[8]

Under Dorsey's successor, "Battlin" Tom O' Malia, Linndale remained a den of vice. O'Malia's extracurricular activities almost robbed him of a chance to even take office![9] Before rising to the office of Mayor, O'Malia served as the village's marshal. In 1927, when O'Malia had officially been elected but not yet sworn into office, he was nearly ousted from his future position by his former deputy marshal, John S. Bourne. Bourne claimed that O'Malia had beaten him, robbed him of $38, and demanded an additional $25 for a poker debt that Bourne had yet to settle. Bourne also claimed that O'Malia had ransacked his home. Somehow O'Malia served as mayor for six years. During this time, he hired a skilled stenographer and lifelong Linndale resident named Ann Lakawitz. When O'Malia's time in city government was up, Lakawitz ran for mayor, and she won.[10]

Lakawitz was the first mayor of Linndale to crusade for a better reputation for the community. She held open office hours where she met with local residents to hear about their day-to-day issues. As she told one reporter, "People come to me with everything. This one is having difficulties with his wife, that one has a child who was hit by a milk bottle thrown through the air. Another…refuses to give his wife his pay because the home isn't kept in shape."[11]

Lakawitz could not fix every problem, but she made a difference. She kept aware of Clevelanders attempting to set up illegal rackets in Linndale and gave the marshal strict orders to prosecute. Linndale continued to harbor gamblers and saloons, but Lakawitz managed to clean up Linndale's act little by little.[12]

The Infamous Linndale Speed Trap

In 1965, Ohio began construction of Interstate 71, and Linndale was quite literally cut in half. Many homes had to be destroyed to make way for the highway, and the village's population plummeted. Suddenly the village government needed a revenue source.[13] The idea that saved Linndale can be credited to Mayor Armand Masten, a dry cleaning store owner and a World War II veteran. Masten ordered the police force to closely monitor the small stretch of highway that passed through Linndale for anyone slightly over the speed limit. Tickets issued in Linndale had to be paid in a mayor's court, and the village got to keep the proceeds. Suddenly the city coffers were full again, and Linndale was able to pay its public employees a wage worth sticking around for.[14] Unfortunately, Masten left office not long after his plan was put into action. In 1969, his son was killed in Vietnam. Masten was beleaguered and upset with the entire political system, and he left office.[15] However he did establish a peace memorial in Linndale, one that still stands today.[16]

In recent years, Linndale has become infamous for its speed traps. For years, various members of the Ohio state legislature have proposed legislation aimed at ending the Linndale speed traps. Most recently, Senator Tom Patton of Strongsville successfully passed legislation stating that Ohio villages under a population of 200 citizens cannot hold a mayor's court. This bill originally had a suggested population of 150 to allow a mayor's court, so Linndale police officers went door-to-door with census forms. Somehow the village hit a population around 179, giving it a 53 percent growth rate. After the census was finished, Patton simply increased the necessary population to 200.[17]

But Linndale's new mayor, Ashlee McLaughlin, found a new way to issue tickets: a speed camera. By setting up this camera at a popular intersection in town, the village began to take in even more money than before. Of course, the Ohio legislature soon passed a law requiring that a police officer had to be present at each camera. Most cities in Ohio removed their cameras at this point, but McLaughlin built a hut with accommodations for Linndale's new round-the-clock officer, including a microwave, mini-fridge, and television.[18]

In October 2017, the crew of *This American Life* showed up in town. Covering the story of traffic tickets in Linndale, the show interviewed current and former mayors, as well as the state representatives intent on killing the policies. The episode, titled "Expect Delays", can be found at the *This American Life* official website.[20]

…through
knowledge
peace…

Population: 247   **Incorporated:** 1841

INSETS L to R: One of the locks that gave Lockbourne its name, found today in Lock Meadows Park • Lockbourne United Methodist Church • A playground found in the center of the village • Lockbourne Veterans' Memorial

Many men from central Ohio served with the Tuskegee Airmen during World War II. Harold Sawyer was one of them; he successfully shot down two Nazi planes during his service. John H. Rosemond attended Howard University after the close of the war, returning to Columbus to open a family medical practice and serve on the city council. His aviation jacket is on display at the Motts Military Museum in Groveport, Ohio.[13]

TOP: A historic marker at Rickenbacker Airport, formerly Lockbourne Airforce Basee

Lockbourne

Building the Columbus Feeder

IN 1825, IN COLUMBUS, OHIO'S CAPITAL, discussions were underway about whether the Ohio and Erie Canal would be routed near the city.[1] While today Columbus is the most populous city in the state of Ohio, in 1825, it was still a very small farming town, despite its status as the capital. Access to a canal would be paramount for businesses in the city, and the citizens were ecstatic.

It was decided that Columbus would connect to the canal via a feeder route. The Columbus Feeder would specifically branch off the canal to bring traffic into the capital city. In July of 1825, construction crews, mostly made up of convicts held at the Ohio Penitentiary, broke ground on the new feeder route. (Convicts only made up the workforce for one year; however, at this time, many court sentences were

specifically listing punishment through work on the canal.)[2] Holes were dug and sandstone was shipped in from Lithopolis.[3]

The Columbus Feeder connected to the Ohio and Erie Canal just south of the city. At this connector, a system of locks near Big Walnut Creek lowered canal boats arriving from Groveport as they made their way south to Circleville, Chillicothe, or Portsmouth. At this point boats could also be sent back north, through the feeder to the city of Columbus. A warehouse was established at this connector to help limit the number of boats traversing the feeder.[4]

A Village on the Canal

In 1831, Colonel James Kilbourne, a well-known Ohio surveyor, began laying out a village at the connector site, on behalf of a group of influential Columbus landholders. The Columbus Feeder was destined to become a key point in the city's economy, so investing in the area seemed obvious. Kilbourne named the new village Lockbourne: a combination of the eight canal locks within its borders and his own last name.[5]

The same year that Kilbourne laid out the village of Lockbourne, water was let into the Columbus Feeder and canal traffic began coming through the city.[6] The village of Lockbourne blossomed. On the eastern side of the village, near locks 28 and 29, visitors to the village would find a granary, whiskey warehouse, and the well-known Moneypenny Distillery. Canal travelers wanting to visit any of these buildings would have to get off their boat, walk along the towpath, and cross a covered bridge to the other side of the canal.[7]

The Moneypenny Distillery was particularly well known. Like many canal towns, the village began to fill with rowdy inns and taverns to accommodate weary travelers. Both travelers and locals wanted a sip (or two) of the whiskey and beer Moneypenny produced in Lockbourne. William Moneypenny was born in Ireland in 1829, coming to the United States as a young man. He began working in distilleries, eventually purchasing one in Lockbourne. He used the Ohio and Erie Canal to ship in grain for his products and ship whiskey to customers. The canal boats he employed were known as *The Magnolia* and *The Cruiser*. The Moneypenny Distillery was a huge employer in the village of Lockbourne, requiring hands not only in the work of making and bottling Moneypenny's wares, but also to work in his cooper's shop, making the barrels that were necessary to produce whiskey. Moneypenny even kept hogs on site to eat the leftover byproducts. Unfortunately, in 1881, distraught over the death of his son, Moneypenny closed up shop, dealing a huge blow to Lockbourne's economy.[8]

The Lockbourne Air Base

In December of 1941, after the United States entered World War II, the War Department sought to build an Army airfield in Lockbourne. This new airfield would be conveniently located near the Wright-Patterson Air Force Base in Dayton and the industrial Curtiss-Wright plant in Columbus. The first soldiers arrived in June of 1942, and training began soon after. The Lockbourne Air Base also boasted a theater, a library, a service club, and day rooms, as well as a biweekly base newspaper.[9]

Today, the Lockbourne Air Force Base is best known for its ties to the Tuskegee Airmen. During the war, the Army Air Corps began a program that allowed African-American men to enlist in a segregated unit and train as pilots. Interested recruits received their training in segregated classrooms and airfields at the Tuskegee Institute in Alabama. Soon these African-American pilots became known as the Tuskegee Airmen. They were extremely successful during the war, damaging more than 409 German airplanes and 950 ground units, and sinking a destroyer.[10]

When the Tuskegee Airmen returned, they continued to experience racial discrimination, both within and outside the armed forces. Many men returned home, but the Tuskegee Airmen who remained in reserve were grouped into the 477th Composite Group and sent to the Lockbourne Air Force Base. Despite their courageous service during World War II, they were still barred from serving with their white colleagues. In 1948, President Truman desegregated the American military; however, the Tuskegee Airmen remained segregated until 1949.[11]

Today the Lockbourne Air Force Base has been renamed for Ohio's World War I flying ace, Eddie Rickenbacker. It now functions as an international airport; however, the Ohio Air National Guard and the Navy Reserve still maintain training grounds on site.[12]

Today visitors to Lockbourne can view Lock 30 on the Ohio and Erie Canal by strolling through the village's Lock Meadows Park. The lock has been integrated into life in Lockbourne, where Ohio's history and Ohio's present share the same space each day.

LOCK AND CANAL CENTER OF CENTRAL OHIO

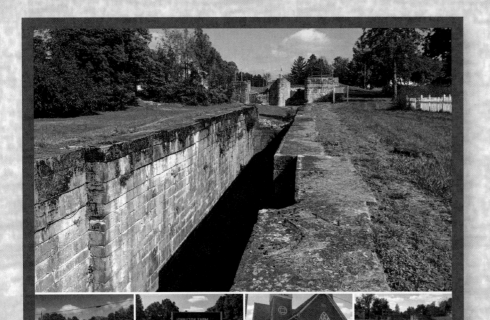

TOP: Two of the four remaining locks in Lockington

Population: 134   **Incorporated:** 1857

INSETS L to R: Lockington Vounteer Fire Department • A sign for
the nearby Johnston Farm • A church in Lockington • A view of
Lock 1, which has been restored

Although it had already been in existence for more
than 100 years, the village of Lockington did
not have a fire department until 1946. In that
year, William Forsythe, owner of Forsythe Dairy,
watched his business succumb to a large fire. After
this experience, he helped found the Lockington Volunteer Fire Association. The Forsythe family rebuilt,
opening up Zero Locker and Forsythe Ice Cream,
run by William's daughter "Tootie" Gilmore and her
husband Junior. The family continues to support the
Lockington Volunteer Fire Association.[16]

Lockington

A Canal Community

IN 1825, THE STATE OF OHIO began construction of the Miami
and Erie Canal, connecting the Ohio River in Cincinnati to Lake
Erie in the northern city of Toledo. Unfortunately, in 1836, construction came to a halt in the city of Piqua of Shelby County when state
funding began to run out.[1] In 1837, taking a bit of a calculated risk
considering the halt in construction, David Mellinger had a surveyor
named Jonathan Counts lay out a town for him just north of the city of
Piqua. He called this town Lockport, for the locks nearby that awaited
the continued canal route. However, Mellinger wasn't the only one
with this idea. As the name Lockport was already taken, the village
was named Lockington.[2]

An Engineering Feat

The locks in Lockington represented a true engineering feat of the
nineteenth century. Each lock was 80 feet long and 14 feet wide, built
from limestone blocks weighing more than 500 pounds each and tied
into the ground below. The floor of the lock was covered in wood, which
could not rot as long as it remained submerged in the canal waters.[3]

In 1839, the Miami and Erie Canal finally came to the town of
Lockington.[4] The village sits atop a 23-mile stretch on the canal deemed
the Loramie Summit. This is the highest point on the canal, and travelers and their cargo needed a way to be lifted uphill (or downhill if
traveling the other direction) about 67 feet.[5] The six locks built near the
village of Lockington essentially served as an elevator for canal boats. It

generally took at least 10 minutes to pass through each lock.[6] Most of the locks at Lockington could lift a boat up to 10 feet, although Lock 1 lifted travelers 15 feet.[7] This 10-minute delay at each of the six locks created a line of travelers waiting to be allowed to continue their journey. Often the canal travelers would leave their boat in line and step onto dry land for a quick drink and perhaps a bit of gossip. For this reason, Lockington became known as "the town of seven saloons."[8] Many saloons were situated near the canal. According to one source, one saloon, known as Fort Sumpter, became a target of female temperance activists brandishing weapons.[9] Ohioans led the early movement for temperance, so such activity probably wasn't surprising to Lockington residents.

A Piece of History Preserved

Visitors to Lockington can still see five of the six locks from the canal days. Now property of the Ohio History Connection, the locks are managed by the Johnston Farm Friends Council. In 2014, Lock 1 was restored, however the other locks show the effects of time and weather.[10] In 1913, Ohio suffered a large flood that destroyed many parts of the Miami and Erie Canal, making these preserved locks one of the last vestiges of this part of the state's history.[11]

Visitors can also visit the nearby Johnston Farm and Indian Agency in Piqua, Ohio. This site, also owned by the Ohio History Connection, features the restored home of John Johnston, a man responsible for negotiating agreements with American Indian nations native to Ohio during the early history of the state. The site also features a museum telling the stories of Ohio's indigenous peoples and a fully functional mule-drawn canal boat, ready for rides.[12]

Petitioning for a Railroad

The canals of Ohio experienced a heyday during the nineteenth century, leading to the incorporation of Lockington in 1857. However, by the 1900s, most Americans were ready for the railroad. In the very early 1900s, the Western Ohio Traction Company planned a railroad through Shelby County. Viewing the route, Lockington residents noticed that it would come near their village but not quite through it. The citizens requested that the railway come through their town. Their petitions were successful, and in 1901, the Western Ohio Traction Company decided to lengthen their track and come through Lockington.[13]

This railway became an asset to the community for many years after, helping residents travel between their homes and the city of Piqua. Many Lockington residents worked in a mill known as Walnut Mills at Piqua and relied on the railroad to get to work each morning.[14]

A Family of Mayors

As the canal system dried up and travelers stopped using Ohio's railways, Lockington began to shrink. However, the residents still have pride in their hometown. In January of 2016, Tracy Johnson was sworn in as the village's newest mayor. Political leadership is a family affair for Johnson. Her grandfather served as mayor of Lockington from 1972 to 1979 and again from 1996 to 1997, and her grandmother served as mayor in 1984.

After Tracy Johnson was officially sworn in, she opened her term by stating, "We are at a crossroad; do we continue to allow the village to deteriorate and become a ghost town, or do we make every effort possible to turn the tide? Do we have the will to foster a new beginning for our 165-year-old village?" Johnson seems to think the answer to this question is a solid yes, also reminding her constituents that "Lockington has a lot of potential."[15]

In 1969, the Lockington Locks historic area was placed on the National Register of Historic Places. In 1975, the Lockington Covered Bridge was also placed on the register. The bridge, an aging thoroughfare over the Great Miami River, burned down in the late 1980s, yet it remains on the list today.[17]

TOP: The Lower Salem Post Office can be found on the main thoroughfare through town

Population: 82   **Incorporated:** 1890s

INSETS L to R: Bob Hauser Community Park next door to Lower Salem Village Hall • A view of the Duck Creek which runs through the village • A sign at village hall states that Amos Porter, an early white settler of the Northwest Territory, is buried nearby • The People's Savings Bank

The corduroy road that linked Lower Salem and the booming metropolis of Marietta made travel between the two quite easy, but what if you had no transportation? Luckily for Lower Salem residents, John Hupp and Jacob Matz, two local men, operated a livery stable in which they rented horses for trips out to Marietta, not unlike the way modern travelers can rent vehicles. Unfortunately, corduroy roads can be harsh on a horse's feet—hopefully the travelers took it easy on their equine companions.[18]

Lower Salem

A Village at the End of the Corduroy Road

THE VILLAGE OF LOWER SALEM, OHIO, was laid out in 1850 on land owned by James Stanley and Moses True. The purpose of the village was to form an endpoint on a corduroy road leading to the much larger port city of Marietta.[1] A corduroy road is made up of wooden planks or logs. These very basic roads have been used for much of human history to traverse swampy or muddy terrain. Lower Salem lies near a tributary of the Ohio River known as Duck Creek and is very prone to flooding. This is likely why the corduroy road was built.[2]

Having a roadway ending in Marietta was very important for Lower Salem and the area in 1850. The city of Marietta was an economic hub, providing a home to almost 2,000 people, two public libraries, one college, and at least 20 different stores. When white settlers first arrived in the Northwest Territory in the late 1700s, Marietta was the first town officially settled. This location on the Ohio River was incredibly important for trade before the advent of canals and railways. In 1850, when Lower Salem was laid out, Marietta's location was just as prized, and the city was still a valuable trade center.[3]

Lower Salem was officially incorporated in the late 1890s, with Dr. Alfred Sturgiss serving as the first mayor. During the 1890s, Lower Salem also built its first-ever prison. The prison was not very high security, considering the few criminals the small town ever had the reason to imprison, and two convicts did manage to escape.[4]

The 1913 Flood

Unfortunately for the residents of Lower Salem, most of the village was washed away in July of 1913. A huge flood swept through the area nearest Duck Creek, with Lower Salem being one of the towns that was hardest hit. Waters cascaded down Front Street, flooding the roadway up to the roofs of its buildings. Residents were forced to flee, seeking shelter with fellow Lower Salem residents on Second Street, where the homes had remained unscathed. The neighboring town of Lowell transferred supplies by hand to the desperate residents.[5]

When the flood struck Lower Salem and the rest of the Duck Creek area, the Red Cross quickly mobilized. Lower Salem residents would have seen Agent E. C. Krecker riding through on horseback, personally interviewing those affected by the flood waters.[6] The Lower Salem Methodist Church also housed an official Red Cross aid station.[7] The Red Cross Ohio Flood Relief Commission was able to provide $7,520 for 66 Duck Creek area families to help rebuild.[8] In 2019, that's about $191,409, or about $2,900 per family.

In Lower Salem alone, five stores, ten houses, and two bridges were completely washed away. Despite these devastating effects, Lower Salem rebuilt and no one died.[9] While 1913 brought one of the worst floods the village has seen, residents of Lower Salem were able to rebuild so swiftly because they were used to the risk of water damage. During a flood in April 1903, residents of Lower Salem weren't the only ones affected by the rising water levels in their town. Just before the flood began, four men from the city of Zanesville had arrived in Lower Salem to investigate oil found about four miles outside of the town. The men were stuck in Lower Salem for two days before they were finally able to return home. As the *Zanesville Times Recorder* reported, the men were "more than ever convinced that oil and water will not mix."[10]

Lower Salem's First Female Mayor

In 1929, a Miss Mary Young became the first female mayor of Lower Salem. Young, a Lower Salem resident by this time, was actually from the Ohio town of Zanesville. Her brother, George F. Young, had become a well-known Ohioan due to his involvement with the pottery business.[11] For many years, Young ran Roseville Pottery out of Zanesville. Originally founded in the town of Roseville, the company was known for its art pottery. Beginning in the 1970s, and today, collectors became very interested in the pottery that Young produced in the early 1900s.[12] Unfortunately for Mary, her brother passed away before he could see her electoral victory.[13]

Before she was mayor, Mary was a milliner, making money by crafting and selling hats to the residents of Lower Salem. She served as Lower Salem's third mayor, and the first that was not a doctor by trade. Four other candidates were up for the office of mayor, including one other woman; however, Mary took the majority with just 15 votes. Also on the ballot that year was the position of town marshal. While the role eventually did go to a male resident, at least one woman was on the ballot.[14]

Lower Salem's Interesting Headlines

Despite its very small size, Lower Salem has been able to attract some unique criminals over the years. In 1886, the town suffered from what one newspaper deemed "devilish work" when a "fire fiend" made his way through the area, burning livestock and property for months.[15] In 1907, a local paper reported a July 4th riot that occurred when men and boys from the rival town of Elba arrived in Lower Salem and began, seemingly without purpose, attacking families enjoying an Independence Day picnic.[16] Almost as bizarre was a bank robbery that occurred in Lower Salem in 1951. The two robbers, not recognized by bank staff, arrived in Wild West-themed costume. As one paper reported, one man wore "a light tan trench coat and black cowboy boots" while carrying twin pistols.[17]

After Lower Salem was incorporated in the 1890s, an official Improvement Society was formed. It quickly succeeded in installing gas street lamps in the village. In 1926, the village installed electric streetlights. While larger cities had electric streetlights well before, this was a big deal for a town so small.[19]

BOB HAUSSER COMMUNITY PARK
In appreciation of his 49 years of public service as our Village Solicitor 1947 - 1996

TOP: The Magnetic Springs Cafe

Population: 291   **Incorporated:** 1883

INSETS L to R: Magnetic Springs baseball park on the edge of the village; the original spring was found nearby • A historic mural painted on Magnetic Springs Town Hall • Magnetic Springs Post Office • Magnetic Springs United Methodist Church

Despite the many attractions in Magnetic Springs, a railroad station was never established in the village. The nearest stations were located in the towns of Delaware (twelve miles away) and Richwood (six miles away). Visitors had to take a train to one of these locales and then call a taxi to take them to Magnetic Springs. With the high number of visitors, a taxi was certainly not hard to find. For particularly ill patients visiting the springs for healing purposes, ambulance services were available.[13]

Magnetic Springs

J. E. Newhouse Accidentally Unearths a Spring

UNTIL THE 1860s, the land around Bokes Creek in Union County, Ohio, remained largely unsettled. Finally in 1864, a man named J. W. Hoskins cleared a spot of land in the area and built a cabin. A few families followed, and in 1872, J. E. Newhouse built a nursery on his land to provide the new local farmers with garden stock. Unfortunately, wet weather often made local roads impassable, damaging Newhouse's profits. He decided to petition Union County to build a pike road (toll road) in the area, offering to donate gravel from his property to cover two miles of the road.[1]

Newhouse was successful in getting the county to build his road to the Bokes Creek area. After excavating the two miles worth of gravel

from his land, he decided to build a pond in the hole left behind. He needed water to fill this new pond, so in April 1879, Newhouse sunk a well on his property. He ended up uncovering a spring so powerful that people came from around the county to see and drink from the solid fountain of water.[2]

Multiple visitors to Newhouse's spring were afflicted with kidney problems, yet somehow after they drank the spring water, they began to feel better. Soon word began to spread about the water's purported healing properties, and more visitors were arriving on Newhouse's property each day. While not scientifically possible, word quickly spread that the water in this spring had magnetic properties. As many sources recorded, "a common pocket knife held in the stream a few moments [would] cause the blade to be magnetized sufficiently to pick up a nail or other small metallic object. Pins [would] readily adhere to the blade for weeks at a time."[3]

Visitors Rush to Magnetic Springs

Due to the growing interest in the spring, Newhouse, and his business partner in his nursery business, M. F. Langstaff, opened a bathhouse on the property. After the bathhouse opened, lots were surveyed nearby and a village began to grow very quickly. The first post office was opened in 1880, under the name of Kokosing. The name was quickly changed to Magnetic Springs to match the village's biggest draw.[4] By 1883, the village of Magnetic Springs was incorporated.[5]

In 1880, perhaps a little exhausted with the rush of visitors, Newhouse and Langstaff offered a plot of land near the spring to anyone would build a first-class hotel. Morgan Savage and A. W. Robinson soon built the Park House, a three-story hotel that featured a billiard parlor, a skating rink, and a spring in the lobby. A night at the Park House was an exciting affair, as one source reported on one average night, "'A party of young folks, 17 couples in all, came to the Park Hotel and were served with a grand supper. They all danced till two a.m., paid their bills—$2.00 a couple—got into their sleighs, and went home rejoicing."[6]

During the early 1900s, the Park Hotel combined with the bathhouse, but unfortunately in 1922, a fire destroyed both buildings. The entire business was just too profitable to leave behind, so by 1923, a new hotel was finished. The new building included horse stables, boating, archery, fishing, and a nine-hole golf course. The Ohio State University football team often stayed at the hotel while practicing.[7]

The Park Hotel was not the only hotel in the village; in fact, it was one of seven. The village even supported an amusement park known as Maple Dell. While the hotels were all luxurious, ultimately most visitors were coming for the healing powers of the spring. In fact, nearly 10,000 visitors passed through the village of Magnetic Springs each summer.[8] As one advertising pamphlet explained, "The water is used both internally and externally." When the water was consumed, "the water acts as a splendid tonic to the digestive organs, removes acidity, fermentation and excess of bile from the stomach and bowels, promoting the secretion of gastric juices, thus correcting unhealthy conditions and stimulating the digestive process." When the water was bathed in, "The mineral properties penetrate the ducts of the body and are assimilated and carried through the system, promoting a general stimulation of the bodily functions, invigorating and improving the general health of the body."[9]

As medical science advanced, mineral baths fell out of fashion, and the village of Magnetic Springs began to suffer. The Park Hotel was converted to the Magnetic Springs Polio Foundation by Dr. Kenneth Keever, but when a vaccine for polio was found, the foundation closed. By the end of the 1980s, all of the hotels from the Magnetic Springs heyday were gone.[10]

Magnetic Springs Today

Unfortunately, once the springs' allure faded, the town began to quickly shrink. However, the community has not given up. In 2015, Sylvia Zimmerman opened the Magnetic Springs Cafe, creating what she calls a destination in the village. She continues to discover new recipes and serve up exciting food for the community.[11] In 2018, the village of Magnetic Springs was awarded a $500,000 Community Development Block Grant from Ohio's Office of Community Development. The entire village worked together to write the grant request. Multiple public meetings were held, and everyone's voice was heard. As Mayor Kathy Cantrell said, "We did a lot of work to accomplish this. We worked all summer and it was just really exciting to get the news on this." The grant will help with projects to redevelop the village.[12]

In 1972, a bottled water company was established in town. During the late 1970s, the company moved to Columbus, but they continued to ship water from Magnetic Springs to the bottling plant. In the 1980s, the company began sourcing their water elsewhere. The Magnetic Springs Bottled Water Company still operates in Columbus today.[14]

TOP: Martinsburg Presbyterian Church

Population: 228   **Approx. Founding:** 1828

INSETS L to R: The Martinsburg Dairy Isle • The Martinsburg Post Office • Martinsburg Tire • Martinsburg Church of Christ

Present-day residents of Martinsburg don't even have to leave the village to treat their sweet tooth. Located on South Market Street, the Martinsburg Dairy Isle is the perfect summer stop. The Dairy Isle serves up milkshakes, ice cream cones, root beer floats, hot fudge sundaes, and more. Not in the mood for something sweet? The Dairy Isle also has burgers and fries. Orders are available for dine-in or carryout.[15]

Martinsburg

Martinsburg's Beginnings

IN 1828, IN KNOX COUNTY, OHIO, two small villages, separated by a road running east and west, decided to join forces. These villages, Hanover and Williamsburg, took the new name Martinsburg (sometimes spelled Martinsburgh). As the years passed, the combined village maintained a steady population of about 300 people, profiting from agriculture.[1] Martinsburg was known for the residents' adherence to the Presbyterian faith, as well as their penchant for temperance. Few strangers came through Martinsburg, as a railway never passed through town, and visitors struggled to find any kind of alcoholic beverage.[2]

In 1838, an institution of higher education opened in the village of Martinsburg, known as the Martinsburg Academy.[3] Most of the students at the academy were young men from Knox County and other nearby locales. For those traveling farther, a limited number of dorms were built, which, according to a course catalog from 1841, could be rented for 62.5 cents per week, with an additional 50 cents per month for washing. Students could also pay about one dollar a week to board with a local family. Each student was compelled to attend weekly church services to keep their place at the academy. While Martinsburg was a majority Presbyterian village, any church would do, as long as the student's moral character was properly managed. In addition, students were charged $10 each month for admission. However they were able to use a library of about 300–400 books for free while enrolled.[4]

William Windom: Alumnus of Martinsburg Academy

Perhaps the best known alumnus of Martinsburg Academy was William Windom. Windom was born in Belmont County, Ohio, in 1827, but he eventually made his way to the Martinsburg Academy, where he began advanced studies.[5] Despite the reluctance of his Quaker parents, Windom took an interest in the law.[6] He was admitted to the Ohio bar in 1850 and opened a practice in Mount Vernon not long after. In 1852, Windom was elected as Knox County Prosecuting Attorney.[7]

Despite his beginnings in Knox County, the state of Minnesota often lays claim to William Windom. In 1855, he moved to Minnesota, which was the Minnesota Territory at the time. After Minnesota officially entered the union in 1858, Windom represented the state in the U.S. House of Representatives and then later in the Senate. In 1881, President James A. Garfield, a fellow Ohio-born public servant, appointed Windom as Secretary of the Treasury. After Garfield's assassination later that year, Windom left his position in the cabinet to return to the Senate and later private legal practice in New York. In 1889, President Benjamin Harrison, another Ohio-born politician, reappointed Windom to the position of Secretary of the Treasury.[8]

In 1891, Windom addressed an eager crowd at the New York Board of Trade. As he was describing the negative effects of an unstable currency, Windom collapsed. He was pronounced dead not long after. Windom was awarded congressional honors, and by order of President Harrison, the Treasury Department remained draped in mourning cloths for weeks after Windom's death.[9] In 1891, Windom was memorialized on a special two-dollar silver certificate that featured his likeness. Today these bills, known as Windoms, are collector's items.[10]

About 30 years after Windom's death, his great-grandson, also named William Windom, was born. He was well known for his long career as a television actor. He appeared in *The Twilight Zone*, *Murder She Wrote*, and *Star Trek*, among many other television shows. Windom often bounced from set to set as a talented guest star, but he spent some time as a series star during the 1960s on the show *The Farmer's Daughter*. Windom stated that this role was particularly important to him, as he played a congressman, making him feel connected to his great-grandfather.[11]

Martinsburg Presbyterian Church

For many years, the village of Martinsburg served as the sort of bedrock for the local Presbyterian community. Most of the early white settlers were Presbyterian. Many of these settlers were veterans of the Revolutionary War, and as a part of their pension, they were granted land in Ohio. These new settlers formed a Presbyterian congregation in Martinsburg as early as 1804, meeting in each other's homes before a simple log church was constructed. The Martinsburg Presbyterian Church was officially registered in 1808. Early residents of the Knox County area were enthusiastic about their faith. By 1843, the Martinsburg Church maintained 300 members.[12]

The second pastor to serve the Martinsburg Presbyterian Church was Reverend Henry Hervey. Hervey was influential in the construction of the Martinsburg Academy in 1838.[13]

As the Civil War dawned and tensions regarding slavery grew, Martinsburg experienced its own inter-village tension. A group of abolitionists, upset that Reverend Hervey had not spoken out against slavery vehemently enough, formed their own congregation, the Free Presbyterian Church. An opposing group, likely families that had originally migrated to the area from Virginia, were angry that Hervey had spoken against slavery at all. They formed the Presbyterian Church at Bladensburg (page 20). While the groups were able to reconcile after the Civil War, the Presbyterian community in Martinsburg never quite recovered from the schism.[14]

Reverend Henry Hervey had a very strange posthumous request: He wanted to be buried on the exact spot of his church's pulpit. In order to do this, the congregation tore down their church, buried Hervey, and built a new church immediately next door. A monument was placed on the spot to mark his grave.[16]

TOP: Mailboxes for sale behind the Miamiville Post Office

Population: 242   **Approx. Founding:** 1849

INSETS L to R: The Rusty Nail • Miamiville Garage • The home offices of Joe Uecker of the Ohio State Senate • A driveway leading to the Miami Boat Club

During the Civil War, a Union Army camp was based just down the road from Miamiville, in the village of Camp Dennison (see page 26). The postal workers in Miamiville were responsible for the Union soldiers' mail. According to a notice published in a local newspaper in 1861, soldiers' families were to address their letters to Miamiville, being careful to note the "company and regiment to which the volunteer is attached." After being sorted at Miamiville, the letters would reach the soldiers "without delay."[10]

Miamiville

Laying out Miamiville

IN SEPTEMBER 1849, on the Little Miami River, Moses F. Robinson laid out the village of Miamiville. White settlers had been moving to the area for a while, thanks to the nearby mills run by the Buckingham family. The Buckinghams had first built a mill in 1810, with updated facilities constructed in 1830. In 1835, the Buckingham family even began running a distillery, but it burned down in 1858 and was never replaced. The new village continued to attract settlers when the Little Miami Railroad laid track through the area. In 1874, a man named A. N. Robinson added 208 new lots to the village so that it reached the train depot.[1]

The Miami Boat Club

In 1897, along the banks of the Little Miami River in the village of Miamiville, 16 interested gentleman formed the Island Canoe Club. The group had actually begun meeting in 1896, having elected Everett Winslow Hobart as their president, but it wasn't until late in 1897 that they finally found a permanent home for their new exclusive country club. After deciding to locate along the Little Miami River, the men had purchased a site known as the Lief Farm, but due to poor weather and high water in 1897, the site was unusable. They secured a piece of land the men called "The Island" and got to work building their new getaway.[2]

The original Canoe Club consisted of only one small house with a kitchen, bedrooms, and a front porch. This setup worked just fine when it was just the men staying at the house; however, when the Island was opened up to female guests for limited times, a problem presented itself: in keeping with decorum of the time, the men and women could not sleep in the same quarters. So when women were staying at the Island House, the men carried their belongings outdoors and spent the night in a row of tents. These tents presented a few issues, including cold weather. The sleeping situation was also somewhat chaotic, as one remembrance stated, "lucky indeed was the man who...should wake up and find all of his belongings where he had last left them. It was no unusual occurrence for a man to find his next-cot-neighbor using his shoes for a pillow, and his only fresh shirt as a foot warmer." This arrangement only lasted about a year before the club members found the money to afford an addition to the house.[3]

The house also included indoor plumbing and showers, provided by a man named Rufus King. The showers were much appreciated, but unfortunately the water emitted a not-so-pleasant odor.[4]

The Island Canoe Club was an exclusive organization, and many southwestern Ohioans were likely barred from visiting. It is very likely that African-American men and women would only have stepped foot on the Island as employees of the Canoe Club, working to cook or clean for the guests at the house. In fact, one remembrance of the club, written for members around the early 1900s, mentions a lead housekeeper named William, describing his services as impeccable, but also using a racial slur of the time period. In the early days, women could only visit the Canoe Club on weekdays, and they were treated as guests rather than club members. While the men of the club quickly decided to rectify this situation, it was only their desire to have the women's company that changed the rules, not any desire for equality.[5]

In 1907, the Island Canoe Club was purchased by members of the Camargo Country Club and renamed the Miami Club. During the 1920s, the club operated as a sort of speakeasy, getting around Prohibition liquor laws. After Prohibition was lifted, during the 1930s, the club members changed their name to the Miami Boat Club, to allow for recognition by other yacht clubs in the United States. During the mid-twentieth century the club was able to feature many big names in jazz, including Frank Sinatra, Count Basie, Cab Calloway, and Harry Belafonte.[6]

Today the Miami Boat Club is still an active organization in Miamiville, with organized events and a recently restored clubhouse. The main entry is nestled tightly within the streets of Miamiville, making it easy to miss. In order to join, potential members must be sponsored by a current member and meet approval by an official board.[7]

Little Miami Scenic Trail

Today, where the Little Miami Railroad once passed through Miamiville, there is now an active bike trail. Known as the Little Miami Scenic Trail, or often the Loveland Bike Trail, this 70-mile paved thoroughfare passes through the towns of villages of southwestern Ohio that were once home to the railway. The trains stopped operating during the 1960s, and as the 1980s dawned, the Ohio Department of Natural Resources got to work on repurposing the path that the railroad tracks left behind.[8]

Many bike riders will start in the nearby community of Loveland, north of Miamiville, where multiple bike rental services are available. Enterprising riders who are willing to spend about an hour on their bike can easily make it from Loveland to Miamiville, with lots of stops for food available on the way. Like the railroad, the Little Miami Scenic Trail often follows the Little Miami River, meaning there are many parks and preserved green spaces available for riders as well.[9]

H. W. Leener, a resident of Miamiville, posted an interesting message in the *Cincinnati Daily Star* in August of 1875. A few days earlier, one of Leener's cows had walked away. The "strayed cow" was white and "speckled about the neck and shoulders." Leener offered a reward, but it isn't clear if she was ever found.[11]

TOP: The Milledgeville Community Center

Population: 110   **Approx. Founding:** 1855

INSETS L to R: A playground near the community center • Kelly's Tavern • Milledgeville-Plymouth Cemetery is also used by nearby Octa (page 138) • A post office nestled in the streets of Milledgeville

One of the most remarkable details about Kelley's Tavern was Arnett Kelley's devotion to his business. He opened the doors of his tavern every single day, 365 days a year. Kelley closed only for one hour each year on Thanksgiving and Christmas, so his family could enjoy a holiday meal together. Nina Kelley recalls that as a child she once begged her father to remain closed all day on Christmas, but, although he tried valiantly, he couldn't stand it. He had the tavern open by noon that day.[17]

Milledgeville

Milledgeville's Early Years

IN 1854, IN FAYETTE COUNTY, OHIO, James Hogue requested that Jacob Creamer, acting for the Fayette County Land Office, lay out the new town of Milledgeville. This village was named for the mill on the edge of the village. During the winter season of 1854–1855, the supplies necessary for the mill began to arrive in town. Over the summer, the mill was erected, and by August, Straley, Creamer & Co. was advertising the new flour mill in the local paper. In anticipation of the incoming growth the mill might bring, Creamer also opened a store for the village.[1]

Unfortunately for Creamer, the development of Milledgeville slowed almost as soon as the village was laid out. In 1861, the United States fell headlong into the Civil War. This greatly limited interest in moving into a new town, and all resources were focused on the battlefront.[2]

However, once the war ended, growth resumed. In the 1870s and 1880s, railroads planned to pass through Milledgeville. With this incoming railway (the Cincinnati, Hamilton and Dayton) in mind, many new citizens moved to town and businesses blossomed.[3] While Milledgeville boomed during the late 1800s, the nearby town of Plymouth, with no access to the railroad, saw a huge population loss. This population shift was so great that the local post office was moved from Plymouth into Milledgeville.[4]

White settlers called this land home long before it was formally organized. In fact, by 1805, a Baptist church was raised in the area that would one day become Milledgeville. The church remained in use until 1955, when it burned down.[5]

Squire Rankin

One of the future Milledgeville's earliest residents was Jacob A. Rankin, eventually known to many in the area as "Squire Rankin." Rankin was born in Ross County, Ohio, in 1800, three years before Ohio gained statehood. He moved with his family to Fayette County as a young boy, discovering Milledgeville at the age of 18. From 1818 to 1833, Rankin worked at clearing land in the future village for his own home. He would become an influential member of the Whig party and a justice of the peace. When not fulfilling his political duties, Rankin attempted to continue clearing land to bequeath to all 10 of his children.[6]

Rankin became a very common name among the residents of Milledgeville. Not long after Milledgeville was officially platted, Smith Rankin drafted a letter to a local medical college, offering a horse and saddle to any doctor that might take up a practice in the new town. Rankin understood that in order for a new town to thrive in the backwoods, there needed to be available medical care.[7] Through most of the late 1800s, the town supported not one but two doctors at a time.[8] Smith Rankin had a keen sense for what the growing village of Milledgeville needed most. As the railways came through town and it began to thrive, he laid out new lots close to the tracks.[9]

Milledgeville's Namesake Destroyed

Unfortunately, in 1970, the mill that gave Milledgeville its name burned to the ground. At 4:25 p.m. on Thursday, November 19, 1970, Mrs. Ed Rankin called the Fayette County Fire Department, alerting them to a large blaze coming from the mill. Owned by L. J. Dill of Westerville since 1940, the mill was filled with about 600 bushels of beans, valued at about $1,800 (about $11,450 in 2019). Luckily for Dill, the corn stored in the mill elevator had been moved the previous day. Dill was the last to leave the mill, shutting down the electric power to the building at 4:00 as he went home for the day. Dill only found out the mill was burning from other town residents.[10]

Fire departments from many local towns and villages helped fight the blaze. Luckily for the Anderson family, who owned the home across the street from the mill, the Jeffersonville Fire Department was able to save their home. The family was unaware of the blaze across the street as they were just sitting down for dinner. During the beginning of their meal, the doorbell rang, and Mr. Anderson answered the door to a child asking him to call the fire department.[11]

The blaze from the mill fire was incredibly hot. The paint on the Anderson home blistered, and their windows cracked from such huge changes in temperature. When the fire finally ended, the sheet metal that had once covered the mill's elevator was a shriveled mess. The blaze burned that day from about 4 to 11 p.m., although it was controlled after about 6 p.m.[12] Dill did not rebuild the mill, and after almost 120 years, the mill that had given Milledgeville its name was no more.[13]

Kelley's Tavern

In August of 1888, Ada Smith purchased a plot of land in Milledgeville, and in 1890 a tavern was erected. Passed from family member to family member, this tavern was eventually purchased by Mr. Arnett Kelley in 1944. Since then, it has been known as Kelley's Tavern.[14] Kelley's Tavern was a central part of Milledgeville life as the highway overtook the railway. For those left in Milledgeville, this was a place they could gather almost 24/7.[15]

Kelley maintained the original coal stove and the wooden booths, adding modern conveniences, such as a pay telephone. His family lived above the tavern, and upon Kelley's death in 2005, his daughter Nina took over operations. Unfortunately, the tavern closed in 2015, but Nina has made clear that she'll never stop appreciating the people of Milledgeville.[16]

Sometimes a small town is the best place to cause some Halloween mayhem. On November 4, 1938, the *Washington Court House Record-Herald* reported on some mischievous midnight activities in Milledgeville: among others, a "discontented cow" was left outside the bank, and chickens were released into a private residence.[18]

TOP: The Millfield Post Office

Population: 341   **Approx. Founding:** 1833

INSETS L to R: Millfield Christian Church • The remains of the Sunday Creek Coal Mine • The former site of the Sunday Creek Coal Mine just outside downtown Millfield • A historic marker placed in 1980 to mark the mine disaster

In July of 1947, a flying saucer was found in Millfield. According to reports, the item, found outside the Millfield Post Office, was "[a]bout 18 inches in diameter... apparently made from an old street light reflector daubed with green paint and a strange collection of automobile and radio parts plus some miscellaneous junk bolted to it." The Athens County Sherriff took on the case and called in a professor from Ohio University who deemed the entire situation to be a hoax. However, in the years since, the flying saucer itself has gone missing. One local man, William Omen, a collector, is now on a mission to find the missing UFO.[21]

Millfield

"It Might Soon Be a Very Thriving Town"

THE EARLY HISTORY OF MILLFIELD is not well recorded. The village was founded around 1833 and originally named Millville, for a nearby mill.[1] During the 1880s, the village was home to a station on the Ohio Central Railroad, a flour mill, a schoolhouse, various shops, and a post office. Yet, as one account wrote at the time, "its growth has not been satisfactory." However, the same author predicted that if "capitalists open coal works in the village it might soon be a very thriving town."[2]

This prediction was correct. Millfield is located in the Hocking Valley, an area known for coal mining in Ohio. As the twentieth century dawned, Millfield became a mining town. With huge mining operations located just on the edge of the village, almost everyone in town had a connection to the mines.[3]

The Sunday Creek Coal Mine Disaster

Unfortunately, Millfield is best known as the site of Ohio's deadliest mine disaster. On November 5, 1930, an explosion at Sunday Creek Coal Mine No. 6 trapped more than 100 miners underground. Sadly, 82 of these 100 men became casualties of the explosion.[4]

November 5, 1930, was a chilly fall day, the day after election day.[5] There were about 300 men on shift at the Sunday Creek Coal Mine, and they had just finished up their lunch and headed back into the mines.[6] Following the miners was a group of businessmen, taking a tour of the Sunday Creek Mine to inspect newly installed safety equipment. The group included mine executives as well as those from the Columbia Cement Company (see page 52). P. H. McKinley, an assistant to the president of the company, arrived late, so he stayed behind to change his clothes before entering the mine. McKinley was the only executive to survive the explosion.[7]

Around noon, there was a rumbling noise, and smoke and flames began swiftly shooting from the mine shaft.[8] Even today, it's still not clear what happened. The official report claims that there was a short circuit between a trolley car and its rails, igniting flammable gas in the mine.[9] However, others believe that a miner carrying an open flame may have triggered the flammable gases.[10]

In most mines, the flow of dangerous gases is controlled by a system of brattices. In the Sunday Creek Coal Mine, wooden poles held up a thick brattice cloth, creating walls at different locations throughout the mine to direct the airflow.[11] This helped prevent methane gas from accumulating and causing explosions. When the explosion occurred, the brattice structure was immediately destroyed. This meant that the toxic gases left over from the explosion, known as afterdamp, spread through the whole mine. Many of the men who died at the Sunday Creek Coal Mine survived the blast but asphyxiated as they tried to escape.[12]

As news of the disaster spread, hundreds of people rushed to the mine. The Ohio National Guard was called in to keep order and direct local traffic. Rescue cars were dispatched on the Panhandle Division of the Pennsylvania Railroad. The railroad engineer, John W. Young, broke rail speed records, traveling 91 miles in 93 minutes.[13]

The Story of H. L. McDonald

Many of the rescue workers entering the mine were local men who wanted to help. This included several miners who typically worked at the Sunday Creek Mine but had not been in the mine when it exploded. Their knowledge of the mine was of utmost importance. H. L. McDonald was an experienced mine foreman who had missed work that morning to take his father to the hospital. His father, also a miner, was suffering from gangrene after a mining accident. His surgery was delayed, so McDonald rushed to the mine where he was immediately conscripted into rescue service.[14]

McDonald and the others were instructed not to retrieve any bodies that they couldn't see with a flashlight from the main mine shaft. This was meant to help them avoid any particularly bad pockets of afterdamp. The gas was unavoidable, however: McDonald remembered feeling weak and fighting a headache. Mine inspectors were sent ahead with oxygen helmets to attempt to find any survivors; however, they returned within the first few hours to tell rescuers that there was no one left to save.[15]

The rescuers began to wrap the bodies they found in discarded brattice cloth.[16] At about 11 p.m., almost 12 hours after the explosion, workers began moving the bodies to the surface using carts pulled by donkeys.[17] Both a company pool room and the mining company store were used as morgues. Today, the ruins of these buildings are all that remain of the Sunday Creek Coal Mine (they are marked with a state historical marker).[18]

Later, McDonald was asked to go on a second rescue trip. Sometime in the early hours of the morning, McDonald and his crew heard a group of men calling out. They ran to the voices and found that 19 men had barricaded themselves with brattice cloth, keeping their air somewhat clean for about 12 hours. Many of the men were unconscious, but rescue workers got them all out.[19] Around 4 a.m., McDonald "emerged from that black chasm that had so ruthlessly taken such a terrible toll of human life." At home that morning, he passed out from carbon monoxide poisoning and had to seek immediate medical treatment. Unfortunately, his father died from gangrene five days later. McDonald eventually returned to work in the mines, but as he said, "like the others, [he] could not shake off that jittery nervous feeling that lingered…"[20]

Millfield is the home of the Athens County Department of Job and Family Services. The main office is located in a historic building, formerly the Athens County Home. The department helps county residents with child-care, financial assistance, medical transportation, food pantries, and an ex-offender reentry program.[22]

16098 Main St
Millfield, Ohio

SITE OF UFO LANDING JULY 12, 1947

ABOUT 1 WEEK AFTER
ROSWELL NEW MEXICO LANDING

TOP: The Fee Villa's location on the Ohio River operated as a stop on the Underground Railroad

Population: 189   **Approx. Founding:** 1816

INSETS L to R: The birthplace of President Ulysses S. Grant in Point Pleasant is only three miles from downtown Moscow • The William H. Zimmer Power Station on the edge of town • This tank is part of a veterans memorial in Moscow • A former Methodist Church in Moscow, recently sold as a renovated commercial property

Just a few minutes down the road from Moscow, Ohio, is the birthplace of President Ulysses S. Grant. The Civil War General-turned-chief-executive was born in a one-room cottage in Point Pleasant, Ohio, where he lived for the first year of his life.[16] The home once traveled around the entire country by train. The house is now the property of the Ohio History Connection (the state historical society) and has been firmly planted back in Point Pleasant, where it is operated as a living-history museum by Historic New Richmond, Inc.[17]

Moscow

Owen Davis Plats Moscow

IN 1816, OWEN DAVIS had a plat of land officially recorded and laid out through his lawyer, John Payne. The land was specifically laid out in the hopes of building a new town, with a lot for a church, a cemetery, and all the other necessities. In 1817, Payne built a hotel, general store, and attached residence in hopes of kickstarting development of the new village of Moscow.[1] Early land buyers came by ferry from Cincinnati to scout out the land. A few buyers took interest, but the village didn't hit its stride until the mid-1800s.[2]

The Wigglesworth Kidnapping

In the early hours of the morning on October 30, 1842, a gang of six armed Kentucky men led by William Moore and William Middletown arrived in the village of Moscow.[3] The men made their way to the banks of the Indian Creek, where Vincent and Fanny Wigglesworth lived with their four children, Maryan (15), Eliza (10), Josiah (5), and an infant of only 16 days.[4,5] Brandishing weapons, Moore, Middletown, and their accomplices tied up Vincent Wigglesworth, kidnapping Fanny and the children. An alarm was sent up, but the men were able to escape, taking Fanny and her children with them.[6]

Moore and Middletown claimed property rights on Fanny, a free black woman who had been living in Moscow for about 16 years. Fanny was originally born into slavery, in Maryland, during the late 1700s. When Fanny's initial slave owner died, they willed her to another woman as property in a life estate. It is believed that this woman brought

Fanny to Ohio in 1826 and filed manumission papers, freeing her. However, because of the use of a life estate, the woman only had ownership of Fanny as long as she lived. Once the Maryland woman died, ownership transferred to the next-named individuals on the estate: William Moore and William Middletown.[7]

A group of outraged Moscow citizens met at the Calvary Methodist Church a few days after the kidnapping and drafted a set of resolutions that were sent to a multitude of Ohio newspapers for printing. Unfortunately, as one historian has pointed out, this was "far from an abolitionist meeting."[8] The group only wanted outsiders to "refrain from intermeddling with any of the laws or institutions of Ohio, and more especially with that of slavery…" They took offense to the Kentucky mob's actions, because it was "an insult to all law."[9] The white residents of Moscow that met at Calvary Methodist Church that day were angry that Ohio law was ignored, but they didn't seem to take issue with slavery itself.

Robert Fee Provides Aid

After losing his family, Vincent Wigglesworth moved to Lebanon, Ohio. Here he caught the eye of a Lebanon local, Governor Thomas Corwin (namesake of the village of Corwin, see page 44). Corwin and his brother, Robert, were able to raise funds to help Vincent find his family. Vincent couldn't go south himself without fear of enslavement, so he turned back to Moscow for aid. He was able to rely on Robert Fee, an abolitionist, who could recognize the family by sight. Fee traced the Wigglesworths to Independence, Missouri.[10]

Fee found Fanny and her children and offered to purchase their freedom from their kidnappers. Had they remained closer to Ohio, Fee may have been able to seek justice in the court system. It is likely Moore and Middletown knew this, and this is why they resorted to kidnapping, rather than litigation. Lacking the total amount, Fee had to turn back with a down payment and a promise. Fee wrote to Vincent with the positive news. It is said that when Robert Corwin read the letter to Vincent, he cried out, "Thanks to God."[11]

Fee returned to Ohio to begin fundraising. After a successful campaign, he returned to Missouri only to find that Moore and Middletown had skipped town and taken Fanny and her children with them. Fee, enraged, had charges of kidnapping levied against the men by the state of Ohio. The state also sent an agent to Missouri on a manhunt for Moore and Middletown, while also asking the Missouri governor to comply by extraditing the kidnappers.[12]

Fee set out again, having traced the kidnappers to Platte City, Missouri. In March 1845, now almost three years later, Fee successfully had the men arrested. Unfortunately, they were soon released and an armed mob came after Fee. He was forced to return to Ohio. Vincent Wigglesworth was never reunited with his family.[13]

It is believed that Fee became an even more ardent abolitionist after this event, running a stop on the Underground Railroad from his home. Violent mobs often surrounded the Fee home, leading the entire family to sleep with pistols on their bedside tables.[14]

A Tornado Hits Moscow

In 2012, a terrible tornado hit the village of Moscow, leaving one-third of the buildings destroyed or uninhabitable and a citizen dead. Five years later, in 2017, the population had dropped from 244 to 170. Many residents reported terrifying experiences. As one resident said, "Everybody was crying, screaming and thinking we weren't going to make it, but we did." The memories are still fresh as the village continues to rebuild today, but not all have lost hope. As one Moscow man said, "I still love the village, and I'm going to stay here until I can't stay here anymore."[15]

Since the 1990s, Moscow has been the home of the William H. Zimmer Power Station. Originally meant to run on nuclear power, it was switched to coal before completion because of the 1979 accident at Three Mile Island. Despite these issues, the plant is able to provide low-cost electricity for many in the Cincinnati area.[18]

TOP: The Red Tomato Market in Mount Eaton

Population: 236   **Approx. Founding:** 1813

INSETS L to R: Mount Eaton Hardware • Mount Easton's Historical Society and Museum • Mount Eaton Community Church • Mount Eaton Medical Center

The bank of Mount Eaton was actually robbed twice in 1920. In December of 1920, just before Christmas, burglars used an acetylene torch to cut out the lock on the bank's vault. They then blew up a safe that held about $4,000. Likely scared off by a harmless noise outside, the robbers left before they were able to retrieve the funds they had freed from the safe, but they did grab exactly $39.84 off of the counter. The robbery was discovered the following morning.[13]

Mount Eaton

Paintville Becomes Mount Eaton

IN 1813, IN WAYNE COUNTY, OHIO, William Vaughn and James Galbraith laid out a new village. Their new community was named Paintville, after the red water that flowed from a local spring. Much like paint, the water colored everything it touched.[1] Residents got to work building their village almost immediately. In fact, Archibald Hanna, the first minister in town, began conducting religious services in a tent before a proper building was available.[2] Galbraith had second thoughts about the village name; in 1829, he worked with Jacob Beam to change it. The two chose Mount Eaton, the village's name today.[3]

Cholera Comes to Mount Eaton

Sadly, in 1833, about one-tenth of Mount Eaton's growing population was wiped out by a cholera epidemic in the village. In August of that year, a family of French immigrants by the name of Brownstine (sometimes Beaverstine) arrived in the village. According to village histories, the Brownstines had the body of their deceased child in their wagon when they first rode into Mount Eaton. The child had succumbed to cholera and still carried the contagion. A local man named David Boyd, who was particularly intoxicated at the time "strutted up to the wagon to see how a cholera victim would look, was soon attacked and died that evening." Soon many residents left Mount Eaton in an attempt to flee the disease. Fortunately, the epidemic ended before it took out all of Mount Eaton. Unfortunately, the final victim of the outbreak was James Galbraith, the village founder.[4]

Dancing and the Dutch War

The ill-fated Brownstines were not the only French family to settle in Mount Eaton. In 1835, a Frenchman named Joseph Boigegrain built a store in the village. Boigegrain often held dances on the store's second floor. It is said that one man once bet that he could dance an entire waltz in wooden shoes at the Boigegrain store without making a "clatter." According to town histories, he won this bet.[5]

Boigegrain wasn't the only one hosting Mount Eaton dances in the early years. In fact, dances were also held at Stinebruner's Grocery, where it seems liquor was also available. One particular dance at Stinebruner's has never been forgotten.[6] In 1844, many of the residents of Mount Eaton could claim either a French or Dutch ancestry. One evening at Stinebruner's, a dance was attended by members of each of these groups. According to village histories, the Dutch became aggressive toward the French, and a brawl began. As one account records, "windows were smashed in and knocked out, teeth were violently jarred from unwilling jaws, many were badly bruised and wounded, and some shooting was done." Luckily, the authorities arrived on time, and the brief "Dutch War" came to a ceasefire without any casualties.[7]

The Mount Eaton Bank

In 1919, a man named John Villard opened a bank in Mount Eaton. During the mid-twentieth century, the independent bank merged with the First National Bank of Orrville-Dalton, now Farmers National Bank. In 1970, Villard's original building was torn down to make more room for the village firehouse. However, a branch of Farmers National Bank was relocated and still operates in Mount Eaton.[8]

In an almost comical chain of events, the bank was robbed in 1920, only about a year after it had opened. On October 7, 1920, poor Edmund Ruch, a cashier at the bank, was locked in a bank vault. Two bandits took about $600 from cash boxes on the counter and then locked Ruch away, apparently not caring to take any cash from the vault as they did so. According to witnesses outside the bank, who were unaware that something illegal had transpired, the bandits calmly got in their car and drove away.[9] Apparently, Ruch remained locked in the vault almost an hour before someone called a repairman about the "unusual noise."[10]

Lightning Strikes in Mount Eaton

Unfortunately, in May of 1982, lightning struck St. Paul United Church of Christ in Mount Eaton, causing a fire that destroyed the building. The fire went unnoticed at first, but eventually fire crews were called in from around the area to deal with the huge blaze. The firemen had to fight the fire over 12 hours. The church was left in ruin. Residents were able to salvage books, church records (dating to the village's early days), furniture, a piano, and the baptismal font. However, these items no longer had a home.[11]

A crew was hired to remove the stained glass windows and bell from the church and to tear the rest of the building down. The community worked together to clean up the site, taking time to enjoy a time capsule that had been placed in the church. Services were held at the local school gym while new construction began. Fortunately, by Christmas Eve of 1982, the congregation of St. Paul's had a brand-new building. As one history recorded, "Bare bulbs hung on loose wires from holes in the ceiling where fixtures had yet to be installed. Unframed windows still carried their shipping stickers and aromas of fresh plaster and sawdust were heavy." But the congregation of Mount Eaton was simply happy to be home.[12]

James Akey Farm is not far from Mount Eaton. Placed on the National Register of Historic Places, this farmstead reflects the experience of early immigrant families. Many of the buildings on this farm have been reconstructed, but one original, a stone house built by Akey after he immigrated from Ireland in 1822, remains.[14]

TOP: The Elizabeth House Mansion Museum

Population: 445   **Incorporated:** 1814

INSETS L to R: Quaker Yearly Meeting House • Freedom Square
in the center of town • Evangelical Friends Church • One of the
many historic buildings of Mount Pleasant

On October 7, 1856, Moses Fleetwood Walker was born in Mount Pleasant, Ohio. As a young man, he attended Oberlin College as well as the University of Michigan Law School. While at Oberlin, Walker played on the varsity baseball team. In 1883, he was offered a spot with the Toledo Blue Stockings. When the Blue Stockings joined the American Association in 1884, Walker became the first African-American player to play major league baseball. His brother, Weldy, was the second. The Walker brothers remained the only African-American players to have entered the major leagues until Jackie Robinson broke this barrier again in 1947.[16]

Mount Pleasant

Moving to Ohio

WITH THE PASSAGE OF THE NORTHWEST ORDINANCE in 1787, the United States declared slavery off-limits in the Northwest Territory. At the time, the territory represented the unknown frontier for white Americans. Despite the risks associated with moving to this new land, the outlawing of slavery made the Northwest Territory attractive for many adamantly abolitionist Quaker communities. Many Quakers began to move west during the late 1790s.[1]

In 1800, settlers from North Carolina established the first major Quaker community in eastern Ohio, in what is now Short Creek Township, of Jefferson County. Another group of white settlers, Presbyterians rather than Quakers, had already settled in the area, but the two groups happily shared the space. In 1803, Jesse Thomas, a Quaker man, and Robert Carothers, a Presbyterian, laid out a town in this new settlement. They gave the town their own names, christening it Jesse-Bob Town. Early settlers quickly changed the name to Mount Pleasant.[2]

The Center of Quaker Life in Eastern Ohio

Mount Pleasant quickly became the center of Quaker life in eastern Ohio. The new settlers in the Mount Pleasant area established three new monthly meetings. These were smaller faith groups, meant to meet with more frequency and provide strong local support. In 1807, these groups formed the Short Creek Quarterly Meeting, coming together a few times a year to address common interests.[3]

Unfortunately, for yearly meetings, the new residents of Mount Pleasant still had to trek all the way to Baltimore. This was quite the journey, but a yearly meeting wasn't established west of the Alleghenies. Quakers in eastern Ohio began to petition for permission to establish a new meeting in their area. In 1813, the petitions were successful, and the first Ohio Yearly Meeting was held.[4]

The first act of the meeting was to design a building for future yearly meetings. Reverend Jacob Ong was hired as the architect, and Mount Pleasant was chosen as the official location. Ong's design mirrored other meeting houses around the country. Despite the familiar architecture, the final building was still awe-inspiring simply for its gigantic size. The brick building housed up to 2,000 people and boasted perfect acoustics. Separate doors and galleries were built for men and women, with a balcony above for children. The meeting house cost $12,345 to build.[5]

The first meeting in the Mount Pleasant Yearly Meeting House was held in 1814. Each August, thousands of Quaker families from around eastern Ohio flocked to the village for the yearly meeting. This gathering soon took on the feeling of an annual fair or a family reunion. Visitors crowded the homes of their families and friends, often sleeping half a dozen to a room, with young children pushed out into the barn. Teenagers were seen late into the night, as new romances filled the air. This behavior was deemed to be "little becoming of the occasion" but somehow continued year after year, like a rite of passage.[6]

Abolitionists in Mount Pleasant

From the earliest days of incorporation, the village of Mount Pleasant was an abolitionist hotspot. Beginning in the 1810s, homes in Mount Pleasant served as stations on the Underground Railroad.[7] The village was also a safe place for free blacks to reside. In fact, the village was even home to a school where free black children could receive an education.[8] In 1817, Charles Osborn of Mount Pleasant began the first anti-slavery newspaper, known as the *Philanthropist*.[9]

One of the frequent contributors to the *Philanthropist* was a man named Benjamin Lundy. Lundy came to Ohio in 1807, where he formed the first anti-slavery organization in the state, the Union Humane Society. Lundy came to Mount Pleasant around 1821 so that he could work on publishing *Genius of Universal Emancipation*, a monthly abolitionist publication. Lundy left in by 1823, but his home continued to serve an important abolitionist purpose.[10]

In 1848, residents of Mount Pleasant formed what they called the Mount Pleasant Free Produce Company of Ohio. This new business was based in part of Lundy's former home.[11] All products sold at the resulting store were "obtained through such channels as will give every attainable degree of certainty that they are clear of the products of slave labor."[12]

Unfortunately, the Free Produce Company never saw financial success. In 1857, the stockholders voted to dissolve the company. As one history points out, it is also possible that the stockholders began to embrace the "growing conviction, especially after 1845, that political action was going to be the only solution [to] slavery."[13]

A Village Preserved

Today much of the village provides a trip back in time. Thanks to the effort of the Historical Society of Mount. Pleasant, the meeting house has been preserved, as have a handful of other historic buildings; today the Mount Pleasant Historical Society offers regular tours for visitors.[14] History is palpable in Mount Pleasant, especially on Union Street, where many of the preserved buildings are located. In 1974, the National Register of Historic Places placed the entire neighborhood on the historic register.[15]

In the 1840s, John W. Gill ran a silk factory in town. It operated for only five years, but it was influential. The factory created a vest for U.S. Senator Henry Clay, who encouraged the government to hire Gill to create a silk flag for Caleb Cushing to carry on the U.S.'s first diplomatic mission to China.[17]

TOP: A train car on the edge of the village serves as a monument to Murray City's coal mining history

Population: 440   **Incorporated:** 1891

INSETS L to R: A local F.O.E. Lodge, which often serves as a social center for Murray City • The Snow Fork Creek runs through the center of the village • The Murray City Coal Mine Museum and History Center • Murray City's coal mining past has almost permanently changed the color of the water that runs off the Snow Fork Creek

During the 1920s, Murray City was home to a semipro football team known as the Murray City Tigers. The team was mostly made up of coal miners who practiced when the work day was done, running plays by the glow of traffic lights, as village officials rerouted traffic. The Tigers were quite the success, winning about 80 percent of their games. The village residents were huge fans, even organizing a special train on the Hocking Valley Railway to travel to Columbus for big games.[12]

Murray City

A Village Built for Mining

AS THE 1870s DAWNED, anticipation grew in Ohio's Hocking River Valley. Previously a sparsely inhabited region, the area blossomed when miners arrived to help excavate the profitable coal that lay beneath the surface. Many locals had been aware of the coal for some time, and when demand for coal increased, entrepreneurs finally decided to do something with the coal of the Hocking region. Many new villages and towns sprang up to support coal mines.[1]

One of them was Murray City, named for its founder, Murray Brown. Around 1875, Brown began laying out the village and corresponding plans for a coal mine. He even built a hotel, anticipating a large influx of business and travel to his new village. Unfortunately,

Brown's start-up capital ran dry, and he abandoned his new village. Not long after, a fire claimed the hotel, the one remaining vestige of Brown's efforts.[2]

Around 1885, Greendale Company, a coal-mining business, took advantage of the village Murray Brown had laid out and opened a mine in Murray City. New residents began to flood in, with hopes of working at Mine No. 7. Even young boys, not yet in high school, began to work in the mines. In 1891, the village of Murray City was officially incorporated. Many of the villages in the area were run by coal businesses; however, this decision to incorporate allowed the residents of Murray City a different kind of autonomy. Perhaps not coincidentally, many leaders of Hocking Valley mining unions came from Murray City.[3]

At the height of the coal boom in the Hocking Valley, Murray City supported more than 2,000 people, a handful of mines, and a stop on the Hocking Valley Railway. The village benefited from the railroad's trade and incoming travel, and in exchange, the railway was able to easily pick up the coal for its engines.[4]

"It Was A Great Place to Grow Up"

Unfortunately, as the coal-mining industry faded in the region, so did Murray City. In 1937, the final mine in Murray City closed. Throughout the middle of the twentieth century, the village's population dwindled. Businesses followed, and as one longtime resident observed, there is now "just nothing, nothing here." As residents left, the population began to age, and there are few children in Murray City to help grow the village in a new generation.[5]

To complicate matters, coal mining has harmed the village's natural landscape. The Snow Fork Creek, which runs through much of the village, has almost permanently adopted a brown-orange hue from the mines' acid runoff. With a small taxpaying population, the village council is struggling to find the funding to put in a sewer system, let alone begin to deal with this environmental legacy.[6]

But longtime residents of Murray City don't want to give up. When interviewed, Rosemarie Pancake, a member of a multi-generational Murray City family, recognized the village's problems, but almost in the same breath recalled, "it was a great place to grow up."[7]

The Legacy of Jack Shuttleworth

One man in Murray City has decided to move forward by preserving the past. Jack Shuttleworth, now in his 80s, has lived in Murray City since he was a young man. When he noticed an interest in mining history from locals and passersby, he began to form a personal collection of historic mining artifacts from the area. Today these artifacts are displayed in the Murray City Coal Mine Museum & History Center, a small white building that Shuttleworth leases for one dollar a year.[8] As Shuttleworth told one interviewer, "If they are rather interested in this equipment, why not start a museum?"[9]

The museum includes many artifacts, including mining equipment, Murray City basketball uniforms, birdcages from the canaries in the coal mine, and family scrapbooks. One interesting set of photographs in the museum had never even been developed until Shuttleworth took an interest. In 2009, Shuttleworth purchased a unique film canister at an estate sale. Murray City resident Gene Six had taken photographs while serving in Germany during World War II, but he had deposited the negatives in this canister and never bothered to have them developed. Shuttleworth developed the film and today the photographs are on display in his museum.[10]

Unfortunately, in 2017, Jack Shuttleworth was in a car accident that affected his memory, making it hard to continue to tell the museum's stories. Luckily a friend, Donnie Cook, has taken an interest and now curates the museum for Shuttleworth. Cook is quick to state that he does not know the stories as well as Shuttleworth. Jack often hosted students on field trips from the nearby Ohio University. He would tell the stories of Murray City and even demonstrate mining equipment for the students. However, it is fortunate that someone has continued to curate his collection, keeping the history of Murray City for its future residents.[11]

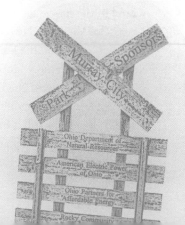

In 1904, Murray City residents opened a co-op. By 1907, about 65 individuals owned stock in the company, with shares valued at $25 and limited to four per person. Customers could buy everything from groceries and furnishings to shoes. The co-op was managed by an R. J. Pinnick, originally of West Virginia.

TOP: Neville Free Will Baptist Church

Population: 107   Approx. Founding: 1808

INSETS L to R: A historic sign welcoming visitors to Neville now hangs in a resident's yard • The Neville Post Office • Misfitland HQ, a monkey rescue in Neville • The Neville Cemetery

In the past decade, many small towns in Ohio have faced the same decision Neville confronted in 2016: find funding or cease to exist. Many of these small towns are left to the nearest township for support, but it is unclear if the townships are ready to take on the responsibility. As a Washington Township trustee told a Cincinnati news outlet in 2016, "We are going to accept the responsibility, we will take care of them, but there's more on our plate now." As more small towns are forced to dissolve across the state, this issue of responsibility will continue to play out from city to city.[11]

Neville

General Presley Neville

IN THE EARLY 1800s, GENERAL PRESLEY NEVILLE, well known for his service during the Revolutionary War, acquired 45 acres of land in the new state of Ohio as a reward for his military service for the state of Virginia. He commissioned a man named Jonathan Taylor to lay out a town on the land in 1808; it was named Neville. In 1812, Neville acquired more land, growing the village.[1]

At first, General Neville was actually a resident of Pennsylvania, by way of Virginia. Neville was born in Winchester, Virginia, in 1755, while the state was still a British colony. Neville had just enough time to finishing his schooling at the University of Pennsylvania before the American Revolution began. Still calling Virginia his home, Presley

Neville enlisted. He served closely with General Marquis de Lafayette, and the two, only a few years apart in age, formed a close friendship. Neville served for the entirety of the war, at one point even spending time as a prisoner of war.[2]

Presley Neville's father, John Neville, was a prominent early American. Consequently, Presley Neville followed in his footsteps after the Revolutionary War. After marrying Nancy Morgan, daughter of General Daniel Morgan, Neville moved with his wife to land in western Pennsylvania that his father owned. The family ended up in Allegheny County, and eventually in the new city of Pittsburgh.[3]

Presley Neville became interested in land speculation while in Pittsburgh. He served as the land-office surveyor of Allegheny County,

Pennsylvania. Unfortunately for Neville, most of the county had already been surveyed. Because of this, Neville sought land in different counties. He used his place in the land office to work as a land agent for men interested in purchasing frontier properties. Neville would help acquire the land patent, and in some cases, helped manage the land. Eventually Neville became interested in trying his own hand at speculation. Neville purchased large portions of land and sold it to new settlers to turn a profit. He became so involved in this land speculation that it is impossible to ascertain exactly how much land Neville owned.[4]

In 1791, the Neville family became involved in one of early American history's best-remembered events: the Whiskey Rebellion. In order to pay the debts accrued during the American Revolution, the new government, under the leadership of President George Washington, passed a tax on distilled spirits. Many Americans weren't pleased with this decision, and protests began. Protestors in western Pennsylvania had a particular issue with the Neville family, as John Neville, Presley's father, was a local tax collector. John Neville's home, known as Bower Hill, was burned to the ground, and Presley was taken prisoner. Eventually the new federal government put down the rebellion, and Presley Neville returned to his very comfortable life in Pennsylvania, where he shaped much of the early development of Pittsburgh and Pennsylvania.[5]

In the early 1800s, Presley Neville's frequent land speculation on the American frontier fell into a downward spiral. Like many other land speculators, Presley Neville found himself in bankruptcy. Neville owed a significant amount of money and had to sell off his lands to make his payments. However, luckily for Neville, he did own one debt-free piece of land in Ohio: the village of Neville. Around 1816, embarrassed by his financial hardships, Presley Neville moved his family to a small log home in the village where he lived out the rest of his days. He died there in 1818, and his body was transferred back to Pittsburgh for burial.[6]

Generations of Flooding

Throughout its history, Neville has flooded frequently, including in 1884, 1913, and 1937. One resident, Emily Camery Leslie, remembered seeking refuge from a flood in the village schoolhouse that her grandfather built in 1883. The residents slept in the schoolhouse, lying side by side with their neighbors, many unable to fall asleep. The village was also forced to store the residents' furniture in the schoolhouse to keep it safe. Mrs. Leslie recalled that "One room was full of pianos…and I remember the noise when they started floating and hitting each other and hitting glass and breaking it."[7]

Most recently a flood tore apart the village of Neville in 1997, leading about 50 percent of the villagers to leave. This huge decrease in population has led to a decrease in funding, especially from the state of Ohio. For this reason, voters in Neville were faced with a tough choice in March of 2016. The residents of Neville had to decide if their village should be dissolved and absorbed by Washington Township.[8]

Only about half of Neville's registered voters cast a ballot on this measure, with 19 voting against dissolution and 11 in favor. These 19 votes saved the village, allowing Neville to remain incorporated. Those who voted against the measure cited interest in the small-town way of life. One voter told the *Clermont Sun*, "They have plenty of funds available for the state of Ohio, they're just trying to close down all the little towns," and another stated, "We're losing so many little villages in this state; I want it to stay the same." However, those who voted in favor recognized Neville's financial struggles, noting that the village just cannot continue to afford the small-town life residents enjoy. As state funding continues to be cut and the population remains low, it is unclear what Neville's fate will be.[9]

During the late 1930s, the Neville Ladies Auxiliary held dances that paid for a very short-lived fire department. Unfortunately, in the late 1970s, the historic schoolhouse, the site of these dances, was damaged by an unknown arsonist. The building, which cost $4,800 to build in 1883, required approximately $20,000 worth of repairs.[10]

INSETS L to R: New Haven United Methodist Church • The New Haven Post Office • The Art Junction • A street in New Haven

When Almon Ruggles and his team arrived in Ohio to survey the Firelands, they were met with a marshy wilderness. They were almost completely alone as they worked, having to travel hours or days just to reach the closest trading post in the city of Huron (today about a 30-minute drive from New Haven). New Haven and many nearby areas are naturally covered in marshlands (see Celeryville page 28, for more on this environment). This meant horses walking away to escape mosquitoes and rattlesnakes appearing on the ground. It's a miracle Ruggles and his crew were able to finish their task![16]

TOP: An outpost of the Huron County Sheriff's Office in New Haven

New Haven

A Revolutionary Beginning

THE HISTORY OF THE VILLAGE OF NEW HAVEN, Huron County, Ohio, began in the state of Connecticut during the American Revolution. In July of 1779, more than four years into the war, General George Washington was entrenched at West Point, New York. Wanting to draw Washington and his men out for battle, and hoping to destroy important supply lines, General Henry Clinton of the British Army ordered a raid on coastal Connecticut.[1]

On July 5, Ezra Stiles, President of Yale College (now University) in New Haven, Connecticut, stood in the steeple of the university's chapel with a telescope, watching British boats arrive in the harbor. Rumors of the invasion had begun to spread that summer, and Stiles had sent many of his students to safety in more-inland towns.[2]

General William Tryon and his 2,600 men tore through New Haven, burning supplies and the homes and businesses of innocent locals.[3] Terrible stories of torture and pillaging were told by the residents of New Haven after the attack.[4] After the destruction of New Haven, Tryon moved on to the cities of Fairfield and Norwalk. Finally, Connecticut militiamen were able to mount a defense at Norwalk and force a retreat. Tryon and his men failed to distract General Washington, but they destroyed swathes of Connecticut.[5]

The men and women of New Haven didn't go down without a fight. The only organized militiamen in the city were the Second Company, Governor's Foot Guard, under the leadership of Captain James Hillhouse. Hillhouse's men were vastly outnumbered. Many able-bodied men quickly came to their aid, including many young men studying at

Yale University.[6] Future Vice President Aaron Burr rallied a group of these university students and marched with them into battle.[7]

When New Haven was attacked, many loyalist residents of the city, still hoping the British might win the war, stayed inside and didn't contest the invasion. After the burning of Connecticut, and loyalist and patriot houses alike, most of these loyalists became patriots. These changes in allegiance ultimately damaged the British war effort.[8]

The Firelands

In 1786, as the United States government began to organize the Northwest Territory, many of the original colonies ceded land in the area to the federal government. However, the state of Connecticut reserved the northeastern portion of the future state of Ohio. This land was aptly named the "Western Reserve." Most of this land was sold to investors, but about 500,000 acres of the westernmost portion were allocated for those who were subjected to Tryon's raid during the war.[9]

The Connecticut Western Reserve as a whole remained unsettled, largely due to conflicts between white settlers and American Indians. In 1805, near present-day Toledo, Ohio, the Treaty of Fort Industry was signed. In exchange for annual payments, members of the Wyandot, Ottawa, Ojibwe, Munsee, Lenape, Potawatomi, and Shawnee were removed from about half a million acres of land in Ohio.[10] Soon after, the Connecticut Western Reserve was officially surveyed and plots prepared to be assigned to land claimants via a lottery system.

The land delegated to the victims of the raids was known as the Fire Lands (later combined to simply one word, Firelands), since the raids had burned the Connecticut cities to the ground. Unfortunately, many actual survivors never made it to the Firelands. The land wasn't actually approved for use until 1808, and by then many survivors had either sold their land claims or passed away.[11]

Early New Haven

The Firelands grew slowly, as the War of 1812 soon distracted possible settlers. As the war ended, new villages began to pop up. In 1815, David and Royal N. Powers drew up a plat for the first village in Huron County, known as New Haven. The plat was modeled after the original New Haven.

One of the first settlers in the New Haven, Ohio, area was Caleb Palmer. Palmer, along with his wife and two children, first settled in Ohio in 1811. Palmer is hard to trace; some sources actually report that he destroyed many of his own papers, not wishing to leave his story to history. Palmer and his family lived through some harrowing moments during the War of 1812, constantly worried that American Indians aligned with the British Army could attack their home. Many sources agree that another historical figure, John Chapman, known to many as Johnny Appleseed, lived with the Palmer family during much of the War of 1812.[12]

The village of New Haven was officially incorporated at the end of the 1830s. As the first village in Huron County, it had great potential. Many travelers stopped through the village, as it was located on a route to Lake Erie.[13] Unfortunately, a decision was made in 1843 that would forever relegate New Haven to small-town status.

In the 1840s, the Sandusky, Mansfield, and Newark Railroad intended to lay track through New Haven, but the railway company expected a financial contribution. Local tavern owners were concerned that a railway would hurt their business, which was largely based on traveling coaches. Furthermore, an influential resident, Judge Ives, insisted that the railway inevitably had to come through town, but the railroad chose to locate elsewhere. The New Haven economy never recovered.[14]

The village of New Haven is part of the larger New Haven Township. In 2017, a township resident ensured that his 105 acres of farmland will be reserved for agriculture forever. The Land Conservancy registered an agricultural easement on property owned by Gene Kurzen. Kurzen plants about 90 acres of his land, but other sections help prevent erosion on the Huron River.[15]

TOP: The New Riegel Cafe in downtown New Riegel

Population: 237　**Incorporated:** 1883

INSETS L to R: Businesses in New Riegel • The historic All Saints Catholic Church • St. Boniface Cemetery, adjacent to the All Saints Catholic Church • A mill in New Riegel

During New Riegel's early years, the village government did everything it could to limit the perceived ill effects of the local saloons. Due to the village's strong religious background, from 1883 to 1888, all saloons and stores were banned from selling liquor from 9 a.m. to 12 p.m., 2 p.m. to 3 p.m., or after 7 p.m. on Sundays. This convoluted language attempted to ensure that no liquor was sold during a church service in the village. These laws never quite stopped the handful of village saloons that continued to turn a profit in New Riegel.[18]

New Riegel

A Settlement on Wolf's Creek

UNTIL 1832, what would become Big Spring Township of Seneca County, Ohio, was a reservation for the Wyandot.[1] During the late 1700s and early 1800s, encroaching white American settlers forced the Wyandot and many other American Indian nations to abandon their homes in the Ohio Territory. While these white settlers spread out across the new state of Ohio, American Indian communities were forced to live in small token spaces that were left over. Soon, even these reservations were at risk. In 1843, the Wyandot people were permanently removed from the state of Ohio.[2]

Soon thereafter, the land quickly went up for sale to white settlers. In September of 1833, a man named Anthony Schindler arrived in Big Spring

Township, emigrating from his birthplace in Germany. He settled in area known as Wolf's Creek. The name was literal; there was a creek and it was frequently surrounded by wolves. In fact, there were so many wolves that Seneca County officials offered six dollars for each wolf shot.[3]

Schindler was soon followed to Ohio by other residents of Riegel, Germany. While the community they lived in was still occasionally colloquially known as Wolf's Creek, the settlers took on the official name of New Riegel as a tribute to their original home.[4] In 1850, Schindler hired G. H. Heming to survey the area around Wolf's Creek, building a village from the plat he received. By 1882, the village was incorporated.[5]

Father Francis de Sales Brunner Arrives in New Riegel

The founding families of the village were largely devout Catholics. In 1836, the settlers built a log church in their new community, complete with a school. The church was known as St. Boniface. Unfortunately, services could not be offered each week, as there were not enough German-speaking priests available in the area. Traveling priests served large territories of the new state, giving services when they could. One of the priests who served the area was Father Francis de Sales Brunner.[6]

Brunner was born in Switzerland, the son of Maria Anna Brunner, an influential force in the Catholic faith.[7] In 1815, a man named Gaspar del Bufalo (now a saint) founded a Catholic missionary society in Italy that he called the Congregation of the Missionaries of the Most Precious Blood. In 1834, one of his followers, Maria Anna Brunner, founded a sister organization in Switzerland, the Sisters of the Precious Blood, allowing women to participate in Bufalo's ministry.[8]

Father Francis de Sales Brunner followed in his mother's footsteps. In 1843, Brunner met Bishop Purcell of Cincinnati, Ohio, while Purcell was traveling through German-speaking countries in Europe, looking for priests who might minister to the German immigrants in Ohio. Brunner agreed to help and brought other priests with him. Brunner quickly took to New Riegel, and he began to build what he thought would be a headquarters for the Missionaries of the Most Precious Blood in the village. However, Purcell told Brunner that he would prefer a convent for the women of the order Brunner's mother founded. Brunner swiftly changed his plans, and by 1844, the convent was complete.[9] On Christmas Eve, 1844, the convent, named "Mary at the Crib," was finally occupied by the Sisters of the Most Precious Blood. As their nightly vigils began, the six sisters marked the opening of the first convent of their order in the United States.

The Sisters of the Most Precious Blood

The convent in New Riegel, growing quickly past its original six inhabitants, was completely self-sufficient. The sisters were active farmers, gardeners, and artisans. They economically supported themselves, and occasionally other village residents who they employed on the convent's farm. The sisters also took in many orphans and opened their own school.[10] In 1860, a new convent was built. The sisters helped to craft and transport its bricks. Eventually the sisters began teaching in the public schools of New Riegel, until 1976.[11]

Unfortunately, in 1979, due to decreased numbers, the sisters had to leave the convent, selling the building in 1980.[12] In 2001, a fire destroyed the building, removing an important part of New Riegel's history.[13]

Modern Landmarks

Today one of the most visible landmarks in the village of New Riegel is the towering All Saints Church. First dedicated in May 1878 as St. Boniface, it was an upgrade from the original log cabin the settlers had built.[14] In 2005, St. Boniface joined with a number of other churches in the area to worship together in this building as the new parish of All Saints.[15]

One of the other well-known landmarks of modern New Riegel is the New Riegel Cafe, known for its barbecue ribs and chicken. The restaurant was first opened in 1953 by W. J. "Pete" Boes, a former Army cook who served during World War II. After the war, he eventually turned to the restaurant business, experimenting with barbecue recipes. Demand grew for Boes's delicious concoctions, and his business expanded.[16]

In addition to delectable barbecue, the New Riegel Cafe serves an interesting type of meat known as New Riegel bologna. In the early 1900s, this bologna, first made by the Smith family, was a common sight in village stores and saloons. It is essentially a "highly spiced, old-fashioned sausage."[17]

Residents of New Riegel have maintained a connection to their roots in Germany. Many residents have visited Riegel, Germany, over the years. Just after World War II, the mayor of Riegel made a special request. That year, residents collected clothes and supplies for their German counterparts and shipped them overseas.[19]

TOP: A mill overlooks New Weston's community park

Population: 130 **Approx. Founding:** 1880s

INSETS L to R: New Weston Community Hall • A busy weekend at Eldora Speedway • A mural in New Weston shows what the town once looked like • A mural and fresh fall apples at Harry Birt's Store

In 1921, residents of New Weston had to work together to save their town from going up in flames. An overheated stove at Luebking Grocery and Hardware store started a blaze that threatened to destroy all of the businesses in the main part of town. Residents quickly formed a bucket brigade and were able to stop the flames. The grocery and the adjoining Peters Hotel could not be saved, but many businesspeople were likely thankful to their neighbors for rescuing their livelihoods.[19]

New Weston

The Cincinnati Northern Railroad

THE VILLAGE OF NEW WESTON, like many of its neighbors in Allen Township of Darke County, was formed thanks to the construction of a new railroad. During the early 1880s, construction began on the Cincinnati Northern rail line. Homes and businesses built up along the new railway, leading to the settlement of New Weston.[1]

For some residents of New Weston, the railroad that ran through their town was a source of employment. In 1910, around the age of 22, Harry W. Randall began working for the rail line as a fireman.[2] As a fireman, Randall was responsible for keeping the fire onboard the locomotive's engine going. Randall fed the flames that fueled the engine of the train during the entire ride, often working closely with the engineer to monitor the controls and operate the train.[3]

In 1914, just four years into his career, Randall received a certification that enabled him to be promoted to an engineer. However, before he could receive this promotion, disaster struck.[4] In the first days of August 1914, Randall and an engineer by the name of A. L. Baldwin were working on the Cincinnati Northern rail line, running a passenger train through Hudson, Michigan. Randall was firing the engine when they hit a broken rail. Randall and Baldwin were thrown from the train into a nearby field. Baldwin, 60 years old and likely nearing his retirement, was found dead. Randall was ailing, with a broken collarbone and a head wound. Luckily for the four passengers on board, their train cars stayed upright. The passengers helped to load Randall and Baldwin into waiting cars.[5]

As Randall was moved to a more comfortable situation, the Cincinnati Northern Railroad sent a special train car to carry his parents from New Weston to his bedside in Michigan. Unfortunately, after twelve hours of suffering from his injuries, Randall passed away.[6]

Randall was taken to New Weston for a funeral and then buried in nearby Ansonia.[7] Unfortunately, the dangers of railroad work took Randall from his family while he was only in his mid-twenties. However, Randall was not forgotten in New Weston. When Harry Randall died, his brother and sister-in-law, Hollis and Vera, were expecting a child. According to census records, the baby, born in February of 1915, was named Harry, just like his uncle.

Eldora Comes to New Weston

In 1954, a man named Earl Baltes, ignoring the worries of his friends and family, began excavating a cornfield in New Weston to build what would become an internationally known racetrack. Baltes had seen a race at the New Bremen Speedway in Auglaize County, and he had become convinced he could also make money on auto racing.[8]

Baltes called his dirt track Eldora Speedway. The quarter-mile track slowly grew over its earliest years, expanding to three-eighths of a mile in 1956, and finally settling at half a mile in 1958. During the late 1950s, Baltes himself took to racing on the half-mile track, despite the fact that he had no experience in the sport. However, Baltes's racing career did not last long. One moment on the track convinced him to leave the driver's seat forever. As the *Hamilton Journal-News* reported, "He was running third when the two cars ahead of him touched and rolled. Baltes made it through the wreck, pulled into the pits and sold his car on the spot. He vowed to never race again."[9]

In 1962, the United States Auto Club (USAC) began racing at Eldora, bringing fans from the entire country with them. Baltes was always known as a skilled promoter, but in the 1970s, he really started upping the bar when he created the World 100, a 100-lap race every dirt track racer wanted desperately to win.[10] This race, first run in 1971, started with a $3,000 prize, and each year the prize grew by $1,000.[11] As NASCAR driver Tony Stewart said of Baltes, "He constantly raised the bar, and he did it by creating events everyone else was afraid to promote."[12]

The World 100 still runs today. Of all the winners over the years, Ohio drivers still hold the top spot with 11 combined wins (followed by Tennessee with 9).[13] The speedway includes 17,782 seats, but it often must accommodate more viewers on the grassy hillside looking down onto the track.[14] Dirt racing fans from all over the country still get excited for this race. As Earl Baltes himself said, "The World 100 is special. Why? I can't tell you exactly, not in words. But it's just the most prestigious, most competitive, most difficult, most exciting event in Dirt Late Model racing. Boy, I love that race."[15]

In 2004, Earl Baltes placed a personal call to Tony Stewart, asking him to drive three hours from his home in Indiana for a conversation. It was during this talk that Baltes asked Stewart to take over the speedway. Stewart took Baltes up on his offer, but he kept the early founder active in Eldora Speedway.[16] Today a life-size statue of Baltes and his wife, Bernice, stands in the entrance of the speedway. Baltes passed away in 2015 at the age of 93, but racing continues in earnest at Eldora.[17]

In 2001, Earl Baltes really had everyone in New Weston talking when he decided to offer a $1 million dollar prize to the winner of a 100-lap race at Eldora Speedway. The race, known as the Eldora Million, was won by newly minted millionaire Donnie Moran.[18]

TOP: St. Louis Catholic Church, now on the National Register

Population: 226   **Approx. Founding:** 1852

INSETS L to R: North Star Park • The North Star Post Office • A sign outside the North Star Fire Department warns residents to watch for farm equipment and motorcycles • Community baseball fields at North Star Park

St. Louis Catholic Church, located in the village of North Star, was added to the National Register of Historic Places during the 1970s, due to its unique architecture. Built during the early 1900s, this church is part of a region of western Ohio known as the "Land of Cross-Tipped Churches." From the mid-1800s until the early 1900s, many churches were built in this region of the state to serve white Catholic settlers. Today the steeples and bell towers of these churches still characterize the local landscape.[15]

North Star

Darke County's Famous Daughter

IN 1852, IN DARKE COUNTY, near the western edge of the state of Ohio, the village of North Star was laid out. It is believed the village was named for its location at the top of the Great Black Swamp. The village also occupies the northernmost part of Darke County that is not also a wetland.[1] Not long after North Star was laid out, its most famous resident was born just a few miles east, between the villages of Woodland (now the unincorporated village of Willowdell) and North Star.[2]

On August 13, 1860, Jacob and Susan Moses welcomed their fourth daughter into the world inside the four walls of a log cabin. They named the girl Phoebe Ann, but, because her older sisters preferred the name Annie, the name Phoebe never stuck.[3] As an adult, Annie Moses

would keep the first name but adopt a last name for the stage. Before her 30th birthday, she would become the internationally known sharpshooter Annie Oakley.[4]

One day, early in 1866, Annie's father loaded up his wagon with corn and wheat to take it to a local mill, about 14 miles from the family cabin. He also intended to stop at the local general store to stock up the family's pantry. After he left, Ohio's rough winter winds picked up, and a large snowstorm covered Darke County. Jacob finally returned at midnight, but as Annie later recalled, "his dear hands had been frozen so he could not use them. His speech was gone." By March 1866, Jacob Moses had passed away.[5]

The Moses family had to move to a smaller farm, as Susan Moses struggled to make ends meet. Annie Moses had always stuck out with her tomboy ways, but luckily for the family, her father had taught her a thing or two about hunting before he passed away. Annie set traps in the woods, where she captured food for her siblings to eat.[6]

It was during this tough time that Annie Moses first fired a rifle. She herself admitted that her memories of the moment had become very romanticized, but as the story goes, Annie was eight years old when she first used her father's rifle to shoot a squirrel in the yard. Annie's mother had always kept her father's rifle above the fireplace in their home. Annie was fascinated with it but had stayed away as her mother had asked. But finally one day, Annie gave into her impulses, grabbed the weapon, fired, and hit the squirrel dead on, with only one shot.[7]

Annie Moses On Her Own

Susan Moses continued to struggle to feed so many children on her own, so at the age of 10, Annie was sent to live at the Darke County Infirmary in Greenville. Not long after her arrival, a family arrived looking to hire a live-in nanny. Annie took on the position, but soon found that the family, whom she called the "Wolves," were abusive employers. Annie was beaten and even left out in the cold where she nearly froze to death.[8] She ran away in 1872, coming back to the Darke County Infirmary, where the superintendent and his wife protected her and offered her a job as a seamstress. Annie made some money, and at 15 was able to move back in with her mother, who was living in North Star.[9]

It was from this home in North Star that Annie Moses's career took off. Annie abandoned her stitching, but she continued to make money for her family, this time through hunting and trapping. During this time period, North Star and Darke County were still largely filled with forested land in which Annie could hunt, wearing her mittens with a trigger finger stitched in. She would send her kills to G. Anthony and Charles Katzenberger, brothers who ran a grocery store in the nearby Greenville. As the story goes, the Katzenberger's customers in

Cincinnati, largely hotelkeepers, preferred Annie's game because she always shot right through the head, keeping any buckshot out of their visitors' meals. Annie also made some money entering shooting competitions, but during her teenage years she was asked to stop entering local contests as she had simply won too many. With her hunting and competing combined, Annie was able to pay off her mother's $200 mortgage on the family home in North Star.[10]

Meeting Frank Butler

In 1875, while visiting her sister Lydia in Cincinnati, Annie Moses took part in one of the most important shooting matches of her life. One of her buyers at a local hotel asked Annie if she would be interested in facing off with a visiting marksman by the name of Frank Butler. Annie accepted the challenge, and she won. Many years later, Frank would recall, "Right then and there I decided if I could get that girl I would do it." The two were married in August 1876.[11]

During the early years of their marriage, Frank was generally on the road performing, while Annie stayed home. However in 1882, Frank's shooting partner fell ill, and he asked Annie to stand in at a performance in Springfield, Ohio. As she said, "I went on with him to hold the objects as he shot, or [so] he thought. But I rebelled." Annie wanted to take her own shots, and the audience was receptive. Soon she took on the name Oakley and became her husband's partner on stage. They joined Buffalo Bill's Wild West Show, leaving North Star behind.[12]

Annie and Frank returned to Darke County in their later years, where Annie passed away in 1926. Annie and Frank are both buried in Brock Cemetery in Greenville.[13] Modern visitors to North Star can find a plaque marking the spot to the east of town where Jacob Moses built the cabin where Annie was born.

It seems North Star has a knack for raising athletes. Craig Stammen, currently a pitcher for the San Diego Padres, was born in the village in 1984. He attended Versailles High School where he stood out as a star athlete, all while helping out his father, Jeff Stammen, at North Star Hardware & Implement Co.[14]

TOP: Norwich Presbyterian Church

Population: 101   **Incorporated:** 1833

INSETS L to R: The National Road and Zane Grey Museum • A village building in Norwich • A headstone marking the final resting place of Christopher Columbus Baldwin in Norwich • Lumi-Lite Candle Company Factory Outlet in Norwich

Former State Representative Chalmers P. Wylie was born in Norwich on November 23, 1920. Wylie went on to study at Otterbein College, The Ohio State University, and Harvard Law School. During his term of higher education, Wylie paused to enlist in the United States military, serving overseas during World War II. Wylie, a Republican, represented his Ohio district in the United States House of Representatives from 1967 to 1993. He passed away in Columbus in 1998 and is buried in Lockbourne (page 102).[17]

Norwich

Capitalizing on the National Road

IN 1827, AN ENGLISHMAN by the name of William Harper purchased a plot of land in Union Township of Muskingum County. He purchased it from a man named John Crawford, and he then laid out a town on the plot. Harper began to plan the town of Norwich, naming it for his own hometown in England. By 1833, Norwich was incorporated and had its first mayor, James Launders, and its first home, a boarding house owned by Samuel McCloud.[1]

A few of the details surrounding the founding of Norwich may seem a bit odd. Why would an Englishman settle in Muskingum County? Why would a brand-new village require a boarding house? To answer both of these questions, we must look to the history of the National Road.

In 1806, the United States Congress passed legislation authorizing the construction of a National Road to connect eastern states to the new western states entering the union. The development began with a long surveying project, and some Americans started to doubt that construction would ever start. As the War of 1812 began, the planning of the National Road was put on hold again, but finally, by 1815, work had begun.[2]

As building commenced, Americans watched the proposed route carefully. Legislators tried shamelessly to encourage federal officials to route the road through towns in their districts. When a surveyor was spotted nearby, a rush of excitement filled American villages, especially in the newest western states, such as Ohio. Land speculators began to purchase large plots where a surveyor had been seen with the hopes of laying out a town on the new road.[3]

Ohioans knew how important the National Road would be for the towns it crossed, as they had already seen villages grow around Zane's Trace. In the late 1700s, following known American Indian trails, Ebenezer Zane felled trees and cleared a rough, but passable, path from Wheeling, Virginia, to Limestone, Kentucky, passing straight through southern Ohio. The road encouraged the growth of trade, western expansion, and the founding of villages along the route.[4]

According to one of Norwich's bygone great collectors of the past, Rollin A. Allen, Mr. William Harper stopped at one of these villages along Zane's Trace in 1827 and began to ask about the plans for the new National Road.[5] Surveying and construction in Ohio had just begun in 1825 and would not finish until 1838.[6] Seeing the economic possibilities in settling near the new road, Harper purchased the future village of Norwich from John Crawford. This plot was directly along the future National Road, making it a common place for travelers to stop. Harper began to clear the land for new homes and settled there himself.[7]

Thanks to the National Road, the village grew quickly. New residents built all of the necessities a traveler could want, from a general store to a boarding house to a tavern. Unfortunately, the town where Harper originally stopped on his journey, Locust Grove, was quickly driven into nonexistence by the new road. The same was true for many communities on Zane's Trace, but those inhabitants often simply moved to the newer villages on the National Road. In fact, Fox McDonald, the postmaster of Locust Grove, simply moved to Norwich and resumed his duties as postmaster of a new village.[8]

Ohio's First Traffic Fatality

As a town built around transportation, it's perhaps not surprising that the village of Norwich was the site of Ohio's first traffic fatality.[9] On August 20, 1835, Christopher Columbus Baldwin, a visitor from the state of Massachusetts, met his end on the National Road as he left town on his way to Zanesville.[10]

In 1835, Baldwin was serving as the librarian of the still-new American Antiquarian Society. In this role he preserved and processed historic papers and artifacts from the early days of the United States, much like an archivist would today. In July of 1835, the American Antiquarian Society raised $150 to send Baldwin to the western United States to research and procure historic artifacts from these areas.[11]

As Harper had predicted, travelers from out of state, including Baldwin, used the village of Norwich as a stopping point on the National Road. After spending time in a local inn, Baldwin decided to travel on to Zanesville. The last entry in his diary reads, "Thursday, August 20, 1835. Set out by stage on the Cumberland Road for Zanesville."[12] (Americans often called the National Road the Cumberland Road, due to its terminus in Cumberland, Maryland.)

Baldwin boarded a stagecoach and asked the driver to take him to his destination. By all reports, the drive was pleasant until a group of hogs appeared on the road. This spooked the horses who began to run off. The driver tried to stop the stagecoach, but the braking mechanism broke right off. Attempting to save himself, Baldwin jumped from the coach, but he was hit by the still-moving vehicle and almost immediately met his end.[13]

Baldwin was buried in Norwich at the Norwich Presbyterian Cemetery. Moved by this story, village historian Rollin Allen decided to better memorialize Baldwin in 1926. As the Scoutmaster of Boy Scout Troop 20, he enlisted his young mentees in the creation of a memorial stone on the site of the accident. He also made efforts to clean the headstone marking Baldwin's grave.[14]

In Norwich, the Ohio History Connection tells the story of the National Road at the National Road & Zane Grey Museum.[15] Across the street, visitors can find the Baker's Motel, a historic building built in the 1930s to accommodate travelers on the National Road (then known as US Route 40).[16]

TOP: A pavilion near the community park welcomes visitors to Octa

Population: 58 **Approx. Founding:** 1876

INSETS L to R: Octa House of Prayer • Octa baseball fields • Octa Town Hall • Benches and green space are plentiful in Octa

When Lawrence Bledsoe first considered his annexation plan, Octa was a wet village in name only. The village had one main market, run by Councilwoman Hazel Gookenbarger and her husband, Mayor G. W. Gookenbarger. But villagers still had to leave Octa if they wanted anything more than a soda. However, the Gookenbargers did not disapprove of Bledsoe's business plan. In fact, his idea was a huge opportunity for the village of Octa. The tax revenue from the hotel could greatly boost village coffers. The residents of Octa celebrated the coming of the Holiday Inn.[14]

Octa

The Many Octas of Allentown

IN 1882, IN A SMALL VILLAGE IN FAYETTE COUNTY known as Allentown, a post office was established, run by the newly minted Postmaster Henry B. Barnes. Barnes's first duty as postmaster? Change the name of his town.[1]

As it turns out, Allentown is a very common name for a city or a village: there have been at least a handful of Allentowns in Ohio, and of course there's the more well-known Allentown, Pennsylvania. This was causing some postal mix-ups for Henry Barnes and his fellow Allentown citizens.[2]

How do you even begin to rename your hometown? This seems like a very big moment for the entire village. However, oddly enough, the renaming of Allentown is only very briefly recognized in most Fayette County histories. The only information that seems to have been recorded is that Allentown took on its new name, Octa, after a Miss Octa Barnes.[3]

But who was Miss Octa Barnes? The most obvious answer seems to be the wife of the postmaster, a Mrs. Octa Vincent Barnes, married to Henry in 1879.[4] If you get to rename your city, why not name it after your wife?

But Mrs. Octa Barnes was not the only Octa in town at the time. In fact, according to census records, another prominent family in Allentown, John and Rebecca Rankin, had just welcomed a new daughter named Octa B. Rankin into the world right around 1882, when the post office name was changed.[5]

Octa was a very small town, never really surpassing 100 people, and it is likely that the Rankin and Barnes family could have been acquaintances. Was baby Octa named for the older Octa Barnes? Was the town named for the Rankins' new child? For the postmaster's wife? Or was it both?

Early Octa

Octa was first laid out in 1876 by Elijah Allen, the man for whom Allentown took its name. William Allen then purchased the very first lot of land, putting up Octa's first building and inaugurating the village. Soon after, John Rankin, Octa B. Rankin's father, opened the first grocery store in 1877. The town grew quickly, hitting a population of 91 by 1910 and accumulating the businesses and necessities that come with a growing town. The town supported multiple general stores, a carpenter, a Methodist church, and even a hotel.[6]

Despite its boom, Octa never grew beyond its small-town nature. In the late 1800s and early 1900s, many counties published official atlases, with landowners noted on a map of each township. In the Fayette County Atlas of 1913, one can find the Village of Octa mapped out in Jasper Township. Spotted across the entire city are the same handful of last names, repeated again and again. Rankin. Allen. Ford. Octa was a village of families.[7]

Both before and after Octa's name change, it served as a main station on various Ohio railroads, including the Dayton and Southeastern Railroad and the Cincinnati, Wooster, & Chicago Railroad.[8] For anyone outside of Octa, this was what the village was known for. In fact, a recently published memoir from a former Octa resident, Robert Steinmetz, is very aptly titled *A Train Ran Through It*.[9]

When looking at the village of Octa on a map today, its shape makes very little sense. It seems to zig and zag awkwardly and resembles a gerrymandered political district, rather than a neatly constructed community. What caused this odd shape?

Octa Grows in the Twentieth Century

In July of 1969, the tiny village of Octa did something more common in big cities: the village annexed a nearby territory. At 12:01 a.m. on July 10, the village of Octa gained about 177.1 acres, 10 citizens, and the potential to double the village's annual revenue.[10]

The original proposal for annexation was actually made by a few nearby residents that were seeking to be annexed by the village of Octa. They had to seek approval from both the Fayette County Commissioners and the Octa Village Council. With some negotiations, an agreement was reached in the spring of 1969, and the village council officially voted yes on the annexation.[11]

The families that lived adjacent to Octa were acting at the suggestion of a man named Lawrence Bledsoe. Bledsoe lived about 30 miles away in the village of Spring Valley, but he owned almost 19 acres of land just outside Octa, near the interchange of Interstate 71 and US Route 35. Bledsoe wanted to develop his land with a brand new Holiday Inn for interstate travelers. Bledsoe hoped that his hotel would include a restaurant, but his land was located in the dry Jefferson Township. He needed Octa, a "wet" village, meaning they legally allowed the sale of liquor, to take on his property if he wanted to serve alcohol in his restaurant.[12]

Unfortunately, the Holiday Inn never came to be. At the end of 1970, the Real Estate Investors Land Corp. of Dayton, Ohio, purchased Bledsoe's land and began to plan for a 120-room motel, a restaurant, and a bank.[13] Not long after their investment, news of Octa's new development disappeared from local newspapers that had been covering the development. Despite the change in plans, Octa still maintains an awkward arm, branching off from the main village to cover Interstate 71.

Unfortunately, in May 1971, the village of Octa lost a resident to the Vietnam War. Sgt. Bruce DeWine, originally of Lima, had made a home in Octa with his wife and young son. DeWine, only 20 years old when he died, was drafted in March 1970. After six weeks in Vietnam, he was a victim of a land mine explosion.[15]

Village of Octa
SUGGESTION BOX

TOP: Old Fort Centennial Park with the Nickel Plate Railroad visible in the background

Population: 186   **Approx. Founding:** 1882

INSETS L to R: Old Fort Church • An original bell outside Old Fort Church • The Old Fort Post Office • The Old Fort Banking Company today

While the village may be unincorporated, Old Fort still maintains its own school district, with a high school in town and an elementary school in nearby Bettsville. Due to a low student count and continuing financial problems, the village of Bettsville merged with the Old Fort District in 2014. The two schools had previously been athletic rivals, but they were able to work together to consolidate. At the time, Old Fort was attempting to raise funds to improve their elementary school; however, consolidation allowed the district to house elementary students in Bettsville while closing the former Old Fort Elementary.[14]

Old Fort

Named for Fort Seneca

THE VILLAGE OF OLD FORT was first platted in 1882 by the Seneca County surveyor. The survey was carried out for R. R. Titus, who owned a large farm in the area. The village was a late bloomer among other towns in Pleasant Township, however with a spot on the Nickel Plate Railroad, there were hopes for success. Villages located on railway stops often blossomed economically, due to visitors and traders passing through.[1] Unfortunately, Old Fort didn't grow as much and remains unincorporated. However, it still maintains a zip code, a post office, and a high school.

The village of Old Fort gets its name from a historic fort that once sat where the village is today. During the War of 1812, General William Henry Harrison (later the ninth U.S. president) oversaw the construction of forts in northwestern Ohio. He used these fortifications to defend against a possible British attack across Lake Erie.[2] Where Old Fort now stands was Fort Seneca (also known as Camp Seneca).[3] Erected in July of 1813, the fort was built in a neat square over about an acre and a half of land. It included a blockhouse and was surrounded by pickets that stood about 12 feet tall.[4]

While Fort Seneca was mainly a supply center for the United States military, Harrison himself was stationed there during both the battle of Fort Stephenson and the Battle of Lake Erie. When Commodore Oliver Hazard Perry claimed victory on Lake Erie, he sent General Harrison a now-famous message stating, "We have met the enemy and they are ours." Harrison received this message at Fort Seneca.[5] (For more on the Battle of Lake Erie, see page 148.)

Today visitors to Old Fort can find a plaque placed by the Daughters of the American Revolution that marks where Fort Seneca is believed to have stood. In downtown Old Fort, next to the Nickel Plate Railroad, there is a model of the fort's blockhouse in Centennial Park.

Old Fort Banking Company

Across the street from Centennial Park, visitors to Old Fort will find the Old Fort Banking Company. While it may be hard to tell from the bank's updated facade, this financial institution has been a part of this community for over 100 years. Founded in 1916, Old Fort Banking Company first opened its doors on April 4, 1917. Forty years after opening, the company was approached by citizens of nearby Bettsville, with requests to open a branch in their village.[6]

The Old Fort Banking Company soon began to spread out even farther, eventually opening branches all along the western half of Ohio. Today, the Old Fort Banking Company is found in many Ohio towns, villages, and cities. The bank is now based in Tiffin, but the original Old Fort building remains an active branch.[7]

The Fry-Gillmor family of Old Fort has been particularly influential for the bank. In 1925, Howard J. Fry began working as a cashier in the original Old Fort Banking Company building on Main Street. By 1940, he had earned the role of board chairman, a role he held until 1969. His son-in-law, P. M. Gillmor, took on the board chairman role from 1969 until 2004, when it was passed down to his son, Paul E. Gillmor (also a former congressman). Unfortunately, Paul passed away in 2007. After his death, Paul's sister, Dianne Gillmor Krumsee, headed up the board.[8]

While the Fry-Gillmor family was always the largest shareholder at the Old Fort Banking Company, they remained dedicated to their community. In fact, in 2015, under Gillmor Krumsee's leadership, the Old Fort Banking Company transitioned to an employee-stock ownership plan, with the company largely owned by its workers.[9] In 2018, Dianne Gillmor Krumsee retired, passing on the title of board chairman to Michael C. Spragg. Spragg is the first board chairman from outside the Fry-Gillmor family since 1940.[10] When the bank celebrated their 100th anniversary, the *Toledo Blade* spoke to a retired Old Fort teacher who has been banking at the Old Fort Banking Company for all her life. She said, "They are always there. If you have a problem or you want to check something, they're always more than helpful."[11]

Pete Mellott

The village of Old Fort is located near Fort Seneca (page 62), which is named for the same fortification from the War of 1812. Fort Seneca itself is covered in this book, but it is hard to discuss one village without the other. Today, visitors to Fort Seneca, especially those with a talent for baseball or softball, are greeted with a touch of the Old Fort community. As players take the field at the local community park, they are greeted with a large sign bearing the smiling face of a well-known Old Fort citizen, Pete Mellott. The ballfield diamonds at Fort Seneca were named in his honor.

Mellott was born in Tiffin in 1936 and graduated from Old Fort High School in 1955. Mellott stayed in Old Fort where he raised his own children while remaining very active in the village community. He served on the school board, as a township trustee, and as a volunteer fireman. Mellott was also a leader in the Old Fort Ex-Hi organization, a group of Old Fort High School alumni dedicated to giving back.[12]

Mellott was an instrumental member of the Old Fort Little League, taking time to prepare the fields each spring. A builder by trade, Mellott helped design the current Old Fort baseball fields and school. Mellott passed away in January 2017.[13]

Paul Gillmor was born in Tiffin, Ohio, in 1939 and graduated from Old Fort High School in 1957. An Air Force vet, Gillmor was elected to the Ohio State Senate in 1967, serving until 1988, when he was elected to the U.S. House of Representatives. He served in Congress from 1989 until his death in 2007.[15]

TOP: The Otway Covered Bridge

Population: 81   **Incorporated:** 1890

INSETS L to R: The Depot, a perfect spot for ice cream on a hot day • Otway Christian Union Church • Otway Post Office • A street in downtown Otway

One resident of Otway, Harry Hoople, fostered his own apple orchards at the Hoople Fruit Farm. Right around 1960, Hoople discovered a new type of Golden Delicious apple growing on one of his trees. Now grown and sold at orchards across the country, this apple is still known as Hoople's Antique Gold. The apple ripens in the mid to late fall and is particularly useful in desserts.[13]

Otway

A Village Named for a Poet

THE VILLAGE OF OTWAY, OHIO, is located in Scioto County's Brush Creek Township, named for the creek that runs through the area. The village was officially incorporated on October 31, 1890. Otway was named by the area postmaster, James Freeman.[1]

It appears Freeman enjoyed reading in his free time, as he named his hometown for a seventeenth-century English poet. Thomas Otway, the town's namesake, was born in 1652 in the British town of Trotton. After a time at Winchester College and the University of Oxford, Otway made his way to the city of London. He briefly flirted with a career on the stage, but after only one performance Otway was too overcome with stage fright to ever act again. Otway moved behind the curtain, embracing his pen and paper to become a well-known playwright. Pausing only briefly to serve in the English military in the Netherlands, Otway wrote many plays, poems, and an autobiography in his short life. Best remembered of these works is *Venice Preserved*, first produced in 1682. Otway died a few years later in 1685, at the age of thirty-three.[2]

The Otway Covered Bridge

In 1874, the Smith Bridge Company of Toledo, Ohio, built a covered bridge in the village of Otway, providing a passageway over Scioto Brush Creek.[3] Bridges were important for small villages like Otway. Without this connection to outside markets, the economy of small villages like Otway could not grow. Today the Otway Covered Bridge is the only bridge of its kind still standing in Scioto County.[4]

Even the best-made bridges eventually need repairs. In 1961, the Ohio Department of Transportation closed the Otway Covered Bridge and built a new bridge to accommodate traffic.[5] Concerned about the loss of this huge piece of Otway history, the Otway Historical Society stepped in and took ownership of the structure.[6]

In 2014, the Otway Historical Society and the Scioto County Engineer were finally able to restore the bridge to its former glory. Keeping as much of the original structure as possible, a firm of restoration experts made the bridge safe again. In August 2014, the bridge was officially reopened to traffic.[7] While covering this reopening, local news outlet WOWK noticed that the president of the Otway Historical Society, Norvel Davis, had collected some trash from around the bridge, signs of late-night gatherings by Otway's younger residents. However, he told WOWK that this is not a negative sign—the bridge has always been a gathering place for Otway's teenagers. In fact, Davis noted a bit of graffiti he himself carved into the bridge in 1947, using his first pocket knife.[8]

The 1916 Fire

April 19, 1916, started out like any other Wednesday in Otway. Men and women filed into work, and schoolchildren made their way to the Otway Public School. One townsperson, a Mrs. Ed Brand, was doing yardwork on Wednesday afternoon. Mrs. Brand had raked some brush from throughout her yard into a pile in anticipation of the arrival of Orval Leath, a laborer set to plow the Brand family garden that day. Despite Mrs. Brand's warnings about the wind, Leath set a match to the brush pile before his work began. The high winds picked up the fire, set a nearby tobacco warehouse on fire, and soon Otway was consumed by flames.[9]

The residents of Otway quickly jumped to action as the fire began to spread. Residents' belongings and livestock soon began dotting the fields of Otway as they raced to save their belongings. Mrs. Odella Upton, the wife of a local reverend in the Methodist Church, helped many residents store their things inside the church building. The Otway bank began moving everything in sight into a large metal vault. One resident, Mrs. Jennie Freeman, ran to call the fire department of the closest large town, Portsmouth. Otway's two telephone companies set up shop in houses outside the fire's radius to allow for continued connection to Portsmouth. Luckily, a student at the Otway Public School noticed the fire in the distance and the children were evacuated.[10]

After Mrs. Freeman's call, the Portsmouth Fire Department loaded up their gear into a specially commissioned railway car and made the 21-mile journey to Otway in just 19 minutes. When they arrived, they saw Otway residents using buckets and water from the Scioto Brush Creek to control the flames. Unfortunately, the Portsmouth Fire Department didn't bring a hose long enough to reach between the creek and the buildings that needed rescuing. Many additional homes and businesses were lost in the time it took to retrieve a longer hose.[11]

In the aftermath of the Otway fire, the ruins of the village were filled with miscellaneous household items. The Otway sheriff was assigned to watch over the belongings of the homeless as they struggled to find a place to stay. Many homes, buildings and businesses were lost, including the bank, school, and mayor's office. The paperwork and cash stored at the bank remained safe in the locked metal vault; however, bankers had to wait a few days for the vault to cool before it could be safely opened. A few days after the fire, Otway mayor, S. T. Unger, called a town meeting to discuss Otway's future. Many local businessmen decided to stick around and rebuild. Luckily, no lives were lost, and the resilient citizens held their ground and remained in the village.[12]

The Otway Covered Bridge used a Smith Truss as patented by Robert W. Smith, the founder of the Smith Bridge Company, in 1867.[14] Smith was an Ohio native, born in Miami County in 1833. His ideas and building plans have become well known among covered bridge enthusiasts and engineers alike.[15]

TOP: Polk Church of Christ

Population: 335   **Approx. Founding:** 1849

INSETS L to R: Polk Market and Deli • Temple Baptist Church
• Polk-Jackson-Perry Fire District Volunteer Fire Station #1
• Polk Post Office

On June 26, 1874, Tully Frederick Hartsel, known as "Topsy," was born in Polk, Ohio. In September, 1898, at the age of 24, Hartsel first began playing Major League Baseball as an outfielder. He spent two years with the Louisville Colonels before joining the Cincinnati Reds in 1900. He was quickly traded to the Chicago Orphans and then again to the Philadelphia Athletics. Topsy spent 1902–1911 with the Athletics.[14] He passed away in 1944 and is buried at Woodlawn Cemetery in Toledo, Ohio.[15]

Polk

The Polk Armory: A Community Landmark

IN MAY OF 1849, IN JACKSON TOWNSHIP, John Kuhn laid out a village named Polk. By the 1880s, the village began to blossom with the arrival of the New York, Pennsylvania, & Ohio Railroad.[1] As the village grew, the state of Ohio built an armory in town.[2]

The Polk Armory, built in 1880, became a destination for Ashland County boys ready to join the armed forces. In 1898, during the Spanish-American War, local soldiers stopped at the Polk Armory for extra training before making their way to Cuba. In 1900, with the war over, the state sold the armory to the village of Polk for $440.

After this sale, the armory became a gathering place for a myriad of different events.[3] In 1903, when the local school burned down, the Polk Armory hosted students until a new building could be constructed. After World War I, the Lucas-Vaughn American Legion Post was housed at the armory, named for Olin Vaughn and Earl Lucas, Polk residents who gave their lives in the war.

Almost everyone in Polk during the twentieth century had at least one memory of the armory. The village's 100th-birthday celebration was held there in 1949. The building also held village council meetings, basketball games, the local fire department, and, briefly, a post office. People came from out of town to attend farmers' institutes at the armory, and local residents traveled to the armory for graduations, school plays, Boy Scout meetings, and holiday get-togethers. It once even had a barbershop! In 1972, the building was razed.[4]

The Murder of Harry Williams

In 1883, the village of Polk was the site of a well-publicized murder. On the evening of Saturday, March 24, 1883, four men from Polk traveled to the nearby village of West Salem. The four men worked at a sawmill together, and some news reports stated that they were going to pick up their paychecks.[5] They spent time in at least one West Salem tavern and didn't leave town until the early hours of Sunday morning. Likely intoxicated, the group began to quarrel. Since Christmas, two of their group, William H. Gribben and George A. Horn, had held a grudge against a third, Harry Williams, for an unknown offense. As they began to bicker, Horn threatened Williams, who hit him in the face. Thinking better of himself and remembering Williams's superior strength, Horn drew back.[6]

Around 2 o'clock in the morning, Horn and Gribben arrived back in Polk by train. Williams and his brother-in-law, Thomas McAvoy, had decided to walk back to the village. Knowing this, Horn and Gribben lay in wait. When Williams and McAvoy arrived, they were confronted by an angry Horn and Gribben. Horn threw a rock at Williams. He then brandished an axe and hit Williams multiple times on the head, fatally wounding him. McAvoy escaped and contacted police. Horn and Gribben were jailed, with angry locals gathering outside.[7]

Gribben and Horn were held in jail for almost an entire year before they were finally tried and sentenced. Horn's actions were considered purposeful and premeditated and Gribben was declared an accessory to the murder. The two were scheduled to hang on May 16, 1884.[8] When the morning of their execution arrived, at least 8,000 people arrived to see Gribben and Horn hang. Local officials predicted this unwieldy situation, so a fence was built around the scaffolding. Less than 150 people were let in through the fence, and the rest were made to wait outside, in a mob that quickly grew restless. Multiple military companies were on site for crowd control.[9]

Horn and Gribben met with friends and family until midnight the night before. Horn was greeted by his parents and sister, and Gribben by his wife and young child. In fact, on the day that Gribben was executed, his infant child turned one. It was a long, emotional evening for Gribben. As one reporter recorded, Gribben and his wife "Clasped each other in an embrace that plainly told the terrible anguish of their hearts," and "moved strong men to tears." Gribben appeared intoxicated the following morning when he was led to the scaffolding.[10]

Before Gribben and Horn were brought out, a riot erupted. The mob became angry upon learning that they would not be viewing the day's events. When the prisoners were led out, shots rang out, and the mob tried to tear down the fence. One soldier, Lew Cook of Wooster, was shot and then carried to the courthouse for medical treatment. He survived. Just after 10:30, Gribben and Horn were declared dead, bringing the saga to an end.[11]

Polk's Own Major General

In September of 1893, Stanley Eric Reinhart was born in the village of Polk. In 1912, Reinhart began classes at West Point. He graduated in 1916 and was sent to Fort Bliss in Texas, where he was made a first lieutenant with the 5th Field Artillery. He served abroad during World War I, first as an aide-de-camp for General Peyton C. March. In July 1918, he was made a Major of Field Artillery, a position he held until the end of the war. When World War I ended, Reinhart began working as an instructor at West Point.[12] Reinhart became best known for his time as a Major General during World War II, leading the 65th Infantry Division. Reinhart was hospitalized when he returned to the United States, and he was forced to retire in 1945. He passed away in 1975 and was buried at West Point.[13]

The village of Polk currently hosts the main fire station for the village of Polk and the townships of Jackson and Perry. The staff of two is on site Monday through Friday from 8 to 5. They respond to both medical and fire calls. In 2017 alone, the department responded to 429 calls, of which 74 percent were medical and 26 percent were fire and rescue.[16]

TOP: The original millstones from Pulaski Flouring Mills

Population: 132   Approx. Founding: 1837

INSETS L to R: Pulaski Methodist Episcopal Church • A historic marker in Pulaski tells the story of the village's namesake • An outdoor supply store in town • Pulaski Township Hall

The village and township of Pulaski were well-represented during the Civil War. According to local stories, the township sent about 100 men who were trained right in town, in the field just east of the M.E. Church. For a time after the war ended, the colors of the 38th Ohio Volunteer Infantry were proudly held by the village.[20]

Pulaski

Founding, and Renaming, The Village of Pulaski

IN OCTOBER OF 1833, Judge John Perkins, his sons, and a few acquaintances set out from the village of Brunersburgh on a journey to Williams County, Ohio.[1] Finding a pleasing piece of land on Beaver Creek, the men settled down and called their new town Lafayette. Perkins hired a surveyor named Miller Arrowsmith, and in 1837 he had the town officially laid out.[2]

Upon settling in Williams County, Perkins began to build a grist and saw mill on Beaver Creek. It's likely it was the first mill in Williams County. It served the village for about 60 years, eventually becoming known as Pulaski Flouring Mills.[3] Unfortunately, in 1897 the mill burned, but the millstone can still be found at the Pulaski Methodist Episcopal Church.[4]

In May of 1837, Perkins also established a post office for the new village, serving as the first postmaster. Unfortunately, another town in Ohio had also chosen the name Lafayette, and the mail was getting mixed up. For this reason, the new village of Lafayette named its Post Office "Pulaski," although the town's name didn't change officially until 1857.[5]

Where did the name Pulaski come from? When the town of Lafayette was originally settled by John Perkins and his acquaintances, their new village was a part of Beaver Township (named for the creek nearby). However, in 1837 Beaver Township split in two, leaving two new townships to be named. One took the name Jefferson and the other Pulaski. Needing a name simply for postal purposes, the village of Lafayette borrowed the new name of their township. Today both the township and the village still have the name Pulaski.[6]

Count Casimir Pulaski

The village of Lafayette was originally named for the Marquis de Lafayette, a French hero who had served in the American Revolution.[7] Fortunately for Pulaski residents, their new name had a similar theme. Born in 1745 in Warsaw, Poland, Casimir Pulaski first gained renown as a military leader during a Polish insurrection against Russia in 1768.[8] In February of 1768, Polish leaders, under heavy Russian influence, had essentially voted to make Poland a Russian protectorate. Unhappy with this turn of events, a group of revolutionaries, including Casimir's father, Josef Pulaski, formed an organization known as the Confederation of Bar.[9] Casimir Pulaski served as a military leader in the ensuing fight against the Polish government, even attempting (unsuccessfully) to kidnap King Stanislaw II. The Confederation earned the support of the Turks and the French, but by 1772 they had been defeated, and Pulaski had to leave his home country.[10, 11]

Pulaski, deflated by his losses in Poland, retired to Paris, France, where he met Benjamin Franklin. The two met in December of 1776 while the American Revolution was in full swing. Franklin saw a great military mind and a respect for democratic rule in Pulaski. He immediately suggested Pulaski to General George Washington as a potential military leader. Pulaski was helpful in many conflicts during the American Revolution, and in 1777 he was promoted to Brigadier General of the cavalry. In fact, due to Pulaski's superior training of the Pulaski Legion, he has been deemed the "father of American cavalry."[12]

In 1779, in an unsuccessful attempt to retake the city of Savannah, Georgia, from British forces, Casimir Pulaski was mortally wounded. Sources are unclear on his date of death and burial; however, it is likely he was taken from the battle to an American ship named the *Wasp*.[13] He died onboard as the ship retreated to Charleston, South Carolina.[14] Today a monument to Pulaski stands in Savannah, and various United States cities celebrate Casimir Pulaski day in October each year.[15] Pulaski also posthumously became one of the eight people in the course of United States history to be named an honorary citizen of the country. Other honorary citizens include Winston Churchill, Mother Teresa, and another foreign leader of the American Revolution—Marquis de Lafayette.[16]

A Monument for a Dear Friend

Just south of Pulaski lies a simple granite stone reading "Old Bill, 38 Y." The stone has been in its place near Beaver Creek since 1878, memorializing the death of a dear friend. Why the moniker "old" for someone who died at only 38? While it isn't clear on the stone, for Bill, a horse, 38 was indeed an advanced age.[17]

Born in 1840, Old Bill (or perhaps just Bill at the time), provided transport for mail and mail carriers traveling between the nearby town of Bryan and Hillsdale, Michigan. After his retirement in 1856, Bill was purchased by a man named Jacob Youse. Youse owned a grocery store in Bryan and a farm in Pulaski. Old Bill found a home on the farm, and the Youse family became very close to their animal companion. According to the family, when Bill died in 1878, Jacob Youse went to his friend, Emmory Willett, who had just opened a tombstone business in Bryan. Willett agreed to carve a tombstone for Old Bill free of charge, as long as Youse could provide the granite stone.[18] The stone that Willett carved in the fall of 1878 has continued to remind Pulaski residents of Old Bill and, more broadly, their shared past. In 1958, the Williams County Historical Society retooled the stone's lettering and placed it on large concrete base so that it can be seen more easily.[19]

During the late 1920s, near Route 127, the village of Pulaski enjoyed a naturally occurring spring. The spring ran down a hill, so a hydraulic ram was built to force the water the opposite direction. Frank Mallory, the owner of the town's general store, often said of his hometown, "Pulaski: where the water runs uphill."

TOP: Downtown Put-in-Bay is busy in the summer season,

Population: 136   **Approx. Founding:** c. 1854

INSETS L to R: The Miller Ferry is one option for visitors trying to get to Put-in-Bay from the mainland • A portion of the ruins of the Hotel Victory • The Boardwalk serves up fresh seafood right on the harbor • Put-in-Bay residents may use the airport to cross to the mainland in the winter when Lake Erie has frozen over

Thousands of tourists flock to Put-in-Bay each year, but there are about 138 permanent residents. According to the 2010 census, about 17 percent of households include children under the age of 18. The village operates Put-in-Bay school for students K–12 on South Bass Island, which serves a few other islands. The island life makes transportation a little complicated: students take ferries, planes, and charter boats to get to and from school and mainland sporting events. This becomes especially complicated in the winter.[16]

Put-in-Bay

Snakes and Raccoons on South Bass Island

FOR MANY YEARS, SOUTH BASS ISLAND, located in Lake Erie just off the Northern edge of Ohio, remained sparsely populated. One history suggests that during the 1700s, American Indian communities living in what is now Detroit, Michigan, occasionally spent winters on the island, when the rattlesnakes that appeared during the summer months were dormant. In the winter, raccoons were also a food source on the island.[1] The island began to see more human contact during the early 1800s. In 1803, a Connecticut judge named Pierpont Edwards purchased South Bass Island as part of a tract in the Connecticut Western Reserve (for more on the Western Reserve see New Haven, page 128). He never made it to the island himself, but he hired field hands to clear land for the raising of sheep, planting of wheat, and the building of a log cabin. However, Edwards's employees were forced to abandon their work when war came to Lake Erie.[2]

Perry's Victory

In 1812, the still-evolving United States Congress declared war on Great Britain for many reasons, chief among them the impressment of American seamen, the interruption of trade with France, and Britain's refusal to remove British soldiers left over from the Revolutionary War. As the War of 1812 began, Oliver Hazard Perry, a 27-year-old Rhode Island native who had been trained as a naval man since his youth, was sent to command American forces on Lake Erie.[3]

In September of 1813, the British Navy held the area near Put-in-Bay. Perry approached with his fleet, and on September 10, the Battle of

Lake Erie began. Perry's men fell behind initially, but after Perry moved to the Niagara, his forces picked up speed, killing or wounding the commander of each British ship. Perry led his men to a decisive victory over the British, who surrendered by nightfall. After his success, Commander Oliver Hazard Perry penned a letter to his superior, William Henry Harrison, including the now-famous line, "We have met the enemy, and they are ours."[4]

Perry's victory was integral for the war effort, cutting off enemy supply lines and pushing the British out of Detroit.[5] Perry has been remembered in many ways across Ohio, from a large painting hanging in the main rotunda at the statehouse to a local beer, brewed by Great Lakes Brewing Company in Cleveland. However, possibly the most well-known remembrance of Perry is located in the village of Put-in-Bay itself: Perry's Victory and International Peace Memorial.

This Doric column on South Bass Island first opened in 1915, after nearly three years of construction (it was begun in 1912 to celebrate the 100th anniversary of the War of 1812). Standing 352 feet high, the monument is the third-tallest national monument in the United States (behind only the Washington Monument and the St. Louis Arch). From the observation deck, visitors can often see the shores of Sandusky or even Canada on a clear day.[6] Today the monument is operated by the National Park Service as a reminder of the peace the United States and Canada have long enjoyed.[7]

Tourism at Put-in-Bay

Not long after the War of 1812, Jose DeRivera St. Jurgo, a Spanish man living in New York, purchased South Bass Island. He encouraged the creation of vineyards on the island, leading to increased tourism and settlement in the 1850s and 1860s. (Today visitors to Put-in-Bay can enjoy a taste of this vineyard history at Heineman's Winery.) As affluent guests continued to flock to the island, investors began to build hotels on Put-in-Bay .[8]

One such investor was J. K. Tillotson, who began raising money for a new project in 1888. On September 10, 1889, Tillotson finally laid the cornerstone for his ambitious Hotel Victory. Built by Toledo architect E. O. Falls and Sandusky-based Feick Construction Company, Hotel Victory was considered to be one of the largest hotels in the world.[9] Due to a nationwide financial panic in 1893, the hotel closed within a year of its grand opening. It was sold at a sheriff's sale, where the head architect, E. O. Falls, purchased the building, reopening to guests in 1896. In 1898, Falls saw some success from adding a freshwater pool. Here he allowed men and women to swim together: a scandalous proposition at the time. However, that same year, the entire island had to be quarantined when a few dozen of Falls's employees came down with smallpox.[10]

Feeling frustrated by his time at the Hotel Victory, Falls sold to two brothers by the name of Ryan, who appointed Thomas McCreary as the hotel manager. They saw the longest success at the head of the hotel, from 1899 to 1907. This was largely due to McCreary's penchant for advertising. After he died in 1907, the hotel slid downhill again. It remained empty for nine years. The hotel was again opened in 1918; however, in August 1919, it caught fire and was ruined. Today the remains of the Hotel Victory can be found by particularly observant campers at South Bass Island State Park.[11]

Year-Round Residents

During the mid- to late-1800s and into the early 1900s, Put-in-Bay was filled with wealthy vacationers. When the Hotel Victory first opened, a room cost four dollars each night (100 dollars a night in 2019), and guests often stayed all summer.[12] During Thomas McCreary's time at the head of the hotel, it was also made clear in advertisements that visitors would encounter "all white servants."[13] Today, Put-in-Bay is still a getaway, but this time it's for everyone.

During the late 1880s, workers at Heineman's Winery began digging a well and discovered the world's largest geode. The rock, deemed "Crystal Cave," can still be toured today.[14] Visitors can also make their way to the Aquatic Visitor's Center at The Ohio State University's Stone Laboratory on Gibraltar Island, where a research center studies Lake Erie wildlife.[15]

Population: 483   Incorporated: c. 1864-1870

INSETS L to R: Quaker City United Methodist Church • Lingos in downtown Quaker City • Thorn-Black Funeral Home • Quaker City Apartments open for lease

The first Ohio Hills Folk Festival hosted one of Ohio's more important musicians and historians, Anne Grimes.[17] Grimes was born in 1912 in Columbus and earned a bachelor's degree in art and music at Ohio Wesleyan University. In the 1950s, Grimes traveled around the state in an effort to preserve Ohio's many folk songs, preserving history that would otherwise likely have been lost.[18]

TOP: Citizens National Bank in Quaker City

Quaker City

Founding (and Naming) Quaker City

AROUND 1805, JOHN HALL moved to Ohio from North Carolina and became the first white settler in what would become Millwood Township.[1] Hall was a Quaker, moving into Ohio as part of a larger migration of Quakers who were interested in living in the Northwest Territory where slavery was illegal. Hall was soon joined by other Quaker settlers, and by 1811 there were 59 people living in the area. In 1818, a man named Jonah Smith arrived from Virginia. As the Quaker community grew, Smith decided to lay out a village.[2]

The area in which Smith laid out his village had been known for many years as Leatherwood.[3] As a result, the first Quaker meeting in town, organized in 1809, took on the name Leatherwood.[4] Despite this, Smith chose to name his new village Millwood, for his hometown in Virginia. Eventually the two names created confusion. In 1871, residents voted for a new name. They looked back to their history and chose Quaker City.[5] This name stuck and is still in use today.

A Festival Kind of Town

Since its earliest days, Quaker City has been known for festivals. The first white settlers began planning annual summer festivals, which came to a stop in 1876. In 1904, the village of Quaker City restarted the old tradition with the first annual Homecoming Festival.[6] These festivals featured parades, baseball games, fair rides, prizes, and even horseshoe-pitching contests.

In 1956, the annual summer festival took on a new meaning. This year was the 150th anniversary of John Hall's arrival in the future Millwood Township. Quaker City wanted to celebrate the event properly. The annual Homecoming Festival was renamed the Ohio Hills Folk Festival, and a new focus was put on celebrating village history. The residents of Quaker City began dressing in historic costume (even holding a beard-and-bonnet contest) and pausing during the festivities to discuss their local history.[7] Today the Ohio Hills Folk Festival is held in Quaker City on the weekend following July 4th each year. The festival celebrates local history and features parades, food, and entertainment.[8]

The Richland Meeting House

In May 2017, a new Ohio Historical Marker was revealed in Quaker City at the former site of the Richland Meeting House. The meeting house was first built in 1828, as the result of an ideological split in the Quaker religious community. The split occurred in 1826, and the Hicksite Friends laid claim to the first Quaker City meeting house. (Today visitors can find this meeting house in the Friends Cemetery.)

The Orthodox Friends needed to find somewhere new to worship, so they built the Richland Meeting House.[9] They used it until 1973, when dwindling numbers meant it was time to officially "lay down" the meeting. The nearby Stillwater Monthly Meeting in Barnesville, Ohio, took ownership of the property at this time. In 1989, they razed the meeting house, but they continue to maintain the nearby burial site, with help from the next-door neighbors. The historical marker makes it clear that for 147 years, residents met, worshipped, and were even laid to rest at the Richland Meeting House.[10]

Mansel Carter and a Life in the Mountains

One of Quaker City's citizens became famous in Arizona in the twentieth century. Mansel Carter was born in Quaker City in 1902. Before his 40th birthday, he had spent time studying photography, working as a pilot, and logging on an American Indian reservation in New Mexico. In 1941, Carter moved to Gilbert, Arizona, opening a camera shop.[11]

It was in Gilbert that Mansel Carter met Marion Kennedy, a member of the Cherokee Nation. The two became close friends, and in 1948 they made the decision to move in together.[12] Carter and Kennedy decided that they wanted to live in the San Tan Mountains. For a while they lived in a cave, but eventually they constructed a shanty. While they were known for their connection to the environment, they also spent much of their days mining.[13]

When they had procured enough copper, gold, silver, and turquoise, Carter and Kennedy took their goods to sell. Carter reinvested his proceeds in mining claims in the San Tan Mountains, claims he has since passed down to his heirs. By purchasing these claims and remaining silent about where they found gold, Carter and Kennedy were able to keep prospectors away and protect the native animals they had grown to love.[14]

Unfortunately, Marion Kennedy went blind and had to stop mining. He still loved to explore, so Carter built him a fence that he could follow with his hands to avoid falling while Carter was away mining. Kennedy eventually developed throat cancer, dying in 1960 at age 86. Carter buried his friend in the mountains, near their home.[15]

Once Carter was on his own, he upgraded from a shack to a trailer. He stopped mining once he hit his 80s and made money by carving and selling "cactus curios." As word spread about Carter, he received visitors from around the U.S. who were enraptured by his connection to the natural life around him. Animals would readily eat out of his hands, and one particularly trusting turtle even laid her eggs under his stove! Carter passed away at the age of 85 and is buried next to Marion Kennedy, on the land the two loved.[16]

The Hall family stayed in Quaker City for generations and was responsible for its early growth. Members of the Hall family were even present in 2017 when the Richland Meeting House historical marker was dedicated.[19]

QUAKER CITY
HOME OF
THE OHIO HILLS
FOLK FESTIVAL
SINCE 1904

TOP: The Taylor Mansion, originally built in 1900 by Lafayette Taylor

Population: 148   **Incorporated:** 1886

INSETS L to R: Rarden Community Park • Rarden Volunteer Fire Department • A mural on the side on the Rarden Volunteer Fire Department building • Rarden is surrounded by rolling hills

During the 1950s, Rarden became known for its infamous town marshal, Sylvanus Daulton. In October, 1955, Daulton unfairly detained three men. On the ride back to the police station, the men threatened Daulton with knowledge of a former sexual assault charge against him.[14] Daulton stopped the car, a scuffle ensued, and Daulton shot one, killing him. Soon thereafter, 116 residents, nearly half of the village's population, signed a petition for Daulton's removal. In 1957, Daulton left town; however, he returned in 1958, kidnapping Mrs. Florence Hoffer and her daughter. A few days later the women were found dead in Adams County, and Daulton's body was found by Clinton County officials.[15]

Rarden

Galena Becomes Rarden

IN 1850, IN AN AREA OF SCIOTO COUNTY occasionally known to white settlers as Moccasin, a new village was officially platted under the name, Galena. Many histories report that one of the village's residents at this time was a man by the name of Orvil Lynch Grant. Orvil came to this new village from Galena, Illinois, and suggested this name for his new home as well. Grant helped run a tannery in town that made cavalry saddles for the U.S. government during the Civil War. This was a particularly fitting position for Grant, as his older brother, Ulysses S. Grant, was serving on the front lines.[1]

In 1883, the Cincinnati and Eastern Railway came to Galena. Like many other new railway stops across the state, Galena grew quickly after the arrival of this mode of transportation. Soon there was need for many new stores and inns to accommodate travelers. As Galena changed, so did its name. With the huge growth caused by the rail line, the village was able to officially incorporate in 1886. Villagers adopted the name Rarden, after an early settler named Thomas Rarden.[2]

Lafayette Taylor

One particular man took advantage of the growth seen in Rarden, and he found fortune for his efforts. Lafayette Taylor (known to friends as "Lafe") had moved to Ohio in 1872 at the age of 16, coming from his childhood home in Pennsylvania.[3] When Rarden began to boom, Taylor opened up a general store in town, complete with an attached ice cream shop. In 1895, Taylor founded his greatest business venture: Rarden

Stone Company. Taylor and the Waller Brothers had joint ownership of the local stone quarry and stone mill. Taylor's new company was able to use the Cincinnati and Eastern Railway to ship his coveted stock around the state.[4]

Taylor's investment in the stone quarry spurred almost immediate financial success for his family. By 1900, Taylor had broken ground on a Victorian-style mansion in Rarden, boasting a total of 22 rooms.[5] Taylor was also a lumber dealer and a big game hunter. As his mansion was under construction, Taylor also commissioned the building of two barns outside his general store. Here he displayed taxidermied animals from his own hunts, as if in a museum.[6]

The Taylor Mansion still stands in Rarden today, a memory of times past. The mansion has been recognized as an official stop on the Scenic Scioto Heritage Trail.[7] The building was briefly used as a haunted house to raise money for the Rarden Volunteer Fire Department in the early 1980s, but the property was purchased by Tom and Shirley Wilkinson in 1982. Since that time, the Wilkinsons have worked on restoring and living in the home.[8]

Raising Funds for the Community: Then and Now

Since the summer of 1960, the village of Rarden has had an active and well-supported Volunteer Fire Department. On July 2 of 1960, Mayor Christian officially organized the fire department, opening a firehouse by October. In May of 1976, the fire department received a new fire truck and equipment. This moment was cause for a parade, in fact, the first parade ever to grace the streets of Rarden. Only four years later, in September of 1980, it was time for a second parade, to honor the Volunteer Fire Department's twentieth anniversary. The village has continued to raise funds for the fire department and ambulance services, particularly through ticket sales for Saturday night bingo.[9]

The village of Rarden has continued to crowdfund many important services, including the Rarden Village Park. Since 2002, the village has annually hosted a festival, known at the Rarden Whitetail Deer Festival, to raise funds. The festival takes its name from the historic importance of hunting in the area. Admission to the festival is free, but visitors are encouraged to make a donation or buy a raffle ticket. Thanks to funds raised at the festival, the park committee has been able to paint the floor of the gymnasium, build an outdoor gazebo, and maintain the grounds. Almost more importantly, the Whitetail Deer Festival gives the community of Rarden a reason to come together once a year. Former residents who have since left the village return during the festival to celebrate with their former neighbors for an entire weekend.[10]

Unfortunately, in the early morning hours of what would have been the final day of the Whitetail Deer Festival of 2018, Rarden was hit with a flash flood. Suddenly the entire festival, including food vendors, campers, and trailers, was waist-deep in water. However, the community of Rarden and helpers from nearby towns rallied to save the festival. People began to drive tractors to the festival site, helping to haul others out of the growing swamp. Vendors whose wares had been saved turned around quickly to help others dig their way out. A local church and the Red Cross brought food to the members of the Rarden community as they continued to work on that unfortunate Sunday.[11]

Despite the ill-effects of mother nature, the citizens of Rarden were still able to have their closing ceremonies. About one month after the flash flood, Rarden held a "festival recovery day." This day included all of the festival activities that would have taken place a month earlier, such as a parade, awards presentations, an auction, and closing ceremonies.[12] The village of Rarden still plans to hold the Whitetail Deer Festival in 2019. A GoFundMe website was created to attempt to recuperate some of the costs of the flash flood in 2018.[13]

For a man with such an auspicious brother, Orvil Grant's life is not well documented. This is likely because the President cut ties with him. Orvil was involved in White House scandals during President Grant's term and was generally known as a swindler. Orvil Grant died at 45 in New Jersey, supposedly in an asylum.[16]

TOP: Rockbridge United Methodist Church

Population: 182 **Approx. Founding:** 1880s

INSETS L to R: Rockbridge's natural namesake • Mini-golf is available at the large Hocking Hills Market in Rockbridge • A view from Clear Creek Metro Park • Good Hope Township Volunteer Fire Department

One of the most recognizable landmarks of the Hocking Hills region is the large Hocking Hills Market in Rockbridge. Most visitors to the region, whether they intend to spend a few days camping, relaxing in a resort cabin, or simply enjoying a day hike, will pass by the market on US Route 33. Included in this large lot is a flea market, a mini-golf course, and Sandy Sue's Silver Diner.

Rockbridge

The Rock Bridge at Millville Station

TODAY THE TOWNSHIP GOOD HOPE in Hocking County, Ohio, has no incorporated villages or towns. However, this was not always the case. In the northeast portion of the tiny township, on the banks of the Hocking River, lies the community of Rockbridge. Now a census-designated place, the village of Rockbridge was once incorporated, holding 250 inhabitants, two churches, and two schools in the 1880s. The community was well known for two things. First, Rockbridge was the site of a station, known as Millville, on the Columbus and Hocking Valley Railroad. That station is gone, but Rockbridge's namesake, a natural 80-foot bridge, continues to draw visitors today.[1]

Rockbridge is part of a region of southeastern Ohio known as Hocking Hills. This area is filled with caves, gorges, and other rock formations

that formed in the area's Black Hand sandstone. This sedimentary rock, first formed millions of years ago while the state of Ohio sat under a large sea, is particularly susceptible to erosion, creating such well-known formations as Old Man's Cave, Ash Cave, Cedar Falls, and Rockbridge. Ohio has at least 12 rock bridges; however, the one in the former village of Rockbridge is considered the most impressive.[2]

The rock bridge in Hocking County was once a large formation of sandstone standing more than 150 feet above the ground.[3] The lower portion of this formation was softer and eroded more easily. It began to break away first, leaving the top portion as a bridge between two cliffs. Today the bridge stands sturdy over a running ravine in the Rockbridge State Nature Preserve. It varies in width from 10 to 20 feet and measures about 100 feet long.[4] About 80 feet of that span is marked by a complete detachment from adjoining rock, the space where the "bridge" occurs.[5] Visitors to the former village of Rockbridge can visit the nature preserve and enjoy 2.75 miles of a hiking trail, including the bridge itself. Courageous hikers can make their way across the bridge.[6]

Plenty of Parks

Also located in Rockbridge is the Clear Creek Metro Park, managed by the Franklin County Metroparks. This park covers almost 5,000 acres of preserved land, including many miles of open hiking trails, ranging in difficulty. Visitors will see more than 2,200 species of plants and animals, as well as a plenitude of Black Hand sandstone formations, ravines, and creeks. The park is also home to Ohio's largest nature preserve, which is named for Columbus businessman Allen F. Beck. During the 1920s, Beck recognized the awe-inspiring features of the Rockbridge area, purchasing the lands that would become the Clear Creek Nature Preserve.[7]

A History of Flooding

Thanks to its location on the Hocking River, the village of Rockbridge is a frequent victim of flooding. Most recently, the community was evacuated in April of 2018 after a particularly bad storm. A number of Rockbridge residents, accustomed to this type of flooding, turned away the firemen and American Red Cross members at their doors and chose to stay at home as the waters rose.[8]

Stories of flooded Rockbridge residents in 2018 echoed the stories of residents past. Throughout the years, residents of nearby Good Hope Township have always been willing to lend a hand. In 1937, as a flood arrived in Rockbridge, a resident named Shad Conkle was very ill. The Hocking County Sheriff and his deputy arrived at Conkle's door, escorting him to the county jail, where they were able to care for the ailing man.[9] In 1959, the *Logan Daily News* reported a horrifying headline, "Hocking River Crests at 14 ½ Ft." According to the same article, "nearly three feet of water was reported in the lower portion of Rockbridge." Soon

two residents showed up in Rockbridge with their own personal boats, escorting at-risk families to a shelter at the Rockbridge High School.[10]

Theresa Hahn, Link Trainer

In February of 1944, the *Logan Daily News* reported that a "Rockbridge WAVE is Speaker at School Assembly."[11] This WAVE, a member of the Women Accepted for Volunteer Emergency Service, a naval unit established during World War II, was a local woman named Theresa Hahn. One of the eldest of many Hahn children, Theresa Hahn was returning to her alma mater to speak about her ongoing service. After graduating in Rockbridge, Hahn had started basic training at Hunter College in New York. From here she transferred to a naval air base in Atlanta, Georgia, where she became a certified Link trainer.[12]

In 1941, low on the necessary supplies and planes to properly train their pilots, the Air Force contacted Link Aviation Devices about a "Combat Crew Trainer" they had begun developing for a contact in Great Britain. This device, eventually known as the Celestial Navigation Trainer (CNT), began appearing on American military bases in 1943. Housed in tall silo-like structures, these trainers simulated a cockpit in all possible situations, including duress.[13]

Someone had to operate these new trainers, and the military turned to the WAVES as their new experts.[14] These women, such as Theresa Hahn, made sure that pilots were combat ready before they were sent abroad. As Hahn told the *Logan Daily News*, she was teaching "pilots to fly blind." Hahn spent most of the war stationed in Patuxent River, Maryland, operating Celestial Navigation Trainers.[15] Over the course of their service, the WAVES trained almost 100,000 pilots.[16]

Since 1992, the village has annually celebrated Lilyfest, a celebration of arts, crafts, music, and gardens. Since 2009, the festival has taken place in the Bishop Educational Gardens, a plot of preserved land donated to the Hocking Soil and Water Conservation District by Bobbi and Bruce Bishop, the founders of Lilyfest.[17]

TOP: The Poultry Barn at Rogers Community Auction and Market

Population: 226   Incorporated: 1895

INSETS L to R: One of the many entrances to the huge Rogers Community Auction and Market • A view of downtown Rogers • A view from one of the highest points in Rogers • Rogers Community Park

In 1883, a professor named A. Y. Taylor constructed Mount Hope College, a new institution of higher learning in Rogers. Taylor's building burned to the ground in 1894, but fortunately, the school was quickly rebuilt. When classes resumed, the college had taken on a new name, this time going by Lincoln College. Unfortunately, Professor Taylor's dream did not last long. By 1905, the college was defunct.[12]

Rogers

A Late Start in Middleton Township

THE VILLAGE OF ROGERS is located in Middleton Township, a part of Columbiana County. Middleton Township grew very slowly during the early years of Ohio statehood. It was sparsely populated, with few incorporated towns and villages during most of the nineteenth century. The county directly borders the state of Pennsylvania, so, as one history notes, many white settlers who arrived in the late 1700s to take advantage of lax rules regarding squatter's rights in Western Pennsylvania, did not realize that they had built their homes in Ohio. Finally, Middleton Township saw some growth in the 1880s when a line of the Pittsburgh, Lisbon & Western Railroad was built within its borders. In 1883, a man named T. G. Rogers had a village laid out near the rail-

road. This village would take on the name of its original owner. It was officially incorporated as Rogers in 1895.[1]

The earliest residents of Rogers were determined to bring industry to their new home. In 1895, the residents raised a total of $5,000, which they gave to John Gould, H. A. Wise, and N. J. Baker, on the condition that they use the money to open a pottery business. They were able to secure four kilns and begin a business, but it shut down after only a few years. After the business sat dormant for three years, it was reopened by the Bradshaw Brothers of East Liverpool, another Columbiana County town known for pottery. The citizens of Rogers again began to raise funds to support the pottery business, in hopes that a successful manufacturing endeavor would help their village blossom. The village of

Rogers gave the Bradshaws $1,100 on the condition that they would run the pottery business for at least one full year.[2]

The Bradshaw Brothers technically kept up their end of the deal—they kept the business open for a year. However, exactly on day 366, the pottery building mysteriously burned to the ground. Not surprisingly, the brothers had taken out a hefty insurance policy on the building. The state fire marshal could not prove foul play, so the Bradshaws collected their insurance, left town, and started a new successful pottery business in Niles, Ohio. They took not only the insurance funds, but every last brick they could salvage from the building. As one resident said, the Bradshaws took "everything but the holes in the ground where the kilns had stood." The residents of Rogers took many years to recover from this betrayal.[3]

A Famous Flea Market

Today the village of Rogers is best known as the home of the largest open air market in the Pittsburgh Tri-State Area (the area on the eastern border of the state of Ohio where it meets Pennsylvania and West Virginia). This market, known as the Rogers Community Auction and Market, has been successfully drawing huge crowds to the village every Friday for over 60 years.[4]

The market originally opened in 1955 when Emmet Baer, an auctioneer by trade, purchased eight acres of land on Old State Route 154, where he built a barn and began to sell produce, eggs, chickens, rabbits, and more each Friday.[5] As Emmet's wife, Lucille, once told a local newspaper, "He was a farmer and a miner, but he always wanted to be an auctioneer, so after we got married he went to school for it. I milked the cows and he went to school." Baer started his own auction business in 1948 (still an active firm today), and he wanted to branch out by opening his own market.[6]

During the 1960s and 1970s, Emmet and Lucille grew the Rogers Community Auction and Market, opening an on site restaurant and

expanding to 200 vendors. After Emmet died in 1971, his son Jim took over the market. Jim was responsible for obtaining many more acres of land for the market and adding multiple buildings for vendors and visitors. Jim passed away in 1999, but the family has kept the business going. Today the market occupies 250 acres (70 of which are free parking) with 1,600 vendor spaces, 5 miles of sales, and up to 50,000 visitors each Friday.[7]

The market is only open on Fridays, except for some large, special Saturday auctions throughout the high season. Originally Emmet Baer only opened his market on Fridays because he needed to be available to travel for auctions for his auction firm on Saturdays. This continues to hold true for the Baer family today.[8] Traditionally, the Friday auction was not a problem for buyers who worked from nine to five. Most vendors would not set up until the afternoon, and visitors would spend their Friday nights gathered at the market. Over the years, flea market culture has changed and many buyers like to show up early in the morning to be sure they get the best deals. This means vendors have started opening earlier and therefore closing earlier. However the Baer family is holding onto the Friday tradition.[9] When you are getting almost 50,000 visitors each week, why change things around?

The Rogers Community Auction and Market has recently caught the interest of a group of filmmakers known as Hollywood Top Productions. In 2018, co-hosts Steve Kreider, Steve Swanson, and Jess Faulstich auditioned hundreds of regular visitors and vendors for a television show they are calling *Flea Market Fanatics*. The hosts are aiming to show viewers the myriad of human stories embedded in the market, whether they be happy, sad, heartwarming, hilarious, or somewhere in between.[10] All of the episodes of the show are currently available at the *Flea Market Fanatics* website (you can even get an official t-shirt with the show's logo).[11]

Today, Baer Auctioneers and the Rogers Community Auction and Market are run by brothers Ken, Will, and Wade, the third generation of Baers to run the business. They graduated from the Reppert School of Auctioneering in Indiana, which also trained their grandfather, Emmet Baer, during the late 1940s.[13]

TOP: Rudolph Christian Church

Population: 458 **Approx. Founding:** 1890

INSETS L to R: Liberty Township Civic Center • Baseball fields for the Rudolph Little League • The famous Rudolph Post Office • A sign welcoming visitors to "the deerest little village in Wood County"

Liberty School was built in the village of Rudolph around 1914, but by the twenty-first century it was long abandoned. Around 2002, locals Scott Rood and Laurie Haas purchased the building and moved in. While the couple worked on renovating the school to make it a proper residence, they rented out rooms to paintball teams, and in the fall, ran a popular haunted house.[15] By 2017, the former school housed 17 tenants, at an affordable price.[16] Unfortunately, late in 2018, due to the expense of keeping a 100-year-old school up to code, the apartments were vacated.[17]

Rudolph

Waiting for a Railroad

THE VILLAGE OF RUDOLPH was laid out much later than many of the other villages represented in this book. It wasn't until May of 1890 that W. H. Wood laid out the town of Mercers for David Mercer. The name of the village was changed very quickly to Rudolph, in honor of a locally recognized merchant named H. J. Rudolph.[1]

Why wait until 1890 to lay out a town? It is likely that David Mercer was hoping to benefit from a new arm of the Cincinnati, Hamilton & Dayton Railroad that was about to pass through his new village. The C. H. & D. began as a commuter line, moving commuters between the three cities mentioned in its name during the 1850s. The nature of the railroad allowed wealthy Cincinnati residents to move into the suburbs and still make it into the city to get to work. By the 1860s, the railway passed north into Toledo, passing through Wood County in villages like Weston, about 10 miles west of the future village of Rudolph.[2]

"At Christmas, we go wild."

Today the village of Rudolph is best known for its post office. No one quite remembers when the tradition began, but for years the Rudolph Post Office has been fielding thousands of customers each Christmas. People travel from across the state of Ohio (and occasionally across the country) to bring their holiday mail to Rudolph, where postal workers place a unique Rudolph the Red-Nosed Reindeer-themed cancellation stamp on each envelope or package. Many people will mail their envelopes directly to the Rudolph Post Office, simply to receive the stamp. Mail comes in from all over, even from other continents.[3]

Residents of Rudolph can agree on one thing: the tradition of the Rudolph postal stamp started with a former postmaster, Joanne Patton, who served the village from the 1970s to the 1990s.[4] While just the red-nosed reindeer's name itself was enough for the village to have a festive postal cancellation, it seems that the United States Postal Service officially gave the village permission to use an image of the reindeer on their cancellation stamps sometime in the early 1990s.[5]

Today, Rudolph's most important tradition is managed by Charlotte Lamb, the resident postmaster. She makes the cancellation stamp available to residents and visitors alike from December 1 until Christmas Eve each year. The stamp design always features Rudolph the Red-nosed Reindeer, but his likeness changes each year. For example, in 2014, a Cincinnati artist was invited to design the stamp.[6]

Rescuing a Tradition

Unfortunately, outside of the month of December, the Rudolph Post Office does not see enough business to warrant more than one employee. In 2012, the United States Postal Service removed Rudolph's second postal employee, leaving Postmaster Charlotte Lamb alone to manage the post office. Lamb feared that this meant the end of Rudolph's Christmas tradition. There was no way for one employee to stamp the close to 80,000 parcels and envelopes that were expected to arrive in December. In fact, she began to turn customers away early in the holiday season. However, the residents of Rudolph were not ready to let their tradition die.[7]

Liberty Township officials contacted Randy Gardner, their representative to the Ohio House of Representatives in 2012. Gardner was able to get in contact with the United States Postal Service and request that special permission be granted to allow volunteers to stamp cancelled mail in the village during December. Gardner was successful, and the tradition was back on.[8]

In that first year, 75 people signed up to help Lamb over the course of December. Many of the volunteers were retired members of the community, looking to help out. As one volunteer said, "That's why we're here, to help one another."[9] Local leaders have also been eager to help out over the years. Lamb has received help from Randy Gardner (who became an Ohio State Senator in 2013 and the Chancellor of the Ohio Department of Education in 2019), Congressman Bob Latta, Ohio State Representative Tim Brown, and Wood County Sheriff Mark Wasylyshyn. Retired postal workers have also been eager to assist.[10]

Volunteers work on shifts, starting by setting out cookies and coffee for the visitors who may have to wait in line, and then getting on to a long day of stamping. Not only do volunteers need to stamp the mail of those who arrive in the front door, but they need to deal with the backlog of items that are mailed to Rudolph for the cancellation stamp.[11] In 2017, one customer walked in with almost 1,000 items to be stamped![12] As Charlotte Lamb says, "At Christmas, we go wild."[13]

The success of Charlotte Lamb and the entire Rudolph community have not gone unnoticed. In 2014, the United States Postal Service decided to hold a national unveiling ceremony for their holiday forever stamps in the "Deerest Little Village in Wood County." That year, 500 million stamps featuring the characters from the holiday classic *Rudolph the Red-Nosed Reindeer* were sent to be sold around the country. The postal service fittingly dedicated these stamps in Rudolph, gifting the village a large display version of a stamp featuring their favorite reindeer.[14]

The village of Rudolph, Wisconsin, is eerily similar to Rudolph, Ohio. Both villages are located in a Wood County, and both have 400–500 people. Rudolph, Wisconsin, also gets in the holiday spirit. On the second Saturday of December, the post office offers a special postmark, processing about 20,000 parcels in one day.[18]

TOP: A street in Rushville

Population: 309   **Approx. Founding:** 1808

INSETS L to R: Rushville United Methodist Church • A storefront at the Rushville Garage displays signs telling visitors about the village's Underground Railroad history • Rushville Masonic Lodge • Kings Grand Central restaurant

Unfortunately, in January 2019, the village of Rushville suffered a serious fire. On January 3, barely into the new year, an insurance office belonging to James Bope caught fire. While the original blaze was tamped down, it reignited later in the evening, collapsing the entire interior of the building, which dated back to 1910. The building also contained apartments on the second floor. Luckily, off-duty Assistant Fire Chief Brian Irwin responded to a text he received about the fire and arrived in time to pull a woman from a locked apartment, likely saving her life.[16]

Rushville

A Village on Rush Creek

BEFORE THE STATE OF OHIO even entered into the Union, white settlers had begun living in the Rushville area. Settlers were drawn to Rush Creek and formed small communities to the west and east of the waterway. In 1802, a man named Moses Plummer erected one of the first mills on the creek, harnessing the power of the water.[1, 2]

In 1808, Joseph Turner officially laid out a village on the eastern side of the creek, giving it the name Clinton. The name was soon changed to East Rushville, while the other side of the creek started going by West Rushville.[3] Today West Rushville has maintained its name; however, East Rushville is now simply Rushville.

The Underground Railroad in Rushville

Before the Civil War, a handful of citizens of Rushville aided escaped slaves on their journey to freedom on the Underground Railroad. The two families whose service was best recorded were the Hanbys and the Hydes. The Hanbys had moved from Rushville to Circleville to Westerville to accommodate Reverend William Hanby's work.[4] During these moves, they maintained their home in Rushville, where at least one source claims William Hanby's mother continued to live.[5] The Hanbys were able to aid escaped slaves, both in Rushville and Westerville.

Dr. Simon Hyde became a very important Underground Railroad figure in Fairfield County and adjacent counties because he could administer medical services. While traveling through the Underground Railroad, many slaves suffered illnesses from exposure to the elements.

According to Wilbur Siebert's well-known history of Ohio's Underground Railroad, compiled via the memories of those involved, Dr. Simon Hyde kept "an articulated human skeleton suspended in an upstairs wardrobe of his house." He had five sons who all knew to open the wardrobe door if any strange men (likely slave-catchers) came through town. The sight of the skeleton seemingly scared away any would-be slavecatchers.[6]

Darling Nelly Gray

In 1842, while the Hanby family was living in Circleville, William Hanby received a notice from his friends in Rushville that his help was needed. A man named Joseph (sometimes recorded as just Joe) Selby had come into town on the Underground Railroad and had been hiding out in Hanby's harness shop. Selby was very ill, and although Dr. Hyde was doing his best, it was likely that the man would die in Rushville.[7]

Seeing that he had little time left, Selby began to tell Hanby and Hyde about his life. As a young man, he had been held in bondage at the same place as a girl named Nelly Gray. Joseph was in love with Nelly, but she had been sold to a master far away. Determined to find the woman he loved, Joseph began a perilous journey to Canada, where he hoped to find a job, make some money, and buy Nelly's freedom. Unfortunately, Joseph Selby died in the Hanby's house in Rushville.[8] He is buried nearby in the Rushville Cemetery (also known as the Pleasant Hill Cemetery), along with several other fugitive slaves who had sought treatment from Dr. Hyde but failed to recover.[9] Hanby's son, Benjamin, later was inspired to enshrine Selby's story in a song titled "Darling Nelly Gray," first released in 1856.[10]

A Complicated Relationship with Racism

Despite the fact that Rushville citizens worked tirelessly on the Underground Railroad, the village had a complicated relationship with racism. On April 15, 1894, the citizens of Rushville arrived at the village prison with the intent of lynching an African-American prisoner who had been accused of rape. The Rushville constable called in the National Guard, but their presence only enraged the village citizens more. The constable asked the National Guard to leave Rushville, but once they were gone, the angry mob overcame the constable, destroying the jailhouse and lynching the accused man in the center of town. After the man died, the woman he had allegedly assaulted "expressed uncertainty about her earlier identification."[11]

Businesses Flourish in Rushville

The modern village of Rushville supports many successful businesses. Just outside the village of Rushville, on a large property of 100 acres, is the Cabin at the Crossroads. Originally a family home built in 1982, this cabin can now be rented by visiting groups for overnight stays or big events.[12] For those Rushville residents looking for a getaway, the Rushville Boarding Kennel, established in 1988, will take care of their furry friends while they hit the road. The kennel was originally founded by Jane and Paul Wildermuth. The couple had previously raised cocker spaniels and figured a kennel would be the perfect new project. After 22 years in business, the couple retired to the city of Lancaster. In 2016, the Winegardners purchased the Rushville Boarding Kennel, and it remains in business today.[13]

Also in Rushville is the Hugus Fruit Farm. This family business began in the early 1900s when William Wikoff gave a plot of farmland to his daughter Bernice and her husband Ray Hugus. Over time the farm has passed down through the family. Today, Ralph Hugus, grandson of Bernice Wikoff Hugus, runs the farm where he sells apples, pears, peaches, plums, and blackberries. He has even added a sawmill on site and now offers lumber as well.[14]

Benjamin Hanby is best known for a Christmas song "Up On the Housetop."[15] Today the house where Hanby's family lived when he was in his twenties and attending Otterbein University is still preserved and open as a historic site in Westerville (a suburb of Columbus).

Population: 383   Incorporated: 1913

INSETS L to R: Rutland Freewill Baptist Church • Rutland Department Store • A Rutland Bottle Gas storefront in the village • Birchfield Funeral Home

TOP: A historic truck from the Rutland Volunteer Fire Department, parked in the village

On 360 acres on the outside of the village of Rutland, an organization known as the United Plant Savers operates the Goldenseal Botanical Sanctuary. The area, formerly known as Paynes Woods, has good-quality soil and a useful topography, making it appealing for the growth of medicinal plants. The United Plant Savers, an organization advocating the cultivation and use of medicinal plants, keeps more than 500 plant species, 120 tree species, and 200 fungi species alive at the sanctuary.[14]

Rutland

Following the Leading Creek to Rutland

IN 1799, BREWSTER HIGLEY OF RUTLAND, Vermont, and John Case, a surveyor, arrived in the future Meigs County, Ohio. Higley and Case were traveling from Belleville, Virginia (now West Virginia), to investigate the land that Higley had recently purchased. For his consulting services, Case was offered a portion of the purchase.[1]

While the two men traveled to the Ohio territory, Higley's wife, Naomi, and their children waited in Belleville. They had been there for 18 months when Higley finally purchased a plot of land for about $1,000.[2]

When Higley and Case returned to Belleville, pleased with what they had seen in Ohio, Higley purchased a boat and traveled with his family to their new home via the Ohio River and the Leading Creek.

When they arrived, Higley tore the boat apart, using the raw materials to build a small lean-to in which his family could temporarily reside.[3]

Higley was appointed a justice of the peace in his new home, per the orders of Arthur St. Clair, Governor of the Northwest Territory. A community began to form near the new Higley family home, and in 1828 the village of Rutland was officially laid out. This name was likely an homage to Higley's former home of Rutland, Massachusetts.[4]

The village of Rutland was not officially incorporated until 1913, but Higley served as an early postmaster for the growing community in the 1800s and as a justice of the peace for the township. He died in 1847, still living in the new Rutland, Ohio.[5]

The Most Famous Brewster Higley

The village of Rutland's most famous resident was a direct descendant of the village's founding family. Born November 30, 1823, in Rutland, Ohio, Brewster Higley VI was the grandson of Brewster and Naomi Higley. In 1841, at the age of 18, Higley began studying medicine. He began his first practice in Pomeroy, a village about seven miles from Rutland and right on the banks of the Ohio River. In fact, Higley's grandparents likely passed right through the future village of Pomeroy on their way to Rutland. Higley eventually moved to Indiana, where he continued to practice medicine.[6]

The romantic endeavors of Dr. Brewster Higley VI were truly a tragic tale. His first wife, Maria Winchell, became ill and soon died in 1852. Most histories report that Higley's second wife, Eleanor Page, died soon after the birth of their son, Brewster Higley VII. However, other sources speculate that Eleanor took Brewster VII and went to live with her ex-husband, David A. Smith. Either way, Brewster and Eleanor were separated by about 1853. Higley and his third wife, Catherine Livingston, had two children together, Estella and Arthur Herman. Unfortunately, Catherine was injured and eventually died from complications from her injury, in 1864, with two small children still at home.[7]

Higley's youngest children soon gained a stepmother, with his marriage to Mercy Ann McPherson. It isn't clear what exactly occurred between Higley and McPherson, but as one source points out, Higley "quite literally ran from the tumultuous marriage." Feeling that his children's lives could be in danger, he left them with relatives in Illinois and, in 1871, made his way to Kansas. Thanks to the Homestead Act, Higley was able to easily acquire a plot of land in Kansas, building a cabin for long-term use in 1872. Higley's marriage to Mercy Ann McPherson legally defaulted into divorce in February 1875. By the end of March he was married again, to Sara E. Clemans.[8] The two had a very successful marriage, living a long life together until their deaths, four months apart, in 1911.[9]

"Home on the Range"— A Claim to Fame

Today Dr. Brewster Higley VI is best known as the author of the well-known song "Home on the Range." In 1872, likely inspired by the peaceful view from his new cabin, Higley penned a poem that he titled "My Western Home." Newspapers around Kansas began printing the poem, beginning with the *Smith County Pioneer*. Soon Higley's friend, Daniel Kelley, put music to the poem, creating a popular dance song. Kelley and his wife, Lulu Harlan Kelley, performed in a musical group known as the Harlan Orchestra, with Lulu's two brothers. The Harlan Orchestra was well known in the Kansas frontier from 1878 to 1885, leading to popularity for "My Western Home." In 1930, Higley's song appeared in a musical and was slightly edited. These edits gave us the song we know today, and the new title: "Home on the Range."[10]

During the 1930s, questions arose about the song's authorship. It had become quite iconic; in fact, in 1933, President Franklin Roosevelt stated that it was his favorite song. Fortunately, all copyright disputes were settled in favor of Higley (although he was deceased by this time). In 1947, "Home on the Range" was declared the state song of Kansas.[11] Today visitors to Athol, Kansas, can visit the cabin, now restored, that Higley lived in when he wrote his poem. In 2016, brothers Mike and Greg Higley, descendants of Dr. Brewster Higley VI, spent a night in the cabin, marveling at the natural landscape that inspired their ancestor to put pen to paper and record the feelings it evoked.[12]

Visitors to Southeast Ohio will notice the name "Rutland" even if they don't ever enter the village. The name "Rutland Bottle Gas" is printed on outdoor propane tanks in 18 Ohio counties and 8 West Virginia counties. Founded in the late 1940s by Arnold Grate, the Rutland company primarily services residential customers.[13]

TOP: Saint Johns United Methodist Church

Population: 185 **Approx. Founding:** 1835

INSETS L to R: A historic building in Saint Johns • The Saint Johns Volunteer Fire Department encourages the community's children to stay safe over the summer • Saint Johns Post Office • A historic bell outside Saint Johns United Methodist

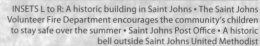

When Catahecassa traveled to Washington, D.C., in 1802, he took along a party of supporters and interpreters. Upon arrival, his companions, particularly some younger Shawnee boys who had not yet been exposed to the disease, were offered a vaccination against smallpox. Local newspapers reported that the American Indians were apprehensive; however, Catahecassa very clearly stated his thanks when speaking to Thomas Jefferson. Another American Indian leader visiting at the time, Michikinikwa, or Little Turtle, of the Miami Nation, had already been vaccinated years earlier.[1,2]

Saint Johns

Building on the Site of a Former Village

IN 1835, THE VILLAGE OF SAINT JOHNS in Auglaize County, Ohio, was platted by two couples with a stake in the area. One of these couples, Daniel and Elizabeth Bitler, had previously lived in Franklin County (in Central Ohio, near Columbus) but moved to Auglaize County in 1834. Daniel Bitler was the first businessman of the new village, having opened a store, a blacksmith shop, and an inn. The other couple, John and Mary Rogers, originally lived in Richland County. They moved to Auglaize County in 1833. In 1834, John Rogers was elected as a township trustee. Most histories record that the founding couples of Saint Johns could not agree on a name for their new village; however, no one knows why exactly they compromised on Saint Johns.[1]

The Bitler and Rogers families were not the first people to build a village on the site of Saint Johns. In the late 1700s, seeking refuge after a forced removal by white settlers, a group of American Indians of the Shawnee Nation settled in this portion of the future Auglaize County. These settlers were led by Catahecassa, or as he was known to most white settlers, Black Hoof. One of the cabins occupied by the new white settlers in Saint Johns had actually been owned by Catahecassa. As one source reports, he'd become close to a group of Quakers who built the home for him in 1822.[2]

Catahecassa's Story

No one is exactly sure when Catahecassa was born, but estimates range from 1717 to 1722. He had established a strong leadership role in his nation during multiple attempts to keep white settlers from pushing the

Shawnee, and other American Indian nations, from their homes. During the French and Indian War, Catahecassa was allied with the French.[3] According to a monument in his honor in the modern-day village of Saint Johns, Catahecassa was present at the Battle of Point Pleasant in 1774, the defeat of Edward Braddock in 1775, Harmar's Defeat in 1790, St. Clair's Defeat in 1791, and the Battle of Fallen Timbers in 1794. Catahecassa was also a signatory of the Treaty of Greenville in 1795.

After an American Indian loss at the Battle of Fallen Timbers and the signing of the Treaty of Greenville, Catahecassa began to express negative feelings about the fate of the Shawnee Nation in what was then the Northwest Territory. He believed that he could only avoid increasingly strict treaty lines that fenced in Shawnee territories by encouraging his village, on the future site of Saint Johns, to adopt the culture of the white settlers. During the early 1800s, visiting Quaker missionaries noted that residents of Catahecassa's town were establishing large farms, cultivating livestock, and building a sawmill and a gristmill. When Tecumseh and his brother, known as The Prophet, attempted to organize the American Indians of Ohio against white settlers, Catahecassa refused to get involved, urging his people to maintain their own lifestyle.[4]

Despite his growing fears, Catahecassa remained a staunch advocate for American Indians in the Ohio Country. In 1802, he traveled to Washington, D.C., to speak with President Thomas Jefferson. He presented to the president, politely, but in no uncertain terms, that he felt the United States had broken multiple tenants of the Treaty of Greenville. Among other issues, the Shawnee Nation was not given the provisions it was promised, white Americans came onto Shawnee land to hunt game, and the land allocated the Shawnee Nation under the treaty was not suitably fertile. Catahecassa also brought more particular issues to Jefferson, such as the kidnapping of a young girl from his village. As he said, "we think it very hard that our children should be taken by force from us..." This would not be Catahecassa's only journey to Washington, D.C., as he continued to represent the Shawnee Nation in the political arena.[5]

Forced Out of Auglaize County

Unfortunately, in 1831, the United States government succeeded in removing the Shawnee Nation from their lands in Auglaize County through the signing of the Treaty of Wapakoneta. In exchange for agreeing to move to Kansas, the Shawnee were promised $13,000 and an annual cut of the profit from selling their former lands to white settlers.[6] Some sources claim that, when asked why he would agree to such a treaty, Catahecassa stated, "because the United States Government wanted to buy and possess our lands, and remove us out of the way. I consented because I could not help myself, for I never knew them to undertake anything without accomplishing it. I knew that I might as well give up first as last, for they were determined to have our lands."[7]

The Shawnee Nation had completely left the future site of Saint Johns by 1832; however, Catahecassa, aged over 100 years at the time, died before he was able to leave for Kansas.[8] Today, Catahecassa's remains are still buried in Saint Johns and marked by a large monument in his honor. This monument is the one remaining vestige of the Shawnee village that Catahecassa founded.

Saint Johns Grows

By 1920, the village of Saint Johns boasted a population of 355 people. This was partly due to the paved roadway, known as the Wapakoneta-Bellefontaine highway that passed through the village.[9] (Wapakoneta, a town near Saint Johns, is now known for being the birthplace of astronaut Neil Armstrong, the first man to walk on the moon.) Today the village is much smaller and has unfortunately been unincorporated. However, Saint Johns still maintains a volunteer fire department, responsible not only for the fighting of fires but for the organization of regular village events.

By the 1920s, Saint Johns supported two grain elevators. Merchants used nearby railways to easily ship their products.[10] The Runkle Grain Company traded primarily in corn, flour, wheat, and coal. Today one of the company's logbooks is preserved at the archives of the Ohio History Connection.[11]

Population: 419   Approx. Founding: 1818

INSETS L to R: Savannah Academy Park • Savannah Post Office •
Cattleman's Restaurant • Savannah Presbyterian Church

The Algeos don't advertise their Johnny Appleseed tree, but they enjoy sharing the exciting story. As Amy Paramore-Sheaffer, an Algeo descendant currently living in a house near the tree, told a reporter, "Last year, an 89-year-old woman said she had wanted to see the last Johnny Appleseed tree her whole life. I gave her a clipping from the tree which she was going to try to grow. I hope she succeeded."[13]

TOP: United Methodist Church of Savannah

Savannah

A Young Man Builds a Village

IN 1815, REVEREND JAMES HANEY moved with his family to present-day Ashland County, Ohio, settling on land previously occupied by the American Indian nations of the Wyandot, Seneca, and Lenape. With Haney was his 16-year-old son, John Haney, the future founder of the village of Savannah, Ohio. On Christmas Day of 1818, at just 19, John Haney laid out the village on a corner of his father's land holdings.[1]

Haney originally named his village "Vermilion" for the river that flowed nearby. It was also known locally as Haneytown. Unfortunately for Haney, Vermilion was a very popular name among early Ohio towns. By the late 1800s, the village post office name was Savannah.[2]

By 1822, five families resided in Haney's new village. The residents of Savannah had very high hopes for their hometown. With its location on a main trading thoroughfare, their hopes were not unfounded.[3] Throughout the early 1800s, many teamsters passed through the village, announcing their arrival by the bells on their horses. One teamster by the name of Loveless Frizzell was particularly well known in the area. All teamsters kept bells on their horses, but if a teamster was ever stuck on the road, he would give his bells to the man who helped him. Legend has it that Frizzell never had to give up any of his bells, and thanks to the help he provided, he could be heard jangling from far away.[4]

Making the Best Out of the Railroad

Railroads were built in communities all around Savannah, but the town itself was overlooked. While a railway depot would have provided an economic boom for the village, the area's three nearby train depots provided some benefit. Goods still needed to be carried to and from outlying villages, like Savannah, to the railway stations. Many Savannah men maintained good jobs as teamsters, moving goods throughout the county.[5]

In the early 1900s, the rise of the automobile made commercial shipping easier, taking away jobs from teamsters. As vehicles became commonplace, the growth of chain stores also took away customers from area businesses.[6]

The Savannah Academy

In 1856, a man named Reverend Alexander Scott brought an institution of higher learning to Savannah. Scott noticed that many young men and women in the village desired further education, but distance was a barrier for many. Knowing this, Scott opened the Savannah Male and Female Academy for the benefit of local students.[7]

In the first year of its existence, the academy met for classes "in a hall over Samuel Gault's storeroom." By the end of the year, about 100 students were enrolled. In 1858, residents of the village began to raise funds to help construct a proper building for the academy. The building was officially erected in 1859, at the cost of $1,565.[8] By the end of the 1800s, the academy had closed, but the building was in use by the village's high school students. Despite the academy's closing, almost 1,000 alumni attended a reunion in 1906, the 50th anniversary of the founding of the Savannah Male and Female Academy. Reverend Scott, the academy's founder, was also in attendance.[9]

In 1924, the academy building was no longer in use as a high school. The school board attempted to sell it, but the residents of Savannah objected. Eventually, between the funds of the village coffers and the offerings of private citizens, the academy property was purchased—technically by a man named William H. Ramsey, although he transferred ownership to the village. The academy's buildings were torn down and the land converted into a park.[10] Academy Park is still a centerpiece of the village of Savannah today.

A Bicentennial Celebration

In 2018, the residents of Savannah gathered at Savannah Park to celebrate the village's first 200 years. While the anniversary technically fell on December 25, 2018, the village, quite understandably, decided to avoid the harsh Ohio winter and celebrate during a summer weekend. The weekend was filled with events. Residents enjoyed a 5K race, a Lions Club breakfast, and live music from the Osborne Brothers and Sugarcreek Bluegrass. Kids from local 4-H organizations sold food to the attendees, and the bicentennial organizers introduced any residents over the age of 85. The Clear Creek Historical Society also remained open for the entire celebration so that residents could enjoy objects and stories from their past. The historical society was opened in 1993 by Liz Densmore and Larry Biddinger, in a home belonging to the Biddinger family.[11]

A Famous Tree

At least four or five groups of visitors make their way to the village of Savannah each year to see the last living tree planted by John Chapman, or as many know him, Johnny Appleseed. The tree is on land that has been owned for generations by the Algeo family. The tree has struggled over the years, but the family has continued to keep it standing. The tree still produces many apples. Chapman wisely planted this particular tree over an underground aquifer that has helped ensure its longevity. In 1991, the American Forests organization confirmed that the tree is legitimately tied to Chapman.[12]

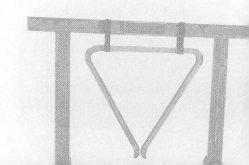

In May of 1846, Sarah Hearst Black was born on a farm just outside of Savannah. Black was best known for her work with the Women's Christian Temperance Union (WCTU), one of the first well-known women's organizations built on social reform. The WCTU, still active internationally, was first founded in Ohio.[14]

TOP: Sinking Spring's unique octagonal schoolhouse

Population: 130   **Incorporated:** 1854, 1894

INSETS L to R: A view inside the schoolhouse • Grace Bible Church • A street in Sinking Spring • Thompson Funeral Home

The village of Sinking Spring is one of many Ohio towns and villages that claims a place along the 1,444 miles of the Buckeye Trail. First started in 1959, and managed by the Buckeye Trail Association ever since, this large looping path goes around the entire state of Ohio. Hikers can follow the "blue blazes," blue painted markers on the trees, to stay on the trail. After passing through Sinking Spring, hikers will find themselves at the Fort Hill Earthworks & Nature Preserve, the site of earthworks built by the Hopewell People about 2,000 years ago.[14]

Sinking Spring

The Ohio Indian Wars

BEFORE WHITE SETTLERS ARRIVED IN OHIO, the land was inhabited by a number of American Indian tribes. After the American Revolution, these western lands were ceded to the United States by the British government, even though they were already inhabited. This created significant conflict between American Indian tribes and white American settlers when they arrived. This conflict played out from 1785 to 1795 in a series of confrontations known as the Ohio Indian Wars.[1]

The wars came to an end in January 1795 with the signing of the Treaty of Greenville. This treaty was a stopgap at best: neither side left the negotiating table feeling satisfied. Per the treaty, a line was drawn across the future state of Ohio. American Indians laid claim to the northern lands, and white Americans could settle the southern portions.[2]

It was this brief moment of peace that drove the earliest settlers of Highland County to travel from their birthplaces in Kentucky to the Ohio frontier.[3] In the spring of 1795, only a few months after the Treaty of Greenville was signed, a man named John Wilcoxen decided to try his luck and move his family to Ohio. Wilcoxen is well known in Highland County, as he would become the first white settler to build a home there.[4]

Wilcoxen and Hiestand

As the story goes, during May of 1795, a storm struck the Ohio frontier, and Wilcoxen's horse ran away. He left his wife, child, and dog behind to search out the horse, but on the way he also found his future home. Wilcoxen happened upon a spring that arose from limestone. Wilcoxen built his home on the sinking spring.[5] Sometime in 1795, the

Wilcoxen family welcomed unexpected visitors from Kentucky into their home. This group was intending to reach Chillicothe, but took a wrong turn and ended up in the Wilcoxen cabin. The Wilcoxens joined this traveling group and continued out of Highland County.[6]

In 1806, a man named Jacob Hiestand brought his family to Highland County from the state of Virginia, and he purchased a large plot of land near the spring that Wilcoxen had found. He began to lay out a town and called it Middletown, as it lay halfway between the bustling city of Chillicothe and Limestone (now Maysville), Kentucky, the town many of its residents hailed from. In 1817, a post office was established, and residents found that another town in Ohio had already claimed the name of Middletown. From 1817 onward, the town was known as Sinking Spring.[7]

The Octagon Schoolhouse

By 1831, the town of Sinking Spring was already building its second schoolhouse, to replace the one-room log cabin that had held the children's earliest lessons. An early version of a school levy was placed on residents to fund the building of the new school. However, as town tradition tells, one man did not want to pay his taxes. Apparently the man claimed he would not give money for "the building of such an ugly-looking smokehouse as that." Not to be outdone, the town treasurer waited until the next day when he saw the man's horse tied up in the street. The treasurer stole the horse and let the man's son know that the ransom was quite simple: pay the tax and you could have the horse back. The man eventually paid up."[8]

This early schoolhouse was, and still is, an architectural marvel. The schoolhouse is octagonal. Inside students sat around a central stove for heat in the winter (eventually the chimney was moved and a school bell placed in the center). Classes were held here until 1844. At that time, not only was the school becoming overcrowded, but laws required the school district, not the village, to own the schoolhouse. A new schoolhouse was built, but the octagonal schoolhouse continued to see use for adult classes, government meetings, and the like. The building still stands in Sinking Spring today.[9]

Charles Willing Byrd

Sinking Spring is the final resting place of a famous early American, Charles Willing Byrd.[10] Born in Virginia to a wealthy family in 1770, Byrd became a land agent for Robert Morris of Kentucky before returning to Philadelphia to practice law. By 1799, Charles and his wife Sarah had moved to the Northwest Territory, where President John Adams appointed Byrd as the Territory's first secretary. In 1802, President Thomas Jefferson made Byrd the Governor of the Northwest Territory, a position he held for only four months, as Ohio became a state in 1803 and the Northwest Territory ceased to exist; the land that wasn't in the new state of Ohio became the Indiana Territory. Byrd served as a delegate to the Ohio Constitutional Convention and finished his career as a justice on the United States District Court of Ohio.[11]

In 1825, Charles Willing Byrd moved with his second wife, Hannah, and their children to Sinking Spring. He believed that the water from the spring held medicinal properties, and he purchased the land on which the spring was located. Byrd built a brick house here where he lived until his death in 1828. Byrd was buried in Sinking Spring, in a cemetery that now bears his name. A monument to Byrd also stands in the cemetery. It was originally unveiled in 1941 by Byrd's great-great-granddaughter, Ruth Gall Fulton.[12]

Byrd's brick home is still standing in Sinking Spring today. In 1946, Jeff and Leona Wylie purchased the home, shortly after Jeff returned from World War II. The couple transformed the home into a funeral home, which they operated until Leona retired in 1985. The business, today known as the Wylie-Thompson Funeral Home is still in operation, run by Steve W. Thompson.[13]

Early residents of Sinking Spring could be indecisive. The village was first incorporated in 1854. However, in 1874, the residents voted to unincorporate. The town was reincorporated in 1894. After 1894, the residents decided to stop bringing the issue up every 20 years: the village has remained incorporated since.[15]

Population: 401   Incorporated: 1901

INSETS L to R: Images of corn line South Vienna's streets in honor of the Corn Festival • Main Street Pizza • The Hangar Sports Center in downtown South Vienna • South Vienna Market and Dairy

On October 5, 1854, Alfretta Ronemus of South Vienna, then only 10 months old, attended the Clark County Fair with her mother. That year at the fair, organizers had planned to hold the first ever baby contest in the United States. One of these organizers approached Ronemus's mother and asked that she enter Alfretta in the contest. Alfretta bested the competition, becoming the first winner of a baby contest in the country. An image of Alfretta Ronemus as a toddler is preserved in the collections of the Ohio History Connection.[16]

TOP: A main intersection in South Vienna

South Vienna

South Vienna Deals with Changing Transportation

IN 1833, JOHN H. DYNES laid out a new village, then known as Vienna, a name taken for the city in Austria. It was no coincidence that Dynes chose 1833 to begin laying out the village; the area had recently been surveyed as a future site on the National Road.[1] This new thoroughfare led to a frenzy of town and village construction, with each clamoring for a piece of the economic success that living near a transportation hub could provide. In 1834, the portion of the road that passed through Vienna was officially opened. Village residents set up toll booths on either side of the village and continued to collect tolls until 1883.[2]

Changes in transportation led to ups and downs for the village of South Vienna over the years. During the late 1800s, when the most popular mode of transportation transitioned from carriage to railroad car, the village saw a decline. Without National Road traffic, the economy faltered. However, in 1901, the Springfield and Columbus Traction Company built a line directly through South Vienna, bringing electric railway cars through town, and growing the economy again.[3] Unfortunately, the traction cars were gone by 1938, and although the village was serviced by a Greyhound bus line, life wasn't the same.[4] In 1970, Interstate 70 was built through the village of South Vienna, displacing portions of the village. Unfortunately, the highway has not had the same economic effect that the original village settlers enjoyed from the National Road.[5]

South of What?

How did the village of Vienna become South Vienna? What exactly is it south of? It turns out the name is a bit misleading. In 1838, when the village first built a post office, the residents decided on the official name "Vienna Crossroads" to differentiate it from another Ohio village named Vienna. However, around 1909, the village residents changed their name again, this time settling on "South Vienna."[6]

Village histories do not shed much light on the reason for the 1909 name change. South Vienna is south of the Trumbull County Vienna, but the name "crossroads" had already differentiated from the other Ohio village. Could this name change have been an attempt to differentiate the village from the capital of Austria? It doesn't seem like that would be a huge problem, with the Atlantic Ocean doing most of the work in separating the two towns. However, in 1909, Austria was embroiled in a conflict known as the Bosnian Crisis, begun when Austria-Hungary attempted to annex Bosnia and Herzegovina.[7] It is possible that residents of South Vienna tired of the confusion that came from reading their local newspaper and wading through stories that concerned both Vienna, Austria, and their own village.

Technically, the village of South Vienna *is* located south of the original Vienna. The village in Ohio is located near latitude 39.927005. The Austrian capital is located around latitude 48.209209. Despite Ohio's distance from Austria, South Vienna is technically the more southern of the Viennas.

The Famous Corn Festival

Today South Vienna is best known for its annual fall Corn Festival. There are even ears of corn painted on the village's streets. The tradition began in 1976, when the United States spent the summer celebrating the nation's bicentennial. The village of South Vienna hosted a parade, and residents were so thrilled with the turnout that they decided the celebration was worth repeating. In September of 1977, the first official South Vienna Corn Festival was held.[8]

Today the Corn Festival still comes to South Vienna each fall, generally in September. The festival can attract anywhere between 80,000 and 100,000 guests over the weekend. Visitors can enjoy parades, shopping, rides, and the competition for Corn Festival Queen. Each year welcomes a new and exciting grand marshal. But most important is the corn: sweet, fresh, and ready to eat.[9]

Planning the Corn Festival is a year-long process. The village of South Vienna maintains a Corn Festival Committee that works on the planning, long before September arrives. The committee is also involved in the community, maintaining relationships with local charity organizations and often donating funds raised from the Corn Festival.[10]

An Auction House on the Edge of Town

Visitors to South Vienna can't miss a large building on the edge of town that bears the name "Ritchie Brothers." This huge building, constructed in 2007, is an auction house.[11] Currently based in Canada, the Ritchie Brothers business was first founded in 1958, by Dave, Ken, and John Ritchie. They branched out into the United States in 1970.[12] In 2007, South Vienna was their 18th United States location. The company maintains over 100 locations around the world.[13]

Today, Ritchie Brothers is the largest auctioneer of heavy equipment and trucks in the world. According to their website, "In 2017...$4.5 billion of heavy equipment was bought and sold at 400+ Ritchie Bros. unreserved public auctions."[14] Because South Vienna has always been a farming community, the company does well in sales of tractors, excavators, backhoes, dump trucks, and similar large equipment.[15] As you might expect, the Ritchie Brothers site takes up a lot of room, as they need to store the large items that they auction.

One business that benefited from the arrival of the Springfield and Columbus Traction Company was a nursery known as Hollandia Gardens. Founded around 1914 by Mark Aukeman, it was located about one and a half miles west of the village, luckily right where the traction line decided to put in a stop.[17]

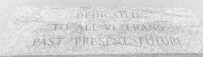

Population: 75   Incorporated: 1904

INSETS L to R: Stafford United Methodist Church • Stafford Park •
A street view in Stafford • Stafford Cemetery

Stafford, Ohio, was the boyhood home of David Kirby, a well-known HIV/AIDS activist. Kirby was estranged from his family due to his sexuality; however, when he was personally struck with AIDS during the 1980s, he called his parents and asked to come home.[10] In 1990, during the last months of his life, Kirby committed one last act of activism by allowing photography student Therese Frare to photograph him on his deathbed in Columbus. One of these photographs was published in *LIFE* Magazine in 1990 and became the face of AIDS activism for years to come.[11]

TOP: The Stafford Post Office

Stafford

William Steel and Early Stafford

THE EARLY HISTORY OF STAFFORD is muddled. All sources agree it was originally named Bethel but soon changed to Stafford due to a postal issue. Whatever the original name, William Steel was a key figure in Stafford history. From the 1840s through the end of the Civil War, Stafford was a wholly abolitionist town, with William Steel as its vocal leader. Steel loudly and publicly protested the Fugitive Slave Law and had at least one bounty placed on his head by disgruntled Southerners.[1]

Steel also served as a lead organizer of the Underground Railroad in town. In 1958, when Steel's former home was renovated (it was the village post office by this point), workers found an underground passage between his home and the neighboring general store. It is likely that this passage was used to move fugitive slaves in secrecy. Village legend tells of many fugitives living in Steel's attic while they waited for a safe moment to continue their travel north.[2]

The Underground Railroad in Stafford

Because operators on the Underground Railroad worked in secret, few details were recorded for future historians. But luckily for historians, Professor Wilbur Siebert of The Ohio State University sought to record the memories of Underground Railroad participants. While many of the men and women he interviewed struggled with aging memories, he was able to put together a map of possible stops.

According to Siebert's map, Stafford was only a small branch on the larger Underground Railroad. Fugitive slaves typically crossed the Ohio River at Reno, a few miles from Marietta, and then traveled to Woodsfield, the seat of Monroe County. Most slaves that traveled through Woodsfield went on to Somerton; however, a small branch extended from Woodsfield to Stafford. Stafford pushed all traffic to Summerfield, from which four branches extended north to freedom.[3]

Those routed to Stafford were met with a very safe stop: the entire town was made up of abolitionist whites and free black residents. No townsperson in Stafford would have stopped the fugitives on their way to freedom. In fact, William Steel often boasted that no fugitive who passed through Stafford was ever caught at any point on their journey.[4]

The Curtis Family

Many fugitive slaves chose to stay in the city of Stafford after their arrival. From 1830 to 1850, the United States Census recorded a sharp increase in the number of free black families living in Monroe County.[5] For example, in 1846, John Curtis and his two younger brothers bravely escaped from a plantation in Rockingham County, Virginia. Due to a particularly harsh winter, the boys were forced to hide out in a cave where they lived on the remains of a bear they killed. One of the boys succumbed to the winter's harsh torment, and his brothers were forced to cover his body with rocks, as the ground was too hard to dig a proper grave. Members of the Feldner family, white abolitionists from nearby Stafford, found the two boys and took them to safety. William Steel negotiated freedom for the Curtis brothers and employed them at his mill. The two surviving Curtis brothers also worked with Steel to move fugitive slaves through the Underground Railroad. In 1863, both Curtis brothers joined the United States Colored Troops and fought in the Civil War, but unfortunately only John returned. John lived in Stafford until his death in 1914 and is today buried in Stafford Cemetery.[6]

Stafford and the Civil War

Many men from Stafford served in the Civil War. A local newspaper, *The Spirit of Democracy*, discussed a recruiting event in May 1861. The day began with the raising of an American flag and a rally with speeches for the Union cause. The crowd was also asked to give "three groans for the Southern Confederacy." Never aiming to disappoint, they uttered "such horrible groans…as were never heard prior to this, in the old hills of Monroe."[7]

At the end of this rally, 44 men offered their services to the Union: a large number for such a small town.[8] Eventually, there were almost 100 volunteers; when they arrived in Columbus, the *Spirit of Democracy* published an excerpt from a Columbus newspaper that stated, "They…are the finest Company we have yet seen: hardy, stout, iron-framed men of large and uniform size; 25 of them, we understand are over six feet in height."[9]

Many free black men in Stafford also desired to serve the Union cause; however, they were largely forced to wait until President Lincoln allowed African American servicemen to enter the military in 1863. After the Civil War ended, many free black residents left the village of Stafford. However, a new tradition developed, beginning around the 1940s. African-American families, formerly of Stafford, began to meet each August at Stafford Park, telling the stories of their brave ancestors who served on the Underground Railroad or took up arms in the Civil War.

William Steel, well-known abolitionist of Stafford, Ohio, had a son who somehow managed to become even more well known than his famous father. William Gladstone Steel was born in Stafford in 1854, during the height of his father's abolitionist activities. As a grown man, he successfully lobbied to have Crater Lake declared a National Park.[12]

TOP: Stockdale United Church of Christ

According to local legend, Stockdale is home to Ohio's most perfect tree, a maple. Standing near State Routes 335 and 32, the tree has been heralded as a perfect specimen by Pike County residents since the 1920s. Today the Pike County Convention and Visitors Bureau lists the tree as a point of interest.[17] In 2005, John and Emily Samson donated the land that the tree stands on to the Arc of Appalachia preserve system. The Samson family had passed the land down through multiple generations, and John wanted to see its natural state preserved.[18]

Stockdale

Early Stockdale—A Large Village

TODAY THE VILLAGE OF STOCKDALE is so small that it is unincorporated, but when the village first appeared in the census in 1850, it boasted 900 residents.[1] When the U.S. Census was taken in 1850, the village of Stockdale was actually known as California. However, letter-writers wishing to contact friends and family in the village directed their letters to the village of "Flat" (a name adopted by the post office). Around 1900, the village officially became Stockdale, taking the name of a well-liked local Methodist minister.[2]

Unlike many small towns and villages at the time, Stockdale wasn't located on a railway. The Ohio Southern Railroad passed through Marion Township, but bypassed the village.[3] Even so, Stockdale was a booming manufacturing town during much of the late 1800s. By the 1880s, the village was home to many businesses, including a flour mill, a blacksmith, a carriage shop, a millinery, a grocery, two shoe shops, and a hotel. One of the most successful was the woolen mill first built in 1860 by William Gordon. In 1862, James McGinniss purchased the mill and added an engine. McGinniss continued to grow the building during the 1860s and 1870s, adding power looms and a shearing machine. The mill made jeans, flannels, yarns, and blankets.[4]

Branch Rickey

The Rickey name appears often in Stockdale's written history, but with the birth of Wesley Branch Rickey in 1881, Rickey was poised to become a household name in the U.S.[5]

At the age of 19, Branch Rickey left home and enrolled in Ohio Wesleyan University, in Delaware, Ohio. Here he embraced a sport he had always loved: baseball.[6] Rickey was the catcher for the Ohio Wesleyan men's baseball team. He was such a good catcher that soon he was offered a spot on a minor league team, with a paycheck for his efforts. By taking this job offer, Rickey became ineligible for college athletics. He instead began coaching the Wesleyan baseball team during his junior and senior years.[7]

During Rickey's time as a coach at Ohio Wesleyan, the men's baseball team's roster included one of the first African-American players in college baseball: Charles Thomas. Thomas, a student from Zanesville, Ohio, was often denied lodging when the team traveled. Some teams wouldn't even take the field, simply because Thomas was on the roster. In one instance, when Thomas was denied lodging in South Bend, Indiana, Rickey forced the hotel manager to allow Thomas to sleep in his room as an unregistered guest. Rickey later recalled watching Charles Thomas sitting on the bed in their shared room, weeping.[8]

After graduating from Ohio Wesleyan University, Rickey was offered a chance to play for the Cincinnati Reds. However, Rickey didn't last long. Raised in a very religious household, Branch Rickey refused to practice on Sundays. The Reds did not like this ultimatum from Rickey, and he soon found himself in St. Louis, playing for the Browns.[9]

Rickey Becomes a Full-Time Coach

Rickey only played for a few years, eventually going back to the University of Michigan where he graduated with a law degree in 1911. From here, Rickey became a full-time coach. He began working for the St. Louis Cardinals in 1917, where he asked that the team buy a few minor league teams so he could recruit upcoming talent. Rickey's idea helped create the idea of the modern farm system for baseball talent development. Such farm systems are commonplace today.[10]

In 1943, Rickey took the most important position of his career: general manager of the Brooklyn Dodgers. After signing on with the Dodgers, Rickey began scouting the Negro Leagues for the perfect player to break the color barrier in baseball. Until this point, African-American players were informally banned from playing in the Major Leagues and instead competed separately in the Negro Leagues. Rickey soon asked Jackie Robinson to sign with the Brooklyn Dodgers.[11]

Breaking the color barrier was not an easy feat for Jackie Robinson, and he endured slurs, abuse, and probably not coincidentally, he was among the league leaders in being hit by pitches. However, by 1952, five years after his 1947 debut with the Dodgers, the Major League had 14 African-American players.[12] During the early 1950s, as more and more African-American players followed Robinson into the Major League, the Negro Leagues disbanded.[13]

Zach Veach Takes on the Indy 500

Stockdale has continued to nurture athletes. During the 2017 and 2018 Indianapolis 500, Zach Veach, born and raised in Stockdale, raced in car number 26.[14] Veach, like many racecar drivers, was often the smallest kid in class, and he speaks openly today about his struggles with bullying. In particular, he recalls one fellow student throwing his hat in a trash can and pouring milk all over it. However, Veach kept a positive attitude through his youth, saying, "Looking back, I'm like, 'One day, I hope I have milk pouring on my hat again.'" (The winner of the Indy 500 is given a glass of milk upon their victory and often pours it over their head.)[15] Now in his early twenties, Veach is living in Indiana and driving for Andretti Autosport. However, he says, "Ohio's always (going to) be home for me."[16] Hopefully Veach will one day find himself bringing another milk-stained hat home to Stockdale.

Stockdale's Eskin Crabtree joined the U.S. Navy in 1917 and was assigned to the *USS Mount Vernon*, a troop transport, in 1918. In September of 1918, the *Mount Vernon* was torpedoed, leaving 36 crew members, including Crabtree, dead. He was only 24 years old. He is buried in Scioto Cemetery in Marion Township.[19]

TOP: One of the man-made lakes in Sugar Bush Knolls

Population: 179　**Incorporated:** 1964

INSETS L to R: The trees in Sugar Bush Knolls are often still found in neat lines left over • Residents from the village's days as a tree farm; residents of Sugar Bush Knolls are surrounded on all sides by natural views • A sign welcomes visitors to the village • Fall colors in Sugar Bush Knolls

Kent State University is famous for its black squirrels, and it holds a Black Squirrel Festival each year. An employee of the Davey Tree Expert Company was responsible for bringing the squirrels to Kent. In the 1950s, the grounds superintendent at the university, Larry Wooddell, was traveling through Chardon and was intrigued by black squirrels he saw. He talked to his friend, Biff Staples, a retired Davey man who had seen black squirrels in Canada on a business trip. The two negotiated with the Canadian government to acquire 10 squirrels that could be moved onto campus. The rest is history![12]

Sugar Bush Knolls

The Father of Tree Surgery

THE DEVELOPMENT OF THE VILLAGE of Sugar Bush Knolls all began with an idea from the "father of tree surgery," John Davey, of Kent, Ohio. Davey was born in England in 1846, moving to the United States as an adult. As the story goes, Davey was a self-made man, even down to the simplest details, like learning to read. After moving to the United States and pursuing a more robust education, Davey became intrigued by the idea of finding a "systematic, scientific way" to save neglected trees. In 1901, Davey published his book, *The Tree Doctor*, to share with the world an interesting idea: trees, like people, became ill, and rather than destroying an ill tree, you could treat it.[1]

Around the time that his father published this book, a young Martin L. Davey was traveling door-to-door near Kent, Ohio, selling typewriters and insurance policies in an attempt to save money for a college education. In addition to his normal sales, Martin started offering his father's book for purchase as well.[2]

By 1908, the two formed the Davey Tree Expert Company and the attached Davey Institute. The company's services were available to businesses and private individuals looking to fix their landscaping. Davey also offered conservation services for public lands, such as parks.[3] When on a call, employees of the Davey Tree Expert Company (often college students on summer break in the early years), performed a myriad of activities including: pruning, bracing, root aeration, spraying for insects, or feeding. One of the most interesting and unique "tree surgeries" that the company offered was the filling of a cavity. If a tree was being eaten away by a fungus, the Davey Company removed the offending fungus, cleaned the open wound, and filled it with concrete, just as a dentist repairs a rotting tooth. Eventually bark would grow over the filling, hiding the work of the tree doctors.[4]

The Davey Company Grows

In 1923, John Davey passed away at the age of 77, leaving Martin at the head of the Davey Tree Expert Company. Throughout the early twentieth century, the company grew immensely, doing three million dollars of business in 1928.[5] In 1930, Martin formed the Davey Investment Company and began to acquire land in Streetsboro Township from the Twin Lakes Land Company. Here he built the company's new headquarters and an institute where employees could be trained in the skills John Davey had left behind, and where scientists were free to make new discoveries. The headquarters was a pleasant place for employees and their families to enjoy, with man-made lakes and picnic grounds. One man, a caretaker of the tree farm on site, lived on the land with his family.[6]

While the family business was booming, Martin L. Davey had some other growing business to attend to. From 1914 to 1918, Davey served as the mayor of the city of Kent, afterwards moving on to a seat in the U.S. House of Representatives. In 1935, Davey became the Governor of Ohio, serving out two terms until 1939.[7]

Building a Subdivision on the Tree Farm

During World War II, the Davey Tree Expert Company experienced a labor shortage because of the war effort. Not long after, in 1946, Martin L. Davey passed away. While the Davey Expert Tree Company would remain a national business (it is still active today), Martin Davey, Jr., had some decisions to make as the 1950s dawned. He eventually moved the tree farm to Wooster and began to look for builders for a residential community on the site in the Kent area.[8]

By the mid-1950s, 158 acres with 111 new lots had been developed in the new Sugar Bush Knolls subdivision, named for the sugar maple trees that once filled the Davey's tree farm. Davey hired a realtor, Bob Meeker, who had grown up playing on the Davey Tree Farm. By the early 1960s, the Davey family was ready to cut ties to the land, and in a famous deal made at the Twin Lakes Country Club (some say Martin Davey, Jr., lost the land in a card game, but this is likely not true), most of the former tree farm was transferred to Cyril Porthouse. In 1963, Cyril and the other founding residents of the new Sugar Bush Knolls subdivision formed a homeowners' association.[9]

The homeowners' association quickly found that the residents of the area were struggling from the inconvenience of being located in two townships (Franklin and Streetsboro). When a heavy snowstorm passed through or a street sign needed to be replaced, it was never quite clear which township was responsible, so neither township sent staff to help the residents of Sugar Bush Knolls. In addition, the children of Sugar Bush Knolls were attending two different schools, sometimes just based on what side of the street they lived on. For these reasons, the homeowners' association quickly suggested the subdivision incorporate themselves as a village.[10]

In June of 1964, the village of Sugar Bush Knolls was officially incorporated. With this new official status, it was time to form a government. The residents of the village elected Cyril Porthouse as the first mayor, and the city council began meeting, hosting each other in their own homes. When it was time to vote, citizens cast their ballots at the home of the Bush family. Former residents recall that Mrs. Bush set up a second fake election each year in which children could practice voting.[11]

Cyril Porthouse was a chemist and became wealthy after taking over Pyramid Rubber in the mid-twentieth century. The company made rubber nipples for baby bottles, a hugely successful endeavor during the baby boom. The Porthouse family funded the construction of the Porthouse Theatre at Kent State University.[13]

TOP: A monument on the former site of the Sulphur Springs school

Population: 194   Approx. Founding: 1833

INSETS L to R: Liberty Township Volunteer Fire Department •
Asnowy street in Sulphur Springs • The final resting place of
Adam Link, one of the final living Revolutionary War veterans •
Sulphur Springs Post Office

One of the last living veterans of the American Revolution resided in Sulphur Springs, Ohio. Adam Link, born in Maryland in 1761, joined the Continental Army as a teenager in 1777. He moved to Crawford County after the war, living to be 102 years old, and dying in August 1864. He is buried in Union Cemetery in Sulphur Springs.[11] While still living, he was photographed and interviewed for an 1864 book titled *The Last Men of the Revolution* that featured seven remaining veterans.[12]

Sulphur Springs

John Slifer Comes to Crawford County

IN 1833 JOHN SLIFER LAID OUT A TOWN that he named Annapolis. Slifer, a native of Maryland, decided to pay tribute to his home state by giving his new town the name of its capital city. Despite Slifer's attempts, most locals called this new village "Slifer Town" in his honor. Any mail directed to the village's residents was addressed to "Sulphur Spring," a name the post office took from a nearby spring with a sulphur-like smell. In July of 1890, the village officially adopted the name of Sulphur Springs, adding an "s" to the postal designation to avoid confusion with similarly named villages.[1]

In 1837, Slifer donated a portion of his land to the village so it could build a small log cabin schoolhouse. It is believed that this school was built near the site of the original spring that gave the village's post office its name.[2]

According to village histories, John Slifer was a loud and impulsive man. Slifer is also remembered for carrying his impetuous nature into his daily interactions.[3] One particular story about Slifer really displays his foolhardy personality. During his time in Sulphur Springs (then Annapolis), Slifer served as justice of the peace for Liberty Township. As the story goes, he once sent a handwritten transcript of his court docket to the Crawford County Court of Common Pleas, where a judge, seeing his poor penmanship, commented, "The people must be fools to elect such an ignorant man as Justice of the Peace." Slifer happened to be in the courtroom at the time, and he asked the clerk for a pen and paper, so that he could copy the docket again, with perfect penmanship this time. Slifer handed over the neatly penned docket to a dumbfounded judge, who asked why he had written so sloppily on his first pass. Slifer acerbically replied that he had "intended [the docket] for use by grown men, not for the entertainment of boys."[4]

Unfortunately for Slifer, his village of Annapolis did not grow fast enough, and he lost money on the venture. In 1841, he sold his land holdings in the village and moved west. Little is known about Slifer after he left Ohio, but many sources agree that within a year he had committed suicide, perhaps distraught over his financial losses.[5]

Transportation in Sulphur Springs

Unfortunately, later in the 1800s, when plans were enacted to build a railroad passing through Crawford County, Sulphur Springs didn't become a railroad stop. That honor was given to New Washington and the nearby Mansfield, in Richland County. Originally, residents of Liberty Township thought that the railway would run through their boundaries. In fact, $35,000 in stock was sold to township residents. On the eastern border of Sulphur Springs, an enterprising farmer by the name of George Teel attempted to build his own town that would sit directly on the railway path. He laid out lots on his farm and even gave his new village a name: Teeltown. When the path of the railroad project was redrawn, Teeltown quickly failed, and it is nothing but a local story today.[6]

While Sulphur Springs never had a railroad, the village was home to a factory that produced horse-drawn carriages and wagons. In 1862, the Sexauer Carriage Works opened at the corner of Paris and Jackson Streets in the village. The business was operated by the four Sexauer brothers of nearby Bucyrus. They built wagons for farming along with carriages, buggies, and light spring wagons for day-to-day transportation.

In 1893, William Sexauer, the only living brother remaining, closed the business and sold the building to Henry Heibertshausen.[7]

Unearthing the Sulphur Spring

For many years the spring that gave Sulphur Springs its name served residents and travelers alike. The spring also helped residents in emergencies, as they carried buckets of fresh spring water to put out fires. Unfortunately, in 1949, when a nearby stream was dredged and cleaned, the spring was affected and began to run dry. Nature took its course, and soon the spring was covered.[8]

In 1983, in celebration of the Sulphur Springs sesquicentennial, Randy Main, a businessman who operated a plumbing, heating, and air conditioning business in the village, began to unearth the original spring. It was believed that the spring was on Main's land, but finding the exact location was complicated. Eventually, Main was able to find an underground steel pipe that town histories said once ran from the spring to a barn owned by a former resident named Elmer Kafer. He was able to follow the pipe east to the spring.[9]

When the spring was found, another Sulphur Springs resident, Kenny Feik, joined Main in his journey, bringing a backhoe to dig out the spring, which was found to be more than a foot below ground and lined with hand-cut sandstone. Main and Feik were able to conduct some emergency restoration work on the sandstone walls to maintain the integrity of the spring. The spring was no longer dry when discovered by Main and Feik; in fact, Main had to pump water from the spring and into a nearby stream a few times a month. This new water flow allowed modern residents to confirm that their ancestors were correct: the spring does give off a strong sulphur odor.[10]

Dr. Frank M. Virtue was a practicing doctor in the early village. In 1926, Virtue passed away, but his wife, Lue, remained in town until her death almost 20 years later. As a widow, Lue invited teachers needing a home to stay with her. For this reason, village residents fondly called her home the "house of virtue."[13]

TOP: A suspension bridge with steel cables built at Cross Mound Park in 1936

Population: 287   Approx. Founding: 1801

INSETS L to R: A sign welcoming visitors to Cross Mound Park • The Crosstown Creamery • Nye's Tavern today with a historic marker dedicated to William Sooy Smith out front • A historic marker telling the story of Zane's Trace can also be found outside the historic Nye's Tavern

Tarlton is home to the Cross Mound. This mound, shaped like a cross, is 90 feet across with a large circular depression, 20 feet wide and 12 inches deep. While the mound has been listed on the National Register of Historic Places, no one really knows much about its history. The mound has no known cultural affiliation, although many scholars have assumed it is of the Mississippian Culture (approximately 800–1500 AD). During this time, the cross symbol was being used to represent the sun. Today the Cross Mound is managed by the Fairfield County Historical Parks Commission.[18]

Tarlton

Early Settlers of Tarlton

TARLTON, OHIO, IS ONE OF THE OLDEST incorporated villages in Ohio. Squatters trying to live near the economically important Zane's Trace initially inhabited the area in the late 1790s. As the nineteenth century dawned, Benjamin Newell of Pennsylvania obtained a portion of land on the Salt Creek. In 1801, Newell laid out a new village on his land, calling it Newellstown. No one is quite sure when or why the name was changed to Tarlton, but that is its name today.[1]

When founded, Tarlton was part of Fairfield County. In 1810, Pickaway County was formed from portions of Fairfield, Ross, and Franklin Counties. When the merge happened, a portion of Fairfield County known as Saltcreek Township was offered to Pickaway. Since Tarlton belonged to Saltcreek Township, Tarlton changed counties, too.[2]

Many early families came to Tarlton from Pennsylvania. In fact, the first white man to lay claim to land in the village of Tarlton was John Shoemaker, from Berks County, Pennsylvania. Many other early residents came from the same place. Shoemaker arrived in 1801, purchased his lot, and then returned to Pennsylvania for his family. It took him five years to return with the entire Shoemaker clan. When he did finally settle into Tarlton, Shoemaker opened the first tavern in town.[3]

Many roads passed through Tarlton in its early days, including the well-known Zane's Trace. This made the village a popular stagecoach stop, leading to success for owners of inns, taverns, and the like. During the War of 1812, a man named Adam Nye came through the village of Tarlton with his regiment. He liked the town so much that after the war he decided to move there. He opened a well-known tavern that was said to be a favorite of both Henry Clay and Andrew Jackson. For anyone traveling from the state of Kentucky to points east, including Washington, D.C., Tarlton was a typical stop. It is very possible that Clay and Jackson made stops in Tarlton.[4]

William Sooy Smith

One of the most well-known residents of Tarlton was William Sooy Smith. Smith was born on July 22, 1830, in Tarlton. During the War of 1812, Captain Sooy Smith, William's father, famously raised a volunteer infantry in Pennsylvania.[5]

At the age of 14, a precocious young William Sooy Smith headed off to Ohio University in Athens, Ohio, with barely any cash in hand. Smith worked hard, managing to pay his way through school. He graduated in 1849.[6] After his time at Ohio University, William Sooy Smith headed to West Point to follow in his father's military footsteps, but in his own unique way: by seeking a degree in engineering.[7] During Smith's studies, he roomed with future Civil War military officers, James B. McPherson and Joshua W. Sill. Smith graduated 6th in his class of 52 pupils, receiving his degree in 1853.[8]

After graduating, Smith was appointed to a frontier post as a lieutenant. Smith found this job incredibly dull and resigned at the end of his first year. Smith began working on the Illinois Central Railroad. An illness took William Sooy Smith to Buffalo, New York, where he met his first wife, welcomed his son Charles into the world, and opened his own engineering business, Parkinson and Smith.[9] Smith began training his son in engineering at the age of six. Smith believed engineering to be both a science and an art, requiring frequent study as well as brawn.[10] Smith's first wife died not long after his son was born, and as a result, father and son likely spent a lot of time together.[11]

As soon as the Civil War began in 1861, William Sooy Smith returned to Ohio to volunteer. He served as a Colonel, leading the 13th Ohio Volunteer Infantry into battle. Smith was made a Brigadier General after the Battle of Shiloh and promoted to Major General after his service at Vicksburg.[12] Due to his training and experience as a mechanical engineer, Smith was often asked to lead expeditions to interrupt Confederate supply lines by altering railways.[13]

William Sooy Smith and the Meridian Campaign

Unfortunately for Smith, he was involved in a major failure during the Meridian Campaign in February 1864. Smith was assigned to fellow Ohioan, Major General William Tecumseh Sherman, who would soon lead his famous March to the Sea. Sherman asked Smith to bring a large group of cavalry (Smith's specialty) from Memphis, Tennessee, to Meridian, Mississippi. At Meridian, Sherman's men would meet Smith's, and as a larger combined force, they would head into Alabama. Smith was defeated on the way by a force led by Confederate leader Nathan Bedford Forrest. Smith wasted valuable time by failing to send a letter to Sherman communicating his loss. Eventually figuring William Sooy Smith would never arrive, Sherman and his men had to give up on their hopes of moving forward to Alabama.[14]

While he would continue to speak positively of Smith's intelligence and bravery, Sherman also submitted an official report on the Meridian Campaign that criticized his actions. Smith would eventually ask Sherman to revoke the report, but he never did. Historians have remained split on William Sooy Smith's culpability for this failure.[15]

In 1864, due to a very painful outbreak of rheumatism, William Sooy Smith was forced to retire.[16] He continued to work as a mechanical engineer, becoming an internationally known expert on bridges and building the world's first all-steel bridge, in Glasgow, Missouri.[17]

According to the *History of Pickaway County*, as written by Aaron Van Cleaf in 1906, the last bear ever shot in Pickaway County was killed in Saltcreek Township in 1840. It was shot by Jonathan Dreisbach and John Reichelderfer. Their two shots landed simultaneously.[19]

TOP: The Tiro Tavern, original home of the Tiro Testicle Festival

Population: 262   **Incorporated:** 1890

INSETS L to R: Tiro-Auburn Volunteer Fire Department • This building in Tiro has a historic sign for Tiro Feed Company on the front • The Doggone Shack is a pet supply store in Tiro • Tiro United Methodist Church

Around 1910, a hatchery was founded in Tiro, under the name Cooperative Breeding and Hatching Company. The company kept several thousand eggs under incubators each year, with a huge hatching season in the spring. Residents of Tiro became accustomed to the site of thousands of day-old chicks being loaded on a truck to be shipped across the country. In 1930, the company even began its own trade publication, *Pay Streak Chick News*. The hatchery was one of the biggest businesses in Tiro at the time.[13]

Tiro

Settlers come to Auburn Township

WHITE SETTLERS CAME to the southwestern corner of Auburn Township fairly early in Ohio's history, but it was not until a railroad arrived that residents began to think about incorporating a village. In December of 1825, Rodolphus Morse became the area's first postmaster, running the operation out of his own cabin. The post office was first called Auburn but eventually renamed Tiro. About a mile and a half south of Morse's cabin was a short-lived community known to the locals as Mechanicsburg. Between 1845 and 1850, many mechanics, including blacksmiths, cabinet makers, coopers, and carpenters, settled in the area.[1]

During the 1870s, the southwestern corner of Auburn Township was chosen as a stop for the Mansfield, Coldwater, and Lake Michigan Railroad. The station in Crawford County was named for the village of De Kalb, about half a mile south of the station's location, in Vernon township. Despite De Kalb's early claim to the station, a new village sprung up around the railway track. Almost immediately after the track was laid, village lots were laid out by J. D. Brown, with additions by John Hillborn a few years later. A store was built in 1872, and in 1874 the local post office moved to the growing community. By this time the post office was going by the name Tiro. This name was brought to the new village, which still today is known as Tiro. The village of Mechanicsburg was absorbed by the new village.[2]

Tiro was incorporated in 1890. The village government was able to jumpstart itself by borrowing some starting capital from a resident named Miss Viola Chapman. She loaned the village $300 in 1890. With cash on hand, the village council was able to assemble and begin drafting a legal code for the community. Tiro's earliest residents were apparently the puritanical sort, as the first ordinance on the books banned the sale of alcohol. By the time an early county history was written in 1912, Tiro was the only village in Crawford County where a saloon had never existed.[3]

The strict morals of Tiro's early residents can be seen in one story passed on from the village's earliest days. Apparently some "wags of the village" thought it would be funny to put up posters around town, declaring that two neighboring towns would be hosting a football game in Tiro the following Sunday. Religious residents of Tiro were visibly upset that anyone would consider taking part in a sporting event on the sabbath. As the story goes, on that Sunday, "Every citizen left his home and was on the streets, crowds gathered everywhere, men and women in indignant protest…" Eventually news leaked that the posters had been only a joke, and everyone was free to go home.[4]

The village of Tiro thrived as the railroad brought prosperity. In 1883, the villagers raised $4,000 to open a mill. In 1921, the village was first wired for electricity, bringing light to the village. In 1930, Tiro made statewide news, as the village of 550 people officially had no debt.[5]

Russell Coffey, A Celebrated Veteran

In 1898, a boy named Russell Coffey was born in Tiro. Little did anyone know, he would live to see three centuries. As a young man, Coffey moved from Tiro to Columbus, to attend The Ohio State University. As he worked on his degree, the U.S. entered World War I. Both of Coffey's brothers entered the military and served overseas, but Coffey did not enlist until October of 1918. As he later said, "I volunteered, because I would have been drafted if I hadn't." Coffey spent about a month in training before the war ended on November 11, 1918. He was discharged in December and returned to Ohio State. While Coffey never actually made it onto a battlefield, he was still a veteran.[6] In fact, at the time of Coffey's death in December 2007, he was the oldest living United States veteran of World War I.[7, 8]

However, Coffey lived to see the age of 109 and outlived his wife and his only child, but he was much prouder of his other lifelong accomplishments. He earned both a bachelor's and master's degree from Ohio State, where he met his wife Bernice. The two moved to New York so that Coffey could earn his Ph.D. at New York University. After his academic training, Coffey spent his career proudly as a teacher. He began in Phelps, Kentucky, teaching grades six through twelve, then moving to a junior high in Findlay, Ohio, and a year at the University of Findlay. Coffey finally settled in Northwest Ohio, teaching at Bowling Green State University from 1948 to 1969. For most of his time at the university, Coffey also directed the graduate program in health and physical education.[9] When Coffey died in December 2007, he received a full military funeral.[10]

An Annual Festival

In the late 1980s, Alan Cramer, the owner of the Tiro Tavern, was visited by a couple of friends who brought along an unusual food: pig and calf testicles. The group fried them up and tried them. Cramer enjoyed the meal, so he brought some to his bar, starting a tradition that would take place annually on the last Saturday of April. Cramer passed away in 2009, but the tradition continues. Each spring the Tiro Tavern brings 600 pounds of calf and pig testicles to the village and fries them up for the annual Testicle Festival. For the squeamish, vendors with other foods are available, along with a weekend of entertainment and, of course, plenty of merchandise. The festival's slogan? "You'll have a ball."[11]

In 1893, the *Tiro American* was first printed, but it didn't last long. In 1911, W. W. Davis took over the printing presses and began publishing the *Tiro World* once a week. The paper published consistently until 1968, including a special 50th anniversary edition in 1961.[12]

TIRO COMMUNITY LIBRARY
in Methodist Church
OPEN
Thurs. 1:00-4:30
Sat. 10:00-1:00

TOP: A veterans' memorial at the Darby Township Cemetery in Unionville Center

Population: 232   Incorporated: 1879

INSETS L to R: The Unionville Center Post Office and UC Signs • The Darby Township Cemetery • Unionville Center Methodist Episcopal Church • A historic marker in a Unionville Center park describes Vice President Charles Warren Fairbanks

Thanks to the creative work of Unionville Center resident Michelle Blevins, the village hosts a family-friendly festival once a year. The festival, named for Charles Fairbanks, takes place on the village green, not far from a state historical marker telling his life story. Originally the festival was hosted each spring; however, Blevins and other festival organizers have officially moved it to the fall, in the hopes of avoiding the spring rainy season.[15]

Unionville Center

Founding Unionville Center

IN 1847, JOHN, FREDERICK, AND DAVID SAGER had the Union County surveyor lay out a village in Darby Township. They called this village Unionville Center. John Sager was the leader of the Sager family, building the village's first store and serving as its first postmaster. By 1879, the population of Unionville Center had reached about 229. In March of that year, the village incorporated.[1]

A Future Vice President Comes of Age in Unionville Center

Today, Unionville Center is best known as the birthplace of former Vice President Charles W. Fairbanks. Fairbanks was born on May 11, 1852, to Loriston Monroe Fairbanks and Mary Adelaide Smith Fairbanks.[2] Charles Fairbanks and his siblings grew up in a one-room log house in Unionville Center on a farm. Eventually, when Fairbanks was still a young man, the family was able to replace their log home with a much more spacious, two-story frame house.[3]

During his childhood, Fairbanks's parents modeled the value of a publicly engaged lifestyle. They were active in the local Methodist Church, Loriston served on local councils, and Mary Adelaide passionately took to the causes of temperance and abolition. She also likely aided refugees passing through on the Underground Railroad.[4]

Fairbanks left Unionville Center at the age of 15 to seek an education at Ohio Wesleyan University, in the city of Delaware.[5] He graduated in 1872, ranking 8th in his class of 44 students.[6] While at Ohio Wesleyan, Fairbanks met Cornelia "Nellie" Cole. Cole came from a very well-to-do family in the nearby Marysville. As the *New York Times* once told the story, "In her class was 'Charlie' Fairbanks, then an awkward farmer. Both took the classical course, both were literary, and when he was elected editor of the college monthly she became associate editor." The two were soon smitten.[7]

Fairbanks Builds His Career

After graduation, Charles worked as a reporter at the *Western Associated Press*, which his uncle managed, while taking night classes at Cleveland Law School. As soon as he passed the bar in 1874, Charlie and Nellie were married and off to Indianapolis,[8] where an uncle had been able to secure Charles a job working as an attorney for the Chesapeake and Ohio Railway.[9]

Fairbanks set up his own practice, and his fortune began to grow, as did his Republican pro-business interests. It is no wonder he began to support large businesses, as a lawyer for railroad managers, he often had to prosecute workers who decided to strike. Fairbanks became a well-known influencer in the Indiana Republican Party. He secretly owned interests in multiple newspapers, and he also funded various candidates.[10]

Trying His Hand at Politics

Eventually Fairbanks made an unsuccessful bid for the U.S. Senate in 1893. Soon after, he got to know fellow Ohioan, and soon to be President-Elect, William McKinley. The two became very close, and McKinley even encouraged Fairbanks to give the keynote speech at the 1896 Republican National Convention. In 1897, McKinley helped Fairbanks finally get elected to the Senate.

When McKinley was choosing a vice president for a potential second term, Fairbanks was mentioned. Like McKinley, Fairbanks represented an older, more conservative, and more business-oriented portion of the Republican Party. However, in order to appeal to the growing progressive wing of their party, Republicans chose Theodore Roosevelt to accompany McKinley on the ticket.[11] In 1901, the nation lost a leader and Charles Fairbanks lost a good friend when President William McKinley was assassinated in Buffalo, New York.[12]

The 26th Vice President of the United States

When President Theodore Roosevelt sought reelection in 1904, the Republican party all but forced him to place Charles Fairbanks on the ticket to please the conservative portion of their electorate. Fairbanks was not pleased: he disliked Roosevelt's progressive policies and likely resented his rise to the Oval Office. Most Republicans had assumed that Fairbanks would have followed his friend McKinley as President, but McKinley's assassination had changed things.

In 1905, Charles and Cornelia Fairbanks moved to Washington, D.C., so that he could serve as vice president. While Charles fell into his role of managing the Senate (Roosevelt wouldn't let him do much else), Cornelia became politically prominent. As the leader of the Daughters of the American Revolution, the politically savvy Cornelia traveled in many political circles in D.C., often discussing progressive policies, such as women's suffrage.[13]

Charles Fairbanks tried desperately to earn his party's nomination for President in 1908, but Theodore Roosevelt made sure that he was defeated by William Howard Taft. Against his wishes, the Republican Party placed Fairbanks back on the Vice Presidential ticket with Charles Evans Hughes in 1916, but the pair lost to incumbent Woodrow Wilson. Fairbanks retired to his home in Indiana, where he passed away in 1918.[14]

Unionville Center once had a traffic light, but it's been gone since the 1950s. As Mayor Denver Thompson told the *Columbus Dispatch* in 2011, "A truck came by and took it out, and the town never put it back up." With only a few major crossroads and only 0.17 square miles of land, the village seems to be doing just fine.[16]

TOP: Storefronts at the Made by Me Art Studio and the Vaughnsville Post Office

Population: 262   **Approx. Founding:** 1847

INSETS L to R: Signs hanging at the Vaughnsville baseball fields mark the village's recent sports history • Vaughnsville Community Church • The front window of the village post office decorated for fall • The Vaughnsville Community Center (formerly Vaughnsville High School's gymnasium)

Vaughnsville may have been the first place where individual cups were used during a church communion service. In 1893, John G. Thomas, a doctor and minister in Vaughnsville, submitted a patent for his "Thomas Individual Communion Service." Vaughnsville's status as the first to use individual cups is hotly contested, but according to some sources, Thomas saw a member of his congregation with a "diseased mouth condition" and decided it would be worth experimenting with separate cups. After trying out his invention, Thomas sought a patent and began selling his new cups during the 1890s.[14]

Vaughnsville

Two Villages Become One

IN 1847, ELI CLEVENGER PLATTED A NEW VILLAGE named Monterey, in Putnam County, Ohio. At the same time, D. C. Vaughn was platting his new town of Vaughnsville, just north of Monterey.[1] The two villages were split by Findlay Road. Vaughn had a slight advantage, as his village was located on the Northern Ohio Railway and was fully equipped with a train station. However, Vaughn and Clevenger were almost certainly not competitors, but friends, and possibly family members. Many Vaughn family members owned land in Monterey, and at least two Vaughns were married to members of the Clevenger families. Just as their two families had merged, Clevenger and Vaughn eventually merged their two villages, taking on the current name of Vaughnsville.[2]

Vaughnsville Throwback Night

In 1906, a new school was built in Vaughnsville, on State Route 12. In 1915, the Vaughnsville High School boys basketball team played its first season at this school. Known as the Vikings, the Vaughnsville team was well known to other Putnam County players. From 1924 through 1949, a period of only 26 years, the Vikings won 10 county titles. However, at the beginning of the 1962–1963 school year, Vaughnsville's students and staff were absorbed into the nearby Columbus Grove school system. The village wasn't large enough to justify operating a school for its residents.[3]

Despite a successful integration with Columbus Grove, Vaughnsville never quite forgot its Vikings. In January of 2015, Nick Verhoff, the Superintendent of Columbus Grove Schools and the nephew of the last Vaughnsville High School principal, turned a regular basketball game into a Vaughnsville Throwback Night. Thanks to local sponsors, the Columbus Grove boys basketball team was able to wear new jerseys that evening, sporting the Viking's blue that had not been seen on the court for over 50 years. Community members pulled Vikings trophies and memorabilia from storage in the former high school gym (now the Vaughnsville Community Center), displaying them in trophy cases at Columbus Grove High School that evening.[4]

Unfortunately, the Columbus Grove boys basketball team lost to Fort Jennings (page 60) that night by a score of 57 to 53. However, Verhoff and his planning team still considered the event a huge success. The event was even attended by a former Vaughnsville teacher, Genevieve Emerson, who was 98 years old in 2015. Emerson was teaching at Vaughnsville when the school consolidated with Columbus Grove. Many people at the event were "coming out of the stands" to approach Emerson, recognizing their teacher from many years ago. For Verhoff, Emerson's presence "made the night."[5]

Stretch Goedde

One of Vaughnsville's best basketball players during the Vikings' heyday was Sylvester Goedde, often known as "Stretch." Sources disagree about his exact height, but he definitely stood at least 6' 8" tall. Goedde was a multi-sport athlete, pitching for the Vikings baseball team at the 1942 state tournament, his senior year. After graduating, Goedde was off to Washington, D.C., having been recruited by the Georgetown basketball team.[6]

Goedde often sat on the bench during his short time at Georgetown. He faced stiff competition for the starting center position from future NBA player John Mahnken. According to one source, Goedde would often request to go home early during evening practices. When

his coach asked why, Goedde explained that, "Basketball was fun, but he'd have to quit the squad if he couldn't get near a radio in time to hear the nightly broadcast of *Superman*."

In February of 1943, Goedde wanted out of Georgetown, so he signed on to play minor league baseball with the Toledo Mudhens.[7] Goedde pitched for Toledo for one year before being traded to Elmira, New York, and the next year, Little Rock.[8] After three years in the minor leagues, Goedde returned to his education, enrolling at the University of Toledo. Here he earned a degree in education in 1948, helping kickstart his career as a high school teacher.[9] Goedde passed away in 2000 in Van Wert, Ohio.[10]

Vaughnsville Communications

Based in the village of Vaughnsville, Vaughnsville Communications works daily to provide fast and efficient service to the rural community. This communications company was originally founded in 1937 as the Vaughnsville Telephone Company and led by a group of local farmers who owned their own telephones, wires, and poles. The farmers had been operating the wires for their own personal use but decided to combine their equipment under one company name, servicing the entire village and saving money on all of the original founders' phone bills.[11] In 2008, the Vaughnsville Telephone Company became Vaughnsville Communications as a small recognition of the changing times and the company's changing services. This connectivity makes Vaughnsville relatively unique among many rural towns, where access to the internet is a real problem.[12]

Many small villages are eager to incorporate as soon as possible, but not Vaughnsville. Residents of Vaughnsville avoided incorporation for business reasons. Vaughnsville was one of the most successful trading points in Sugar Creek Township by the early 1900s, and locals worried that a government and its regulations would get in the way of this financial success.[13]

TOP: Welsh flags hang at many homes in the village

Population: 119   Incorporated: 1897

INSETS L to R: The crowd inside Salem Presbyterian during the 2018 Gymanfa Ganu • A baseball park in Venedocia, complete with lights for nighttime play • A view of Salem Presbyterian over a field of soybeans from the edge of Venedocia • The Venedocia Post Office

Some of the best singers at the Gymanfa Ganu over the years were members of the Venedocia Male Chorus. Formed in 1890, this group competed in (and won) many an Eisteddfod, a day of competition for Welsh singers and other artists. As the story goes, the original conductor of the chorus, Bob Thomas, once took the group to Columbus for a statewide Eisteddfod, but upon arriving, found he was short one man. He went out onto the streets of the capital city, found a willing participant, and told him to stand still among the normal chorus members and keep his mouth shut.[13]

Venedocia

Welsh Immigrants with Ohio Connections Arrive in Van Wert County

IN 1847, William Bebb, Thomas Morris, Richard Jervis, and their families boarded a ship leaving North Wales. After six weeks and three days of travel, the group reached New York. Upon disembarking from their ship, the group immediately made their way to Ohio. Within two weeks, the new Welsh settlers made it to the Butler County village known as Paddy's Run (today the unincorporated community of Shandon).[1]

By the time the families reached Paddy's Run, the village had become a well-established center of Welsh culture in the new state of Ohio. It was an obvious first stop for a new group of Welsh settlers, but this enterprising group of travelers wanted to form their own settlement.[2]

The group would use Paddy's Run as a planning ground for a future foray into the Ohio wilderness. Luckily for them, one of their members, William Bebb, had friends in high places in the state.[3] In 1846, Bebb's cousin and a former resident of Paddy's Run, also named William Bebb, had been sworn in as Ohio's 19th Governor. The governor was born at Paddy's Run in 1802 to Welsh immigrant parents. This first-generation American spent much of his time fostering a community in his hometown. He was one of the first teachers in Paddy's Run, and he opened a boarding school along with his wife, Sarah. After breaking into politics in the 1840s, Bebb was nominated for governor by the Whig Party.[4]

Bebb took a brief break from his governing duties to return to his hometown and meet his cousin for the first time. The two William Bebbs knew they were related, but they had grown up with an ocean between them; this would have been quite the family reunion. After getting to know each other, the two William Bebbs quickly set out from Paddy's Run to find a place for the newly arrived Welsh settlers to live. Most of the traveling group stayed that year in Paddy's Run while the Bebb cousins traveled to Van Wert county. Here they found and purchased a yet-undeveloped portion of land for the new Welsh settlers.[5]

Early Life in Venedocia

Bebb returned to Paddy's Run to bring his family and traveling partners back to Van Wert County. The settlers found that life on the Ohio frontier was not easy. As Richard Jervis wrote in his recollection of the time "…the land was thick with trees, and it was wet and uninhabited….The only means of transporting goods to the communities was by the slow boat; and when the canal would freeze at the beginning of the winter, everything had to be at a standstill until the ice would melt again."[6]

To trade for necessary goods, the residents of the new Venedocia had to travel to nearby Delphos. The new settlers had no cash, but they were able to exchange butter and eggs for a few cents a pound. A trip to Delphos became a multiple-day journey, as the settlers needed to also take advantage of the village's flour mill. As Jervis wrote, the group would have to leave Venedocia by noon to be sure they made it to Delphos by nightfall. They would sleep in the mill overnight and then take their goods home in the morning.[7]

Night was a dangerous time for the early settlers of Venedocia. They all wrote of restless nights filled with the howls of wolves and the claws of wildcats scratching at their newly constructed log homes. As one local story says, on the first night in Venedocia, the Jervis family heard animals scratching at the door and chimney of their little cabin. Richard Jervis went to the door, weapon in hand, ready to shoot the beasts. He

took a quick shot, but only after he killed one of the animals did the family realize that the "threat" was simply a few porcupines.[8]

Venedocia grew steadily over the course of the nineteenth century. A mill was erected, new businesses came to town, and a railroad was routed through the county. By the late 1890s, talk was circulating about officially incorporating the village. On September 7, 1897, that dream was finally realized and the village of Venedocia gained its official legal status.[9]

The Salem Presbyterian Church Yesterday and Today

Worship has always been an important part of life in Venedocia. From the time that the first settlers arrived, they were certain to carve out time each week to hold church services in their homes. In 1853, the residents of Venedocia built the first Salem Presbyterian Church, and it has been a center of Welsh culture in the community ever since. The church itself has been rebuilt and moved various times over its history. The current structure was dedicated in 1898. All church services were conducted in the Welsh language until 1885, and only in 1917 did the Salem Church begin to print their annual reports in English.[10, 11]

Welsh culture is alive and well in Venedocia today. The most important event of the year for the small community is known as Gymanfa Ganu, or the festival of sacred hymns. This festival is held each year on the Sunday of Labor Day Weekend. The event centers around the singing of traditional Welsh hymns in four-part harmony by the entire community. Residents of Venedocia and visitors from all over the country crowd the rows of pews at the Salem Presbyterian Church and begin to sing together. The doors are left open, and it is said you can hear the singing up to a mile away. Gymanfa Ganu celebrations are common in Wales and in Welsh settlements around Ohio and the world.[12]

Interested in learning more about Venedocia? It boasts the title of smallest Ohio village with a website. Since 1996, Charles Good, a retired professor who has lived in town since 1977, has run the village's website. It covers current events as well as hundreds of historical documents. Visit at www.venedocia.org.[14]

TOP: The West Farmington Fire Dept. and a park where Western Reserve Seminary once stood

Population: 491   Approx. Founding: 1807

INSETS L to R: West Farmington Town Hall • West Farmington United Methodist Church • Hillside Cemetery • Bylers Groceries and Bulk Foods

C. E. W. Griffith was one interesting resident of West Farmington. Griffith traveled the world performing all of Shakespeare's works from memory. When not traveling, he lived in West Farmington. Griffith's obsession with Shakespeare took over the architecture of his home in town. It became known as the Shakespeare cottage, as Griffith worked to turn it into a replica of Shakespeare's home in Stratford-upon-Avon. Griffith almost always traveled with his manager, John P. Callahan. It is unconfirmed, but the two are generally considered to have been romantic partners.[17]

West Farmington

The Curtis and Wolcott Families Arrive in Trumbull County

IN 1806, THE FIRST WHITE SETTLERS arrived in what would become Farmington Township. To get there, David Curtis and Captain Lewis Wolcott walked from their homes in Connecticut. Wolcott stopped for a year just outside the future Farmington to work for a man named Joel Humiston in Vienna Township. After a year, Wolcott bid Mr. Humiston adieu and continued on to unfamiliar territory.[1]

Soon after, another man, Josiah Wolcott, made his way to this "New Connecticut." He was approached by a man named Samuel Bond, who at this time owned a large portion of the future Farmington. Bond convinced Josiah Wolcott to purchase 1,000 acres in Farmington, sight unseen. Wolcott then traveled to Ohio with some friends and

family. The group set off in the winter of 1806–1807, struggling on their way, but safely arriving. The group built a log cabin on the land and settled in for the winter.[2] In summer of 1807, Josiah made his way back to Connecticut to retrieve the women and children of the Wolcott family. The Wolcott family was large and growing. During the very early years of Farmington's existence, most of the population carried the surname Wolcott.[3]

Unfortunately, Josiah Wolcott's trip back to Ohio with his family was accompanied by a great loss. During the journey, Josiah's daughter, Mary (also known as Polly), fell off a log while crossing a stream. She was drenched in water and developed a serious cold. This eventually led to the tuberculosis that took Mary's life in 1808. A plot of land was cleared to bury Mary Wolcott.[4] Today this plot has grown and stands as the Hillside Cemetery in West Farmington. Mary's headstone can still be found here.[5]

When the Wolcott family arrived and built their new primitive homes, the land they settled on was known not as Farmington, but Henshaw. The township was owned by about 11 different men during the early 1800s, including one by the name of Samuel Henshaw. As the story goes, either Josiah Wolcott's son (E. P. Wolcott) or a man named Dennis Lewis changed the name to Farmington for the city of Farmington, Connecticut. By the 1820s, the Wolcott's new home was known as West Farmington, a village in Farmington Township.[6]

The Western Reserve Seminary

In 1828, residents of Farmington Township began fundraising to build a college known as Farmington Academy.[7] This school was so popular with northeastern Ohio students that a new building was needed by 1850. This new school was known as Farmington Normal School. In 1854, the school came under the leadership of the Methodist Church, and its name was changed to the Western Reserve Seminary. For over 70 years, the Western Reserve Seminary educated both men and women, preparing them for a myriad of careers.[8]

With interested students traveling from around the area, The Western Reserve Seminary built two dormitories in 1868.[9] According to an advertisement produced by the seminary in 1869, each room included a stove, table, and bedstead. Most students could acquire a room for $3.50–$4.00 per week, sometimes less if they formed Boarding Clubs.[10] In the men's dorm, known colloquially as "Thunder Caste" a professor was asked to live-in and "subdue high spirits."[11]

Among the graduates of the Western Reserve Seminary were Asa Jones, Ohio Lieutenant Governor; Charles E. Kennedy, director of the *Cleveland Plain Dealer*; and Clarence A. Darrow, a lawyer made famous for the Scopes Trial.[12]

The Western Reserve Seminary graduated its final class in 1906. Unfortunately, not long after, all three buildings on campus burned to the ground. It is suspected that the buildings were well insured, and the owners sought their benefits. All three buildings were gone by the early 1910s.[13] Today visitors to West Farmington will see a fire station and a park where the Western Reserve Seminary once stood.

Saving West Farmington's History From the Flames

Unfortunately, in the summer of 2017, the village of West Farmington lost a portion of its history when a fire struck Bontrager's Grocery. Not only did residents rely on this store for a quick shopping trip in town, but the building was also essentially serving as the village's museum.[14]

The building, one of the oldest in the town, was built in 1878. It had served as a dance hall and various grocery stores before the Bontragers took over in 2010. The grocery store was also storing ledgers, photographs, clothing, and various other physical items that told the story of the village. When the building went up in smoke, Julie Bontrager told Fire Chief John Bland, "We don't care what happens to the rest, can we please get to that stuff?"[15]

Bland understood Bontrager's desire to save the village's history; in fact, at one point, his grandparents had owned the local grocery store that was now in flames. Children from around the village, equally concerned, rushed to the scene of the fire and began to help fire crews move the damaged items out of the area. Many of these pieces of West Farmington history were saved, but unfortunately Bontrager's Grocery Store was lost.[1]

Almon Bruce French was born in West Farmington in 1838, enrolling at Western Reserve Seminary by the age of 16. When on summer break, French discovered that he could communicate with spirits. Using this supposed newfound power, French traveled the country conducting seances.[18]

TOP: Wharton United Methodist Church

Population: 342   **Approx. Founding:** 1848

INSETS L to R: Wharton Village Hall • A mill in the center of Wharton • A mural marks Boden's Garage in the village • A memorial to the former Wharton High School found near Wharton Community Park

While the village of Wharton was once home to Richland Township's first schoolhouse, today local children are bussed out of the village to get to school. However, residents of Wharton have successfully preserved the memory of their former school system. In the village's community park, visitors will find a plaque bearing an image of Wharton's former high school, home of the Dragons. In the sidewalk nearby, the letters "WHS" have been formed with bricks from the former schoolhouse.

Wharton

Building Around the Mad River and Lake Erie Railroad

WHARTON'S FOUNDING WAS TIED specifically to the construction of the Mad River and Lake Erie Railroad. This railway, meant to travel from Dayton to Sandusky by way of Tiffin, was first financed in 1836. The railway company incorporated in 1832, but it took a few extra years to secure state and county funding.[1]

The railway company made plans to lay track in Wyandot County, through Richland Township. Early residents of the county organized Richland Township in 1813, choosing a name that reflected the fertile soil in Wyandot County. Just over 30 years later, in 1844, railway construction was finishing up and the township was poised to grow. The Mad River and Lake Erie Railroad wasn't quite finished until the 1850s, but once construction finished in Richland Township, it became obvious to the residents that a new village was also on the way.[2]

Records conflict as to the official date that Samuel Rathburn laid out the town of Whartonsburg (sometimes spelled Whartensburgh). Some say 1846, while others stick to 1848. Either way, he was just in time to take advantage of the railroad. The village was centered on the railway depot, covering both sides of the tracks that ran northeast and southwest through town. The Whartonsburg depot would become a central hub of the railroad.[3]

Thanks to the railway, the village of Wharton prospered in its early years. Soon a hotel, known as the Wharton House, was established. The village also boasted three newspapers, the first school in the township, and by 1915, electric street lamps.[4]

It is believed that Rathburn chose the name of his new village to honor an early resident, but the mysterious Wharton has remained unidentified to this day.[5] In 1879, the Whartonsburg Post Office officially dropped the "burg" from its name, sticking with the name the village still uses today: Wharton.[6]

Delbert Rummel Goes Missing

By 1913, the village of Wharton was home to about 500 residents.[7] One of these residents was Delbert Rummel, a successful barber. Rummel was part of a longtime Wharton family: his last name was littered among the village's most important founding documents. Rummel himself had grown up in the village and knew his customers very well.[8] He was 35 years old but had not married.[9] His closest relatives were his brothers.[10]

On November 17, 1915, as *The Union County Journal* recorded, "just as a customer entered his shop, Rummel put on his hat and coat and said he would be back in a minute."[11] He was going just about half a mile down the road to collect a debt from a local farmer.[12] However, after he left his shop that day, Delbert Rummel was never seen again.

It took Rummel's brothers a few days to realize that something was amiss. They simply assumed that Delbert had forgotten to check in before he went to visit an out-of-town friend or family member. Two weeks after his disappearance, they began to worry. The brothers penned letters to all of their family members, asking after Delbert's location. With each reply they became more and more certain that something was wrong.[13]

The citizens of Wharton, many who had known Delbert Rummel since he was born, began a thorough manhunt. Worried that Rummel had been murdered, the searchers, numbering 75, spent a January day digging out a 40-foot sewer and dragging a nearby swamp. The residents also contacted the county government, insisting that a reward be offered for any information that could lead to Delbert's whereabouts. As the search continued, wild rumors spread, but no clues materialized.[14]

As the frustration grew among searchers, mania took hold. A local spiritualist dropped a clue about Delbert's case that encouraged a group of about 150 farmers to lead a lynch mob against the named kidnapper. Fortunately, they were stopped.[15]

By February of 1916, about three months since Delbert was last seen, one of his brothers decided to consult a fortune teller in the city of Bucyrus. John F. Rummel may have been a spiritualist, or he may have been desperate. Since the brothers' childhood in Wharton, Rummel had moved to the city of Dayton. He was likely traveling back and forth frequently, trying to help search for his brother from afar. Unfortunately, his chosen fortune teller believed that Delbert had been murdered and his body hidden.[16]

The Rummel family, and the many citizens of Wharton who searched alongside them, never solved the mystery. No one confessed and Delbert Rummel was never found.[17]

Mennel Milling Company

Today the village of Wharton is the location of one of six successful flour mills operated by the Mennel Milling Company. Mennel was originally founded in 1886 as the Harter Milling Company, about 40 minutes north of Wharton in the city of Fostoria, Ohio. In 1917, when Alphonse Mennel and sons purchased the business, the name was changed.[18]

According to the Mennel Milling Company, just one day at their six mills requires 2,200 acres of wheat, or at the end of the day, six million pounds of flour. Wharton Grain works with Northwest Ohio farmers to process not only wheat but soybeans and corn as well. With a storage capacity of 847,000 bushels, the mill in Wharton can do quite a bit of business.[19]

The first house in Wharton was built by a couple named Nicholas and Anna Depew. They were able to purchase a lot in the village in 1849 for just five dollars. Anna, born in 1805, lived to watch the village of Wharton grow and change. She lived to be 102 years old, remaining an avid reader well into her old age.[20]

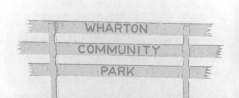

TOP: Willshire United Methodist Church

Population: 383   **Approx. Founding:** 1822

INSETS L to R: Willshire Drive-In • River's Edge Carry Out and Drive Thru • A branch library in downtown Willshire • Becky's Village Restaurant featuring "the best pie anywhere"

On January 27, 1971, on his seventh birthday, Matthew Winkler of Willshire left a hospital in Lima, Ohio, as the first person recorded to ever survive rabies without any permanent damage. In October 1970, while at home in Willshire, Winkler was bitten by a rabies-infected bat. Unfortunately, the vaccine wasn't administered in time. Winkler spent months in the hospital as the disease took hold. He survived and went on to a normal childhood. As an adult, the *Washington Post* checked in with Winkler, who still happily resided in Willshire with his family, and two small children.[14]

Willshire

American Indian Removal in Northwest Ohio

THE HISTORY OF THE UNITED STATES during the eighteenth and nineteenth centuries is filled with stories of white Americans removing American Indian nations from their ancestral lands, whether through war or via treaties. In 1817 and 1818, many American Indian communities were removed from Northwest Ohio and Indiana.

In 1817, the United States signed the Treaty of the Maumee Rapids with the Wyandot, Seneca, Lenape, Shawnee, Potawatomi, Ottawa, and Ojibwe Nations. The terms of the treaty promised annual stipends but required the tribes to move to specified reservations. The largest of these reservations, allotted for the Seneca, covered 30,000 acres. However, many nations only received a fraction of that, between about 5,000-7,000 acres of land.[1]

The Treaty of the Maumee Rapids was further finalized in 1818 through the St. Mary's Treaty, a document that also included the Miami Nation. Once the treaty was finalized, the U.S. government began to seek surveyors to help plot and settle this new land that they had laid claim to.[2]

Captain James Riley

One of the surveyors who answered this call was Captain James Riley. Recently trained as a surveyor, he was able to make about $1,200 a year by contracting with the government to plot out their new lands.[3] A Connecticut native, Riley and his son, James Watson Riley, traveled to Ohio and got to work.[4]

Captain Riley had turned to surveying thanks to a harrowing experience with his first occupation. In 1815, Captain Riley helmed a trade ship that traveled to the Cape Verde Islands by way of Gibraltar. Poor weather shipwrecked Riley and his crew off the western coast of Morocco. Here they were enslaved by a group of Berber tribesmen passing through the area. Luckily, Riley was able to send a message to a group of British men in the city of Mogador (today Essaouira). The men, particularly a consul named William Willshire, worked to secure the freedom of Riley's surviving crew by offering a ransom to their captors. Within two months of their shipwreck, the remaining crew was safe and sound. However, Captain Riley understandably chose to leave the sea behind and turned to surveying.[5]

When Riley began working in Northwest Ohio, he decided to maintain a portion of the land that he was surveying to build his own village. He platted this village in Van Wert County in March of 1822, on land that previously belonged to the Miami and Shawnee Nations.[6] Riley chose this land in the hopes that the nearby St. Marys River would encourage the state to construct the proposed Ohio and Erie Canal through the area. Riley named his new village Willshire, for the man that had saved his crew in Morocco.[7]

Riley built a dam and a mill in his new village, in hopes of bringing new settlers to the area. He then moved his family from Connecticut and settled in Willshire. Unfortunately, without any major transportation in the area, the village grew very slowly in its first 10 years. By the early 1830s, Captain Riley was bankrupt, and he was forced to travel to New York, where he took command of a vessel traveling to the East Indies. He died at sea on that journey.[8]

Despite the loss of their founder, Willshire grew. In January of 1836, the first schoolhouse opened in the village. Among the first children to receive an education here was a boy named Willshire Reichard. Reichard had been the first child born in the village, so his parents named him for the new town.[9]

Unfortunately, in the summer of 1854, the village of Willshire was struck with drought and disease. The winter of 1853–1854 was unusually cold. When spring arrived and the St. Marys River thawed, the village flooded, priming the area for disease. Beginning in May of 1854, the village of Willshire received absolutely no precipitation. After this weather whiplash, the wells and fountains of the village were left "covered with the almost ever-present green scum, the [harbinger] of disease and death.[10]

The village fell into a crisis mode during this drought. Malaria and cholera began taking lives, and even the animals of the village began showing signs of extreme thirst. As one history records, "the cattle were lowing to and fro, as if in search of food and water." As "pungent sorrow reigned supreme," Willshire residents began burying their deceased family members in their backyards and praying for rain. The local saloon keeper began offering free whiskey for medicinal purposes.[11] Finally, on July 28, 1854, rain came to the village of Willshire. The infectious diseases that had plagued the village residents subsided, and Willshire was able to start again with a clean slate.[12]

During the 1870s, a railroad came to Willshire, boosting its economy. In 1880, the residents formed a mutual insurance company. Willshire did slow down when highways took over railways, but it continues to maintain many businesses today. Open since 1954, the Willshire Drive-In, an ice cream shop, is managed today by Mike Schumm. Schumm keeps the drive-in open most of the year, closing up only between Thanksgiving and the beginning of March. He has been managing the very successful business since 1997. Schumm has a large staff and enjoys giving teenagers their first shot at employment. He told a local reporter in 2018, "I love what I do. I wake up every morning and get to work to give it a good effort…"[13]

When Captain Riley returned from his harrowing experiences in Morocco, he published his story in a book with the help of a friend named Anthony Bleecker. Riley's story, and this book, continue to fascinate readers. It is still in print 200 years later.

TOP: The Wilderness Center

For years, Vernon Craig worked in Wilmot at the Alpine Alpa, a former cheese shop. Later, he turned to a completely different career: he began performing death-defying stunts. Performing under the name "the Amazing Komar," Craig gained Guinness World Records for the longest fire walk in bare feet, the longest time on a bed of nails, and the most weight borne on a bed of nails. When he returned to Wilmot in 2000 (at age 68) for a performance, he told reporters, "It sounds like a dumb thing. But it is spectacular showmanship. It's been fun." Unfortunately, Craig passed away in 2010.

Wilmot

The Gateway to Amish Country

IN APRIL OF 1836, JACOB AND HENRY WYANT, landowners in Stark County, Ohio, worked with the county surveyor to lay out a new village on their land. Initially the village took the name of Milton. Today the Wyant family's village is known as Wilmot, although no one is sure when the name change took place.[1] The village grew quickly in its early years, supporting many businesses and industries. The village was home to manufacturers of agricultural machinery, a woolen mill, a carriage works, a foundry, and a gristmill, among other ventures.[2]

Today the village of Wilmot is well known as the home of the Amish Door Village. In March 1977, Milo and Anna Kathryn Miller opened a small restaurant in Wilmot by the name of Stucki's. Stucki's only seated about 48 patrons. By 1982, the couple needed to add on a new barn to their restaurant to increase seating to 325. From here the business just continued to blossom. The restaurant was rebuilt, now seating 450, and over the years a gift shop, bakery, bed and breakfast, banquet center, and inn were added. Today the Miller family's large business complex is known as the Amish Door Village.[3]

It's not a surprise that Wilmot's largest business is known for their Amish fare. Southwestern Stark County is known locally as the gateway to Ohio's Amish Country. Stark County borders Holmes County, where Ohio's largest population of Amish families can be found. In 1809, Jonas Stutzman, an Amish man from Somerset County, Pennsylvania, settled on the Walnut Creek in Holmes County, Ohio. Since Stutzman's arrival, the Walnut and Sugar Creeks have been home to a growing Amish population.[4] Many non-Amish Ohioans enjoy a visit to Amish Country for food, shopping, or a peaceful getaway.

Mayor Pulley's Annexation

Parts of the Amish Door Village only recently became part of Wilmot proper. In recent years, Milo Miller of the Amish Door and Wilmot's mayor, Bob Pulley, have been working together to grow the small town through annexation. For Mayor Pulley, annexation of nearby territories allows the village of Wilmot to grow their tax base. Without a larger tax base, it is impossible to afford necessities such as police protection (now contracted out to nearby Beach City) or sidewalk maintenance. For Miller, moving more of his business into Wilmot territory means a large cut in utility costs. Above all, both men want to see Wilmot prosper.[5]

Mayor Pulley has been involved in Wilmot government for most of his life. He moved to Wilmot in 1970, as a child, from Tennessee. Pulley met Milo Miller as a young boy, while Miller was still serving meals at the original Stucki's. At the age of 26, Pulley began serving on the village council, until eventually he ran unopposed for mayor. Pulley is a passionate and active mayor. Since his election he has already accomplished two annexations and paved multiple roads. Next on his list is another annexation and addressing the few abandoned homes on Main Street. As Pulley says, "If I get my way, I'd love to double the size of the town."[6]

The Wilderness Center

Since the mid-1960s, visitors from around the area have come to Wilmot to enjoy a piece of Ohio's natural landscape. In 1963, members of the Canton Audubon Society began to propose an outdoor education center.[7] The president of the Canton Audubon Society, Arnold Fritz, working with Dr. Charles King of Malone College, went to Ralph Regula, an Ohio Representative in the United States Congress, to request funding for this project.[8]

Around the same time, Charles Sigrist of Wilmot was selling about 250 acres of land that his family had owned for 84 years. Sigrist had insisted that the trees on the property remain standing and had resisted the profit of lumbering. This made the Sigrist land a prime location for the wildlife center.[9] Unfortunately, a strip-mining company was also interested.[10]

Fritz, King, and Regula were able to acquire a large grant from the Timken Foundation, which, in combination with community funds raised, was able to fund the original purchase of the Sigrist land in 1964. With this purchase, on June 19, 1964, the managing organization was officially incorporated as the Stark Wilderness Center (in 1979, the name was changed to The Wilderness Center, Inc. and is still in use today).[11]

The first hiking trail developed at the Wilderness Center, measuring about 0.75 mile, was the aptly named Sigrist Woods Trail. A few of the center's well-known natural markers can be found on this trail. Most of the trees on the trail are thought to be over 300 years old, but one particularly magnificent bur oak, measuring 16 feet around, is likely over 400 years old. This tree has been named "Ole Bur" for its remarkable age.[12] Also present on the trail is "The Grand Yankee," an American beech tree of almost perfect symmetry. The beech tree has become rare, as it prefers deep, fertile soil, which farmers also seek out for fields.

The Wilderness Center continued to grow, and at present, the Wilderness Center boasts 10 miles of hiking trails and an Astronomy Education building, including a digital planetarium. Admission is now, and has always been, completely free for the public.[13]

When Charles Sigrist's father passed away, Sigrist dug out a huge stone on his land to serve as a gravesite marker. The local cemetery wouldn't let him use it, so now it sits on the Sigrist Woods Trail, completely unearthed.[14]

TOP: The Yankee Lake Inn is the first thing most visitors to Yankee Lake see today

Population: 75   Approx. Founding: 1930

INSETS L to R: A view of the grounds where Yankee Lake hosts entertainment • A view of the main road that runs past Yankee Lake and brings visitors for summer entertainment • The front door of the Yankee Lake ballroom • The spectator entrance on the Yankee Lake grounds

In 1941, about 4,500 people made their way to the Yankee Lake Ballroom to see Glenn Miller and his band. Miller drew huge crowds, but he also proved to be one of the most expensive acts at Yankee Lake, commanding a large advance plus 60 percent of the evening's profits. Miller was paid a total of $2,500 for his performance, which, adjusted for inflation, would be about $44,700 today![14]

Yankee Lake

John Jurko Comes to Ohio

THE STORY OF YANKEE LAKE is also the story of its founding family. Both stories begin on October 15, 1885.[1] On that day, in Romania, John Jurko entered the world. Within a generation, Jurko made a major impact on Trumbull County.

In 1905, Jurko left his home in Romania, made his way to the port of Bremen in Germany, and set sail for the United States. On December 29, 1905, he arrived New York City. Shortly after, he married his wife, Anna, and the couple settled in Sharon, Pennsylvania, where they ran a boarding house and welcomed a son, Paul Jurko.[2]

By 1910, the Jurko family had settled in Brookfield Township. Here John Jurko owned a farm, but he also began his first foray into a lifelong

business of leisure. On his farm, John Jurko served as a brewmaster of sorts, making and selling alcohol, mostly whiskey. At the time, Prohibition was in full swing, but Jurko had the police of multiple cities in his pocket. He made regular runs between Cleveland, Brookfield, and Pittsburgh to ferry contraband to his customer.[3]

Recently, one of Jurko's descendants, John Jurko II, has begun to perform research for a documentary about the town his family built. He conducted various oral histories, and one man spoke of his experience riding with John Jurko to Pittsburgh on one of his bootlegging runs. The man remembers noticing that as they drove through the city of Pittsburgh, Jurko was frequently running red lights. He stopped to ask Jurko if he was worried about being pulled over. Finally, Jurko was stopped by the police, but upon recognizing his face, they sent him on his merry way.[4]

Building Yankee Lake

Perhaps hoping to capitalize on his already lucrative bootlegging endeavors, in 1924, John Jurko partnered with another nearby farmer, Ernest Houston Stewart, to build what would become a center of entertainment in their area. The two men owned farmland that included the Yankee Run Creek.[5] By damming up this waterway, they were able to create a lake that measured 55 acres. According to another oral history recorded by John Jurko II, some of the young men helping to build the dam stole rail tracks from a nearby project to bury in the dam and make it stronger.[6]

The men held a contest for the naming of the lake, opening the new getaway under the winning moniker: Ligamore Lake. Jurko's friends quickly pointed out to him that Ligamore just didn't roll off the tongue. He needed a much more marketable name. Finally, Jurko settled on Yankee Lake, in honor of the creek that had been altered to build the new site.[7]

An inn was built at Yankee Lake, and on Labor Day of 1928, with Whitey Kaufman and his band providing the music, a brand new ballroom was opened in Trumbull County. With illegal booze flowing and big band music playing, the residents of Brookfield certainly enjoyed the new addition of Yankee Lake.[8]

Becoming a Village

As it turns out, if Jurko and Stewart hadn't opened a ballroom, the Village of Yankee Lake might never have existed. In 1928, when Yankee Lake was just starting out, Ohio law stated that Sunday dances could not be held in unincorporated territory. Most dancehalls got around this by simply paying a fine. By 1930, Jurko had taken over the operations of Yankee Lake, and as one newspaper article reported, he "didn't want to be known as a lawbreaker." If a city was incorporated, its mayor could issue a license for Sunday dancing.[9] Jurko managed to pull the 25 signatures he needed to get the new village of Yankee Lake incorporated, barely squeaking by on the population minimum. And somehow, just like that, John Jurko had managed to essentially turn his farm into a legally incorporated village.[10]

So who was to be mayor of this new village? It seems obvious that the choice would be John Jurko himself; however, he turned instead to Mrs. Elizabeth Crowe. Crowe was also the manager of the Yankee Lake Inn, and she very quickly proclaimed Sunday as a free day for all dancing in the new village. In 1931, once he had turned 21, John Jurko's son Paul became mayor of Yankee Lake, a position he would hold most of his life.[11]

Running Yankee Lake really was a family affair. At one point during the 1970s, Paul was mayor, his wife was the clerk of council, his son was the police chief, and almost every family living in Yankee Lake was represented on the village council. The Jurkos also owned most of the land and businesses in town, including the Village Party Center: a more modern and legal version of John Jurko's bootlegging business. At one point, the Jurko family had to collect more signatures from their neighbors to put another Sunday issue on the ballot: beer and wine sales.[12]

In 1955, regular dancing ended at Yankee Lake, and in 1979, the lake was permanently drained.[13] Today the area where the lake once stood is frequently used to host rock concerts, motocross races, and monster truck rallies. While the big band dancing of John Jurko's era has long disappeared, his legendary entertainment and fun has had a long-lasting impact on this part of Trumbull County.

John Jurko II is currently in the process of writing and producing a documentary about his family's village. While the documentary is not out yet, Jurko has carefully curated an online gallery full of news clippings, documents, and gorgeous photographs telling the story of Yankee Lake at yankeelakehistory.com.[15]

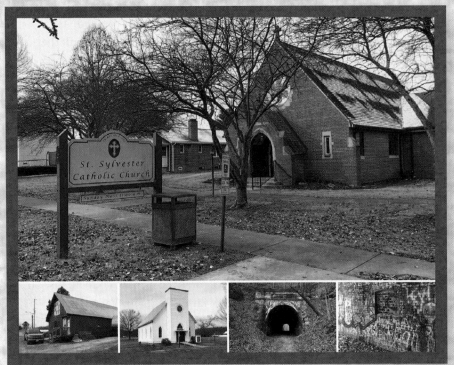

TOP: St. Sylvester Catholic Church

Population: 271 **Approx. Founding:** 1856

INSETS L to R: Zaleski Candle Works • Zaleski Methodist Church • The Moonville Tunnel • The walls inside the Moonville Tunnel are covered with colorful notes and graffiti

Peter Zaleski apparently intended to live in Ohio at one point, as he had a castle built in the village that bore his name. The castle included two and a half stories, about a dozen rooms, and eight fireplaces with mantels made of slate shipped from Liverpool, England. Zaleski never made it to the United States, but the castle was still maintained until the 1890s. Local lore suggests that the castle was once visited by Charles Dickens on a trip through Ohio.[15]

Zaleski

Noah Wilson Goes to Paris

IN 1856, THE VILLAGE OF ZALESKI was laid out by H. B. Robison on the grounds of the Zaleski Mining Company.[1] The company (and town) were named for Peter Zaleski, a mining shareholder and resident of Paris, France. During the mid-1850s, a local named Noah Wilson, representing The Marietta and Cincinnati Railroad, went abroad looking for the funding that was needed to extend a railway into Vinton County. He found Zaleski, a Polish man exiled in Paris; Zaleski and his friends were interested in making some large investments, but they were more interested in mining than a railroad. Zaleski purchased mortgages from Wilson, who turned around and invested this money in 2,000 acres of land, purchased in Zaleski's name. Soon the Zaleski Mining Company was formed.[2]

In the early years, the village of Zaleski was mostly owned by the mining company. Homes were made available for employees of the mine and their families. Most of these homes were likely log cabins with dirt floors. About 250 men were employed by Zaleski, requiring quite a bit of living space. Each day these 250 men would have encountered the Zaleski Furnace, built in 1858 and used to process iron ore.[3] Today the Zaleski Furnace is gone, but interested visitors can see another successful blast furnace of the time, the Hope Furnace, in the Zaleski State Forest.[4]

Zaleski was a very prosperous village during the 1860s and 1870s, growing along with the successful Zaleski Mining Company. During this heyday, the village had three newspapers, a two-story schoolhouse, a hotel, and a flour mill, among many other businesses. But a large portion of the company's business came from mining iron ore, and as the demand for iron waned, so did business.[5] The Zaleski Mining Company continued to mine coal, but by the 1890s, the village had begun to shrink.[6] By 1967, it had rebounded and the village maintained a population of 1,200.[7] However, as of the 2010 census, only 278 people call Zaleski home.

The Village of Moonville

The village of Zaleski only came into existence because Noah Wilson of the Marietta and Cincinnati (M&C) Railroad traveled to Paris looking for funding for the railway. Despite Peter Zaleski's lack of interest in the railway, Samuel Coe, of the neighboring village of Moonville, made the M&C Railroad an offer they couldn't refuse. Moonville was populated by only about 100 people, and most of them worked at Coe's coal mine. Coe wanted an easier way to transport his coal out of town for a profit, so he offered a plot of his land to the M&C Railroad for free. In 1856, the M&C Railroad finally crossed Vinton County, by way of Coe's Moonville property.[8]

Coe's mine remained successful for many years, providing coal for the nearby Hope Furnace and shipping out the remainder on the M&C Railroad (the Baltimore & Ohio Railroad after 1883). Unfortunately, Moonville began to run out of coal, and the mines were forced to close in the early 1900s. The last family left Moonville in 1947, making it a ghost town. The tracks were active until 1988.[9]

A True Ghost Town in the Zaleski State Forest

Today, Moonville is a part of the Zaleski State Forest. Occasionally small pieces of buildings or belongings from Moonville residents are found, but the biggest reminder of the village's existence is the Moonville Tunnel, an interesting stop for hikers in Zaleski. The tunnel was built under a large hill on Henry Ferguson's property to allow trains to pass through.[10] Visitors today can still see the words "Moonville Tunnel" on large arches above the entryway, amid years of vibrant graffiti.

The Moonville Tunnel is a particularly popular destination for Ohio's ghost hunters. Although the population of Moonville was very small, the village's cemetery (another site visitors can see in the Zaleski State Forest) was quite large.[11] The village was the site of many fatal accidents, especially surrounding the train tracks. Reports of about half a dozen different well-known ghosts are common.[12]

Perhaps one of the most well-known ghost stories of the Moonville Tunnel is the story of the brakeman. Apparently, during the late 1800s, a drunken brakeman, on the way home from a good night with his friends, decided to walk through the tunnel. A train came through, so the brakeman violently shook his lantern in an attempt to catch their attention. He was unsuccessful. The train came through the tunnel and killed him on impact. It is believed that the brakeman now haunts the tunnel, continuing to swing his lantern back and forth. So many people have seen a ghostly light in the tunnel that a special signal had to be installed in 1981. Railway engineers were seeing a light in the tunnel and breaking unnecessarily. After the signal was installed, they were asked to ignore any other lights that may appear in the tunnel.[13]

The story of the haunted Moonville Tunnel has been featured in songs, books, and television shows. Of particular note is a song by the bluegrass band The Rarely Herd, titled "The Ghost of Moonville Tunnel." The story has also been featured on the SyFy channel, in a show called *Haunted Highway*.[14]

The Moonville Tunnel and the Hope Furnace are located along the trails of the Zaleski State Forest. Named for the village, this preserve is the second-largest state forest in Ohio. It provides more than 25 miles of hiking trails, with a focus on backpacking trips.

In 2017, the Zaleski General Store was torn down. Residents took to Facebook to share memories of it. Letha Toops, one of the store's final owners, was the subject of many memories The store was robbed in 2009 and 2010; both times Toops pulled a gun, making headlines. As the sheriff once said of Toops, "She's a pistol-packing momma."[16]

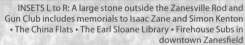

INSETS L to R: A large stone outside the Zanesville Rod and
Gun Club includes memorials to Isaac Zane and Simon Kenton
• The China Flats • The Earl Sloane Library • Firehouse Subs in
downtown Zanesfield

By the late 1800s, many railroads passed through
Logan County in the city of Bellefontaine, a few
miles from Zanesfield. According to a historical marker placed in the village today, a group of
Chinese immigrants who worked for one of these
railways lived in a Zanesfield hotel in 1885. The
hotel eventually burned down and was replaced
in the 1940s. It now houses a shop with antiques
and gifts known as China Flats. The shop takes its
name from the hotel, which was known around the
village as the "China Flats."[16]

TOP: A modern reconstruction of the Ebeneezer Zane Cabin

Zanesfield

The Story of Isaac Zane

THE STORY OF THE VILLAGE OF ZANESFIELD begins long
before a plat was laid out in 1819, possibly as far back as 1762, in Virginia, with a boy named Isaac Zane, the youngest of the five Zane
brothers.[1, 2] One of Isaac's eldest brothers, Ebenezer Zane, would become
famous for plotting an early road, Zane's Trace, through the Northwest
Territory.[3] This road would become integral to early trade in Ohio.

At age nine, Isaac Zane was kidnapped by a group of American
Indians from the Wyandotte Nation. Many histories of his time with the
Wyandotte Nation have been written, including one account by Ebenezer's great-grandson, the writer Zane Grey (a native of Zanesville, a city
named for his great-grandfather).[4]

Some histories suggest that both Isaac and his older brother
Jonathan were kidnapped as they walked home from school. Jonathan
returned home within a few years, but Isaac, possibly by his own voli-
tion, continued to live with a Wyandotte leader named Tarhe whose
daughter, Myeerah, was only a few years younger than Isaac. When
they reached adulthood, Isaac and Myeerah married.[5] After the American Revolution, as the United States and American Indian nations
came into conflict, Isaac Zane served as an interpreter between the two
groups. For his services, the U.S. government gave him a tract of land
in what would one day become Zanesfield.[6] When Zane settled here
around 1795, he became the first white settler in the area.[7]

Forced Removal From Wapatomica

Before Zane arrived in Logan County, the area was largely occupied by members of the Shawnee Nation. Beginning in the 1780s, the United States continuously pushed the native Shawnee from this territory, eventually completely removing American Indians from the area (see page 165 for more about this). The Shawnee settlement closest to modern-day Zanesfield was found just a few miles away at Wapatomica. This village served as a political center for the Shawnee Nation during the 1700s, until 1786 when Colonel Benjamin Logan of the Virginia Militia led a raid through Wapatomica and other nearby Shawnee villages. The residents of this village were forced to seek refuge farther north. Members of the Shawnee Nation didn't return to Wapatomica until 2007, when members of the Eastern Shawnee Tribe visited from their current residence in Oklahoma.[8]

The Next Zane Generation Plats Zanesfield

Issac and Myeerah Zane raised their children in Logan County, in an area that became known as Zanestown, in their honor.[9] Their son, Ebenezer, became an important member of the community, leaving home and building his own cabin in 1805. A reconstructed version of this cabin is still visible to visitors at the Helen Wonders Blue Memorial Park today. In 1819, Ebenezer hosted the First Methodist Quarterly Conference in his home. The conference was attended by 300 white settlers and 60 members of the Wyandotte Nation. Little is known about the Zane family's private life, but evidence suggests they maintained a positive relationship with the Wyandotte Nation.[10]

In 1819, Ebenezer Zane and Alexander Long began to lay out a new village in Zanestown, changing the name to Zanesfield. Zane and Long owned much of the land in the area, some of which was purchased from Lucas Sullivant, another well-known early Ohioan.[11]

Zane and Long largely left each other to their own devices, working separately on their own halves of the village plat. However, this changed when Long and another early settler of Zanestown, Lanson Curtis, found themselves in a heated quarrel. Seeking retribution, Long attempted to organize the new village so that when leaving from his home, Curtis could only reach the main road, Sandusky Street, if he were to use Locust Street, which was only 24 feet wide. Curtis, a merchant, needed a wider road to conveniently move his wares.[12]

Zane got wind of Long's attempted skullduggery when Long attempted to purchase the lot that lay between Curtis's property and Sandusky Street, which Zane owned. As the story goes, Long offered Zane $100 for the lot, to which Zane replied, "Mebby not." When Zane next saw Curtis, he asked if the merchant would want to buy the lot. When Curtis inquired to an offering price, Zane stated, "Mebby $10." The land was sold to Curtis, and Long's attempted retribution was foiled.[13]

The Earl Sloan Library

One of the most striking buildings in downtown Zanesfield is the Earl Sloan Library. Built with "buff press brick and grey Bedford stone," the library has a striking red tile roof. The library first opened in 1913, thanks to financial support from a former Zanesfield resident, Earl Sloan. Sloan was born in Zanesfield in 1848 and grew up going to school at the current site of the library that bears his name.[14] His father, "Doc" Andrew Sloan, was a harness-maker turned veterinarian, specializing in horses. Andrew developed a liniment to ease joint pain in horses. Earl took the liniment to St. Louis as a young man, where he and his older brother, Foreman Sloan, began to sell the invention, which became wildly successful. The library still operates today, both lending books and providing a home for many historic artifacts.[15]

Zanesfield was home to an active Quaker population. A Quaker schism occurred in the 1820s. Followers of Elias Hicks (aka Hickites) split off from the main church, building a small church on the edge of town in 1828; the two groups rejoined in 1913. The old Hicksite Church still stands today in the Zanesfield Cemetery.[17]

Population: 178   Approx. Founding: 1817

INSETS L to R: The Zoar Store • A view of the historic streets
of Zoar Village • Zoar Hotel • The Number One House, where
Joseph Bimeler lived at Zoar

During his time as the leader of the village of Zoar, Joseph Bimeler designed a seven-pointed star that became a symbol of the community. The star is encased in a circle and features an acorn in the center. The star, always in red, blue, and yellow, can be seen throughout the village even today. Occasionally historians have located stars with additional points, leading many to believe that when a particular Zoarite deserved special recognition, they were given an extra point on their star.[17]

TOP: Zoar United Church of Christ

Zoar

The Zoarites Come to America

DURING THE EARLY 1800s, a group of religious separatists in what is now Germany were persecuted under King Frederick II. Banding together, they left their homes in 1817, traveling to the U.S. in hopes of finding religious freedom.[1] The Separatists had similar beliefs to most American Quakers, especially concerning nonviolence. When the Separatists arrived in the United States, they settled in Philadelphia, Pennsylvania, where a local group of Quakers helped them.[2] The Separatists were thankful, but they also wanted to forge their own path, so their leader, a man named Joseph Bimeler, began to seek a new home.

By the end of 1817, Bimeler had purchased 5,500 acres in Tuscarawas County, Ohio, at about $3 per acre. This was a very expensive purchase, so Bimeler had to agree to a three-year payment plan. Group members soon traveled to Ohio to begin construction on the new community's first buildings. The rest of the members arrived in 1818, putting the total population at around 225. Seeking their own refuge from religious persecution, the Separatists decided to name their new village "Zoar," after the Biblical city that provided Lot a refuge as he escaped Sodom and Gomorrah.[3]

A Dedication to Communal Living

The Zoarites, as they were now called, struggled financially at first. For this reason, in May of 1819, the residents of Zoar formed the Society of Separatists of Zoar, opting to live communally.[4] Under this new system, all wealth and property was owned by the community as a whole, rather than by any one individual. Joseph Bimeler was chosen as a leader, and he, along with a group of trustees, managed the entire commune's finances.[5] Many of the homes in the village were known by a number, assigned for the purpose of collecting products for sale.[6]

The village of Zoar built and operated all the hallmarks of a growing village economy— mills, foundries, bakeries, and artisan shops among them. In fact, it was once said that Zoarites made everything they needed except rice and coffee. They even raised silkworms and made their own silk! Any surplus items were sold to make money for the commune.[7]

Profiting From the Canal

The arrival of the Ohio and Erie Canal during the 1820s and 1830s boosted the Zoar economy. The Society contracted with the state of Ohio to help build the canal. The completed canal helped the Zoarites move marketable goods throughout the state. In addition, Zoarites profited from visitors and travelers patronizing Zoar's hotel or general store.[8]

One of the goods that Zoarites shipped across Ohio was beer. Zoarites raised their own hops; often the harvesting of hops was a job for young boys and girls. The Separatists rationed their own consumption: one beer at lunch each day during the hot summer months was the average. Instead of drinking the beer themselves, Zoarites sold the drink at the Zoar Hotel, to local farmers and to interested buyers along the canal.[9] Apparently the beer produced at the brewery was quite enjoyable: summer visitors to the hotel often found themselves intoxicated. When this occurred, they often found themselves in a bed at the village jail.[10]

The Society Disbands

Unfortunately, the commune slowly deteriorated over the second half of the nineteenth century. In 1853, the town's leader, Joseph Bimeler died, and in 1875, the Cleveland, Tuscarawas Valley, and Wheeling Railway came through the village, disrupting the communal lifestyle.[11,12] Commune members began to fight about pay and status, and to add to

this confusion, one of the village's newest tourists, a retired Cleveland businessman named Alexander Gunn, permanently settled in the Zoar Hotel and formed a fraternal society with many of the village's leaders. He held meetings in "the Hermitage," a log cabin that was among the first few buildings built in Zoar. Many Zoarites resented that the trustees had sold this building to Gunn, an outsider.[13] Finally, the new generations of Zoarites, removed from the original persecution their parents and grandparents had faced in Germany, began to seek involvement in the outside world.

When the Society of Separatists of Zoar disbanded, a third party was hired to split up the assets fairly. The Society had become quite prosperous, and a full share was valued at $2,000. In addition, families kept their own homes and about 50 acres of land.[14] Today Zoar is considered one of the most successful communal experiments in the U.S.

Preserving Zoar Today

Many of the original buildings built by the Society of Separatists of Zoar still stand in the village. Some are used as private residences, bed and breakfasts, businesses, and restaurants. Others are owned by the Ohio History Connection and managed as public museums. More than 100 people still call the village of Zoar home, many of them descendants of the original settlers, such as Mayor Scott Gordon.[15]

Zoar's major foe in recent years has been water. During the 1930s, the Army Corps of Engineers built a levee to protect the historically significant buildings from frequent flooding. However, the levee deteriorated; in 2008, residents were on a 24/7 flood watch. Fortunately, the Army Corps has decided to rebuild the levee and is now actively working in the village, now an official National Historic Landmark.[16]

Visitors can't miss the Zoar Garden, which covers an entire block. The garden itself represents the deep faith that was central to life in Zoar. It is intended to mirror New Jerusalem, as described in the 21st chapter of the Book of Revelation. In the center stands a large evergreen tree, representing the Tree of Life.[18]

Sources

ADELPHI

1. Overman, William D. *Ohio Town Names*. Akron, OH: Atlantic Press, 1959, pg. 1.

2. Adelphi, Colerain Twp. Sesquicentennial Celebration at Adelphi, Ohio, Oct. 1, 2, 3, 1954: Memorializing Its Founders of 1804, PA Box 778 5, Ohio History Connection.

3. Overman. *Ohio Town Names*.

4. May, Debbie. "Bologna Has Trail of History." *Chillicothe Gazette*, May 24, 1985.

5. "Adelphi Community Band." Adelphi, Ohio. http://adelphiohio.com/adelphi-community-band/.

6. "Tella Kitchen: Southern Ohio's 'Grandma' Moses." *The Pike County News Watchman*, September 20, 2013.

7. "Mrs. Kitchen Named Mayor at Adelphi." *Chillicothe Gazette*, Feb. 5, 1964.

8. Wertkin, Gerard C. *Encyclopedia of American Folk Art*. Florence: Routledge, 2004.

9. "Tella Kitchen: Southern Ohio's 'Grandma' Moses."

10. Wertkin. *Encyclopedia of American Folk Art*.

11. "Tella Kitchen: Southern Ohio's 'Grandma' Moses."

12. "Purdue, John, 1802–1876." Purdue University Archives and Special Collections. https://archives.lib.purdue.edu/agents/people/529.

13. Ibid.

14. Adelphi, Colerain Twp. Sesquicentennial Celebration at Adelphi, Ohio, Oct. 1, 2, 3, 1954.

15. "Mrs. Kitchen Named Mayor at Adelphi."

AMESVILLE

1. "Ohio Company of Associates." Ohio History Central. Ohio History Connection. www.ohiohistorycentral.org/w/Ohio_Company_of_Associates.

2. Hunter, Gary E. *Athens County: The Second Century, 1905–2005*. Taylor Publishing Company, 2005.

3. "Ephraim Cutler." Ohio History Central. Ohio History Connection. www.ohiohistorycentral.org/w/Ephraim_Cutler.

4. "The Coonskin Library." Amesvilleohio.org. Sarah J. Cutler. www.amesvilleohio.org/uploads/9/1/6/2/9162814/sarahcutlerarticle.pdf.

5. Ibid.

6. Ibid.

7. Ibid.

8. "Coonskin Library." Ohio History Central. Ohio History Connection. www.ohiohistorycentral.org/w/Coonskin_Library.

9. "The Coonskin Library." www.amesvilleohio.org/uploads/9/1/6/2/9162814/sarahcutlerarticle.pdf.

10. Kuresman, Kia. Amesville History. Countdown to Millennium: An Oral History Collection Project. www.seorf.ohio.edu/~xx125/history.html.

11. "Visitors Guide for Amesville, Ohio." Amesvilleohio.org. www.amesvilleohio.org/uploads/9/1/6/2/9162814/amesvillevisitorguide2016.pdf.

12. "Thomas Ewing." Find A Grave. www.findagrave.com/memorial/4113.

13. "About Us." Homecoming Farm. www.homecomingfarmohio.com/about-us.html.

BEALLSVILLE

1. Ibid.

2. Maienknecht, Theresa A., and Stanley B. Maienknecht. *Monroe County, Ohio: a History*. Windmill Publications, 1989.

3. Ibid.

4. Ibid.

5. Monroe County Chapter of the Ohio Genealogical Society. *Monroe County, Ohio Families*. Taylor Publishing Company, 1992.

6. Ibid.

7. Kneeland, Douglass E. "Ohio Town That Lost 7 Men in Vietnam Now Worries More About Economy." *The New York Times*, April 4, 1975, p. 8.

8. Wagner, Mike. "Beallsville's Loss of Vietnam War Soldiers Still Felt." *Columbus Dispatch*, April 26, 2015, www.dispatch.com/content/stories/local/2015/04/26/six-sons-not-forgotten.html.

9. *Monroe County, Ohio Families*.

10. Wagner. "Beallsville's Loss of Vietnam War Soldiers Still Felt."

11. *Monroe County, Ohio Families*.

12. Ibid.

13. Ibid.

14. *A Small Town Loses Six Young Soldiers in Vietnam*. Archival Film. New York, NY: NBC Universal, 10/15/1969. Accessed Sept. 16, 2017, from NBC Learn: https://archives.nbclearn.com/portal/site/k-12/browse/?cuecard=5081.

15. Ibid.

16. Maienknecht and Maienknecht. *Monroe County, Ohio: a History*.

17. Kneeland. "Ohio Town That Lost 7 Men in Vietnam Now Worries More About Economy." *The New York Times*, April 4, 1975, p. 8.

18. "A Pronunciation Guide to Places in Ohio." *The E. W. Scripps School of Journalism at Ohio University*, 2016, scrippsjschool.org/pronunciation/.

19. Ross, Bobby. "Rich, in Name and Spirit, in Rural Ohio." *The Christian Chronicle*, Sept. 5, 2013, christianchronicle.org/rich-in-name-and-spirit-in-rural-ohio/.

BELL VALLEY

1. *History of Noble County, Ohio: With Portraits and Biographical Sketches*...Chicago: L.H. Watkins & Co., 1887.

2. Pickenpaugh, Roger. *A History of Noble County, Ohio 1887–1987*. Baltimore: Gateway Press, 1988.

3. Pickenpaugh. *A History of Noble County, Ohio 1887–1987*.

4. Pickenpaugh, Roger. *Noble County, Ohio: A History*. Baltimore, MD: Otter Bay Books, 2012.

5. Ibid.

6. Ibid.

7. "Two Gas Explosions in Mine Kill Fifteen." *Perrysburg Journal*, May 23, 1913.

8. Pickenpaugh. *A History of Noble County, Ohio 1887–1987*.

9. Ibid.

10. Ibid.

11. "Two Gas Explosions in Mine Kill Fifteen."

12. Pickenpaugh. *A History of Noble County, Ohio 1887–1987*.

13. "Babes, Too Small to Know Left Orphans." *The Times Recorder* (Zanesville, OH), May 20, 1913.

14. Pickenpaugh. *A History of Noble County, Ohio 1887–1987*.

15. Ibid.

16. Pickenpaugh. *Noble County, Ohio: A History*.

17. "Rumor of Quest for Gold Vein Near Belle Valley." *Times Recorder* (Zanesville, OH), June 2, 1930.

BENTON RIDGE

1. Beardsley, D. B. *History of Hancock County: From Its Earliest Settlement to the Present Time, Together with Reminiscences of Pioneer Life, Incidents, Statistical Tables, and Biographical Sketches*. Springfield, OH: Republic Printing Company, 1881.

2. Ibid.

3. Britannica, The Editors of Encyclopædia. "Thomas Hart Benton." *Encyclopædia Britannica*. www.britannica.com/biography/Thomas-Hart-Benton-American-writer-and-politician.

4. "Historic Missourians—The State Historical Society of Missouri." Senator Thomas Hart Benton. https://shsmo.org/historicmissourians/name/b/bentonsenator/.

5. "About Us." Benton Ridge Telephone Company. www.brtelco.com/about.htm.

6. Latson, Jennifer. "The Woman Who Made History by Answering the Phone." *Time Magazine*, September 1, 2015. http://time.com/4011936/emma-nutt/.

7. "About Us."

8. "AT&T Challenged by Tiny Company." *The Newark Advocate*, December 29, 1965.

9. Ibid.

10. "About Us."

11. Ibid.

12. Solt Speedway. www.soltspeedway.com.

13. "Uses a Puppet." *The Marion Star*, January 6, 1967

BENTONVILLE

1. Evans, Nelson W., and Emmons B. Stivers. *A History of Adams County, Ohio*. West Union, OH: E.B. Stivers, 1900.

2. Ibid.

3. Beardsley, D. B. *History of Hancock County, from Its Earliest Settlement to the Present Time*. Springfield, OH: Republic Printing Company, 1881.

4. Evans and Stivers. *A History of Adams County, Ohio*.

5. Ibid.

6. Ibid.

7. Ibid.

8. Francis, Jason. "Bentonville Anti-Horse Thief Society Celebrates 165 Years." *The Adams County Informer*, April 26, 2018. www.informerpress.com/2018/04/26/bentonville-anti-horse-thief-society-celebrates-165-years.

9. "Bentonville Anti-Horse Thief Society." Ohio History Central. www.ohiohistorycentral.org/w/Bentonville_Anti-Horse_Thief_Society.

10. "Anti-horse Thief Society Not Too Active Anymore." *Wilmington News Journal*, January 15, 1976.

11. "Bentonville Anti-Horse Thief Society."

12. Francis. "Bentonville Anti-Horse Thief Society Celebrates 165 Years."

13. Beech, Patricia. "Bentonville: A Community at the Crossroads of Adams County History." *The People's Defender*, October 11, 2017. www.peoplesdefender.com/2017/10/11/bentonville-a-community-at-the-crossroads-of-adams-county-history/.

14. Ibid.

15. Ibid.

16. "Anti-horse Thief Society Not Too Active Anymore."

BEULAH BEACH

1. *Beulah Beach Beacon*, 1928, PA Box 389 2, Ohio History Connection.

2. Hildebrandt, H. John and Marie. *Lake Erie's Shores and Islands*. Arcadia Publishing, 2015, pg. 56.

3. "Then & Now." The Alliance. 2018. www.cmalliance.org/about/history/.

4. "A. W. Tozer." The Alliance. 2018. www.cmalliance.org/about/history/tozer.

5. Ritter Public Library. "Through the Trees at Beulah Beach." YouTube video, 1:05:03. Dec 6, 2017. https://youtube.com/kUCLftGHxcA.

6. Whipple, Dick. "Tiny Fourth Class Post Offices Envision True Cross Section of 'Rural America'." *Sandusky Register*, April 23, 1958.

7. "Hobby Brightens Up Man's Future." *Sandusky Register*, January 30, 1965.

8. Beulah Beach. 2015. www.beulahbeach.org.

9. https://www.beulahbeach.org/, also available through Google Play and the Apple App Store

10. Tichnor Quality Views. *Baptismal Scene at Convention, Beulah Beach, Ohio*. 1930-1945. The Tichnor Brothers Collection, Digital Commonwealth, Worcester, Massachusetts, https://www.digitalcommonwealth.org/search/commonwealth:sj1394917.

11. "Hope Church Annual Picnic at Beulah Beach." Hope Church. Accessed August 07, 2019. https://hopebrunswick.org/event/hope-church-annual-picnic-at-beulah-beach/.

BLADENSBURG

1. Davidson, Christina. "Wherefore Art Thou Bladensburg?" *The Baltimore Sun*, September 9, 2014. www.baltimoresun.com/news/opinion/oped/bs-ed-bladensburg-battle-20140909-story.html.

2. Bladensburg Community Institute, Bladensburg, Ohio, 1974: Knox County, the nation and the world. Dwight W. Horn, PA Box 759 18, Ohio History Connection.

3. "Bladensburg." American Battlefield Trust. www.battlefields.org/learn/war-1812/battles/bladensburg.

4. Ibid.

5. Ibid.

6. Davidson. "Wherefore Art Thou Bladensburg?" *The Baltimore Sun*, September 9, 2014. https://www.baltimoresun.com/news/opinion/oped/bs-ed-bladensburg-battle-20140909-story.html.

7. Ibid.

8. Ibid.

9. Ibid.

10. Massa, Paul. "Oilmen Flock to Knox Village." *The Newark Advocate*, March 26, 1965.

11. Ibid.

12. Haneberg-Diggs, Dominique M. "The 'Clinton' Oil-and-Gas Play in Ohio." *GeoFacts*, published by the Ohio Department of Natural Resources, Division of Geological Survey, 30 (June 2015), https://geosurvey.ohiodnr.gov/portals/geosurvey/PDFs/GeoFacts/geof30.pdf.

13. Massa, Paul. "Oilmen Flock to Knox Village." *The Newark Advocate*, March 26, 1965.

14. Haneberg-Diggs. "The 'Clinton' Oil-and-Gas Play in Ohio."

15. "Our History." Lasater Funeral Homes. www.lasaterfuneralhomes.com/our-history.

BOWERSVILLE

1. *Greene County, 1803–1908*. Xenia, OH: Aldine Pub. House, 1908.

2. Broadstone, M. A. *History of Greene County, Ohio: Its People, Industries and Institutions*. Indianapolis: B.F. Bowen & Company, 1918.

3. Ibid.

4. *Greene County, 1803–1908*.

5. Broadstone. *History of Greene County, Ohio*.

6. Ibid.

7. Ibid.

8. Ibid.

9. *Greene County, 1803–1908*.

10. Broadstone. *History of Greene County, Ohio*.

11. Ibid.

12. Kilner, Arthur R. *Greene County, Ohio—Past and Present*. Bowie, MD: Heritage Books, 1997.

13. "Robbers Blow Safe in Bank." *The Evening Independent* (Massillon, Ohio), March 21, 1933.

14. "Bandits Raid Ohio Village." *Marysville Journal-Tribune*, March 21, 1933.

15. Kilner. *Greene County, Ohio—Past and Present*.

16. Yoakam, Rosalie. "Dr. Norman Vincent Peale Was Born in Greene County." *Dayton Daily News*. August 5, 2015. www.daytondailynews.com/news/local/norman-vincent-peale-was-born-greene-county/ASJeJlabXFB4X9AyjL1TgO/.

17. "Business Mirror." *The Daily Times-News* (Burlington, NC), November 2, 1977.

BRADY LAKE

1. Orlousky, Paul. "Small Village to Disappear after Citizens Vote." *Cleveland 19 News*, May 3, 2017. www.cleveland19.com/story/35329622/small-village-to-disappear-after-citizens-vote/.

2. "Brady's Lake." *Akron Beacon Journal*, December 27, 1902.

3. Ibid.

4. Ballou, Nancy. "Brady Lake Place of Legend and History." *Daily Kent Stater* (Kent State University), February 22, 1980.

5. *History of Portage County, Ohio: Containing a History of the County, Its Townships, Towns, Villages, Schools, Churches...Chicago: Warner, Beers & Co., 1885.

6. Orlousky."Small Village to Disappear after Citizens Vote." *Cleveland 19 News*, May 3, 2017. http://www.cleveland19.com/story/35329622/small-village-to-disappear-after-citizens-vote/.

7. "Kent Folks like to Go to Lake Brady." *Akron Beacon Journal,* June 14, 1912.

8. "News of Akron Resorters at Nearby Lakes." *Akron Evening News*, May 24, 1919.

9. Ibid.

10. "News of Akron Resorters at Nearby Lakes." *Akron Evening News*, June 21, 1919.

11. Melton, J. Gordon. "Spiritualism." Encyclopædia Britannica. www.britannica.com/topic/spiritualism-religion.

12. Lake Brady Spiritualists Camp meeting, PA Box 645 29, Ohio History Connection.

13. Orlousky."Small Village to Disappear after Citizens Vote." *Cleveland 19 News*, May 3, 2017. www.cleveland19.com/story/35329622/small-village-to-disappear-after-citizens-vote/.

14. Merchant, Matthew. "Brady Lake Still a Village ... for Now." *Record Courier* (Kent, OH), July 9, 2017. www.record-courier.com/news/20170709/brady-lake-still-village--for-now.

15. "Séances and Slot Machines: The Story of Brady Lake Park." Western Reserve Public Media. June 2014. westernreservepublicmedia.org/brady_lake_park.htm.

16. "'Slots' Are Locked at Brady Lake." *Evening Independent* (Massillon, OH), June 10, 1946.

17. Bugel, Andrew. "What's next for Brady Lake?" *Record Courier* (Kent, OH), May 4, 2017. www.record-courier.com/news/20170504/whats-next-for-brady-lake.

18. Smith, Diane. "Brady Lake: One year later." *Record Courier* (Kent, OH), May 13, 2018. www.record-courier.com/news/20180513/brady-lake-one-year-later.

19. Merchant. "Brady Lake Still a Village ... for Now."

20. "Eddie Morgan." Baseball Reference. www.baseball-reference.com/players/m/morgaed02.shtml.

21. "Home Run in First At-Bat." Baseball Almanac. www.baseball-almanac.com/feats/feats5.shtml.

22. "Eddie Morgan."

CAMP DENNISON

1. Sloan, Mary R., *History of Camp Dennison, 1796–1956*. PA Box 78 18, Ohio History Connection.

2. "Symmes Purchase." Ohio History Central. www.ohiohistorycentral.org/w/Symmes_Purchase.

3. Sloan. *History of Camp Dennison.*

4. Ibid.

5. Starr, Stephen Z. "Camp Dennison, 1861–1865." *Bulletin of the Historical and Philosophical Society of Ohio Cincinnati* vol. 19, no. 3 (July 1961): 167–190. http://library.cincymuseum.org/topics/c/files/civilwar/hpsobull-v19-n3-cam-167.pdf.

6. Ibid.

7. Ibid.

8. Ibid.

9. Ibid.

10. "Camp Dennison." Ohio History Central. Accessed February 01, 2019. www.ohiohistorycentral.org/w/Camp_Dennison.

11. Starr. "Camp Dennison, 1861–1865."

12. Sloan. *History of Camp Dennison, 1796–1956.*

13. The Schoolhouse Restaurant. 2019. https://theschoolhousecincinnati.com.

14. "Welcome to the Christian Waldschmidt Homestead." Ohio Society Daughters of the American Revolution. November 3, 2016. www.ohiodar.org/waldhouse.shtml.

CELERYVILLE

1. Wecker, David. "Small Ohio Town Is Famous for Its Celery." *Deseret News,* June 14, 1988. www.deseretnews.com/article/7362/SMALL-OHIO-TOWN-IS-FAMOUS-FOR-ITS-CELERY.html.

2. Ibid.

3. Ibid.

4. Ibid.

5. "History of Buurma Farms." Buurma Farms. www.buurmafarms.com/about/history.

6. "Our Story." Wiers Farm. www.wiersfarm.com/our-story.html.

7. Jordan, Miriam. "One Ohio Town's Immigration Clash, Down in the Actual Muck." *New York Times*, June 18, 2017. www.nytimes.com/2017/06/18/us/willard-ohio-migrant-workers.html.

8. "History of Buurma Farms."

9. "Our Story."

10. "The History of Holthouse Farms." Holthouse Farms of Ohio, Inc. www.holthousefarms.com/about.

11. "History of Buurma Farms."

12. "Our Story."

13. Wecker. "Small Ohio Town Is Famous for Its Celery."

14. "The History of Holthouse Farms."

15. Jordan. "One Ohio Town's Immigration Clash, Down in the Actual Muck."

16. Ibid.

17. Ibid.

18. "Our Story."

19. "About." Celeryville Christian School. www.celeryville.org/about.

CHESTERHILL

1. Hoopes, Minta. *Collected Traditions of "Ye Olde Log Cabin Town" At Chesterhill, Ohio: Founded by the Quakers from Belmont County.* McConnelsville, OH: Herald Printing, 1957.

2. Robertson, Charles, M.D. *History of Morgan County, Ohio: With Portraits and Biographical Sketches of Some of Its Pioneers and Prominent Men.* Chicago: L.H. Watkins &, 1886.

3. Hoopes. *Collected Traditions.*

4. Robertson. *History of Morgan County, Ohio.*

5. Hoopes. *Collected Traditions.*

6. McCoy, Erin L. "How a Fruit and Vegetable Auction in Rural Ohio Helps Appalachian Farmers Thrive." *Yes Magazine,* January 13, 2014. www.yesmagazine.org/new-economy/how-a-fruit-and-vegetable-auction-in-rural-ohio-helps-appalachian-farmers-thrive.

7. Ibid.

8. Chesterhill Produce Auction: A Rural Appalachia Case Story. The Voinovich School of Leadership and Public Affairs, Ohio University. Central Appalachian

Network, 2010, http://ruralaction.org/wp-content/uploads/2011/05/CPA_casestudy-ordered.pdf.

9. McCoy. "How a Fruit and Vegetable Auction in Rural Ohio Helps Appalachian Farmers Thrive."

10. Chesterhill Produce Auction: A Rural Appalachia Case Story.

11. Ibid.

12. Marinova, Viktoria. "Hidden Figures of SE Ohio: Chesterhill Preserves History of African-American Community." *Zip It. News*, August 23, 2018. http://zipit.news/stories/hidden-figures-of-se-ohio,4.

13. "Tour Explores Area's Rich History with Underground Railroad." *The Athens News*, April 24, 2008. www.athensnews.com/news/local/tour-explores-area-s-rich-history-with-underground-railroad/article_5032352e-49ee-501a-a410-4de04e5a383e.html.

14. McCoy. "How a Fruit and Vegetable Auction in Rural Ohio Helps Appalachian Farmers Thrive."

15. Hoopes. *Collected Traditions*.

CHESTERVILLE

1. Morrow County History Book Committee. *History of Morrow County, Ohio*. Don Mills Inc., 1989.

2. Ebersole, Pat. "History of Chesterville." Selover Public Library. 1995. http://selover.lib.oh.us/history-of-chesterville.

3. Morrow County History Book Committee. *History of Morrow County, Ohio*.

4. Ibid.

5. Ibid.

6. Ibid.

7. Ibid.

8. Ebersole. "History of Chesterville."

9. Ibid.

10. Morrow County History Book Committee. *History of Morrow County, Ohio*.

11. Ebersole. "History of Chesterville."

12. Ibid.

13. Pedersen, Ginger. "Hugh Dillman and His Dream – Sandy Loam Farm." Palmbeachpast.org. January 28, 2014. Accessed December 01, 2018. www.palmbeachpast.org/2010/09/hugh-dillman-and-his-dream-sandy-loam-farm/.

CLIFTON

1. Kilner, Arthur R. *Greene County, Ohio—Past and Present*. Bowie, MD: Heritage Books, 1997.

2. Ibid.

3. A Committee of the Home Coming Association, ed. *Greene County, 1803–1908*. Xenia, OH: Aldine Publishing House, 1908.

4. Kilner. *Greene County, Ohio—Past and Present*.

5. Historic Village of Clifton. www.villageofclifton.com.

6. *Greene County, 1803–1908*.

7. Broadstone, Hon. M. A., ed. *History of Greene County, Ohio: Its People, Industries, and Institutions*. Vol. 1. Indianapolis, IN: B.F. Bowne & Company, 1918.

8. Kilner. *Greene County, Ohio—Past and Present*.

9. "Historic Clifton Mill." https://cliftonmill.com.

10. "Clifton Gorge State Nature Preserve." ODNR Division of Natural Areas and Preserves. http://naturepreserves.ohiodnr.gov/cliftongorge.

11. "Clifton Opera House." Historic Village of Clifton. www.villageofclifton.com/clifton-opera-house/.

12. Kilner. *Greene County, Ohio—Past and Present*.

13. "Clifton Opera House."

14. Britannica, The Editors of Encyclopædia. "Isaac Kauffman Funk." Encyclopædia Britannica. www.britannica.com/biography/Isaac-Kauffman-Funk.

15. Britannica, The Editors of Encyclopædia. "Woody Hayes." Encyclopædia Britannica. www.britannica.com/biography/Woody-Hayes.

16. Hutslar, Donald A. "'God's Scourge:' The Cholera Years in Ohio." *Ohio History Journal* 105 (1996): 174–191. http://resources.ohiohistory.org/ohj/search/display.php?page=2&ipp=20&searchterm=clifton&vol=105&pages=174-191.

17. Clifton Garden Cabin. www.cliftongardencabin.com.

COALTON

1. *History of Coalton and Coal Township: The Town with More Future than Past*. Coalton, OH, 1953.

2. Ibid.

3. Ibid.

4. Ibid.

5. "James A. Rhodes." Ohio History Central. www.ohiohistorycentral.org/index.php?title=James_A._Rhodes&mobileaction=toggle_view_mobile.

6. Ibid.

7. Ibid.

8. Ibid.

9. Ibid.

10. Bernstein, Mark. "John H. Patterson–John Patterson Rang up Success with the Incorruptible Cashier."

Dayton Innovation Legacy. Reprinted with the author's permission from *Smithsonian Magazine*, June, 1989. www.daytoninnovationlegacy.org/patterson.html.

11. *History of Coalton and Coal Township*.

12. Bernstein. "John H. Patterson–John Patterson Rang up Success with the Incorruptible Cashier."

13. Ibid.

14. Ibid.

15. Ibid.

16. "Isham Jones." Songwriters Hall of Fame. www.songhall.org/profile/Isham_Jones.

17. "Pat Duncan." Baseball Reference. www.baseball-reference.com/players/d/duncapa01.shtml.

18. "Coalton Wildlife Area." Ohio DNR Division of Wildlife. http://wildlife.ohiodnr.gov/coalton.

COLLEGE CORNER

1. Springer, Craig. "College Corner: A Place on the Map." *Ohio's Electric Cooperatives*, January 3, 2019. https://ohioec.org/ohio-cooperative-living/college-corner-a-place-on-the-map/.

2. "Ohio National Register Searchable Database." Ohio History Connection. http://nr.ohpo.org/Details.aspx?refnum=76001376.

3. Bartlow, Bert S., W. H. Todhunter, Stephen D. Cone, Joseph J. Pater, and Frederick Schneider. *Centennial History of Butler County, Ohio: To Which Is Appended a Comprehensive Compendium of Local Biography and Memoirs of Representative Men and Women of the County*. B.F. Bowen & Co., 1905.

4. Ibid.

5. Ibid.

6. Springer. "College Corner: A Place on the Map."

7. "College Township." The Lane Libraries. https://sites.google.com/a/lanepl.org/butler/home/c/college-township.

8. Springer. "College Corner: A Place on the Map."

9. Ksander, Yaël. "West College Corner." Moment of Indiana History. July 14, 2008. https://indianapublicmedia.org/momentofindianahistory/west-college-corner/.

10. Wheeler, Lonnie. "College Corner Journal; Singular Loyalty for Divided School." *The New York Times*, August 28, 1988. www.nytimes.com/1988/08/23/us/college-corner-journal-singular-loyalty-for-divided-school.html.

11. Dakss, Brian. "Town In Two Time Zones." CBS News. April 08, 2005. Accessed February 18, 2019. www.cbsnews.com/news/town-in-two-time-zones/.

12. Ibid.

13. Ksander. "West College Corner."

14. Dakss. "Town In Two Time Zones."

15. "Indiana's Complicated History with Daylight Saving Time." *RTV6 Indianapolis*, March 13, 2017. www.theindychannel.com/news/local-news/indianas-complicated-history-with-daylight-saving-time.

16. Dakss. "Town In Two Time Zones."

17. Wheeler. "College Corner Journal; Singular Loyalty for Divided School."

18. Ibid.

19. Pfeiffer, Casey. "Justice for a G-Man: The FBI in College Corner." The Indiana History Blog. August 16, 2017. https://blog.history.in.gov/tag/college-corner/.

CONESVILLE

1. Hill, N. N., Jr. *History of Coshocton County, Ohio: Its Past and Present, 1740–1881*. Newark, OH: A.A. Graham & Publishers, 1881.

2. Ibid.

3. Ibid.

4. Bahmer, William J. *Centennial History of Coshocton County, Ohio*. Chicago: S.J. Clarke Publishing Company, 1909.

5. "Stolen Car Recovered; 2 Men Held." *The Tribune* (Coshocton, Ohio), September 27, 1935.

6. Ibid.

7. Ibid.

8. Waitkus, Dave. "Conesville Coal Prep Plant to Close, to Be Offered for Sale." AEP Retirees & Alumni. January 20, 2012. https://aepretirees.com/2012/01/20/conesville-coal-prep-plant-to-close-to-be-offered-for-sale/.

9. "Group Claims Cancer Risk High around Conesville Power Plant." *Times Reporter*, May 12, 2009. www.timesreporter.com/x1194167142/Group-claims-cancer-risk-high-around-Conesville-power-plant.

10. Proctor, Darrell. "AEP Will Close Ohio Coal Plant Early." *POWER Magazine*. October 10, 2018. www.powermag.com/aep-will-close-ohio-coal-plant-early/.

11. Hayhurst, Leonard. "American Electric Power Conesville Plant to Close by May 2020." *Coshocton Tribune*, October 5, 2018. www.coshoctontribune.

com/story/news/local/2018/10/05/aep-conesville-plant-close-may-2020/1536021002/.

12. "Group Claims Cancer Risk High around Conesville Power Plant."

13. "Conesville Coal Lands." American Electric Power. 2019. www.aep.com/Recreation/Areas/Conesville.

COOLVILLE

1. Hunter, Gary E. *Athens County: The Second Century*. Taylor Publishing Company, 2005.

2. Hill, Agnes. "Speech titled Early Coolville History" (1968), transcribed.

3. Beatty, Elizabeth Grover., and Marjorie S. Stone. *Getting to Know Athens County*. Athens, Ohio (49 Graham Dr., Athens): Stone House, 1984.

4. Hunter. *Athens County: The Second Century*.

5. Beatty and Stone. *Getting to Know Athens County*.

6. Heagney, Meredith. "Smallest Church, Open Door." *The Columbus Dispatch*, January 20, 2012. www.dispatch.com/content/stories/faith_and_values/2012/01/20/smallest-church-open-door.html.

7. Hunter. *Athens County: The Second Century*.

8. "History and Staff." White-Schwarzel and Ewing-Schwarzel Funeral Home. Accessed March 30, 2019. www.white-schwarzelfuneralhome.com/who-we-are/history-and-staff.

9. Ibid.

10. Hill, Agnes. *The History of Coolville, Ohio 1818–1968*. Self-published.

11. "Coolville – Now That's an Awesome Name!" Less Beaten Paths of America Travel Blog. March 03, 2016. http://lessbeatenpaths.com/coolville/.

12. Blue Heron Campground, www.blueheroncoolville.com.

CORWIN

1. Campbell, Karen. "Corwin, Ohio ~ Waynesville's Sister Village." Waynesville, Ohio ~ Connections with the Past. 2005. http://waynesgenhis.blogspot.com/2005/08/corwin-ohio-waynesvilles-sister.html.

2. Ibid.

3. Ibid.

4. Miami Cemetery—Corwin, Ohio. www.swohioweather.org/corwin/miami/index.htm.

5. "Thomas Corwin." Ohio History Central. www.ohiohistorycentral.org/w/Thomas_Corwin.

6. Ibid.

7. Ibid.

8. Ibid.

9. "Thomas Corwin." Encyclopædia Britannica. December 14, 2018. www.britannica.com/biography/Thomas-Corwin.

10. "Thomas Corwin."

11. Corwin, Thomas. Speech before the United States Senate, February 11, 1847.

12. "Bowman Park." Warren County Park District. www.co.warren.oh.us/parks/Parks_List/Bowman.aspx.

CYNTHIANA

1. *History of Lower Scioto Valley, Ohio: Together with Sketches of Its Cities, Villages and Townships, Educational, Religious, Civil, Military, and Political History...* Chicago: Inter-State Publishing, 1884.

2. Ibid.

3. Ibid.

4. Ibid.

5. Backs, Jean. "Two Faces of Robert McKimie." *Ohio State Parks*, Fall 2011/Winter 2012, 4–5.

6. Ibid.

7. Ibid.

8. Ibid.

9. Ibid.

10. Ibid.

11. "McKimie's Trial in Pike County." *The Highland Weekly News*, March 20, 1879.

12. Backs. "Two Faces of Robert McKimie."

13. *History of Lower Scioto Valley*.

14. "McKimie's Trial." *Waverly Watchman*, March 11, 1879.

15. *History of Lower Scioto Valley, Ohio*.

16. Backs. "Two Faces of Robert McKimie."

17. "Court Matters." *Waverly Watchman*, March 18, 1879.

18. "McKimie's Trial." *Waverly Watchman*, March 11, 1879.

19. "Court Matters."

20. Ibid.

21. Backs. "Two Faces of Robert McKimie."

22. *History of Lower Scioto Valley, Ohio*.

23. "Attempt to Break Jail." *Waverly Watchman*, March 25, 1879.

24. Backs. "Two Faces of Robert McKimie."

DAMASCUS

1. Damascus thru the years, 1808–1958. *Historical sketch compiled for the sesqui-centennial celebration of*

Damascus, Ohio, PA Box 498 23, Ohio History Connection.

2. Ibid.

3. Ibid.

4. White, Lois. "Damascus History Retraced on Eve of Sesqui Observance." *The Salem News*, July 1, 1958.

5. Damascus thru the years, 1808–1958.

6. Ibid.

7. Ibid.

8. "Sacred Ground: Archeological Dig Sifts 150-year-old Quaker Burial Site." *Farm and Dairy*, July 3, 2002. www.farmanddairy.com/news/sacred-ground-archeological-dig-sifts-150-year-old-quaker-burial-site/6196.html.

9. Ibid.

10. Ibid.

11. Ibid.

12. "Friends Burying Grounds Historical Marker." Historical Marker Database. www.hmdb.org/marker.asp?marker=78942.

13. "Ervin George Bailey Papers, 1908–1991." Lemelson Center for the Study of Invention and Innovation. http://invention.si.edu/ervin-george-bailey-papers-1908-1991.

14. White. "Damascus History Retraced on Eve of Sesqui Observance."

15. Damascus thru the years, 1808–1958.

DEERSVILLE

1. Poulson, Homer C. *History of the Village of Deersville, Ohio 1815–1952*. Not published.

2. Ibid.

3. "Delaware Indians." Ohio History Central. www.ohiohistorycentral.org/w/Delaware_Indians.

4. "Gnadenhutten." Ohio History Central. www.ohiohistorycentral.org/w/Gnadenhutten.

5. "Gnadenhutten Massacre." Ohio History Central. www.ohiohistorycentral.org/w/Gnadenhutten_Massacre.

6. Britannica, The Editors of Encyclopædia. "Gnadenhutten Massacre." Encyclopædia Britannica. www.britannica.com/event/Gnadenhutten-Massacre.

7. Poulson, Homer C. *History of the Village of Deersville, Ohio 1815–1952*. Not Published.

8. "Gnadenhutten Massacre."

9. Poulson. *History of the Village of Deersville, Ohio 1815–1952*.

10. "The Moravian Trail Historical Marker." Historical Marker Database. www.hmdb.org/marker.asp?marker=79828.

11. "Story Map Tour." Tappan Moravian Trail. http://gis3.dot.state.oh.us/ScenicByways/TMT.html.

12. Baker, Jon. "Deersville's Union Bell Hotel Restored, Open for Business." *Times-Reporter* (New Philadelphia, OH), August 19, 2013. www.timesreporter.com/x1676649435/Deersvilles-Union-Bell-Hotel-restored-open-for-business.

13. "Lake Covers Towns, Not People's Efforts." *The Times Leader* (Martins Ferry, OH), August 2, 2015. www.timesleaderonline.com/news/community/2015/08/lake-covers-towns-not-people-s-efforts/.

14. "History." Muskingum Watershed Conservancy District. www.mwcd.org/get-to-know-us/history.

15. "About Us." Tappan Lake Park. https://tappanpark.mwcd.org/park-and-marina-info.

16. "Story Map Tour." Tappan Moravian Trail. http://gis3.dot.state.oh.us/ScenicByways/TMT.html.

17. "Lake Covers Towns, Not People's Efforts."

18. "Mary Jobe Akeley." Connecticut Women's Hall of Fame. www.cwhf.org/inductees/arts-humanities/mary-jobe-akeley#.XKJCtJhKiUk.

EAST FULTONHAM

1. Schneider, Norris F. *Y Bridge City: The Story of Zanesville and Muskingum County, Ohio*. Cleveland, OH: World Publishing Company, 1950.

2. Cavanaugh, James M. "The Zanesville & Western - Columbus's 'Backyard Railroad.'" Columbus Railroads. www.columbusrailroads.com/new/pdf/Z&W final.pdf.

3. Schneider. *Y Bridge City: The Story of Zanesville and Muskingum County, Ohio*.

4. Ibid.

5. Woodward, Virginia Beal. "Columbia Cement Helps to Build Uncle Sam's Airports." *Sunday Times Signal* (Zanesville, Ohio), April 22, 1945.

6. Ibid.

7. Ibid.

8. Lake Isabella. www.lake-isabella.org.

9. Donovan, Katie. "Quasar Energy Group Has East Fultonham Up In Arms." *Whiz News*, July 8, 2015. www.whiznews.com/2015/07/quasar-energy-group-has-east-fultonham-up-in-arms/.

10. Snyder, Kate. "Construction Begins on Medical Marijuana Farm." *Zanesville Times Recorder*, April 25, 2018. www.zanesvilletimesrecorder.com/story/

news/local/2018/04/26/construction-begins-medical-marijuana-farm/535900002/.

11. Snyder, Kate. "State Grants Right to Build Medical Marijuana Farm in Newton Township." *Zanesville Times Recorder*, November 30, 2017. www.zanesvilletimesrecorder.com/story/news/local/2017/11/30/state-grants-right-build-medical-marijuana-farm-newton-township/910054001/.

12. Snyder. "Construction Begins on Medical Marijuana Farm."

13. Ibid.

14. Snyder. "State Grants Right to Build Medical Marijuana Farm in Newton Township."

15. Snyder. "Construction Begins on Medical Marijuana Farm."

16. "Birthplace of Thomas A. Hendricks." Remarkable Ohio. http://remarkableohio.org/index.php?/category/1161.

17. "Building Razed With Estimated Loss of $18,000." *Times Recorder* (Zanesville, Ohio), February 14, 1929.

EAST LIBERTY

1. McCormick, Todd, and David Wagner. *Historic Glimpses of Logan County, Ohio*. Evansville, IN: M.T. Pub., 2003.

2. *History of Logan County and Ohio*. Chicago: O.L Baskin & Co., 1880.

3. McCormick and Wagner. *Historic Glimpses of Logan County, Ohio*.

4. Ibid.

5. Ibid.

6. [Central Ohio College] Catalogue, with announcements and calendar., PA Box 49 23, Ohio History Connection.

7. Ibid.

8. McCormick and Wagner. *Historic Glimpses of Logan County, Ohio*.

9. "Acura Was Born in Ohio." Acura Columbus. 2019. www.acuracolumbus.com/acura-born-ohio/.

10. "Honda's East Liberty Auto Plant Marks 20 Years of Automotive Innovation." Honda of America Mfg., Inc. December 18, 2009. https://ohio.honda.com/article/hondas-east-liberty-auto-plant-marks-20-years-of-automotive-innovation.

11. Malone, JD. "Acura's Redesigned, Sporty RDX Now Rolling out of East Liberty Plant." *Columbus Dispatch*, May 15, 2018. www.dispatch.com/business/20180515/acuras-redesigned-sporty-rdx-now-rolling-out-of-east-liberty-plant.

12. Sanctis, Matt. "Honda Begins Production of Latest RDX in East Liberty." *Springfield News-Sun*, May 16, 2018. www.springfieldnewssun.com/news/local/honda-begins-production-latest-rdx-east-liberty/v3V2WN8Wa3X6f497kCVP4K/.

13. "Ohio Breaks Ground on New Smart Mobility Facility in East Liberty." WBNS-10TV Columbus, Ohio. July 9, 2018. www.10tv.com/article/ohio-breaks-ground-new-smart-mobility-facility-east-liberty.

14. Baier, Miriam. "Small Town Living Heralded." *Bellefontaine Examiner*, June 24, 2017. www.examiner.org/news/83379-small-town-living-heralded.

15. "The Ackleys." Drink-Milk.com. 2019. www.drink-milk.com/farm_family/ackley-family/.

16. "Home of John Garwood / Garwoods Mill Site Historical Marker." Historical Marker Database. June 16, 2016. Accessed January 28, 2019. www.hmdb.org/marker.asp?marker=35071.

FLAT ROCK

1. "Bishop John Seybert/Flat Rock Cluster." Archives & History, The United Methodist Church. www.gcah.org/research/travelers-guide/bishop-john-seybert-flat-rock-cluster.

2. Ibid.

3. "United Methodist Church." Ohio History Central. www.ohiohistorycentral.org/w/United_Methodist_Church.

4. Seneca County Genealogical Society. *Seneca County, Ohio: History & Families*. Paducah, KY: Turner Publishing Company, 1998.

5. Baughman, A. J. *History of Seneca County, Ohio: A Narrative Account of Its Historical Progress, Its People, and Its Principal Interests*. Vol. I. Chicago-New York: Lewis Publishing Company, 1911.

6. "Our History." Flat Rock Homes. www.flatrockhomes.org/about-us/history-of-flat-rock-childrens-home/.

7. Ibid.

8. Ibid.

9. Ibid.

10. Ibid.

11. Baughman. *History of Seneca County, Ohio*.

12. Seneca Caverns Ohio. https://senecacavernsohio.com.

13. Ibid.

FLETCHER

1. *The History of Miami County, Ohio, Containing a History of the County ... Portraits of Early Settlers and Prominent Men; History of the Northwest Territory; History of Ohio ... Constitution of the United States...* Chicago: W.H. Beers & Co., 1880.

2. Hill, Leonard U., comp. *A History of Miami County, Ohio (1807–1953)*. Miami County, Ohio, Sesquicentennial Committee, 1953.

3. *The History of Miami County, Ohio*.

4. Ibid.

5. Hill. *A History of Miami County, Ohio*.

6. "Burglars Looted a Little Village." *The Lima News*, December 18, 1908.

7. "Curfew Set at Fletcher." *The Piqua Daily Call*, October 3, 1969.

8. "Halloween Curfew on in Fletcher." *The Piqua Daily Call*, September 28, 1972.

9. "Fletcher Fire Loss Estimated at $11,000; Rogers Grocery Entirely Destroyed Along with All Stock." *The Piqua Daily Call*, October 24, 1930.

10. "Ambulance Service Brown Township Topic." *The Piqua Daily Call*, August 24, 1976.

11. "Brown Trustees Bow out of Cemetery Situation." *The Piqua Daily Call*, November 9, 1976.

12. "Fletcher Presbyterian Church Cemetery." Findagrave.com. www.findagrave.com/cemetery/2652682/fletcher-presbyterian-church-cemetery.

13. "Brown Trustees Bow out of Cemetery Situation."

14. "Fletcher Presbyterian Church Cemetery."

15. "United States District Court, District of Nebraska." Munger, Thomas Charles. www.ned.uscourts.gov/public/judicial-archive/munger-t-c.

16. "End of the Road Farm." Local Harvest. www.localharvest.org/end-of-the-road-farm-M62514.

FORT JENNINGS

1. Martin, Evelyn. "This and That — The Fort of Fort Jennings." *Delphos Herald*, August 14, 2016. https://delphosherald.com/Content/Social/Social/article/this-and-that-the-fort-of-fort-jennings/-2/-2/199251.

2. "Fort Defiance." Ohio History Central. www.ohiohistorycentral.org/w/Fort_Defiance.

3. Elwer, Imogene. *Historical Fort Jennings*. Fort Jennings Area Bicentennial Committee, 1976.

4. Martin. "This and That — The Fort of Fort Jennings."

5. Elwer. *Historical Fort Jennings*.

6. Kinder, George D. *History of Putnam County, Ohio: Its Peoples, Industries, and Institutions*. Indianapolis, IN: B.F. Bowne & Company, 1915.

7. "Jennings Memorial Hall." Ohio History Connection - State Historic Preservation Office. www.ohiohistory.org/preserve/state-historic-preservation-office/hpawards/past-recipients/2014-shpo-awards/jennings-memorial-hall.

8. Fort Fest. http://fjfortfest.com.

9. Verhoff, Roselia Deters, and Putnam County Historical Society. *Putnam County, Ohio History & Families*. Evansville, IN: M.T. Pub., 2006.

10. "Fort Jennings High School." U.S. News & World Report. www.usnews.com/education/best-high-schools/ohio/districts/jennings-local/fort-jennings-high-school-15689.

11. Bates, Kim. "Fort Jennings Has a Face to Put with Its Community." *The Toledo Blade*, April 19, 2001. www.toledoblade.com/frontpage/2001/04/19/Fort-Jennings-has-a-face-to-put-with-its-community.html.

12. Ibid.

13. Ibid.

14. Elwer, Imogene. *Historical Fort Jennings*.

15. Verhoff and Putnam County Historical Society. *Putnam County, Ohio History & Families*.

FORT SENECA

1. "Seneca Indians." Ohio History Central. Accessed March 03, 2019. www.ohiohistorycentral.org/w/Seneca_Indians.

2. *Fort Seneca Sesquicentennial 1836–1986*, PA Box 649 11, Ohio History Connection.

3. Ibid.

4. Ibid.

5. Ibid.

6. *History of Seneca County, Ohio: Containing a History of the County, Its Townships, Towns, Villages...* Chicago: Warner, Beers & Co., 1886.

7. *Fort Seneca Sesquicentennial 1836–1986*.

8. Ibid.

9. Ibid.

10. Ibid.

11. Ibid.

FREEPORT

1. Overman, William D. *Ohio Town Names*. Akron, OH: Atlantic Press, 1959, pg. 47-48.

2. Harrison County Ohio Sesquicentennial Celebration, PA Box 771 6, Ohio History Connection.

3. "John J. Ashenhurst." Prohibitionist Party. http://www.prohibitionists.org/history/votes/John_J_Ashenhurst_bio.html.

4. Ibid.

5. Ibid.

6. Ibid.

7. "History Of Printing, A Time for Reflecting, Celebrating the History of Printing in Ohio and N. Kentucky." *The Communicator* 12, no. 3. http://epro2.com/article/History Of Printing/1272152/140358/article.html.

8. Ibid.

9. "Freeport Press Buys Scio Paper." *The Daily Times* (New Philadelphia, OH), February 6, 1961.

10. "History Of Printing."

11. Morrison, Lee. "Making His Mark – Freeport Press Owner Pilcher Inducted into Printing Hall of Fame." *Times Reporter* (New Philadelphia, OH), November 25, 2013. www.timesreporter.com/article/20131125/NEWS/131129595.

12. "History Of Printing."

13. Morrison. "Making His Mark."

14. Ibid.

15. "Freeport Press up and running at new site in New Philadelphia." *Times Reporter* (New Philadelphia, OH), December 21, 2015. www.timesreporter.com/article/20151221/NEWS/151229924.

16. 'Post Boy' Murder, Revived in Discovery of Death's Head, Told in Old Newspaper." *The Daily Times* (New Philadelphia, OH), March 17, 1911.

17. "Trails." Harrison County, Ohio. www.harrisoncountyohio.org/trails.

18. Adams, Ian. *A Photographers Guide to Ohio*. Athens: Ohio University Press, 2011, pg. 127.

FRESNO

1. Coshocton County Genealogical Society. *The 1985 History of Coshocton County, Ohio*. Taylor Publishing Company, 1985.

2. "Koquethagechton." Ohio History Central. www.ohiohistorycentral.org/w/Koquethagechton.

3. McEachern, Janelle. "Friday Reprise: Koquethagechton/White Eyes of the Lenape/Delaware." Great Warriors Path. August 4, 2017. http://greatwarriorspath.blogspot.com/2016/06/koquethagechton-white-eyes-of.html.

4. "Koquethagechton."

5. Zotigh, Dennis. "A Brief Balance of Power—The 1778 Treaty with the Delaware Nation." Smithsonian.com. May 21, 2018. www.smithsonianmag.com/blogs/national-museum-american-indian/2018/05/22/1778-delaware-treaty/.

6. "Koquethagechton."

7. Ibid.

8. *The 1985 History of Coshocton County, Ohio*.

9. Ibid.

10. "Our Story." Pearl Valley Cheese. https://pearlvalleycheese.com/pages/about-us.

11. Ibid.

12. Ibid.

13. Wooly Pig Farm Brewery. www.woolypigfarmbrewery.com.

14. Ibid.

15. Old Ohio Schools - Coshocton County. www.oldohioschools.com/coshocton_county.htm.

16. Forest Hill Lake. www.foresthilllake.com.

17. Historic Roscoe Village. https://roscoevillage.com.

GILBOA

1. Calvin, Marguerite. *People and Places—Putnam County, Ohio, 1800–1900*. 1981.

2. Ibid.

3. Kinder, George D. *History of Putnam County, Ohio: Its Peoples, Industries, and Institutions*. Indianapolis, IN: B.F. Bowen & Co., 1915.

4. Calvin. *People and Places—Putnam County, Ohio, 1800–1900*.

5. Ibid.

6. Kinder. *History of Putnam County, Ohio*.

7. Little Red Bakery. www.littleredbake.com.

8. Reynolds, Bryan. "Gilboa Chef Brings Treats to Area." Limaohio.com, September 22, 2017. www.limaohio.com/news/261369/gilboa-chef-brings-treats-to-area.

9. Ibid.

10. Ibid.

11. Little Red Bakery.

12. Reynolds. "Gilboa Chef Brings Treats to Area."

13. Gilboa Quarry Scuba Diving. www.divegilboa.com.

14. Blake, Erica. "The Quarries of Northwest Ohio." Alert Diver Online. 2011. www.alertdiver.com/The_Quarries_of_Northwest_Ohio.

15. Gilboa Quarry Scuba Diving.

16. Blake. "The Quarries of Northwest Ohio."

17. Gilboa Quarry Scuba Diving.

18. Blake. "The Quarries of Northwest Ohio."

19. Killea, Frances. "The Gilboa Bull." Ohiomagazine.com, August 2015. www.ohiomagazine.com/ohio-life/article/giant-bull.

20. Scinto, Maria. "Haunted Places to Go in Putnam County, Ohio." Classroom. September 29, 2017. https://classroom.synonym.com/haunted-places-to-go-in-putnam-county-ohio-12082133.html.

GIST SETTLEMENT

1. Wright, Paula Kitty. *Gist's Promised Land: The Little-Known Story of the Largest Relocation of Freed Slaves in U.S. History*. Seaman, OH: Sugar Tree Ridge Publishing, 2013.

2. Ibid.

3. Ibid.

4. Ibid.

5. Ibid.

6. Ibid.

7. Ibid.

8. Ibid.

9. "Gist Settlement Keeps Alive Days of Long Ago." *Wilmington News Journal*, July 25, 1936. https://www.wnewsj.com.

10. Williams, Kevin. "Slavery's Long Legacy in a Corner of Ohio." *Aljazeera America*, October 25, 2015. http://america.aljazeera.com/articles/2015/10/25/legacy-slavery-corner-ohio.html.

11. "The Gist Settlement." Washington Court House City Schools. www.wchcs.org/GISTSettlement Project.aspx.

12. Williams. "Slavery's Long Legacy in a Corner of Ohio."

13. Ibid.

14. Ibid.

15. Ibid.

16. Samuel Gist, VFM 6411, Ohio History Connection.

17. Wright. *Gist's Promised Land*.

18. Samuel Gist.

19. "Gist Settlement Keeps Alive Days of Long Ago." *Wilmington News Journal*, July 25, 1936.

GLENMONT

1. Holmes County Genealogical Society. *Holmes County Ohio Celebrating 175 Years*. Paducah, KY: Turner Publishing Company, 1999.

2. *Holmes County Ohio to 1985*. Holmes County History Book Committee, 1985.

3. Ibid.

4. Ibid.

5. Holmes County Genealogical Society. *Holmes County Ohio Celebrating 175 Years.*

6. *Holmes County Ohio to 1985.* Holmes County History Book Committee, 1985.

7. Holmes County Genealogical Society. *Holmes County Ohio Celebrating 175 Years.*

8. Briar Hill Stone Company. 2007. www.briarhill-stone.com.

9. Mangus, Mike. "Battle of Fort Fizzle." Ohio Civil War Central. January 9, 2011. www.ohiocivilwarcentral.com/entry.php?rec=227.

10. Brown, Gary. "The Monday After: Telling the Tale of the 'Battle of Fort Fizzle.'" *Canton Repository*, June 11, 2017. www.cantonrep.com/news/20170611/monday-after-telling-tale-of-battle-of-fort-fizzle.

11. Zurcher, Neil. *Strange Tales from Ohio: True Stories of Remarkable People, Places and Events in Ohio History.* Cleveland, OH: Gray & Co., 2008.

12. Ibid.

13. Mangus. "Battle of Fort Fizzle."

14. Ibid.

15. Ibid.

16. Zurcher. *Strange Tales from Ohio.*

17. Evans, Michael. "Spend the Night in a Treehouse at the Mohican Cabins in Ohio." Ohio. Find It Here. March 12, 2018. http://ohio.org/treehouses-and-cabins-at-the-mohicans/.

18. di Costanzo, Lily. "Crack a Beer Way Up in This Treehouse Brewing Company." Curbed. January 17, 2014. www.curbed.com/2014/1/17/10153392/crack-a-beer-way-up-in-this-treehouse-brewing-company.

19. Zurcher. *Strange Tales from Ohio.*

20. Ancestry.com. Ohio, Soldier Grave Registrations, 1804–1958 [database on-line]. Lehi, UT, USA: Ancestry.com Operations, Inc., 2017. Original data: Graves Registration Cards Collection, Ohio History Connection, Columbus, Ohio.

GRATIOT

1. Hill, N. N., Jr., comp. *History of Licking County, O., Its past and Present. Containing a Condensed, Comprehensive History of Ohio, including an Outline History of the Northwest; a Complete History of Licking County, a History of Its Soldiers in the Late War, Biographies and Histories of Pioneer Families, Etc.* Newark, OH: A. A. Graham & Co., 1881.

2. Ibid.

3. "Commanders of the Corps of Engineers." U.S. Army Corps of Engineers. https://web.archive.org/web/20090522191037/http://www.usace.army.mil/History/Pages/Commanders.aspx.

4. "Gratiot Named After General." *The Times Recorder* (Zanesville, OH), April 16, 1972.

5. "Commanders of the Corps of Engineers."

6. "Hamilton, Cornelius Springer." Biographical Directory of the United States Congress. http://bioguide.congress.gov/scripts/biodisplay.pl?index=H000106.

7. Ibid.

8. Ibid.

9. "The Murder of Mr. Hamilton." *The New York Times*, December 23, 1867. https://timesmachine.nytimes.com/timesmachine/1867/12/26/80209652.pdf.

10. Ibid.

11. Ibid.

12. Ibid.

13. Ibid.

14. DeOreo, Dave. "Photographer Re-imagines History in Gratiot, Ohio." *Ideastream*, October 25, 2017. www.ideastream.org/news/photographer-re-imagines-history-in-gratiot-ohio.

15. "Jesse Yarnell Dead." *Los Angeles Times*, January 20, 1906.

HANOVERTON

1. *History of Hanover (Hanoverton) Columbiana County, Ohio, 1914–1976.* Hanover Township Historical Society.

2. Sandy and Beaver Canal, PA Box 764 14, Ohio History Connection.

3. Ibid.

4. Ibid.

5. "Tavern & Inn History." Spread Eagle Tavern. 2019. http://spreadeagletavern.com/history/tavern-inn-history.

6. *History of Hanover (Hanoverton) Columbiana County, Ohio.*

7. Ibid.

8. Ibid.

9. Sandy and Beaver Canal.

10. *History of Hanover (Hanoverton) Columbiana County, Ohio.*

11. Ibid.

12. Ibid.

13. Ibid.

14. "Tavern & Inn History."

15. "Hanoverton Canal Town District." LandmarkHunter.com. 2018. Accessed February 18, 2019. http://landmarkhunter.com/188629-hanoverton-canal-town-district/#NRHP.

16. "Newt Gingrich's Ohio Days: December Nights Spent at Historic Spread Eagle Tavern & Inn." *Cleveland.com*, January 29, 2012. www.cleveland.com/open/index.ssf/2012/01/newts_ohio_days_december_night.html.

17. "Tavern & Inn History."

18. Stratford, Suzanne. "Ghost Stories Surround Ohio Tavern Where U.S. Presidents Visited." Fox 8 Cleveland, June 27, 2016. https://fox8.com/2016/06/27/ghost-stories-surround-ohio-tavern-where-u-s-presidents-visited/.

19. *History of Hanover (Hanoverton) Columbiana County, Ohio.*

HARBOR VIEW

1. Sumner, Casey. "Oregon Historical Museum Takes Shape." *The Toledo Blade*, August 7, 2012. www.toledoblade.com/East/2012/08/07/Oregon-historical-museum-takes-shape.html.

2. Romaker, Janet. "Tiny Lucas Co. Village Has Big Vote Ahead." *The Toledo Blade*, October 28, 2013. www.toledoblade.com/Politics/2013/10/28/Tiny-Lucas-Co-village-Harbor-View-has-big-vote-ahead.html.

3. The E.H. Close Realty Company. "A Lot Free." Advertisement. *The Lima News*, July 14, 1913.

4. "Who's up for a Harbor View Orgy?" Toledo History Box. May 30, 2012. www.toledohistorybox.com/2012/05/30/harbor-view-orgy/.

5. The E.H. Close Realty Company. "A Lot Free."

6. "Who's up for a Harbor View Orgy?"

7. Ibid.

8. Ibid.

9. "Were Not Careful Enough." *Portsmouth Daily Times*, April 10, 1924.

10. "Crabbe Would Hit Liquor Courts." *Marysville Journal-Tribune*, March 29, 1924.

11. Ibid.

12. "Deputy Marshal Ralph J. Zahnle." The Officer Down Memorial Page (ODMP). www.odmp.org/officer/14648-deputy-marshal-ralph-j-zahnle.

13. Ibid.

14. Ibid.

15. "Rummer Tells About Killing Toledo Marshal." *The Sandusky Register*, March 22, 1930.

16. "Deputy Marshal Ralph J. Zahnle." The Officer Down Memorial Page (ODMP).

17. Sumner."Oregon Historical Museum Takes Shape."

18. Romaker, Janet. "Tiny Lucas Co. Village Has Big Vote Ahead."

HARROD

1. *History of Allen County, Ohio: Containing a History of the County, Its Townships, Towns, Villages, Schools, Churches, Industries, Etc....* Chicago: Warner, Beers & Co., 1885.

2. Ibid.

3. "Harrod's Veteran's Memorial Park." Touring Ohio. http://touringohio.com/northwest/allen/harrods.html.

4. Information recorded on a plaque in the Harrod Veterans' Memorial Park.

5. "Harrod's Veteran's Memorial Park."

6. Ibid.

7. *History of Allen County, Ohio.*

8. "Harrod Railroad Park." Auglaize Township Historical Society. 2011. www.auglaizetownship historicalsociety.com/harrod-railroad-park/.

9. Lackey, Mike. "From Harrod to Hollywood." *The Lima News.* June 30, 2015. www.limaohio.com/features/lifestyle/60751/from-harrod-to-hollywood.

10. Ibid.

11. Ibid.

12. Ibid.

13. Ibid.

14. "Louise Clapp." All-American Girls Professional Baseball League. 2017. www.aagpbl.org/profiles/louise-clapp/255.

15. Harrod's Veteran's Memorial Park."

16 "Pork Rind Heritage Fest." Ohio Traveler. www.ohiotraveler.com/pork-rind-heritage-fest/.

17. "About." Pork Rind Heritage Festival. www.porkrindfest.com/about.

18. Bush, John. "Belvedere Emporium: A modern boutique inside a historic building." *The Lima News.* Dec 2, 2016. www.limaohio.com/news/217130/belvedere-emporium-a-modern-boutique-inside-a-historic-building.

HARTFORD

1. "Village History." Village of Hartford. www.villageofhartford.org.

2. Hill, N. N., Jr. *History of Licking County, O., Its past and Present.* Newark, OH: A.A. Graham & Co., Publishers, 1881.

3. Overman, William D. *Ohio Town Names.* Akron, OH: Atlantic Press, 1959. pg. 58.

4. "Village History."

5. Ibid.

6. "History of the Hartford Independent Fair." The Hartford Fair - The Biggest Little Fair In The World! www.hartfordfair.com/history.htm.

7. Ibid.

8. Ibid.

9. Ibid.

10. Massa, Paul. "Advocate Salutes Croton." *The Newark Advocate,* August 11, 1965.

11. King, Andrew. "Hartford Back in Business, but Dissolution Try Still Stings." *ThisWeek Community News,* November 17, 2014. www.thisweeknews.com/content/stories/johnstown/news/2014/11/14/grant-money-lost-hartford-back-in-business-but-dissolution-try-still-stings.html.

12. Ibid.

13. "About." IronGate Equestrian Center. http://irongateequestriancenter.com/about/.

14. "Doyt Perry." BGSUSports.com. www.bgsusports.com/mambo/content/view/24/53.

HOLIDAY CITY

1. Jefferson Township Holiday City Visitor's Bureau (Home). www.holidaycityohio.org.

2. Wise, Jean. "VillageVoice: Holiday City, Newest Village Still Evolving." *The Bryan Times,* January 4, 2010. www.bryantimes.com/news/local/villagevoice-holiday-city/article_6b2c3623-acd8-51d0-baaa-01ec89a39325.html.

3. Ibid.

4. Jefferson Township Holiday City Visitor's Bureau (Home).

5. "Menards Plans $28M Plant in Williams Co." *Toledo Business Journal,* July 1, 2017. www.toledobiz.com/Files/major_stories/2017featured/1707featured/tbj_featured1707menards_holiday_city.html.

6. Osburn, Ron. "Holiday City Visitors Bureau Seeks to Promote Holiday City and Williams County." *The Bryan Times,* February 28, 2015. www.bryantimes.com/news/local/holiday-city-visitors-bureau-seeks-to-promote-holiday-city-and/article_0f5f69d8-59df-56cc-b18a-60af71f86e4f.html.

7. Ibid.

8. Ibid.

9. Ibid.

10. "Ohio Plastics Company Taking over Closed Bluffton Factory." Wane.com, August 31, 2017. www.wane.com/news/local-news/ohio-plastics-company-taking-over-closed-indiana-factory/1000409492.

11. "Product Development." 2020 Custom Molded Plastics, Ltd. www.2020cmp.com/product development.htm.

12. "Menards Plans $28M Plant in Williams Co."

13. Thompson, Lynn. "Holiday City Celebrates 20th Anniversary." *The Bryan Times,* November 9, 2017. www.bryantimes.com/news/local/holiday-city-celebrates-th-anniversary/article_3188e8cc-7f65-5046-a8a6-f38435401c82.html.

14. Miller, Rebecca. "Holiday City Congratulated on Village Status." *The Bryan Times,* April 30, 2011. www.bryantimes.com/news/local/holiday-city-congratulated-on-village-status/article_3933ede5-24b6-57bd-a381-5b9a4b78cf41.html.

15. Thompson. "Holiday City Celebrates 20th Anniversary."

16. Spangler Candy Company. www.spanglercandy.com.

17. Ibid.

18. Cherry, Dan. "Ohio Reporter Authors Book on Skelton Brothers' Disappearance." *The Daily Telegram (Adrian, MI),* February 16, 2019. www.lenconnect.com/news/20190216/ohio-reporter-authors-book-on-skelton-brothers-disappearance.

HOLLANSBURG

1. Wilson, Frazer Ellis. *History of Darke County, Ohio: From Its Earliest Settlement to the Present Time. In Two Volumes. Volume I.* Milford, OH: Hobart Pub., 1914.

2. Miltenberger, JoKay C. *Calling Hollansburg Home: Celebrating 150 Years, 1838–1988.* Ohio: Hollansburg Sesqui-Centennial Committee, 1987.

3. Wilson. *History of Darke County, Ohio.*

4. Miltenberger. *Calling Hollansburg Home.*

5. Ibid.

6. Ibid.

7. Ibid.

8. Ibid.

9. Reese, Matt. "Downing Family Tree Full of Apple Growers." Ohio Ag Net | Ohio's Country Journal. October 13, 2015. http://ocj.com/2015/10/downing-family-tree-full-of-apple-growers/.

10. Ibid.

11. Ibid.

12. Ibid.

13. Miltenberger. *Calling Hollansburg Home.*

IBERIA

1. Morrow County History Book Committee. *History of Morrow County, Ohio.* Don Mills, 1989.

2. Ibid.

3. *History of Morrow County and Ohio.* Chicago: O.L. Baskin & Co., 1880.

4. *History of Morrow County, Ohio.*

5. Ibid.

6. Ibid.

7. Ibid.

8. Ibid.

9. Ibid.

10. Predmore, Dorothy. *Stories We Tell Our Children About Iberia.* Bucyrus, OH: Eichelberger Print., 1969.

11. *History of Morrow County, Ohio.*

12. Ibid.

13. Lace, David. "Iberia: Little Town With Big History." *Marion Star,* February 14, 1970.

14. Kent, Russell. "Iconic Iberia Business Changing Hands." *Galion Inquirer,* January 9, 2018. www.galioninquirer.com/uncategorized/25856/iconic-iberia-business-changing-hands.

15. *History of Morrow County, Ohio.*

JACKSONBURG

1. Bartlow, Bert Surene, W. H. Todhunter, and Stephen D. Cone., et al. *Centennial History of Butler County, Ohio: To Which Is Appended a Comprehensive Compendium of Local Biography and Memoirs of Representative Men and Women of the County.* B. F. Bowen & Co., 1905.

2. Cox, James M. *Journey Through My Years.* New York: Simon and Schuster, 1946.

3. "Rural: Jacksonburg Is Small, and That's Fine with Residents." *The Cincinnati Enquirer,* December 19, 1999.

4. Ibid.

5. Cox. *Journey Through My Years.*

6. "James M. Cox." Ohio History Central. www.ohiohistorycentral.org/w/James_M._Cox.

7. Cox. *Journey Through My Years.*

8. Ibid.

9. "About Us." Jacksonburg United Methodist Church. www.jacksonburgumc.org/717611.

10. Bartlow, Todhunter, and Cone, et al. *Centennial History of Butler County, Ohio.*

11. "Rural: Jacksonburg Is Small, and That's Fine with Residents."

12. Bartlow, Todhunter, and Cone, et al.

13. "Wayne School Demolition In Tiny Ohio Town Brings About Impromptu Reunion." Huffington Post, December 6, 2012. www.huffpost.com/entry/wayne-school-demolition-i_n_2250983.

14. Ibid.

15. Cox. *Journey Through My Years.*

16. Guerrieri, Vince. "The Election of 1920." Ohiomagazine.com, February 2015. www.ohiomagazine.com/ohio-life/article/the-election-of-1920.

KILBOURNE

1. *History of Delaware County and Ohio.* Chicago: O.L. Baskin & Co., 1880.

2. "James Kilbourne." Ohio History Central. www.ohiohistorycentral.org/w/James_Kilbourne.

3. Berquist, Goodwin F., and Paul C. Bowers. *The New Eden: James Kilbourne and the Development of Ohio.* Lanham, MD: University Press of America, 1983.

4. *History of Delaware County and Ohio.*

5. Lytle, James R., ed. *20th Century History of Delaware County, Ohio, and Representative Citizens.* Chicago: Biographical Publishing Company, 1908.

6. Botkin, D. Anthony. "Kilbourne Post Office Closing." *The Delaware Gazette,* August 17, 2017. www.delgazette.com/news/60027/kilbourne-post-office-closing.

7. Ibid.

8. Ibid.

9. Botkin, D. Anthony. "Brown Township Breaks Ground on $1.4 Million Hall." *The Delaware Gazette,* June 3, 2017. www.delgazette.com/news/58635/brown-township-breaks-ground-on-1-4-million-hall.

10. Botkin, D. Anthony. "Brown Township celebrates dedication of new hall." *The Delaware Gazette,* November 14, 2017. www.delgazette.com/news/63496/brown-township-celebrates-dedication-of-new-hall.

11. Hapner, Breck J. "Kilbourne Resident Has Colorful History." The Associated Press, October 20, 2010. https://newsok.com/article/feed/193034/kilbourne-resident-has-colorful-history.

12. Ibid.

13. Buckeye Valley Summer Baseball. https://buckeyevalleysummerbaseball.weebly.com.

14. Lytle. *20th Century History of Delaware County, Ohio and Representative Citizens.*

KIPTON

1. *History of Lorain County, Ohio, with Illustrations & Biographical Sketches...* Philadelphia: Williams Brothers, 1879.

2. "North Coast Inland Trail." Lorain County Metro Parks. 2012. http://metroparks.cc/north_coast_inland_trail.php.

3. Pope, Nancy. "The Great Kipton Train Wreck." National Postal Museum. April 22, 2013. https://postalmuseumblog.si.edu/2013/04/the-great-kipton-train-wreck.html.

4. "Awful Disaster. Express and Mail Train on the Lake Shore Road Collide..." *The News-Herald* (Hillsboro, OH), April 23, 1891.

5. "Terrible Railroad Wreck—Eight Men Killed." *Democratic Northwest and Henry County News* (Napoleon, OH), April 23, 1891.

6. Ibid.

7. "Fearful Fate. Six Postal Clerks and Two Engineers Meet an Awful Death..." *News-Journal* (Mansfield, OH), April 19, 1891.

8. "Terrible Railroad Wreck—Eight Men Killed."

9. "Fearful Fate. Six Postal Clerks and Two Engineers Meet an Awful Death..."

10. "Terrible Railroad Wreck—Eight Men Killed."

11. "Fearful Fate. Six Postal Clerks and Two Engineers Meet an Awful Death..."

12. Ibid.

13. Pope. "The Great Kipton Train Wreck."

14. Ibid.

15. "Webb C. Ball Co." Encyclopedia of Cleveland History | Case Western Reserve University. https://case.edu/ech/articles/w/webb-c-ball-co.

16. Wysochanski, Joe. "Anniversary Commemorated of Fatal Kipton Train Wreck That Prompted Widespread Reforms." *The Chronicle* (Elyria, OH), April 21, 2016. www.chroniclet.com/news/2016/04/21/Anniversary-commemorated-of-fatal-Kipton-train-wreck-that-prompted-widespread-reforms.html.

17. "Webb C. Ball Co."

18. "Great Kipton Train Wreck." Historical Marker Database. www.hmdb.org/marker.asp?marker=96536.

19. "Untitled." *The Democratic Press* (Ravenna, OH), April 22, 1891.

20. Welcome to Ball Watch. www.ballwatch.com/global/en/home.html.

LAKE SENECA

1. "About Lake Seneca." Lake Seneca. www.lakeseneca.org/About-Lake-Seneca-s/136.htm.

2. *Williams County, Ohio: A Collection of Historical Sketches and Family Histories*. Montpelier, OH: Williams County Historical Society, 1978.

3. "Resort Developer Files as Bankrupt." *The New York Times*, September 6, 1975. www.nytimes.com/1975/09/06/archives/resort-developer-files-as-bankrupt.html.

4. Pakulski, Gary. "Bargain Values at Troubled Lake Seneca." *Toledo Blade*, August 22, 2004. www.toledoblade.com/Real-Estate/2004/08/22/Bargain-values-at-troubled-Lake-Seneca.html.

5. *Williams County, Ohio: A Collection of Historical Sketches and Family Histories*.

6. Pakulski. "Bargain Values at Troubled Lake Seneca."

7. *Williams County, Ohio: A Collection of Historical Sketches and Family Histories*.

8. Pakulski. "Bargain Values at Troubled Lake Seneca."

9. "Resort Developer Files as Bankrupt."

10. Pakulski. "Bargain Values at Troubled Lake Seneca."

11. Ibid.

12. Ibid.

13. Ibid.

14. Ibid.

15. Lakeside Cafe. www.lakesenecacafe.com.

16. Ibid.

17. Shinn, William Henry. *The County of Williams: A History of Williams County, Ohio, from the Earliest Days...*Madison, WI: Northwestern Historical Association, 1905.

LEESVILLE

1. Eckley, H. J., and William T. Perry. *History of Carroll and Harrison Counties, Ohio. Vol. 1.* Chicago and New York: Lewis Publishing Company, 1921, p. 195–196.

2. Papers, 1912 August 15, VFM 979, Ohio History Connection (notes compiled for Centennial Celebration of Leesville in 1912).

3. Baker, Jon. "Local History: Coal Mines, Oil Boom Brought Prosperity to Leesville at Beginning of 20th Century." *Times-Reporter (New Philadelphia, OH)*, January 7, 2019.

4. Ibid.

5. Baker, Jon. "Jon Baker History Column: Camp at Leesville Lake Provided Work Training for Young Men during Great Depression." *Times-Reporter (New Philadelphia, OH)*, August 8, 2016.

6. Ohio Department of Natural Resources Division of Wildlife. "Leesville Lake." Ohio.gov. 2012. http://wildlife.ohiodnr.gov/public-hunting-fishing-wildlife-viewing-areas/lake-and-reservoir-fishing-maps/leesville-lake#tabr2.

7. Baker. "Jon Baker History Column: Camp at Leesville Lake Provided Work Training for Young Men during Great Depression."

8. Ibid.

9. "'Black Diamonds' Will Bring a Merry Christmas." *The Daily Times* (New Philadelphia), December 18, 1947.

10. Ibid.

11. "Dog On Hand For Opening Of All Jones Mines In Last 13 Years." *The Evening Independent* (Massillon, OH), July 5, 1947.

12. Baker, Jon. "Historic Leesville House Demolished as Part of Interstate Pipeline Project." Canton Rep, February 25, 2017. https://www.cantonrep.com/news/20170225/historic-leesville-house-demolished-as-part-of-interstate-pipeline-project

13. Ibid.

14. Ibid.

15. "A history of Leesville, Ohio," PA Box 474 5, Ohio History Connection.

16. Eckley and Perry. *History of Carroll and Harrison Counties, Ohio. Vol. 1.*

17. "A history of Leesville, Ohio," PA Box 474 5, Ohio History Connection.

LINNDALE

1. Johnson, Crisfield, comp. *History of Cuyahoga County, Ohio: In Three Parts...with Portraits and Biographical Sketches of Its Prominent Men and Pioneers*. D.W. Ensign & Co., 1879.

2. Robert Linn. "Linndale." Advertisement. *The Tiffin Tribune*, July 3, 1873.

3. Johnson. *History of Cuyahoga County, Ohio*.

4. "Mayor Ann and Her Lady Cabinet Tamed the 'Toughest Town in Ohio.'" *Portsmouth Daily Times*, February 9, 1936.

5. "Youth Admits Shooting Man." *Marysville Journal-Tribune*, November 13, 1930.

6. "Ohio Mayor Is Sent to Prison." *News-Journal* (Mansfield, OH), December 1, 1926.

7. "Takes Steps to Oust Its Mayor." *News-Journal* (Mansfield, OH), October 6, 1926.

8. "Ohio Mayor Is Sent to Prison." *News-Journal* (Mansfield, OH), December 1, 1926.

9. "Linndale Politics in Uproar Again." *The Daily Times* (New Philadelphia, OH), December 30, 1927.

10. "Mayor Ann and Her Lady Cabinet Tamed the 'Toughest Town in Ohio.'"

11. Ibid.

12. Ibid.

13. Trickey, Erick, and Mark Demarino. "Greetings From Linndale." *Cleveland Magazine*, July 21, 2011. https://clevelandmagazine.com/in-the-cle/the-read/articles/greetings-from-linndale.

14. Ibid.

15. "Mayor Quits After Son Dies in Vietnam." *The Circleville Herald*, May 8, 1969.

16. Trickey and Demarino. "Greetings From Linndale."

17. "Expect Delays." This American Life. October 20, 2017. www.thisamericanlife.org/629/expect-delays.

18. Ibid.

19. "Mayor Ann and Her Lady Cabinet Tamed the 'Toughest Town in Ohio.'"

20. Ibid.

LOCKBOURNE

1. Droege, John, Barnett Golding, and Richard Anderson. *The Ohio and Erie Canal from Lockbourne to Carroll, and the Columbus Feeder Canal*. Akron, OH: Canal Society of Ohio, 1974.

2. Ibid.

3. Meyer, David A. *Life Along the Ohio Canal: Licking Reservoir to Lockbourne and the Columbus Feeder*. Canal Winchester, OH: Canal Winchester Historical Society, 1998.

4. Ibid.

5. *History of Franklin and Pickaway Counties, Ohio, with Illustrations and Biographical Sketches...* Williams Bros., 1880.

6. Droege, Golding, and Anderson. *The Ohio and Erie Canal from Lockbourne to Carroll, and the Columbus Feeder Canal*.

7. Meyer. *Life Along the Ohio Canal- Licking Reservoir to Lockbourne and the Columbus Feeder*.

8. Ibid.

9. Stroup, Robert M., II. *Crossroads of Liberty: A Pictorial Tribute to Lockbourne/Rickenbacker AFB-ANGB-IAP*. Missoula, MT: Pictorial Histories Publishing Company, 2008.

10. "Tuskegee Airmen." Motts Military Museum. www.mottsmilitarymuseum.org/Tuskegee_Airmen.html.

11. Stroup. *Crossroads of Liberty: A Pictorial Tribute to Lockbourne/Rickenbacker AFB-ANGB-IAP.*

12. "Historical – Lockbourne Air Force Base." Ohio Exploration Society. www.ohioexploration.com/miscellaneous/historical-lockbourneafb/.

13. "Tuskegee Airmen."

LOCKINGTON

1. Piqua Historical Area: John Johnston farm and buildings, restored section of Miami and Erie Canal, canal boat Genl Harrison, Historic Indian Museum, PA Box 763 46, Ohio History Connection

2. Hitchcock, A.B.C. *History of Shelby County, Ohio and Representative Citizens.* Chicago, IL: Richmond Arnold Publishing, 1913, pp. 393–394.

3. Wallace, Rich. "Canals - Making the Canal Locks." Traveling Through Time—Archived Articles of People, Places and Events. Shelby County Historical Society, 1998. www.shelbycountyhistory.org/schs/canal/makingthelocks.htm.

4. Piqua Historical Area: John Johnston farm and buildings.

5. Wallace. "Canals - Making the Canal Locks."

6. "How a Lock Works." National Parks Service. Accessed September 29, 2018. www.nps.gov/choh/learn/kidsyouth/how-a-lock-works.htm.

7. Wallace. "Canals - Making the Canal Locks."

8. The Miami & Erie Canal, pathway through the wilderness / Great Miami River Corridor Committee of Miami & Shelby Counties, Inc., PA Box 778 9, Ohio History Connection.

9. Wallace, Rich. "Lockington." Traveling Through Time—Archived Articles of People, Places and Events. Shelby County Historical Society, 1998.

10. "Lockington Locks." Museum and Historic Site Locator. Ohio History Connection, www.ohiohistory.org/visit/museum-and-site-locator/lockington-locks.

11. The Miami & Erie Canal, pathway through the wilderness.

12. "Johnston Farm & Indian Agency." Museum and Historic Site Locator. Ohio History Connection. www.ohiohistory.org/visit/museum-and-site-locator/johnston-farm-and-indian-agency.

13. "Through Village of Lockington: Western Ohio People Will Build Their Line." *The Piqua Daily Call,* June 03, 1901.

14. "Lockington At The Turn Of The Century," *The Piqua Daily Call,* August 15, 1963.

15. "Johnson Sworn in as Lockington's Mayor." Shelby County Post. January 6, 2016. www.shelbycountypost.com/johnson-sworn-in-as-lockingtons-mayor/.

16. Ibid.

17. "National Register of Historic Places." National Parks Service. Accessed September 29, 2018. https://npgallery.nps.gov/nrhp.

LOWER SALEM

1. *Washington County, Ohio, to 1980: A Collection of Topical & Family Sketches.* Washington County Historical Society, 1980.

2. Ibid.

3. "Marietta, Ohio." Ohio History Central. www.ohiohistorycentral.org/w/Marietta,_Ohio.

4. *Washington County, Ohio, to 1980.*

5. Ibid.

6. "Aids Flood Victims." *The Greenville Journal,* August 14, 1913.

7. *Washington County, Ohio, to 1980.*

8. "Aids Flood Victims."

9. "3,000 People Fled For Their Lives in Flood Regions Along Duck Creek." *The Times Recorder* (Zanesville, OH), July 17, 1913.

10. "Home Again, Are the Four Flood Sufferers." *The Times Recorder* (Zanesville, OH), April 15, 1903.

11. "Former Resident, Milliner at Lower Salem, Woman Mayor." *The Times Recorder* (Zanesville, OH), November 11, 1929.

12. Maloney, Pete. "Roseville Art Pottery." The Arts and Crafts Antique Gallery. www.gustavstickley.com/roseville-pottery.html.

13. "Former Resident, Milliner at Lower Salem, Woman Mayor."

14. Ibid.

15. "Fire." *The Spirit of Democracy* (Woodsfield, OH), December 7, 1886.

16. "Rioters Arrested." *The Greenville Journal,* July 11, 1907.

17. "Cowboy-Booted Two-Gun Desperado and Partner Escape with $4,969 Cash." *The Times Recorder* (Zanesville, OH), April 5, 1951.

18. *Washington County, Ohio, to 1980.*

19. Ibid.

MAGNETIC SPRINGS

1. Curry, W. L. *History of Union County, Ohio: Its People, Industries and Institutions.* Indianapolis, IN: B.F. Bowen and Company, 1915.

2. Ibid.

3. Ibid.

4. Ibid.

5. Union County History Book Committee. *Family Heritage Union County, Ohio 1985.* Dallas, TX: Taylor Publishing Company, 1985.

6. Ibid.

7. Ibid.

8. Ibid.

9. Magnetic Springs Ohio Famous Health Resort, PA Box 337 33, Ohio History Connection.

10. Union County History Book Committee. *Family Heritage Union County, Ohio 1985.*

11. Blundo, Joe. "Magnetic Springs Cafe Is Woman's Labor of Love." *Columbus Dispatch,* October 23, 2018. www.dispatch.com/entertainmentlife/20181023/magnetic-springs-cafe-is-womans-labor-of-love.

12. Cordell, Mac. "Magnetic Springs Receives $500,000 Grant." *Marysville Journal-Tribune,* September 12, 2018. www.marysvillejt.com/news/magnetic-springs-receives-500000-grant/.

13. Magnetic Springs Ohio Famous Health Resort, PA Box 337 33, Ohio History Connection.

14. "About Magnetic Springs - Water Delivery Company." Magnetic Springs. https://magneticsprings.com/about/.

MARTINSBURG

1. Massa, Paul. "Advocate Salutes Martinsburg." *The Newark Advocate,* April 14, 1965.

2. Hill, N. N., and A. A. Graham. *History of Knox County, Ohio: Its past and Present, Containing a Condensed, Comprehensive History of Ohio, including an Outline History of the Northwest; a Complete History of Knox County...* Mount Vernon, OH: A.A. Graham & Publishers, 1881.

3. Massa. "Advocate Salutes Martinsburg."

4. Martinsburg Academy. *Catalogue of the Officers and Students of the Martinsburg Academy.* Martinsburg, OH, 1841, Ohio History Connection.

5. "Windom, William." Biographical Directory of the United States Congress. http://bioguide.congress.gov/scripts/biodisplay.pl?index=w000629.

6. Christenson, Erin. "Throwback Thursday: William Windom: The Man on the $2 Bill." *Winona (Minnesota) Daily News,* March 23, 2017. www.winonadailynews.com/news/local/throwback-thursday-william-windom-the-man-on-the-bill/article_3164dd7d-520b-5461-a8fc-594915fc03d0.html.

7. "Windom, William."

8. Ibid.

9. Christenson. "Throwback Thursday: William Windom: The Man on the $2 Bill."

10. "Value of 1891 $2 Silver Certificate – Windom." AntiqueMoney.com. www.antiquemoney.com/value-of-1891-2-silver-certificate-windom/.

11. Bergan, Ronald. "William Windom Obituary." *The Guardian*, August 23, 2012. www.theguardian.com/tv-and-radio/2012/aug/23/william-windom.

12. "Zanesville Presbytery Group In Pilgrimage to Martinsburg." *Zanesville Times Recorder*, May 31, 1955.

13. Ibid.

14. Ibid.

15. Martinsburg Dairy Isle Facebook page. https://www.facebook.com/dairyisle6682046/

16. "Zanesville Presbytery Group In Pilgrimage to Martinsburg."

MIAMIVILLE

1. Everts, Louis H. *History of Clermont County, Ohio, with Illustrations and Biographical Sketches of Its Prominent Men and Pioneers*. Philadelphia: J. B. Lippincott & Co., 1880.

2. "Island Canoe Club Charter." Miami Boat Club. www.miamiboatclub.com/files/Island_Canoe_Club_Charter.doc.

3. Ibid.

4. Ibid.

5. Ibid.

6. "History." Miami Boat Club. www.miamiboatclub.com/History.html.

7. "Membership." Miami Boat Club. www.miamiboatclub.com/Membership.html.

8. "Home." Loveland Bike Trail. www.lovelandbiketrail.com/.

9. Ibid.

10. "Letters for the Volunteers." *Highland Weekly News*, May 16, 1861.

11. "Lost." *Cincinnati Daily Star*, August 11, 1875.

MILLEDGEVILLE

1. "Milledgeville Grew from Hogue's Settlement." *Washington Court House Record-Herald*, September 18, 1976.

2. Ibid.

3. Dills, R. S. *History of Fayette County, Together with Historic Notes on the Northwest, and the State Of Ohio...* Dayton, OH: Odell & Mayer, 1881.

4. "Milledgeville Grew from Hogue's Settlement."

5. Ibid.

6. Ibid.

7. Ibid.

8. Dills. *History of Fayette County*.

9. "Milledgeville Grew from Hogue's Settlement."

10. "Fire Razes Milledgeville Landmark." *Washington Court House Record-Herald*, November 20, 1970.

11. Ibid.

12. Ibid.

13. Ibid.

14. Mullen, Bev. "Kelley's Tavern in Milledgeville to Close This Weekend." *Washington Court House Record-Herald*, October 30, 2015. www.recordherald.com/news/3052/the-end-of-an-era.

15. Ibid.

16. Ibid.

17. Ibid.

18. "Celebrators Active." *Washington Court House Record-Herald*, November 4, 1938.

MILLFIELD

1. Beatty, Elizabeth Grover, and Marjorie S. Stone. *Getting to Know Athens County*. Athens, Ohio: Stone House, 1984.

2. *History of Hocking Valley, Ohio: Together with Sketches of Its Cities, Villages and Townships, Educational, Religious, Civil, Military, and Political History, Portraits of Prominent Persons, and Biographies of Representative Citizens*. Chicago: Inter-State Publishing, 1883.

3. Beatty and Stone. *Getting to Know Athens County*.

4. Hunter, Garry E., Lisa A. Eliason, and Ed Venrick. *Athens County: The Second Century, 1905–2005*. Taylor Publishing Company, 2005.

5. Watkins, Damon D. *Keeping the Home Fires Burning, a Book about the Coal Miner*. Columbus, OH: Ohio, 1937, Chapter 1.

6. Jaworowski, J. Frank. "4 From Here Among Victims Of 1930 Athens Co. Explosion." *The Times Recorder* (Zanesville), November 5, 1972.

7. "Flames Follow Near Athens, Ohio; Bodies Lie Everywhere in Inferno; Officials Fall Beside Workmen." *The Sandusky Register*, November 6, 1930.

8. Watkins. *Keeping the Home Fires Burning, a Book about the Coal Miner*.

9. Beatty and Stone. *Getting to Know Athens County*.

10. The Millfield mine explosion, Nov. 5, 1930 / H. L. McDonald, PA Box 552 10, Ohio History Connection.

11. Ibid.

12. Ibid.

13. Watkins. *Keeping the Home Fires Burning, a Book about the Coal Miner*.

14. Ibid.

15. Ibid.

16. Ibid.

17. Ibid.

18. Jaworowski. "4 From Here Among Victims Of 1930 Athens Co. Explosion."

19. Ibid.

20. Ibid.

21. Powell, Dennis E. "You've Heard of Roswell – How 'bout the Millfield Flying Saucer?" *The Athens News*, October 11, 2015. www.athensnews.com/opinion/columns/the_view_from_mudsock_heights/you-ve-heard-of-roswell-how-bout-the-millfield-flying/article_8dd69ae4-702e-11e5-9ca3-57d7b393560f.html.

22. "About Us." Athens County Job and Family Services. www.jfs.athensoh.org/explore_athens_jfs/about_us/index.php.

MOSCOW

1. *History of Clermont County, Ohio: With Illustrations and Biographical Sketches of Its Prominent Men and Pioneers*. Philadelphia: Louis H. Everts, 1880.

2. Ibid.

3. Knepp, Gary L. *Freedom's Struggle, A Response to Slavery from the Ohio Borderlands*. Milford, OH: Little Miami Publishing, 2008, Chapter 8.

4. Clermont County Convention and Visitors Bureau. *Clermont County, Ohio Freedom Trail*. 2017, www.visitclermontohio.com/wp-content/uploads/Clermont-Freedom-trail-WEB.pdf.

5. Palmer, D. P. "Untitled." *The Democratic Standard* (Georgetown, OH), December 6, 1842.

6. Knepp, Gary L. *Freedom's Struggle, A Response to Slavery from the Ohio Borderlands*. Milford, OH: Little Miami Publishing, 2008, Chapter 8.

7. Ibid.

8. Ibid.

9. Palmer, D. P. "Untitled." *The Democratic Standard* (Georgetown, OH), December 6, 1842.

10. Knepp, Gary L. *Freedom's Struggle, A Response to Slavery from the Ohio Borderlands*. Milford, OH: Little Miami Publishing, 2008, Chapter 8.

11. Ibid.

12. Ibid.

13. Ibid.

14. Ibid.

15. "Will Moscow Ever Be Able to Recover from 2012 Tornado?" *WCPO Cincinnati*, March 2, 2017. www.wcpo.com/news/local-news/clermont-county/moscow/will-moscow-ever-be-able-to-recover-from-2012-tornado.

16. "Ulysses S. Grant." Ohio History Central. www.ohiohistorycentral.org/w/Ulysses_S._Grant.

17. "U. S. Grant Birthplace." Ohio History Connection. www.ohiohistory.org/visit/museum-and-site-locator/us-grant-birthplace.

18. "William H. Zimmer Power Station." Ohio History Central. www.ohiohistorycentral.org/w/William_H._Zimmer_Power_Station

MOUNT EATON

1. *The History of Paint Township & Mount Eaton, Ohio, 1829–2003*. Sugarcreek, OH: Carlisle Press, 2003.

2. *History of Wayne County, Ohio Volume 1*. Indianapolis, IN: B. F. Bowen & Co., 1910.

3. *The History of Paint Township & Mount Eaton, Ohio, 1829–2003*.

4. *History of Wayne County, Ohio Volume 1*.

5. *The History of Paint Township & Mount Eaton, Ohio, 1829–2003*.

6. Ibid.

7. Ibid.

8. Ibid.

9. "Cashier Locked in Safe; Robbers Loot Ohio Bank." *Akron Beacon Journal*, October 8, 1920.

10. *The History of Paint Township & Mount Eaton, Ohio, 1829-2003*.

11. Ibid.

12. Ibid.

13. "Find N.O.T. Property Near Bank Robbery Scene at Wooster." *Akron Beacon Journal*, December 24, 1920.

14. State History Publications, LLC. *Ohio Historic Places Dictionary, Vol. 2*. North American Book Dist. LLC, 2008, pg. 1402.

MOUNT PLEASANT

1. "Quaker Meeting House Historical Marker." Historical Marker Database. www.hmdb.org/marker.asp?marker=37047.

2. Friends Meeting House State Memorial, PA Box 763 28, Ohio History Connection

3. Burke, James L., and Donald E. Bensch. *Mount Pleasant and the Early Quakers of Ohio*. Columbus, OH: Ohio Historical Society, 1975.

4. Ibid.

5. Ibid.

6. Ibid.

7. Friends Meeting House State Memorial, PA Box 763 28, Ohio History Connection.

8. "Aboard the Underground Railroad—Mt. Pleasant." National Parks Service. www.nps.gov/nr/travel/underground/oh4.htm.

9. Friends Meeting House State Memorial.

10. "Benjamin Lundy." Ohio History Central.. www.ohiohistorycentral.org/w/Benjamin_Lundy.

11. Burke and Bensch. *Mount Pleasant and the Early Quakers of Ohio*.

12. Articles of Association of the Mount Pleasant Free Produce Company, PA Box 20 30, Ohio History Connection

13. Burke and Bensch. *Mount Pleasant and the Early Quakers of Ohio*.

14. Baker, Jon. "Mount Pleasant, Ohio — a Step Back in Time." *Times-Reporter (New Philadelphia, OH)*, July 4, 2016. www.timesreporter.com/news/20160704/mount-pleasant-ohio---step-back-in-time.

15. Burke and Bensch. *Mount Pleasant and the Early Quakers of Ohio*.

16. "Moses Fleetwood Walker." Negro League Baseball Players Association. www.nlbpa.com/the-athletes/walker-moses-fleetwood.

17. Burke and Bensch. *Mount Pleasant and the Early Quakers of Ohio*.

MURRAY CITY

1. *Murray City, Ohio, Historical and Industrial, 1907*. 1966.

2. Ibid.

3. Ibid.

4. Ibid.

5. *Murray City, Ohio: A Legacy of Coal*. WOUB Public Media. Vimeo. https://vimeo.com/92555760.

6. "Legacy." The Water Project. http://ouwaterproject.org/issues/legacy/.

7. *Murray City, Ohio: A Legacy of Coal*.

8. Thompson, Justin. "Murray City Man Keeps Mining Museum's Lights on." WOUB Digital, November 5, 2018. https://woub.org/2018/11/05/murray-city-man-keeps-mining-museums-lights-on/.

9. "Murray City: All Worked Out." Carolyn Rogers Photojournalist. www.carolynrogersphotography.com/murray-city-ohio/.

10. Thompson. "Murray City Man Keeps Mining Museum's Lights on."

11. Ibid.

12. "Murray City Tigers Were Grid Power in 1920s." *The Messenger* (Athens, OH), December 1, 1963. https://littlecitiesarchive.org/tag/murray-city/.

NEVILLE

1. Rockey, J. L., and R. J. Bancroft. *History of Clermont County, Ohio: With Illustrations and Biographical Sketches of Its Prominent Men and Pioneers*. Philadelphia: Louis H. Everts, 1880.

2. Hogg, J. Bernard. "Presley Neville." *The Western Pennsylvania Historical Magazine* 19, no. 1 (March 1936): pg. 17–26. https://journals.psu.edu/wph/article/viewFile/1761/1609.

3. Ibid.

4. Ibid.

5. Ibid.

6. Ibid.

7. *Clermont County, Ohio, 1980: A Collection of Genealogical and Historical Writings*. Batavia, OH: Clermont County Genealogical Society, 1984.

8. Underwood, Brad. "Vanishing Villages: Floods and State Funding Cuts Hurt Neville." Local 12 (Cincinnati, OH), March 11, 2016. https://local12.com/news/local/vanishing-villages-floods-and-less-state-funding-hurting-neville.

9. "Neville to Remain a Village." *The Clermont Sun*, March 17, 2016. www.clermontsun.com/2016/03/17/neville-to-remain-a-village/.

10. *Clermont County, Ohio, 1980*.

11. Underwood. "Vanishing Villages: Floods and State Funding Cuts Hurt Neville."

NEW HAVEN

1. "Connecticut Raids." George Washington's Mount Vernon, Digital Encyclopedia. www.mountvernon.org/library/digitalhistory/digital-encyclopedia/article/connecticut-raids/.

2. Lilienthal, Sal, and Mary Collins. "New Haven: 1779 Invasion (Bike Tour)." Revolutionary Connecticut. 2013. www.ctamericanrevolution.com/images/maps/5_New_Haven_July_2013_PDF.pdf.

3. "Connecticut Raids."

4. Hermes, Katherine. "Daggett's Charge: The Revolution in New Haven." Digital Farmington Blog.

December 16, 2017. https://digitalfarmington.org/religion/daggetts-charge-the-revolution-in-new-haven/.

5. "Connecticut Raids."

6. Hermes. "Daggett's Charge: The Revolution in New Haven."

7. Parton, J. *The Life and Times of Aaron Burr.* New York: Mason Brothers, 1861, pg. 123–125.

8. Lilienthal and Collins. "New Haven: 1779 Invasion (Bike Tour)."

9. "Firelands." Ohio History Central. www.ohiohistorycentral.org/w/Firelands.

10. "Treaty of Fort Industry (1805)." Ohio History Central. www.ohiohistorycentral.org/w/Treaty_of_Fort_Industry_(1805).

11. "Firelands History." *Norwalk Reflector*, October 29, 2015. www.norwalkreflector.com/News/2010/07/26/Firelands-history.

12. Williams, William. *History of the Fire Lands.* Cleveland: Press of Leader Printinc Company, 1879.

13. Baughman, A. J. *History of Huron County, Ohio: Its Progress and Development, with Biographical Sketches of Prominent Citizens of the County.* Chicago: S. J. Clarke Publishing Company, 1909.

14. Williams. *History of the Fire Lands.*

15. Western Reserve Land Conservancy. "105-acre Huron County Farm Permanently Preserved." August 10, 2017. www.wrlandconservancy.org/articles/2017/08/10/huroncountyfarmpreserved/.

16. "Firelands History."

NEW RIEGEL

1. Wagner, Elaine Lafontaine. *A Century of Growth in Pride, Prayer and Progress: A Centennial History of New Riegel.* New Riegel, OH: Centennial History Committee, 1983.

2. "Wyandot Indians." Ohio History Central. www.ohiohistorycentral.org/w/Wyandot_Indians.

3. Wagner. *A Century of Growth in Pride, Prayer and Progress.*

4. Ibid.

5. *History of Seneca County, Ohio: Containing a History of the County, Its Townships, Towns, Villages...*Chicago: Warner, Beers & Co., 1886.

6. Wagner. *A Century of Growth in Pride, Prayer and Progress.*

7. "The Sisters of the Precious Blood." Maria Stein Shrine of the Holy Relics. www.mariasteinshrine.org/the-sisters-of-the-precious-blood.html.

8. "Our Founder St. Gaspar Del Bufalo." Missionaries of the Precious Blood. www.cppsmissionaries.org/about-us-cpps/our-founder/.

9. Wagner. *A Century of Growth in Pride, Prayer and Progress.*

10. Ibid.

11. "New Riegel Parish and Convent." Remarkable Ohio. www.remarkableohio.org/index.php?/category/1316.

12. Wagner. *A Century of Growth in Pride, Prayer and Progress.*

13. "New Riegel Parish and Convent."

14. Wagner. *A Century of Growth in Pride, Prayer and Progress.*

15. "New Riegel Parish and Convent."

16. "History." New Riegel Cafe. www.newriegelcafe.com/history.html.

17. Wagner. *A Century of Growth in Pride, Prayer and Progress.*

18. Ibid.

19. Ibid.

NEW WESTON

1. Wilson, Frazer E. *History of Darke County, Ohio: From Its Earliest Settlement to the Present Time.* Vol. 1. Milford, OH: Hobart Publishing Company, 1914.

2. "Funeral of Harry W. Randall, Victim of Railroad Wreck, Held at New Weston." *Dayton Daily News*, August 7, 1914.

3. Sperandeo, Andy, Kevin P. Keefe, and David C. Lester. "The People Who Work on Trains." *Trains Magazine.* May 1, 2006. http://trn.trains.com/railroads/abcs-of-railroading/2006/05/the-people-who-work-on-trains.

4. "Funeral of Harry W. Randall, Victim of Railroad Wreck, Held at New Weston."

5. "Engineer Killed in Train Wreck." *The Yale Expositor* (Yale, MI), August 6, 1914.

6. "Funeral of Harry W. Randall, Victim of Railroad Wreck, Held at New Weston."

7. Ibid.

8. Billing, Greg. "Legend Fueled Sport's Growth." *The Journal-News* (Hamilton, OH), March 24, 2015.

9. Ibid.

10. Ibid.

11. "Eldora Speedway - History of the World 100 (1971 - 1987)." YouTube. March 24, 2014. www.youtube.com/watch?v=bVzrTmwxiPI.

12. Billing. "Legend Fueled Sport's Growth."

13. "World 100 Driver History." Eldora Speedway. www.eldoraspeedway.com/world-100-driver-history/.

14. Billing, Greg. "Eldora Ready for NASCAR Invasion." *The Journal-News* (Hamilton, OH), July 22, 2014.

15. "World 100 Driver History."

16. Billing. "Eldora Ready for NASCAR Invasion."

17. "Press Release—Earl Baltes, Eldora Speedway Founder, Passes at Age 93." Eldora Speedway. www.eldoraspeedway.com/2015/03/23/earl-baltes-eldora-speedway-founder-passes-at-age-93/.

18. Billing. "Legend Fueled Sport's Growth."

19. "Fire Threatens to Wipe Out New Weston." *Dayton Daily News*, February 25, 1921.

NORTH STAR

1. "North Star, Ohio." MyDarkeCountyOhio. http://mydarkecounty.com/communities/north-star.

2. Kasper, Shirl. *Annie Oakley.* Norman, OK: University of Oklahoma Press, 1992.

3. Ibid.

4. Macy, Sue. *Bull's-Eye: A Photobiography of Annie Oakley.* National Geographic Society, 2001.

5. Ibid.

6. Ibid.

7. Kasper. *Annie Oakley.*

8. Ibid.

9. Macy. *Bull's-Eye: A Photobiography of Annie Oakley.*

10. Kasper. *Annie Oakley.*

11. Macy. *Bull's-Eye: A Photobiography of Annie Oakley.*

12. Ibid.

13. Kasper. *Annie Oakley.*

14. Kilgore, Adam. "Craig Stammen Works through Injury to Make Washington Nationals' Starting Rotation." *Washington Post*, March 28, 2010.www.washingtonpost.com/wp-dyn/content/article/2010/03/27/AR2010032703053.html.

15. Brown, Mary Ann, and Mary Niekamp. *National Register of Historic Places Inventory/Nomination: Cross-Tipped Churches Thematic Resources*, 2–5. National Park Service, July 1978, https://npgallery.nps.gov/NRHP/GetAsset/NRHP/64000616_text.

NORWICH

1. *History of Muskingum County, Ohio: With Illustrations and Biographical Sketches of Prominent Men and Pioneers.* J. F. Everhart & Co., 1882.

2. "National Road." Ohio History Central. www.ohiohistorycentral.org/w/National_Road.

3. Jordan, Philip D. *The National Road.* Indianapolis and New York: Bobbs-Merrill Company, 1948.

4. Ibid.

5. "Daniel Washington." *Tales of a Tavern; or, The House on the Hill.* Rollin A. Allen, 1956.

6. "National Road."

7. "Daniel Washington." *Tales of a Tavern.*

8. Ibid.

9. Cartaino, Carol. *It Happened in Ohio: Remarkable Events That Shaped History.* Rowman & Littlefield, 2010, pg. 54.

10. Allen, Jim. *Tall Tree Tales: The First Recorded Traffic Accident in Ohio.* 1990.

11. Ibid.

12. Ibid.

13. Ibid.

14. Ibid.

15. "National Road & Zane Grey Museum." Ohio History Connection. www.ohiohistory.org/visit/museum-and-site-locator/national-road-and-zane-grey-museum.

16. Baker's Motel. http://bakersmotel.com.

17. "Wylie, Chalmers Pangburn." Biographical Directory of the United States Congress. Accessed March 30, 2019. http://bioguide.congress.gov/scripts/biodisplay.pl?index=W000781.

OCTA

1. Allen, Frank M. *History of Fayette County, Ohio: Her People, Industries and Institutions.* B. F. Bowen & Co., 1914.

2. Ibid.

3. Overman, William Daniel. *Ohio Town Names.* Akron, OH: Atlantic Press, 1958.

4. Ancestry.com. *Ohio, County Marriage Records, 1774–1993* [database on-line]. Lehi, UT, USA: Ancestry.com Operations, Inc., 2016.

5. Ancestry.com. *1900 United States Federal Census* [database on-line]. Provo, UT, USA: Ancestry.com Operations Inc, 2004.

6. United States of America, Bureau of the Census. *Twelfth Census of the United States, 1900.* Washington, D.C.: National Archives and Records Administration, 1900. T623, 1854 rolls.

7. Allen. *History of Fayette County, Ohio.*

8. *Plat Book of Fayette County, Ohio.* Des Moines, IA: The Company, 1913.

9. Allen. *History of Fayette County, Ohio.*

10. Steinmetz, Robert. *A Train Ran Through It: A Boy's Life in Octa, Ohio, 1940–1953,* and a *History of the Small Rural Village.* 2018.

11. "It's 'Expansion Day' For Octa!" *Washington Court House Record-Herald,* July 10, 1969.

12. Ibid.

13. Ibid.

14. "Octa Motel Appears Nearer." *Washington Court House Record-Herald,* April 7, 1970.

15. "It's 'Expansion Day' For Octa!" *Washington Court House Record-Herald,* July 10, 1969.

16. "Former Octa Man Killed in Vietnam." *Washington Court House Record-Herald,* May 20, 1971.

OLD FORT

1. Baughman, Abraham J. *History of Seneca County, Ohio: A Narrative Account of Its Historical Progress, Its People, and Its Principal Interests.* Vol. 1. Lewis Publishing Company, 1911, pg. 472.

2. "Fort Seneca." Touring Ohio. http://touringohio.com/history/fort-seneca.html.

3. Baughman. *History of Seneca County, Ohio.*

4. Butterfield, Consul W. *History of Seneca County: Containing a Detailed Narrative of the Principal Events That Have Occurred since Its First Settlement...*Sandusky, OH: D. Campbell & Sons, 1848.

5. "Fort Seneca - Harrison Trail Historical Marker." Historical Marker Database. www.hmdb.org/marker.asp?marker=21948.

6. "About Old Fort Banking Company." Old Fort Banking Company. www.oldfortbank.com/about-us/about-old-fort-banking-company.html.

7. Stengle, Janet. "Old Fort Bank Celebrates 100 Years." *Toledo Blade,* July 15, 2016. www.toledoblade.com/business/2016/07/15/Old-Fort-Bank-celebrates-100-years/stories/20160714265.

8. Ibid.

9. Ibid.

10. "About Old Fort Banking Company."

11. Stengle. "Old Fort Bank Celebrates 100 Years."

12. "Marion "Pete" Mellott of Old Fort, Ohio." Engle-Shook Funeral Home & Crematory. 2017. www.engleshookfuneralhome.com/obituary/4090891.

13. Ibid.

14. McCray, Vanessa. "Bettsville Schools to Merge with Old Rival." *Toledo Blade,* June 22, 2014. www.toledoblade.com/Education/2014/06/22/Bettsville-schools-to-merge-with-old-rival.html#pJImEmJK2z4cR9O2.99.

15. "Gillmor, Paul Eugene." Biographical Directory of the United States Congress. http://bioguide.congress.gov/scripts/biodisplay.pl?index=G000210.

OTWAY

1. *A History of Scioto County, Ohio: A Narrative Account of Its Beginning, Its Development, and Its People.* Portsmouth, OH: Portsmouth Area Recognition Society, 1986.

2. Britannica, The Editors of Encyclopædia. "Thomas Otway." Encyclopædia Britannica. www.britannica.com/biography/Thomas-Otway.

3. "Otway Covered Bridge." Ohio History Connection—2015 State Historic Preservation Office Awards. www.ohiohistory.org/preserve/state-historic-preservation-office/hpawards/past-recipients/2015-recipients-(1)/otway-covered-bridge.

4. *A History of Scioto County, Ohio.*

5. "Otway Covered Bridge."

6. Nandy, Ben. "Otway, Ohio Residents save and Restore Area's Only Covered Bridge." 13 WOWKtv.com (Huntington, WV), December 17, 2015. www.wowktv.com/archives/otway-ohio-residents-save-and-restore-area-s-only-covered-bridge/865525310.

7. "Otway Covered Bridge."

8. Nandy, Ben. "Otway, Ohio Residents save and Restore Area's Only Covered Bridge."

9. "Fire at Otway." *Portsmouth Daily Times,* April 22, 1916.

10. Ibid.

11. Ibid.

12. Ibid.

13. Burford, Tom. *Apples of North American: 192 Exceptional Varieties for Gardeners, Growers, and Cooks.* Portland: Timber Press, 2013, pg. 84.

14. "Otway Covered Bridge."

15. "Bridge Builders: Robert W. Smith." Indiana Covered Bridge Society. www.indianacrossings.org/builders/rwsmith.html.

POLK

1. Baughman, Abraham J. *History of Ashland County, Ohio.* Vol. 1. S. J. Clarke Publishing Company, 1909.

2. Plank, Betty. *Historic Ashland County: A Collection of Local History Accounts about People, Places and Events from 1812–1987.* Endowment Committee of the Ashland County Historical Society, 1987.

3. Ibid.

4. Ibid.

5. "Two Men Hang For $1.50." *The Summit County Beacon* (Akron, Ohio), May 21, 1884.

6. "A Chapter of Crime, in Which Whiskey Plays a Prominent Part." *The Marion Star*, March 27, 1883.

7. Ibid.

8. Baughman. *History of Ashland County, Ohio.*

9. Ibid.

10. "Two Men Hang For $1.50."

11. Ibid.

12. Cullum, George W. *Biographical Register of the Officers and Graduates of the U.S. Military Academy at West Point, N.Y.: Since Its Establishment in 1802.* Saginaw, MI: Seemann & Peters Printers, 1920, pg. 1810.

13. "Historic Ashland: County Native Reinhart Had a Decorated Military Career." *Times-Gazette*, May 29, 2010. www.times-gazette.com/news/20100529/historic-ashland-county-native-reinhart-had-decorated-military-career.

14. "Topsy Hartsel Stats." Baseball Almanac. 2018. www.baseball-almanac.com/players/player.php?p=hartsto01.

15. "Tully Frederick "Topsy" Hartsel." Find A Grave. Accessed January 22, 2019. www.findagrave.com/memorial/46276293.

16. Polk-Jackson-Perry Fire Department. http://polkjacksonperryfd.com/?fbclid=IwAR3AEUgNNr_NmLhGlNnEG1W7p04YGvGRU6uqBtyZt3oPxD-Hxpzr9Lnbv7xI.

PULASKI

1. Goodspeed, Weston A., and Charles Blanchard. *County of Williams, Ohio: Historical and Biographical: With an Outline Sketch of the Northwest Territory, of the State, and Miscellaneous Matters: Illustrated.* Chicago: F.A. Battey & Co., 1882.

2. Bowersox, Charles A. *A Standard History of Williams County, Ohio: An Authentic Narrative of the Past...*Chicago and New York: Lewis Publishing Company, 1920.

3. Goodspeed and Blanchard. *County of Williams, Ohio.*

4. Williams County Historical Society, comp. *Williams County, Ohio: A Collection of Historical Sketches...*Vol. 1. 1978.

5. Ibid.

6. Ibid.

7. Bowersox. *A Standard History of Williams County, Ohio.*

8. Britannica, The Editors of Encyclopædia. "Kazimierz Pulaski." Encyclopædia Britannica. www.britannica.com/biography/Kazimierz-Pulaski.

9. Britannica, The Editors of Encyclopædia. "Confederation of Bar." Encyclopædia Britannica. www.britannica.com/topic/Confederation-of-Bar.

10. Ibid.

11. Britannica, The Editors of Encyclopædia. "Kazimierz Pulaski."

12. "Casimir Pulaski." Polish American Center. www.polishamericancenter.org/Pulaski.htm.

13. Britannica, The Editors of Encyclopædia. "Kazimierz Pulaski."

14. "Casimir Pulaski." National Parks Service. www.nps.gov/fopu/learn/historyculture/casimir-pulaski.htm.

15. "Casimir Pulaski."

16. Brown, David W. "The 8 Honorary Citizens of the United States." Mental Floss, March 9, 2015. http://mentalfloss.com/article/62058/8-honorary-citizens-united-states.

17. "(1840) – Old Bill's Grave (Pulaski, Ohio)." *The Village Reporter (Williams and Fulton Counties, OH)*, March 21, 2018. www.thevillagereporter.com/1840-old-bills-grave-pulaski-ohio/.

18. Ibid.

19. Ibid.

20. Ibid.

PUT-IN-BAY

1. Frohman, Charles E. *Put-in-Bay: Its History.* Columbus, OH: Ohio Historical Society, 1971.

2. "History." OhioPutInBay.com. www.ohio-put-in-bay.com/history/.

3. "Oliver Hazard Perry." National Parks Service. www.nps.gov/pevi/learn/historyculture/perry.htm.

4. "Battle of Lake Erie." Ohio History Central. www.ohiohistorycentral.org/w/Battle_of_Lake_Erie.

5. Ibid.

6. Stuckey, Ronald L. *Lost Stories: Yesterday and Today at Put-in-Bay: Including Theresa Thorndales "Island Jottings" of the 1890s.* Columbus, OH: RLS Creations, 2002.

7. "Perry's Victory and International Peace Memorial Ohio." National Parks Service. www.nps.gov/pevi/index.htm.

8. Stuckey. *Lost Stories: Yesterday and Today at Put-in-Bay.*

9. "The History and Mystery of Put-in-Bay's Hotel Victory." Midwest Guest. October 29, 2015. www.midwestguest.com/2015/10/the-history-and-mystery-of-put-in-bays-hotel-victory.html.

10. Ibid.

11. Ibid.

12. Hotel Victory and Victory Park, PA Box 631 6, Ohio History Connection.

13. The World Famous Hotel Victory, PA Box 785 6, Ohio History Connection.

14. "Crystal Cave—The World's Largest Geode." Heineman's Winery. www.heinemanswinery.com/crystalcave.asp.

15. Stone Lab, https://ohioseagrant.osu.edu/education/stonelab.

16. "District Information." Put-in-Bay School. www.put-in-bay.k12.oh.us/district.

QUAKER CITY

1. Sarchet, Col. Cyrus P.B. *History of Guernsey County Ohio. Vol. 1.* Indianapolis, IN: B. F. Bowen & Co., 1911.

2. Booth, Russell H., Jr. *A Brief History of Guernsey County, Ohio: Including the Morgan Raid Claims.* Cambridge, OH: Gomber House Press, 1998.

3. Ibid.

4. Yarnall, Bruce. "Richland Quaker Meetinghouse Historical Marker Dedicated." *The Daily Jeff (Cambridge, OH)*, June 7, 2017. www.daily-jeff.com/news/20170607/richland-quaker-meetinghouse-historical-marker-dedicated.

5. Booth. *A Brief History of Guernsey County, Ohio.*

6. Schneider, Norris F. "Quaker City's Hill Folk Festival To Attract Thousands of Visitors." *Zanesville Times Recorder*, July 10, 1966.

7. Schneider. "Quaker City's Hill Folk Festival To Attract Thousands of Visitors."

8. "Ohio Hills Folk Festival." Ohio Traveler. www.ohiotraveler.com/ohio-hills-folk-festival/.

9. "Historical Marker Dedication Sunday at Quaker City." *The Times Leader (Martins Ferry, OH)*, May 27, 2017. www.timesleaderonline.com/news/community/2017/05/historical-marker-dedication-sunday-at-quaker-city/.

10. Yarnall. "Richland Quaker Meetinghouse Historical Marker Dedicated."

11. Bale, Mary Peirce. "Exploring Carter and Kennedy's San Tan Mountains." Bushducks. September 2005. http://bushducks.com/tripreps/santan.htm.

12. Ibid.

13. Ibid.

14. Ibid.

15. Ibid.

16. Ibid.

17. Schneider. "Quaker City's Hill Folk Festival To Attract Thousands of Visitors."

18. "Anne Grimes." Ohio History Central. www.ohiohistorycentral.org/w/Anne_Grimes.

19. "Historical Marker Dedication Sunday at Quaker City."

RARDEN

1. Evans, Nelson W. *A History of Scioto County, Ohio: Together with a Pioneer Record of Southern Ohio.* Portsmouth, OH, 1903.

2. Portsmouth Area Recognition Society. *A History of Scioto County, Ohio, 1986: A Narrative Account of Its Beginning, Its Development, and Its People.* Dallas, TX: Taylor Publishing Company, 1986.

3. Scenic Scioto Heritage Trail. "The Taylor Mansion." Historic marker located in Rarden, OH.

4. Portsmouth Area Recognition Society. *A History of Scioto County, Ohio, 1986.*

5. Scenic Scioto Heritage Trail. "The Taylor Mansion."

6. Portsmouth Area Recognition Society. *A History of Scioto County, Ohio, 1986.*

7. Scenic Scioto Heritage Trail. "The Taylor Mansion."

8. Portsmouth Area Recognition Society. *A History of Scioto County, Ohio, 1986.*

9. Ibid.

10. Rarden Whitetail Deer Festival. http://rardendeerfest.com/site/.

11. Ibid.

12. Ibid.

13. "Rarden Festival Flood Relief." Gofundme.com. www.gofundme.com/rarden-festival-flood-relief.

14. "Marshal Held For Murder Is Known Locally." *The Press-Gazette* (Hillsboro, OH), January 3, 1956.

15. Christian, Helen. *Echo of Rarden History.* Vantage Press, 1980.

16. "Untitled Obituary." *The Middleburgh Post*, August 18, 1881.

ROCKBRIDGE

1. *History of Hocking Valley, Ohio: Together with Sketches of Its Cities, Villages and Townships...*Chicago: Inter-State Publishing, 1883.

2. "Rock Bridge." Hockinghills.com. www.hockinghills.com/rock_bridge.html.

3. *History of Hocking Valley, Ohio.*

4. "Rockbridge State Nature Preserve." ODNR Division of Natural Areas and Preserves. Accessed March 27, 2019. http://naturepreserves.ohiodnr.gov/rockbridge.

5. *History of Hocking Valley, Ohio.*

6. "Rockbridge State Nature Preserve."

7. "Clear Creek Metro Park." www.hockinghills.com/rock_bridge.html.

8. Wells, Rob. "Hocking County Village Submerged in Floodwater." Fox 28 (Columbus, OH), April 4, 2018. https://myfox28columbus.com/news/local/hocking-county-village-submerged-in-floodwater.

9. "Flood Refugee at Jail." *The Logan Daily News*, January 25, 1937.

10. "Hocking River Crests at 14 1/2 Ft. in Logan." *The Logan Daily News*, January 22, 1959.

11. "Rockbridge WAVE Is Speaker at School Assembly." *The Logan Daily News*, February 4, 1944.

12. Huske, Ruth M. "Rockbridge Club Celebrates Third Anniversary Date." *Lancaster Eagle-Gazette*, February 4, 1944.

13. Connor, Roger. "Women Guided the Way in the [Simulated] Sky During WWII." Smithsonian National Air and Space Museum. March 31, 2017. https://airandspace.si.edu/stories/editorial/women-guided-way-simulated-sky-during-wwii.

14. Ibid.

15. "Rockbridge WAVE Is Speaker at School Assembly."

16. Connor. "Women Guided the Way in the [Simulated] Sky During WWII."

17. "Lilyfest – A Celebration of Arts, Crafts, Music, and Gardens in the Hocking Hills." www.lilyfest.com.

ROGERS

1. McCord, William B. *History of Columbiana County, Ohio, and Representative Citizens.* Chicago: Biographical Publishing Company, 1905.

2. Ibid.

3. Ibid.

4. "History." Rogers Community Auction | Open Air Market. http://rogersohio.com/about-rogers/media-guide/.

5. Ibid.

6. "FAQS—I Remember When the Flea Market Was Late on Friday Night." Rogers Community Auction | Open Air Market. http://rogersohio.com/faqs/.

7. "History." Rogers Community Auction.

8. "FAQS—Why Fridays?" Rogers Community Auction | Open Air Market. http://rogersohio.com/faqs/.

9. "FAQS—I Remember When the Flea Market Was Late on Friday Night."

10. "Casting for Humorous Series to Shoot at Rogers Flea Market." *Youngstown Vindicator*, February 24, 2018. www.vindy.com/news/2018/feb/24/humorous-series-will-shoot-at-rogers-fle/.

11. https://fleamarketfanatics.com/

12. McCord. *History of Columbiana County, Ohio.*

13. "About Baer." Baer Auctioneers Realty, LLC. http://baerauctions.com/about-baer/.

RUDOLPH

1. *Commemorative, Historical and Biographical Record of Wood County, Ohio: Its past and Present, Early Settlement and Development ... Biographies and Portraits of Early Settlers and Representative Citizens..*Chicago: J.H. Beers & Co., 1897.

2. "Cincinnati, Hamilton, and Dayton Railroad." Ohio History Central. www.ohiohistorycentral.org/w/Cincinnati,_Hamilton,_and_Dayton_Railroad.

3. Lindstom, Lauren. "Postal Service Honors 'Rudolph' the Reindeer in Rudolph, Ohio." *Toledo Blade*, November 29, 2014. www.toledoblade.com/local/2014/11/29/Postal-Service-honors-Rudolph/stories/20141128220.

4. Hannah, Jay. "The Most Famous Reindeer Still a Mailing Staple in Rudolph." NBC 24 News, December 22, 2017. https://nbc24.com/news/local/the-most-famous-reindeer-still-a-mailing-staple-in-rudolph.

5. Associated Press. "Rudolph the Red-Nosed Reindeer Postmark: Ohio Town Unites to save Holiday Tradition." *The Oregonian*, December 3, 2012. www.oregonlive.com/today/2012/12/rudolph_the_red-nosed_reindeer.html.

6. Lindstrom. "Postal Service Honors 'Rudolph' the Reindeer in Rudolph, Ohio."

7. Associated Press. "Rudolph the Red-Nosed Reindeer Postmark: Ohio Town Unites to save Holiday Tradition."

8. Ibid.

9. Ibid.

10. Konecny, Tom. "Volunteers Keep Rudolph Post Office Humming Every December." *Toledo City Paper*, December 14, 2015. https://toledocitypaper.com/the-city/volunteers-keep-rudolph-post-office-humming-every-december/.

11. Ibid.

12. Hannah. "The Most Famous Reindeer Still a Mailing Staple in Rudolph."

13. Konecny. "Volunteers Keep Rudolph Post Office Humming Every December."

14. Lindstrom. "Postal Service Honors 'Rudolph' the Reindeer in Rudolph, Ohio."

15. Murphy, Steve. "Rentals, Apartments Put New Life into Old Liberty School." *Toledo Blade*, November 25, 2003. www.toledoblade.com/frontpage/2003/11/25/Rentals-apartments-put-new-life-into-old-Liberty-School.html.

16. Rogers, Debbie. "Liberty School Building Owner Says Beauty of Property in Eye of Beholder." *Sentinel-Tribune*, Bowling Green, August 28, 2017. www.sent-trib.com/news/front_page/liberty-school-building-owner-says-beauty-of-property-in-eye/article_f3e55054-84c8-5cfa-b40d-2590c7d37eea.html.

17. Rogers, Debbie. "Liberty School vacant once again." *Sentinel-Tribune*, Bowling Green, December 6, 2018. www.sent-trib.com/news/liberty-school-vacant-once-again/article_9e4eeb24-f95b-11e8-8d9a-e792605ab077.html.

18. Konecny. "Volunteers Keep Rudolph Post Office Humming Every December."

RUSHVILLE

1. Scott, Hervey. *A Complete History of Fairfield County, Ohio*. Columbus, OH: Siebert & Lilley, 1877.

2. Miller, Charles C., Ph.D. *History of Fairfield County, Ohio and Representative Citizens*. Chicago: Richmond-Arnold Publishing, 1912.

3. Graham, A. A. *History of Fairfield and Perry Counties, Ohio: Their past and Present...*Chicago: W. H. Beers & Co., 1883.

4. "Benjamin Hanby." Ohio History Central. www.ohiohistorycentral.org/index.php?title=Benjamin_Hanby&rec=202.

5. Siebert, Wilbur H. "Tiers of Midway Counties from West to East" in "The Mysteries of Ohio's Underground Railroad," MSS 116 AV Box 52 Folder 8, Ohio History Connection, https://www.ohiomemory.org/digital/collection/siebert/id/955. Title changed per https://www.ohiomemory.org/digital/collection/siebert/id/1011

6. Ibid.

7. Ibid.

8. "Benjamin Hanby and His Anti-Slavery Song, Darling Nelly Gray." Westerville Public Library. www.westervillelibrary.org/underground-hanby.

9. "Pleasant Hill Cemetery." National Parks Service. 2010. www.nps.gov/subjects/ugrr/ntf_member/ntf_member_details.htm?SPFID=4436849&SPFTerritory=NULL&SPFType=NULL&SPFKeywords=NULL.

10. "Benjamin Hanby and His Anti-Slavery Song, Darling Nelly Gray."

11. Benedict, Michael Les, and John F. Winkler. *The History of Ohio Law*. Athens, OH: Ohio University Press, 2004, pg. 793.

12. "Features." Cabin at the Crossroads, Rushville, Ohio. www.cabinatthecrossroads.com/crossroads_features.htm.

13. "About Us." Rushville Boarding Kennel. 2016. www.rushvilleboardingkennel.com/About-Rushville-Boarding-Kennel.html.

14. "Hugus Farm History." Hugus Fruit Farm. www.hugusfruitfarm.com/history.html.

15. "Benjamin Hanby."

16. Barron, Jeff, and Matthew Berry. "Fire Severely Damages Rushville Insurance Business Building." *Lancaster Eagle-Gazette*, January 4, 2019. www.lancastereaglegazette.com/story/news/2019/01/04/fire-severely-damages-rushville-insurance-business-building/2481615002/.

RUTLAND

1. Larkin, Stillman Carter. *The Pioneer History of Meigs County*. Berlin Printing Company, 1908.

2. Ibid.

3. Ibid.

4. Ibid.

5. Ibid.

6. Ibid.

7. Pickens, Jordan D. "The Roots in Rutland of Home on the Range." *Meigs Independent Press*, January 3, 2019. http://meigsindypress.com/2019/01/03/the-roots-in-rutland-of-home-on-the-range/.

8. Ibid.

9. "Dr. Brewster Higley VI." Home on the Range Cabin. www.homeontherangecabin.com/dr-higley.

10. "Home on the Range." Kansapedia. Kansas Historical Society. www.kshs.org/kansapedia/home-on-the-range/19076.

11. Ibid.

12. Schoone, Ivan. "Higley Brothers Return to Relative's 'Home on the Range.'" *Hastings Tribune*, October 24, 2016. www.hastingstribune.com/news/higley-brothers-return-to-relative-s-home-on-the-range/article_55ab2d7c-9a14-11e6-8713-4710a4933cae.html.

13. "About Us." Rutland Bottle Gas. www.rutlandbottlegas.com/about.html.

14. "United Plant Savers Botanical Sanctuary, Rutland, Ohio." United Plant Savers. April 13, 2011. https://unitedplantsavers.org/160-goldenseal-botanical-sanctuary-rutland-ohio/.

SAINT JOHNS

1. McMurray, William J., ed. *History of Auglaize County Ohio. Vol. 1*. Indianapolis, IN: Historical Publishing Company, 1923.

2. Williamson, C. W. *History of Western Ohio and Auglaize County*. Columbus, OH: W. M. Linn & Sons, 1905.

3. "Catahecassa." Ohio History Central. www.ohiohistorycentral.org/w/Catahecassa.

4. Ibid.

5. "I. Address of Black Hoof, [5 February 1802]." Founders Online, National Archives and Records Administration. https://founders.archives.gov/documents/Jefferson/01-36-02-0331-0002.

6. "Treaty of Wapakoneta." Ohio History Central. www.ohiohistorycentral.org/w/Treaty_of_Wapakoneta_(1831).

7. Lodge, David. "Chief Blackhoof." Shelby County Historical Society. 1997. www.shelbycountyhistory.org/schs/indians/chiefblackhoof.htm.

8. "Catahecassa."

9. McMurray. *History of Auglaize County Ohio. Vol. 1*.

10. Ibid.

11. Account ledger, 1909–1915, VOL 1396, Ohio History Connection.

12. "I. Address of Black Hoof, [5 February 1802]."

SAVANNAH

1. Bailey, Rae. *Old Keys: An Historical Sketch of Clear Creek Township, Ashland County, Ohio, and of Savannah, the Townships Only Village*. Washington, D.C., 1941.

2. Historical data of Clear Creek Township and village of Savannah, Ohio. Prepared for Civic improvement club of Savannah, Ohio, by John Gibson and Mrs. W.S. Wert as a supplement to historical pageant presented June 27 and 28, 1928, PA Box 26 8, Ohio History Connection.

3. Bailey. *Old Keys*.

4. Ibid.

5. Ibid.

6. Ibid.

7. Ibid.

8. Ibid.

9. Ibid.

10. Ibid.

11. Ibid.

12. Sangiacomo, Michael. "Ohio Tiny Towns: Last Living Johnny Appleseed Tree Is Pride of Savannah." *Cleveland.com*, May 7, 2018. www.cleveland.com/metro/index.ssf/2018/05/tiny_towns_ohio_last_living_jo.html.

13. Ibid.

14. Willard, Frances E. *American Women: Fifteen Hundred Biographies with over 1,400 Portraits: A Comprehensive Encyclopedia of the Lives and Achievements of American Women during the Nineteenth Century.* Vol. 1. Mast, Crowell & Kirkpatrick, 1897, pg. 89.

SINKING SPRING

1. "Ohio Indian Wars," Ohio History Central, www.ohiohistorycentral.org/w/Ohio_Indian_Wars.

2. Ibid.

3. Klise, Rev. J. W. *The County of Highland: A History of Highland County, Ohio, From the Earliest Days...*Edited by A. E. Hough. Madison, WI: Northwestern Historical Association, 1902.

4. "Sinking Spring, Brushcreek Township History Recalled." *The Press Gazette* (Hillsboro, OH), May 21, 1975.

5. Ibid.

6. Ibid.

7. Ibid.

8. Wallis, Jean. "One of a Kind 'Octagonal' in Sinking Spring." *The Times-Gazette (Hillsboro, OH)*, July 13, 2016. www.timesgazette.com/news/8921/one-of-a-kind-octagonal-in-sinking-spring.

9. Ibid.

10. "Sinking Spring, Brushcreek Township History Recalled."

11. "Charles W. Byrd," Ohio History Central, www.ohiohistorycentral.org/w/Charles_W._Byrd.

12. "Sinking Spring, Brushcreek Township History Recalled."

13. "Our Story." Thompson Funeral Service, Inc. www.thompsonfuneralhomes.com/our-story.

14. "Sinking Spring Section." Buckeye Trail Association. www.buckeyetrail.org/sections/sections.php?section=sinkingspring.

15. "Sinking Spring, Brushcreek Township History Recalled."

SOUTH VIENNA

1. "Welcome to South Vienna." The Village of South Vienna...a Short History. 2016. www.southvienna.org.

2. Shoemaker, Ron, and Greg Smith. "1833–1912." History of South Vienna. https://southvienna.webs.com/1833-1912.

3. Ibid.

4. Shoemaker, Ron, and Greg Smith. "Home." History of South Vienna. https://southvienna.webs.com.

5. Shoemaker, Ron, and Greg Smith. "1912–2014." History of South Vienna. https://southvienna.webs.com/1912-2014.

6. "Welcome to South Vienna."

7. Encyclopædia Britannica. "Bosnian Crisis of 1908." www.britannica.com/event/Bosnian-crisis-of-1908.

8. Shoemaker, Ron, and Greg Smith. "Corn Festival." History of South Vienna. https://southvienna.webs.com/corn-festival-2.

9. Ibid.

10. Ibid.

11. Shoemaker and Smith. "1912–2014."

12. "History." Ritchie Bros. Auctioneers. www.rbauction.com/aboutus/history.

13. Shoemaker and Smith. "1912–2014."

14. "Home." Ritchie Bros. Auctioneers. www.rbauction.com.

15. Shoemaker and Smith. "1912–2014.".

16. "Alfretta Ronemus Ambrotype." Ohio Memory. www.ohiomemory.org/digital/collection/p267401coll32/id/108.

17. Hollandia Gardens, PA Box 544 42, Ohio History Connection.

STAFFORD

1. Burke, Henry Robert, and Charles Hart Fogle. *Washington County Underground Railroad.* Arcadia Publishing, 2004.

2. Maienknecht, Theresa A., and Stanley B. Maienknecht. *Monroe County, Ohio: A History.* Mt. Vernon, IN: Windmill Publications, 1989.

3. MSS 116 AV Box 52 Folder 7, Wilbur Siebert Collection, Ohio History Connection. https://ohiomemory.org/digital/collection/siebert/id/1239/rec/2.

4. Maienknecht and Maienknecht. *Monroe County, Ohio.*

5. "Stafford (Franklin Twp) Monroe County, Ohio." Lest We Forget - African American Military History by Researcher, Author and Veteran Bennie McRae, Jr. http://lestweforget.hamptonu.edu/page.cfm?uuid=9FEC4E6D-F15E-0E0C-5C2B-4716B4A55CFD.

6. Burke, Henry Robert. "John Curtis and Family." Links to the Past. http://henryburke1010.tripod.com/id20.html.

7. "Untitled." *The Spirit of Democracy* (Woodsfield, OH), May 15, 1861.

8. Ibid.

9. "A splendid company of volunteers." *The Spirit of Democracy* (Woodsfield, OH), July 31, 1861.

10. Curry, Cheryl. "Pictures Of Son Cause Pain, Do Good -- Parents Of Dead Man Say Ads May Help Control Fear Of Aids." *The Seattle Times*, April 23, 1992. http://community.seattletimes.nwsource.com/archive/?date=19920423&slug=1487969.

11. Cosgrove, Ben. "The Photo That Changed the Face of AIDS." *Time Life*, November 25, 2014. http://time.com/3503000/behind-the-picture-the-photo-that-changed-the-face-of-aids/#1.

12. "William Gladstone Steel." Crater Lake Institute. www.craterlakeinstitute.com/cultural-history/people/william-gladstone-steel.htm.

STOCKDALE

1. *History of Lower Scioto Valley, Ohio.* Chicago: Inter-State Publishing, 1884.

2. "Stockdale." City Guide Information - Piketon, OH. www.piketoninfo.net/stockdale.html.

3. "Pike County." Ohio Railroad Stations Past and Present. www.west2k.com/ohstations/pike.shtml.

4. *History of Lower Scioto Valley, Ohio.*

5. "Branch Rickey," Ohio History Central, www.ohiohistorycentral.org/w/Branch_Rickey.

6. "Branch Rickey." Biography.com. July 7, 2014. www.biography.com/people/branch-rickey-9458118.

7. "Branch Rickey." Ohio Wesleyan University. www.owu.edu/about/history-traditions/branch-rickey/.

8. Ibid.

9. "Branch Rickey." Biography.com.

10. Ibid.

11. Ibid.

12. Treder, Steve. "Sociology of the MLB Player: 1952." *The Hardball Times.* August 30, 2005. https://tht.fangraphs.com/sociology-of-the-mlb-player-1952/.

13. Ibid.

14. Allan, Mark. "2 with Ohio Roots on the Grid for Indy 500." 2news Wdtn.com (Dayton, OH), May 24, 2018. www.wdtn.com/sports/2-with-ohio-roots-on-the-grid-for-indy-500/1197124236.

15. Wilson, Phillip B. "Veach Looks to Inspire With His Story of Overcoming Bullying." *Indycar*, July

21, 2018. www.indycar.com/News/2018/07/07-21-Veach-overcomes-bullying.

16. Allan. "2 with Ohio Roots on the Grid for Indy 500."

17. "Enjoy Some of Pike County's Many Attractions." Pike County Convention and Visitors Bureau. www.piketravel.com/cvb-Attractions.html.

18. Blundo, Joe. "I Really Did See Ohio's Most Perfect Tree." *Columbus Dispatch*, August 20, 2009. www.dispatch.com/article/20090820/LIFESTYLE/308209574.

19. "Stockdale."

SUGAR BUSH KNOLLS

1. *The Davey Bulletin*. Vol. XVI. No 10. Kent, Ohio, 1928: Davey Expert Tree Company.

2. Ibid.

3. Ibid.

4. Ibid.

5. Ibid.

6. Beal, James R., and Nancy K. Stillwagon. "The History of the Village of Sugar Bush Knolls." The Village of Sugar Bush Knolls, Ohio. 2017. http://sugarbushknollsohio.org/wp-content/uploads/2017/12/History-of-the-Village-of-Sugar-Bush-Knolls_2017-ed.pdf.

7. "Martin L. Davey." Ohio History Central. www.ohiohistorycentral.org/w/Martin_L._Davey.

8. Beal and Stillwagon. "The History of the Village of Sugar Bush Knolls."

9. Ibid.

10. Ibid.

11. Ibid.

12. Farkas, Karen. "Kent State University Celebrates 50 Years of Black Squirrels on Campus." *Cleveland Plain Dealer*, January 6, 2011. http://blog.cleveland.com/metro/2011/01/kent_state_university_celebrat.html.

13. McDonald, Kyle. "Sheriff's Sale Looms for Porthouse Mansion in Sugar Bush Knolls." *Record Courier*, March 17, 2013. www.record-courier.com/news/20130317/sheriffs-sale-looms-for-porthouse-mansion-in-sugar-bush-knolls?start=8.

SULPHUR SPRINGS

1. *History of Crawford County and Ohio.: Containing a History of the State of Ohio, from Its Earliest Settlement to the Present Time...*Chicago: Baskin & Battey, 1881.

2. McJunkin, James E., ed. *History of Crawford County, Ohio, Horizons '76*. Bucyrus, OH: Crawford County Historical Foundation, Inc., 1976.

3. Longsdorf, Jim. "From Slifertown to Sulphur Springs, This Crawford Village Has Survived." *News Journal* (Mansfield, OH), June 30, 1974.

4. Ibid.

5. Cannon, Rev. Paul L., and William A. Marquart. *Sulphur Springs Sesquicentennial: A History of the past 150 Years of Sulphur Springs, Ohio*. Sulphur Springs Sesquicentennial Committee, 1983.

6. Longsdorf. "From Slifertown to Sulphur Springs, This Crawford Village Has Survived."

7. Cannon and Marquart. *Sulphur Springs Sesquicentennial*.

8. Ibid.

9. Ibid.

10. Ibid.

11. Ibid.

12. Finefield, Kristi. "The Last Men of the Revolution." Library of Congress. November 07, 2013. https://blogs.loc.gov/picturethis/2013/11/the-last-men-of-the-revolution/.

13. Ibid.

TARLTON

1. Dawley, Betty. "Zane Trace Is Significant Factor of Tarlton History." *The Circleville Herald*, July 23, 1968.

2. Ibid.

3. Van Cleaf, Hon. Aaron R. *History of Pickaway County, Ohio, and Representative Citizens*. Chicago: Biographical Publishing Company, 1906.

4. Dawley. "Zane Trace Is Significant Factor of Tarlton History."

5. Fischer, Frank. "General William Sooy Smith." *Pickaway Quarterly*, Summer 1965, pg. 10–19.

6. Ibid.

7. "Major General William Sooy Smith Historical Marker." Historical Marker Database. www.hmdb.org/marker.asp?marker=13495.

8. Fischer. "General William Sooy Smith."

9. Ibid.

10. Smith, General William Sooy. "How To Succeed; As a Civil Engineer." In *How to Succeed: In Public Life, As a Minister, As a Physician...A Series of Essays*, pg. 41–47. New York: G. P. Putnam's Sons, 1882.

11. Fischer. "General William Sooy Smith."

12. "Major General William Sooy Smith Historical Marker."

13. Fischer. "General William Sooy Smith."

14. Ibid.

15. Ibid.

16. Ibid.

17. "Major General William Sooy Smith Historical Marker."

18. "Tarlton Cross Mound." Ohio History Central. www.ohiohistorycentral.org/w/Tarlton_Cross_Mound.

19. Van Cleaf. *History of Pickaway County, Ohio, and Representative Citizens*.

TIRO

1. Hopley, John E. *History of Crawford County, Ohio, and Representative Citizens. Vol. 1.* Chicago: Richmond-Arnold Publishing Co., 1912.

2. Ibid.

3. Ibid.

4. Ibid.

5. McJunkin, James E. *History of Crawford County, Ohio: Horizons 76.* Bucyrus, OH: Crawford County Historical Foundation, 1976.

6. Phillips, Jeb. "Oldest WWI-era Vet Joined Weeks before War's End." *Columbus Dispatch*, April 2, 2007. www.pressreader.com.

7. McKinnon, Julie M. "WWI Vet Is Recalled for His Life of Service." *The Toledo Blade*, December 23, 2007. www.toledoblade.com/news/deaths/2007/12/23/WW-I-vet-is-recalled-for-his-life-of-service/stories/200712230036.

8. Courson, Paul. "Last Living U.S. World War I Veteran Dies." CNN, February 28, 2011. www.cnn.com/2011/US/02/27/wwi.veteran.death/index.html.

9. Phillips. "Oldest WWI-era Vet Joined Weeks before War's End."

10. McKinnon. "WWI Vet Is Recalled for His Life of Service."

11. "Tiro Testicle Festival Review – May 19, 2013." Ohiofestivals.net. https://ohiofestivals.net/4-tiro-testicle-festival-may-19-2013/.

12. McJunkin. *History of Crawford County, Ohio: Horizons 76*.

13. Ibid.

UNIONVILLE CENTER

1. *The History of Union County, Ohio, Containing a History of the County; Its Townships, Towns, Churches, Schools, Etc...Vol. II*. Chicago: W. H. Beers & Co., 1883.

2. Senate Historical Office. "Charles Warren Fairbanks, 26th Vice President (1905–1909)." United States Senate. www.senate.gov/artandhistory/history/common/generic/VP_Charles_Fairbanks.htm.

3. "Charles Warren Fairbanks Birthplace Historical Marker." Historical Marker Database. www.hmdb.org/marker.asp?marker=87103.

4. "Charles W. Fairbanks." UVA Miller Center. https://millercenter.org/president/roosevelt/essays/fairbanks-1901-vicepresident.

5. Ibid.

6. Senate Historical Office. "Charles Warren Fairbanks, 26th Vice President (1905–1909)."

7. "Mrs. C. W. Fairbanks Dead." *The New York Times*, October 25, 1913.

8. "Charles W. Fairbanks."

9. Senate Historical Office. "Charles Warren Fairbanks, 26th Vice President (1905–1909)."

10. Ibid.

11. Ibid.

12. Senate Historical Office. "Charles Warren Fairbanks, 26th Vice President (1905–1909)."

13. "Mrs. C. W. Fairbanks Dead." *The New York Times*, October 25, 1913.

14. "Charles W. Fairbanks."

15. "Tiny Towns." *Columbus Dispatch*, May 21, 2011. www.dispatch.com/content/stories/life_and_entertainment/2011/05/21/tiny-towns.html.

16. Ibid.

VAUGHNSVILLE

1. Kinder, George D. *History of Putnam County, Ohio: Its Peoples, Industries, and Institutions.* Indianapolis, IN: B.F. Bowen & Company, 1915.

2. Calvin, Marguerite. *People and Places Putnam County, Ohio, 1800–1900.* 1981.

3. The Findlay Courier. Accessed 2018. http://sportsbuzzohio.com/prep-basketball-vaughnsville-remembered/.

4. Ibid.

5. Ibid.

6. Ibid.

7. Ibid.

8. "Sylvester Goedde Minor Leagues Statistics & History." Baseball Reference. www.baseball-reference.com/register/player.fcgi?id=goedde001syl.

9. "Player Bio: Sylvester Goedde (1942–1943)." Georgetown Basketball History Project: Top 100 Players. www.hoyabasketball.com/players/s_goedde.htm.

10. "Sylvester Franklin 'Stretch' Goedde." Find A Grave. www.findagrave.com/memorial/129388932/sylvester-franklin-goedde.

11. "About Vaughnsville Communications." Vaughnsville Communications. http://vaughnsvillecomm.com/about.html.

12. Ibid.

13. Kinder. *History of Putnam County, Ohio.*

14. "Who First Adopted Individual Cups as a Regular Communion Practice?" Sharper Iron. March 30, 2011. https://sharperiron.org/article/who-first-adopted-individual-cups-as-regular-communion-practice.

VENEDOCIA

1. "Chapter 1: 'Beginnings' A Preview of the History of Salem Presbyterian Church." Venedocia Church History Project. www.venedocia.org/salem/begin.html.

2. Ibid.

3. Ibid.

4. "William Bebb." Ohio History Central. www.ohiohistorycentral.org/w/William_Bebb.

5. "Chapter 1: 'Beginnings'

6. "Recollections of the First Welsh Settlement in Venedocia, Van Wert Co., Ohio -Translated from 'Y Cyfaill'", 1894-J.T.W. by Mr. R. Jervis." History of Venedocia, Ohio — 1847–1852. www.venedocia.org/1847-52.html.

7. Ibid.

8. Ibid.

9. "The History of Venedocia from the 1830's through 1974." Venedocia. www.venedocia.org/york.html.

10. "History of the Salem Presbyterian Church." Venedocia. www.venedocia.org/salem/churhist.html.

11. "Annual Reports and Publications of Venedocia Ohio's Salem Presbyterian Church." Venedocia. www.venedocia.org/salem/salemannualreports/index.html.

12. "Venedocia Community." Venedocia. www.venedocia.org.

13. "The History of Venedocia from the 1830's through 1974."

14. Mayer, Vickie. "Venedocia, Ohio: Small Village, Big Web Page." *The Municipal*, May 9, 2012. www.themunicipal.com/2012/05/venedocia-ohio-small-village-big-web-page/.

WEST FARMINGTON

1. Upton, Harriet Taylor. *A Twentieth Century History of Trumbull County, Ohio: A Narrative Account of Its Historical Progress, Its People, and Its Principal Interests. Vol. 1.* Chicago: Lewis Publishing Company, 1909.

2. Ibid.

3. Ibid.

4. Ibid.

5. "Mary 'Polly' Wolcott." Findagrave.com. www.findagrave.com/memorial/35755614/mary-wolcott.

6. Upton. *A Twentieth Century History of Trumbull County, Ohio.*

7. Anthony, Dorothy Sloan. "History of Farmington- Farmington Ending Its Second Century." Bristol Public Library. http://www.bristollibrary.org/farmington/farmingtonhistory.htm.

8. Upton. *A Twentieth Century History of Trumbull County, Ohio.*

9. Ibid.

10. Western Reserve Seminary, VFM 3817, Ohio History Connection.

11. Anthony. "History of Farmington- Farmington Ending Its Second Century."

12. Ibid.

13. Ibid.

14. Sess, Dave. "Fire Strikes Historic Small Town Grocery Store in Trumbull County." WKBN First News 27 (Youngstown, OH), July 10, 2017. www.wkbn.com/local-news/fire-strikes-historic-small-town-grocery-store-in-trumbull-county/1067889963.

15. Ibid.

16. Ibid.

17. Anthony. "History of Farmington- Farmington Ending Its Second Century."

18. Tuttle, Hudson. "A Sketch of the Life of A. B. French." In *Gleanings from the Rostrum.* Press of Hann & Adair, 1892.

WHARTON

1. *Whartensburgh 1846 and Wharton 1971: Historical Sketch Prepared for the 125th Celebration of Wharton, Ohio, August 14, 1971.* 1971, https://archive.org/details/whartensburgh18400.

2. Ibid.

3. Ibid.

4. Ibid.

5. Ibid.

6. "Wharton." Wyandot Chamber of Commerce. http://wyandotchamber.com/wyandot-county-information/wharton.

7. Baughman, A. J., ed. *Past and Present of Wyandot County, Ohio: A Record of Settlement, Organization,*

Progress and Achievement. Chicago: S. J. Clarke Publishing Company, 1913.

8. "Search for Missing Man." *News Journal* (Mansfield, OH), January 25, 1916.

9. "Posse to Prosecute Search." *Union County Journal* (Marysville, OH), January 27, 1916.

10. "Search for Missing Man."

11. "Posse to Prosecute Search."

12. "Dayton Man Now Hunting Brother, Deemed Murdered." *Dayton Herald*, February 10, 1916.

13. "Search for Missing Man." *News Journal* (Mansfield, OH), January 25, 1916.

14. Ibid.

15. Dayton Man Now Hunting Brother, Deemed Murdered."

16. Ibid.

17. Ibid.

18. "The Mennel Milling Company." Mennel Milling. https://mennel.com/locations/whartongrain.

19. Ibid.

20. *Whartensburgh 1846 and Wharton 1971*.

WILLSHIRE

1. "Treaty of the Maumee Rapids (1817)." Ohio History Central. www.ohiohistorycentral.org/w/Treaty_of_the_Maumee_Rapids_(1817).

2. O'Daffer, Floyd C. *History of Van Wert County*. Lima, OH: Fairway Press, 1990.

3. Ibid.

4. Van Wert County Historical Society. *History of Van Wert County Ohio*. Taylor Publishing Company, 1981.

5. Davis, Robert C. "Slavery in North Africa – the Famous Story of Captain James Riley." The Public Domain Review. https://publicdomainreview.org/2011/10/03/slavery-in-north-africa-the-famous-story-of-captain-james-riley/.

6. O'Daffer. *History of Van Wert County*.

7. Van Wert County Historical Society. *History of Van Wert County Ohio*.

8. Ibid.

9. Ibid.

10. Ibid.

11. Ibid.

12. Ibid.

13. Langham, Jim. "Willshire Residents Find Cool Change at Ice Cream Shop." *Times Bulletin* (Van Wert, OH), June 30, 2018. https://timesbulletin.com/Content/News/News/Article/Willshire-residents-find-cool-change-at-ice-cream-shop/2/4/215577.

14. "Intensive Treatment Helped Ohio Man Survive Childhood Bat Bite." *Washington Post*. www.washingtonpost.com/archive/lifestyle/wellness/1995/11/07/intensive-treatment-helped-ohio-man-survive-childhood-bat-bite/3994575f-35d9-4ec8-b445-ad8ff81d74e7/?utm_term=.a10038e997e6.

WILMOT

1. Perrin, William Henry. *History of Stark County: With an Outline Sketch of Ohio*. Chicago: Baskin & Battey, Historical Publishers, 1881.

2. Lehman, John H., ed. *A Standard History of Stark County, Ohio: An Authentic Narrative of the Past, with Particular Attention to the Modern Era in the Commercial, Industrial, Civic and Social Development: A Chronicle of the People, with Family Lineage and Memoirs. Vol. I*. Chicago and New York: Lewis Publishing Company.

3. Amish Door Village. http://amishdoor.com.

4. "Amish & Holmes County History." Ohio Amish Country. www.visitamishcountry.com/Learn/AmishHeritage.

5. Shaheen, Joe. "Wilmot Seeks to Grow through Annexation." *IndeOnline (Massillon, OH)*, November 14, 2017. www.indeonline.com/news/20171114/wilmot-seeks-to-grow-through-annexation.

6. Ibid.

7. Sigrist Woods trail guide: Stark Wilderness Center, Wilmot, Ohio / text by Charles C. and Nicky King; sketches by Freda Case; photographs by Howard Oberlin, PA Box 280 22, Ohio History Connection.

8. "About Us." The Wilderness Center. www.wildernesscenter.org/about-us/.

9. Sigrist Woods trail guide.

10. "About Us."

11. Sigrist Woods trail guide.

12. Ibid.

13. The Wilderness Center. www.wildernesscenter.org/about-us/.

14. Sigrist Woods trail guide.

YANKEE LAKE

1. Jurko, John, II. "Yankee Lake: The Documentary." https://store.yankeelakehistory.com/old/history.html.

2. Ibid.

3. Jurko, John. "Yankee Lake: The History and The Legend." Raw Interview Footage. Indiegogo. www.indiegogo.com/projects/yankee-lake-the-history-and-the-legend#/comments.

4. Ibid.

5. Jurko, John, II. "Yankee Lake: The Documentary."

6. Jurko, John. "Yankee Lake: The History and The Legend."

7. Jurko, John, II. "Yankee Lake: The Documentary."

8. Ibid.

9. Ibid.

10. Ibid.

11. Ibid.

12. Ibid.

13. Ibid.

14. Ibid.

15. Vesey, Steve. "Wild History Behind Why Yankee Lake Became Its Own Village." 21 WFMJ (Youngstown, OH), September 28, 2017. www.wfmj.com/story/36435666/wild-history-behind-why-yankee-lake-became-its-own-village.

ZALESKI

1. Biggs, Louise Ogan. *A Brief History of Vinton County*. Columbus, OH: Heer Printing, 1950.

2. Cullen, William M. *A History of Moonville, Ohio and a Collection of Its Haunting Tales: Revised Edition*. Xlibris Corporation, 2013.

3. Biggs. *A Brief History of Vinton County*.

4. "Lake Hope." Hockinghills.com. www.hockinghills.com/lake_hope.html.

5. Biggs. *A Brief History of Vinton County*.

6. Family Heritage. *Vinton County, Ohio History & Families*. Paducah, KY: Turner Pub., 1996.

7. Cullen. *A History of Moonville, Ohio and a Collection of Its Haunting Tales: Revised Edition*.

8. Quackenbush, Jannette. "History of Moonville and Moonville Tunnel." Moonville Tunnel. www.moonvilletunnel.net/Moonville_History.htm.

9. "Moonville Tunnel." Ohio Exploration Society. www.ohioexploration.com/structures/moonvilletunnel/.

10. Quackenbush. "History of Moonville and Moonville Tunnel."

11. Ibid.

12. "Moonville Tunnel." Ohio Exploration Society.

13. Ibid.

14. Ibid.

15. Family Heritage. *Vinton County, Ohio History & Families*.

16. Buchanan, Tyler. "Zaleski General Store Torn Down." *The Courier* (Vinton and Jackson Counties), January 4, 2017. www.vintonjacksoncourier.com/spotlight/zaleski-general-store-torn-down/article_d7665e9c-482d-55b2-b837-54119e462888.html.

ZANESFIELD

1. Perrin, William Henry, and J. H. Battle. *History of Logan County and Ohio: Containing a History of the State of Ohio, from Its Earliest Settlement to the Present Time* ...Chicago: O. L. Baskin & Co., 1880.

2. Reames, O.K., ed. *History of Zanesfield and Sketches of the Interesting and Historical Places of Logan County, Ohio*. Zanesfield, OH: O.K. Reames, 1929.

3. "Isaac Zane Tract." Ohio History Central. www.ohiohistorycentral.org/w/Isaac_Zane_Tract.

4. Grey, Zane. *Betty Zane*. New York: Grosset & Dunlap, 1903.

5. Reames. *History of Zanesfield and Sketches of the Interesting and Historical Places of Logan County, Ohio*.

6. "Isaac Zane Tract."

7. Perrin and Battle. *History of Logan County and Ohio*.

8. Bremer. "Shawnee Trail of Tears Began at Wapatomica." https://www.tsbremer.com/shawnee-trail-of-tears-began-at-wapatomica/

9. Reames. *History of Zanesfield and Sketches of the Interesting and Historical Places of Logan County, Ohio*.

10. "Ebenezer Zane Cabin." Remarkable Ohio. http://remarkableohio.org/index.php?/category/881.

11. Perrin and Battle. *History of Logan County and Ohio*.

12. Ibid.

13. Ibid.

14. Reames. *History of Zanesfield and Sketches of the Interesting and Historical Places of Logan County, Ohio*.

15. "Earl Sloan Library, Zanesfield." www.sloanlibraryoh.org/contact-us.html.

16. "China Flats." Historical Marker Database. www.hmdb.org/marker.asp?marker=98744.

17. "Hicksite Quaker Church." Historical Marker Database. www.hmdb.org/marker.asp?marker=98842.

ZOAR

1. Mansfield, John Brandt. *The History of Tuscarawas County, Ohio, Containing a History of the County; Its Townships, Towns, Churches, Schools, Etc; General and Local Statistics; Military Record; Portraits of Early Settlers and Prominent Men; History of the Northwest Territory; History of Ohio; Miscellaneous Matters, Etc., Etc.* Chicago: Warner, Beers & Co., 1884.

2. Ibid.

3. Ibid.

4. Sarbaugh, Howard A. *A Brief History of Zoar*. 2nd ed. Columbus: Ohio State Archaeological and Historical Society, 1935.

5. Mansfield. *The History of Tuscarawas County, Ohio*.

6. Rosenberg. "Zoar Village, Two Centuries After Founding, Survives The Floods." https://radio.wosu.org/post/zoar-village-two-centuries-after-founding-survives-floods#stream/0

7. Sarbaugh. *A Brief History of Zoar*. 2nd ed.

8. Mansfield. *The History of Tuscarawas County, Ohio*.

9. Morhart, Hilda Dischinger. *The Zoar Story: Sesquicentennial Edition*. Dover, Ohio: Seibert Printing Company, 1967.

10. Ibid.

11. Rosenberg. "Zoar Village, Two Centuries After Founding, Survives The Floods."

12. Ibid.

13. *Zoar: An Ohio Experiment in Communalism*. 3rd ed. Columbus, OH: Ohio Historical Society, 1960.

14. Ibid.

15. Rosenberg. "Zoar Village, Two Centuries After Founding, Survives The Floods."

16. Ibid.

17. Burkhart, JoAnne. *A Walking Tour of Historic Zoar Structures, 1817–1898: A History of the Original Structures Still Standing in Historic Zoar, Ohio*. Zoar, OH: Syl and Anna Bachtel, 1985.

18. Ibid.

Towns/Villages and Their Respective Counties

Adelphi: Ross
Amesville: Athens
Beallsville: Monroe
Belle Valley: Noble
Benton Ridge: Hancock
Bentonville: Adams
Beulah Beach: Erie
Bladensburg: Knox
Bowersville: Greene
Brady Lake: Portage
Camp Dennison: Hamilton
Celeryville: Huron
Chesterhill: Morrow
Chesterville: Morrow
Clifton: Clarke and Greene
Coalton: Jackson
College Corner: Butler and Preble
Conesville: Coshocton
Coolville: Athens
Corwin: Warren
Cynthiana: Pike (Perry Township)
Damascus: Mahoning
Deersville: Harrison
East Fultonham: Muskingum
East Liberty: Logan
Flat Rock: Seneca
Fletcher: Miami
Fort Jennings: Putnam
Fort Seneca: Seneca
Freeport: Harrison
Fresno: Coshocton
Gilboa: Putnam

Gist Settlement: Highland
Glenmont: Holmes
Gratiot: Licking and Muskingum
Hanoverton: Columbiana
Harbor View: Lucas
Harrod: Allen
Hartford: Licking
Holiday City: Williams
Hollansburg: Darke
Iberia: Morrow
Jacksonburg: Butler
Kilbourne: Delaware
Kipton: Lorain
Lake Seneca: Williams
Leesville: Carroll
Linndale: Cuyahoga
Lockbourne: Franklin
Lockington: Shelby
Lower Salem: Washington
Magnetic Springs: Union
Martinsburg: Knox
Miamiville: Clermont
Milledgeville: Fayette
Millfield: Athens
Moscow: Clermont
Mount Eaton: Wayne
Mount Pleasant: Jefferson
Murray City: Hocking
Neville: Clermont
New Haven: Huron
New Riegel: Seneca
New Weston: Darke
North Star: Darke
Norwich: Muskingum

Octa: Fayette
Old Fort: Seneca
Otway: Scioto
Polk: Ashland
Pulaski: Williams
Put-in-Bay: Ottawa
Quaker City: Guernsey
Rarden: Scioto
Rockbridge: Hocking
Rogers: Columbiana
Rudolph: Wood
Rushville: Fairfield
Rutland: Meigs
Saint Johns: Mercer
Savannah: Ashland
Sinking Spring: Highland
South Vienna: Clark
Stafford: Monroe
Stockdale: Pike
Sugar Bush Knolls: Portage
Sulphur Springs: Crawford
Tarlton: Fairfield/Pickaway
Tiro: Crawford
Unionville Center: Union
Vaughnsville: Putnam
Venedocia: Van Wert
West Farmington: Trumbull
Wharton: Wyandot
Willshire: Van Wert
Wilmot: Stark
Yankee Lake: Trumbull
Zaleski: Vinton
Zanesfield: Logan
Zoar Village: Tuscarawas

About the Author

Karen Robertson is proud to have been born and raised just outside the historic city of Cleveland, Ohio. Trading in the shores of Lake Erie for the banks of the Olentangy, Karen earned her Master's degree in Public History from the Ohio State University in 2015. She is currently a Curator of Manuscripts at the Ohio History Connection, where she enjoys sharing the stories of Ohio's amazing history each day. When she isn't reading and writing about the past, Karen enjoys diving into a new board game with her husband, Jake, lacing up her tennis shoes for a run, or exploring the depths of her Netflix queue.